From media history to today's rapid-fire changes . . . your best source is right here:

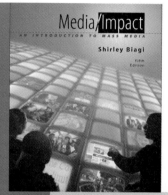

Lively and visual, Shirley Biagi's new Fifth Edition of *Media/Impact* keeps your students current with both established and emerging media—while at the same time offering an exciting look at the *entire* mass media panorama. More than any other text, *Media/Impact* pinpoints the intersection of media business, technology, and social impact, giving students one of the most complete pictures of the changing landscape of mass media today. And to keep pace with the rapid-fire advances in the mass media, this new Fifth Edition offers more online resources than ever before, helping students access the latest news and research *as it happens*!

Timely, intriguing, interactive . . .
this new Fifth Edition includes:

- In-depth coverage of the impact of digitization in each media, including emerging forms of new media technology

- Up-to-date information regarding the latest media mergers

- Updated information on recent FCC rulings

- A strong historical foundation that provides students with perspective and gives them a basis of comparison to recent related developments, especially to technology's effect on media

- Strong coverage of multicultural issues throughout

- A *Student Resource Guide* at the end of the text that includes a comprehensive list of media Web sites for further research

- And much, much more!

Featuring an exciting, state-of-the-art collection of online, video, multimedia, and print resources to make your classroom come alive like never before! See pages 5–8.

> "I like the idea of integrating the three themes very much. The author has hit the nail on the head by putting these together. The defining aspect of the American media system is its ownership by private industry. So for her to pull these together with the advance of technology is great. . . . I applaud her."
>
> **Edgar P. Trotter**
> **California State University, Fullerton**

The most recent advances in digital technology . . .

Up-to-the-minute coverage of the impact of digitization in each media gives students a sense of the latest advances in equipment and techniques and a look at the trend towards media convergence. Biagi provides current information on: MP3 technology for recording downloads; DVRs; digital projectors for feature film production; digital movie downloads; and new media technologies including immersive virtual reality systems, holographic theaters, personal channels, intelligent video agents, digital paper, and portable tablets.

Digital Video Records (DVRs). DVRs can download programming, using a device called a "set-top box" (which looks much like today's cable boxes and sits on or near the TV).

Scheduled to be introduced in fall 1999, DVRs use hard-drive computer storage to receive information from any program service (including the broadcast networks, satellite and cable programmers) to send viewers up-to-date information about what's on TV. DVRs transfer the information to an on-screen program guide, where viewers can decide what to watch and when, a practice called **time-shifting**. One of the biggest features of a DVR is that it allows viewers to hit the "pause" button for a show they're watching, leave the TV set on, and then start up the program again when they return, or fast-forward through the recorded portion.

Because DVRs could change viewers' control over which programming they watch (and, most importantly, which commercials), all of the major TV networks have invested in the companies that are producing this technology. The networks want to be able to influence what consumers can record and when, but the value of total viewer control is one of DVRs' most attractive features for consumers.

time-shifting recording a television program on a DVR or VCR to watch at a more convenient time.

TECHNOLOGY AND THE FUTURE

From the beginning, profits in the recording industry have been tied to technology. Ever since William Paley and David Sarnoff decided to produce LPs and 45s, the consumer has tracked the equipment manufacturers, looking for better, more convenient sound.

Today, recording companies worry that music pirates will copy digitized music, which can be sent over the Internet. Online subscribers can now browse through online music catalogs, downloading samples of music they like. But once digitized, the music is available to anyone and can be sent over the Internet around the world. The challenge for music company executives is to develop a way to protect this new technology with an even newer technology that will make copying impossible. "The information highway could be bad news if we don't control the right of distribution and receive fair renumeration," says James Fifield, president of EMI Music. "I want my hands on the wheel."[13]

The expansion of MP3 digital technology in 1999 signaled a new era for music lovers, making music available on the Internet. MP3 software allows any computer user with an Internet connection to download the latest music.

Singer Tori Amos is among the first performers to offer live performances on a website devoted to MP3 music.

Ebet Roberts

. . . and new Impact/Digital boxes to keep students on the forefront of change

"Impact/Digital" boxes, eight new to this edition, keep students on the cutting edge with essays on ways the new technology influences the media.

You in the Digital Age

IMPACT

digital *Living Dorm Life in the Camera's Eye*

Students Put Themselves in Focus on the Internet 24 Hours a Day

By Mary Beth Marklein
USA TODAY

For tech-savvy, trend-setting college students, the place to see and be seen...is through the eye of a Webcam.

Through the wonders of this tennis-ball-size piece of technology that hooks to a personal computer, just about any student can capture his or her image live, 24 hours a day, seven days a week, and upload it to the Internet for all the world to behold.

Who, besides Mom and Dad, would care?

field (Ill.) College junior Ben Miller, 20, who set up a Webcam in November as the host of a college-oriented Web site for about.com.

This year, he is living off campus, so Jason Davis, his former roommate, offered to operate a camera with his laptop. As a bonus, the school just went wireless, so the camera is no longer tethered to a dorm-based personal computer.

In the past year or so, pockets of students like Miller were independently installing Webcams, video cameras that, when hooked up to computers, transmit images in intervals ranging from seconds to minutes to hours. But as word spreads, costs dro

Online all the time: The Webcam, top, is used to send images of college students live on the Internet 24 hours a day, seven days a week. Those students include Melissa Gaunt, below, in San Antonio.

With so many compelling articles, it's like a text plus a reader in one!

In every chapter, students will find engaging and stimulating articles from noted communications writers and from primary sources such as the *Freedom Forum, Wired Magazine, The Wall Street Journal, TIMEdigital.com,* and many more. Two-thirds of the readings are new to this edition, making Biagi's text one of the most current sources of media information you'll find.

"Impact/On You" boxes, nine new to this edition, keep students in touch with how the mass media affect the everyday lives of ordinary people and how the media are doing business differently based on new advances in technology.

IMPACT
on you   *If Only DeMille Had Owned a Desktop*

The camera glides in on a tableau: Jesus and his apostles gathered solemnly at a long table, each frozen in painterly poses familiar from *The Last Supper*. Then Jesus suddenly comes to life, and in a flurry of special effects that owes more to Dali than da Vinci, he miraculously provides a banquet of breads, crackers and grapes from thin air and transforms water into a blood-red wine cooler called New Testament. Along the way, he transforms himself into a caked pitch man

the entire project with an ordinary 16-millimeter camera, two Power Macs and some off-the-shelf software at a cost of $1,700.

There's nothing new these days about digital technology's marriage with the movies. Moviegoers have been getting an eyeful of digital wonders on the big screen, from *Titanic* to *A Bug's Life*. But those displays of digital wizardry were managed by filmmakers with tens of millions of dollars at their disposal for the tedious tasks involved

film to video, where images, once digitized, can be cut with editing software and enhanced with easy-to-use animation programs. Others use digital video camcorders—small, relatively inexpensive cameras that can load their already digitized images onto computer hard drives—to breathe cinematic life into what had once flickered only in their imaginations, then transfer the result to film. Some moviemakers have given up film altogether, choosing instead to shoot, edit and, in some cases,

---

"Impact/Point of View" boxes, six new to this edition, challenge students to think critically and debate the issues. These provocative short essays reflect current and emerging trends on media topics such as this one on the 1999 Jenny Jones trial.

IMPACT
point of view   *It's Time Shock-Talk TV Took Some Responsibility*

$25 Million 'Jenny Jones' Verdict Should Help
By John Carman

The *Jenny Jones* verdict threatens to introduce a disturbing new element into TV's shock-talk jungle—responsibility.

Naturally, the industry is aghast.

If yesterday's verdict somehow stands up on appeal, it could spoil the long and lavish party for Jones, Jerry Springer, Ricki Lake and their ilk.

Jenny Jones, and Warner Bros. Television, which syndicates it. Both are units of the entertainment giant Time Warner.

Ruling that the defendants negligently caused Amedure's death, the jury awarded his family $5 million for his pain and suffering, $10 million for their loss of his companionship, $10 million for the loss of his future earnings, and $6,500 for funeral expenses.

Jones issued a statement calling the verdict "outrageous," she

ing effect on television's burgeoning realm of reality programs.

Good. This is a corner of TV that needs not only a good chill, but maybe a chest cold, a full bout of pneumonia and a funeral dirge.

Shows that stage outlandish surprises and spontaneous confrontations ought to take responsibility for the consequences. Amedure's death was a consequence.

But in the circus world of TV today, responsibility is a stuffy and antiquated notion. *Jenny Jones* and

---

"Impact/Profile" boxes, four new to this edition, highlight people who have shaped the mass media and made it what it is today, including names like Jeff Bezos, Ernie Pyle, Ida Tarbell, Edward R. Murrow, Tim Berners-Lee, and, featured here, Michael Robertson of MP3.com.

IMPACT
profile   *Capturing Ears on the Internet*

Musicians Love Him. Labels Are Skeptical
By Alce Foege

"Hell's Bells," a raucous anthem by the rock group AC/DC, blared from loudspeakers as Michael Robertson, the chief executive of MP3.com, walked to the podium. It seemed an unlikely introduction at last month's New York Music and Internet Expo for a man who wore a conservative camel hair sports jacket—and who had an evangelical Christian background.

Yet after his keynote speech, Mr. Robertson, a 32-year-old entrepreneur in

"I've got a lot of respect for him because he zigged when everybody else zagged, and that's what we're doing."

MP3.com began two-and-a-half years ago as the Z Company, a Yahoo-syle search engine founded by Mr. Robertson. In October 1997, Greg Flores, now MP3.com's director of sales, showed the MP3 software to Mr. Robertson, who was impressed enough to buy the rights to the MP3.com domain name and to rename his company.

At that point, MP3.com had four employees, including Mr. Robertson, working out of their Last summer, it expanded

Enticing visuals draw students in . . .

Dozens of new photographs, cartoons, and Web displays capture both the history and modernization of the mass media, giving students a real feel for the media's past, present, and future and making the content come alive like never before.

New **"Impact/Industry"** visuals summarize major highlights of each media through striking collages like this one from Chapter 9, "New Media, On-line Media, and the Web." This chapter has been praised by reviewers for treating emerging media with the same attention given to established media.

> *"The use of visuals to help explain various aspects of media history is useful."*
>
> **Marshel D. Rossow**
> **Minnesota State University, Mankato**

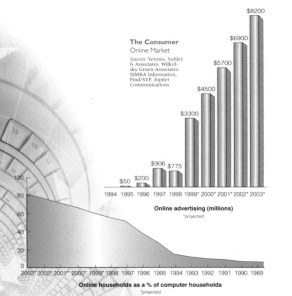

... and "TimeFrames" add historical context

"TimeFrames" for each of the mass media industries give important dates and milestones that begin today and move backward in time—adding a unique, historical perspective to the material.

> *"Chapter 9 is great! This makes new media a full-fledged part of the mass communications array."*
>
> **Debra Merskin**
> **University of Oregon**

Keep pace with the rapid advances in media with *InfoTrac® College Edition*—free with every student copy of the text!

Updated daily and dating back four years, this world-class, virtual library gives you and your students access to full-length articles (not abstracts) from hundreds of popular and scholarly publications. And now, for the first time, *InfoTrac College Edition* comes automatically packaged with each copy of *Media/Impact!* Your students receive four months of **FREE** access to this fully searchable database, giving them an incredible research tool right at their fingertips.

INFOTRAC COLLEGE EDITION EXERCISES

Using InfoTrac College Edition, a fully searchable online database of articles and abstracts, do the following exercises as directed by your instructor.

1. Read "Digital/Impact Technology: So What Exactly is Digital TV?" in Chapter 7. Then using the key words "HDTV " or "digital TV," choose one article from the list of citations on InfoTrac College Edition.

INFOTRAC COLLEGE EDITION EXERCISES

Using InfoTrac College Edition, a fully searchable online database of articles and abstracts, do the following exercises as directed by your instructor.

1. Read "Digital/Impact Technology: So What Exactly is Digital TV?" in Chapter 7. Then using the key words "HDTV " or "digital TV," choose one article from the list of citations on InfoTrac College Edition. Write a brief summary of the article (no more than 300 words) and include some discussion of whether you think HDTV will gain popular support. Be sure to sum up the article's major points or conclusions in your overview.

2. Choose two or three other students in class to make up a small group. Then choose one of the following TV personalities:

   1. Edward R. Murrow
   2. Lucille Ball (or "I Love Lucy")
   3. David Brinkley
   4. Flip Wilson
   5. Milton Berle
   6. Ed Sullivan
   7. David Sarnoff

Special exercises link text and database

Now you can expand your course beyond the pages of the text and challenge your students to do research as they read! Each chapter of *Media/Impact* contains *Impact/InfoTrac College Edition Exercises*—highlighted by a special icon—which ask students to expand their knowledge and explore contemporary media issues even further by accessing articles from *InfoTrac College Edition*. Assign them for homework, extra credit, or as the beginning of a term paper. These special exercises provide students with the vital link to relevant research.

Efficient, easy to use, reliable

Students can begin using *InfoTrac College Edition* instantly, anywhere, anytime. A simple key word search yields relevant articles drawn from across the entire interdisciplinary database of thousands of articles. Ideas and content from the complete set of journals, magazines, and newspapers are indexed in the database, making searches incredibly quick, easy, and efficient. Content is rich, diverse, and above all, reliable. Students can even print out or e-mail complete articles whenever it's convenient.

InfoTrac College Edition *is available to North American colleges and universities only. Specific journals subject to change.*

Here are just some of the periodicals available with InfoTrac College Edition:

American Journalism Review
American Visions
Americas
Broadcasting
Broadcasting & Cable
Campaigns & Elections
Columbia Journalism Review
Contemporary Policy Issues
Historical Journal of Film, Radio & Television
Insight on the News
Interpretation
Interview
Journal of Advertising
Journal of Advertising Research
Journal of Consumer Affairs
Journal of Leisure Research
News Photographer
Newsline
Online Magazine
PC Magazine
Public Interest
Public Relations Journal
Public Relations Quarterly
Public Relations Review
Publishers Weekly
Society News
Society Perspectives
USA Today
Video Age International
Video Marketing News
Vital Speeches
Washington Journalism Review
World Press Review

InfoTrac® College Edition Student Activities Workbook for Mass Communication
by Chris Allen
ISBN 0-534-56087-3

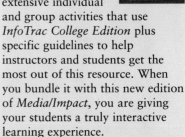

With a focus on mass communication topics, this invaluable workbook features extensive individual and group activities that use *InfoTrac College Edition* plus specific guidelines to help instructors and students get the most out of this resource. When you bundle it with this new edition of *Media/Impact*, you are giving your students a truly interactive learning experience.

If you wish to bundle the text with the workbook, use ISBN 0-534-71382-3.

An expanded, full-service Web site connects you and your students to even more communications resources

Communication Café

http://communication.wadsworth.com

When you adopt *Media/Impact* for your course, you and your students can log on to the *Communication Café*, <u>the</u> online resource for communications students and faculty. Our newly re-designed Web site features everything from online testing to tutorials to discussion forums. You'll be able to connect with other faculty members and discuss relevant topics, download supplements online, explore custom publishing options, and find out more about

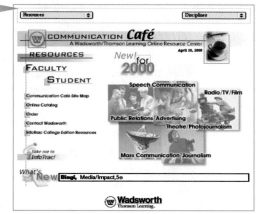

our large selection of communications titles through our online catalog. You'll also have access to many hot links relevant to mass media and all other communication disciplines, to communication associations, and other student and instructor resources.

"Working the Web" sections

A list of 5-10 Web sites at the end of each chapter give the title and URL of sites related to chapter content—a great tool for further research online.

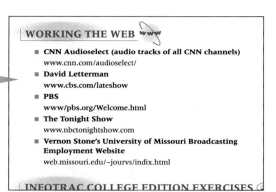

WORKING THE WEB www

- **CNN Audioselect (audio tracks of all CNN channels)**
  www.cnn.com/audioselect/
- **David Letterman**
  www.cbs.com/lateshow
- **PBS**
  www.pbs.org/Welcome.html
- **The Tonight Show**
  www.nbctonightshow.com
- **Vernon Stone's University of Missouri Broadcasting Employment Website**
  web.missouri.edu/~jourvs/indix.html

INFOTRAC COLLEGE EDITION EXERCISES

With these excellent resources, you have everything you need!

CNN Today Videos, a Wadsworth exclusive, updated annually!

Launch a lecture or spark a discussion with riveting footage from CNN, the world's leading 24-hour global news television network. These high-interest, one- to four-minute video clips give you the power to integrate the newsgathering and programming power of CNN into the classroom to show students the relevance of mass communication topics to their everyday lives. Adopters receive one new, updated video containing current, timely footage each year.

CNN Today, Mass Communication Volume I
ISBN 0-534-54813-X
CNN Today, Mass Communication Volume II
ISBN 0-534-54818-0
New! CNN Today, Mass Communication Volume III
ISBN 0-534-54823-7

Wadsworth Communication Video Library

When you adopt this text, you can select from a variety of videos covering key communication topics such as public speaking, family and gender communication, and mass communication. Contact your Wadsworth/Thomson Learning representative for more information and a complete list of titles. You will also have access to *The Effects of New Technologies*, a unique video that examines three new technologies that have revolutionized the world of mass communication: the fax machine, the cellular phone, and the Internet. Each segment provides the history of the technology and a discussion of its impact on daily life.

ISBN 0-534-25832-8 PAT MAST – 1-800-225-4804

Instructor's Resource Manual with Test Items

by Jan Haag and Shirley Biagi
This all-inclusive resource features chapter objectives, *InfoTrac College Edition* exercises, worksheets for in-class discussion, a test bank of multiple-choice and essay questions, suggested student assignments, and a correlation guide of CNN videos for classroom use.
ISBN 0-534-57512-9

ExamView®, including online testing

Create, deliver, and customize tests and study guides (both print and online) in minutes with this easy-to-use assessment and tutorial system for both Windows® and Macintosh® systems. This cross-platform CD-ROM offers both a *Quick Test Wizard* and an *Online Test Wizard* to guide you step-by-step through the process of creating tests, while its unique WYSIWYG (What You See Is What You Get) capability allows you to see the test you are creating on the screen exactly as it will print or display online. You can build tests of up to 250 questions using up to 12 question types. Using *ExamView*'s complete word-processing capabilities, you can enter an unlimited number of new questions or edit existing questions.
ISBN 0-534-57513-7

ExamView® and *ExamView Pro®* are trademarks of *FSCreations*, Inc. Windows is a registered trademark of the Microsoft Corporation used herein under license. Macintosh and Power Macintosh are registered trademarks of Apple Computer, Inc. Used herein under license.

Media Link: Presentation Tool for Mass Communication

Add punch to your visual presentations with this dual-platform CD-ROM. This dynamic presentation tool contains a searchable database of *PowerPoint* slides featuring text art and CNN video clips, plus the ability to import information from previously created lectures. You can add your own slides, make changes to or delete existing slides, and rearrange slide order.
ISBN 0-534-57514-5

Take your course beyond the classroom with even more Web-based tools

WebTUTOR™

Thomson Learning's Web Tutor 2.0 *on WebCT and Blackboard*

Designed to complement and expand Biagi's text, this content-rich, Web-based teaching and learning tool helps students succeed by taking the course beyond the classroom boundaries to an anywhere, anytime environment. *Web Tutor* is rich with study and mastery tools, communication tools, and course content. For your students, *Web Tutor* offers real-time access to a full array of study tools, including chapter objectives and summaries, flashcards with audio, practice quizzes, online tutorials, and Web links.

You can customize the content in any way you choose, from uploading images and other resources, to adding Web links, to creating your own practice materials. *Web Tutor* also provides rich communication tools to instructors and students, including a course calendar, asynchronous discussion, 'real time' chat, gradebook, and an integrated e-mail system. In addition, students will have access to the online *Newbury House Dictionary*, which includes audio pronunciations and complete definitions. Students can also easily link to *InfoTrac College Edition* from within the *Web Tutor* interface.

To order *Web Tutor* on WebCT packaged with the student text, use ISBN 0-534-71418-8. To order *Web Tutor* on Blackboard packaged with the student text, use ISBN 0-534-70066-7.

© 2001 Thomson Learning, Inc. All Rights Reserved. Thomson Learning™ *Web Tutor*™ is a trademark of Thomson Learning, Inc.

The electronic version of Shirley Biagi's *Media/Impact*, Fifth Edition

Combine a remarkable text like Shirley Biagi's *Media/Impact* with the technological wizardry and the immediate, interactive nature of the computer and what do you have? The entire textbook delivered over the Internet—a fast, fun, visual, and affordable option to the traditional text. Every page from Biagi's text is here, with art, tables, and boxed material. Students can purchase the entire text online, and print out the pages they need . . . or they can purchase chapters individually.

e-Biagi gives your students so much more!

- Exercises linked to various sources on the Web

- Easy notetaking and highlighting—with a click of the mouse, the cursor becomes an electronic highlighter that works just like a highlighting marker

- Discussion group capability—with their own classmates and with other campuses across the nation

- A bookmarking feature so students can create their own custom hyperlinks to pages of the text and any other source (such as *InfoTrac College Edition*)

- Links to *InfoTrac College Edition*, *Thomson Learning Web Tutor*, and CNN videos

- And much, much more!

Contact your local Wadsworth/Thomson Learning sales representative for a demo and for more information.

www.wadsworth.com

wadsworth.com is the World Wide Web site for Wadsworth and is your direct source to dozens of online resources.

At wadsworth.com you can find out about supplements, demonstration software, and student resources. You can also send e-mail to many of our authors and preview new publications and exciting new technologies.

wadsworth.com
Changing the way the world learns®

FROM THE WADSWORTH SERIES IN MASS COMMUNICATION AND JOURNALISM

General Mass Communication
Shirley Biagi, *Media/Impact: An Introduction to Mass Media,* 5th Ed.
John Craft, Frederic Leigh, and Donald Godfrey, *Electronic Media*
Louis Day, *Ethics in Media Communications: Cases and Controversies,* 3rd Ed.
Robert S. Fortner, *International Communications: History, Conflict, and Control of the Global Metropolis*
Donald Gillmor, Jerome Barron, and Todd Simon, *Mass Communication Law: Cases and Comment,* 6th Ed.
Donald Gillmor, Jerome Barron, Todd Simon, and Herbert Terry, *Fundamentals of Mass Communication Law*
Kathleen Hall Jamieson and Karlyn Kohrs Campbell, *The Interplay of Influence,* 5th Ed.
Paul Lester, *Visual Communication,* 2nd Ed.
Cynthia Lont, *Women and Media: Content, Careers, and Criticism*
Joseph Straubhaar and Robert LaRose, *Media Now: Communications Media in the Information Age,* 2nd Ed.
Ray Surette, *Media, Crime, and Criminal Justice: Images and Realities,* 2nd Ed.
Edward Jay Whetmore, *Mediamerica, Mediaworld: Form, Content, and Consequence of Mass Communication,* Updated 5th Ed.
John D. Zelezny, *Communications Law: Liberties, Restraints, and the Modern Media,* 3rd Ed.

Journalism
Paul Adams, *Writing Right for Today's Mass Media: A Textbook and Workbook with Language Exercises*
Douglas Anderson, *Contemporary Sports Reporting*
Dorothy Bowles and Diane L. Borden, *Creative Editing,* 3rd Ed.
John Catsis, *Sports Broadcasting*
Jean Chance and William McKeen, *Literary Journalism: A Reader*
Raymond Dorn, *How to Design and Improve Magazine Layouts,* 2nd Ed.
Heintz-Dietrich Fischer, *Sports Journalism at Its Best: Pulitzer Prize-Winning Articles, Cartoons, and Photographs*
Lionel Fisher, *The Craft of Corporate Journalism*
William Gaines, *Investigative Reporting for Print and Broadcast,* 2nd Ed.
Carl Hausman, *The Decision-Making Process in Journalism*
Robert L. Hilliard, *Writing for Television, Radio & New Media,* 7th Ed.
Lauren Kessler and Duncan McDonald, *When Words Collide,* 5th Ed.
Alice M. Klement and Carolyn Burrows Matalene, *Telling Stories/Taking Risks: Journalism Writing at the Century's Edge*
Ray Laakaniemi, *Newswriting in Transition*
Fred S. Parrish, *Photojournalism: An Introduction*
Carole Rich, *Writing and Reporting News: A Coaching Method,* 3rd Ed.
Carole Rich, *Workbook for Writing and Reporting News,* 3rd Ed.

Photojournalism and Photography
Fred S. Parrish, *Photojournalism: An Introduction*
Marvin Rosen and David DeVries, *Introduction to Photography,* 4th Ed.

Public Relations and Advertising
Jerry A. Hendrix, *Public Relations Cases,* 5th Ed.
Jerome A. Jewler and Bonnie L. Drewniany, *Creative Strategy in Advertising,* 7th Ed.
Eugene Marlow, *Electronic Public Relations*
Doug Newsom and Bob Carrell, *Public Relations Writing: Form and Style,* 6th Ed.
Doug Newsom, Judy VanSlyke Turk, and Dean Kruckeberg, *This Is PR: The Realities of Public Relations,* 7th Ed.
Juliann Sivulka, *Soap, Sex, and Cigarettes: A Cultural History of American Advertising*
Gail Baker Woods, *Advertising and Marketing to the New Majority: A Case Study Approach*

Research and Theory
Earl Babbie, *The Practice of Social Research,* 8th Ed.
Stanley Baran and Dennis Davis, *Mass Communication Theory: Foundations, Ferment, and Future,* 2nd Ed.
Sondra Rubenstein, *Surveying Public Opinion*
Rebecca B. Rubin, Alan M. Rubin, and Linda J. Piele, *Communication Research: Strategies and Sources,* 5th Ed.
Roger D. Wimmer and Joseph R. Dominick, *Mass Media Research: An Introduction,* 6th Ed.

Media/Impact

AN introduction TO MASS MEDIA

FIFTH EDITION

SHIRLEY BIAGI
California State University, Sacramento

Wadsworth
Thomson Learning

Australia • Canada • Mexico • Singapore • Spain • United Kingdom • United States

Mass Communication Editor: Karen Austin
Executive Editor: Deirdre Cavanaugh
Publisher: Clark Baxter
Executive Marketing Manager: Stacey Purviance
Project Editor: Cathy Linberg
Print Buyer: Barbara Britton
Permissions Editor: Joohee Lee
Technology Project Manager: Jeanette Wiseman
Production Service: Electronic Publishing Services Inc., NYC
Text Designer: Studio Montage
Photo Researcher: Terri Wright
Copy Editor: Electronic Publishing Services Inc., NYC
Cover Designer: Gary Palmatier
Cover Images: Tony Stone Images/Chicago and PhotoDisc
Cover Printer: Phoenix Color
Compositor: Electronic Publishing Services Inc., NYC
Printer: Quebecor World, Versailles

Chapter Opener Photo Credits: *Chapter 1*
Brooks Kraft/Sygma; *Chapter 2* Michael Newman/
PhotoEdit; *Chapter 3* Francis Hogan/Electronic
Publishing Services Inc., NYC; *Chapter 4* PhotoDisc,
Inc.; *Chapter 5* Deborah Davis/PhotoEdit; *Chapter 6*
Francis Hogan/Electronic Publishing Services Inc.,
NYC; *Chapter 7* Peter Beck/Uniphoto; *Chapter 8*
Francis Hogan/Electronic Publishing Services Inc.,
NYC; *Chapter 9* Francis Hogan/Electronic
Publishing Services Inc., NYC; *Chapter 10* Goodby,
Silverstein & Partners; *Chapter 11* AP/Wide World
Photos; *Chapter 12* John Neubauer/PhotoEdit;
Chapter 13 Courtesy of The *New York Daily News*;
Chapter 14 N. Tully/CORBIS Sygma; *Chapter 15*
Reuters/Ian Waldie/Archive Photos; *Chapter 16*
Ulrike Welsch/Stock, Boston

ExamView® and *ExamView Pro®* are trademarks of
FSCreations, Inc. Windows is a registered trademark of
the Microsoft Corporation used herein under license.
Macintosh and Power Macintosh are registered trademarks of Apple Computer, Inc. Used herein under license.

Library of Congress Cataloging-in-Publication Data
Biagi, Shirley.
    Media impact : an introduction to mass media /
Shirley Biagi.--5th ed.
        p. cm.
Includes bibliographical references and index.
ISBN 0-534-57510-2 (pbk.) -- ISBN 0-534-57511-0
(instructor's ed.)
1. Mass media.
P90.B489 2000
302.23—dc21   00-027152

Wadsworth/Thomson Learning
10 Davis Drive
Belmont, CA 94002-3098
USA

For information about our products, contact us:
Thomson Learning Academic Resource Center
1-800-423-0563
http://www.wadsworth.com

International Headquarters
Thomson Learning
International Division
290 Harbor Drive, 2nd Floor
Stamford, CT 06902-7477
USA

UK/Europe/Middle East/South Africa
Thomson Learning
Berkshire House
168-173 High Holborn
London WC1V 7AA
United Kingdom

Asia
Thomson Learning
60 Albert Street, #15-01
Albert Complex
Singapore 189969

Canada
Nelson Thomson Learning
1120 Birchmount Road
Toronto, Ontario M1K 5G4
Canada

♻ *This book is printed on acid-free recycled paper.*

Brief Contents

Detailed Contents

Chapter 2

Newspapers   35

Chapter 3

Magazines   61

Chapter 4

Books 81

Chapter 5

Radio   101

Chapter 6

Recordings   127

Chapter 8
Movies   177

Chapter 9

Digital Media and the Web   203

Chapter 10

Advertising   227

Chapter 11

Public Relations   247

Chapter 12

Mass Media and Social Issues   267

Chapter 13

Media Ownership and Press Performance   291

Chapter 14

Law and Regulation   309

Chapter 15

Ethics   345

Chapter 16

A Global Media Marketplace   365

Impact/Critical Insights

Preface

In spring 1997, an extraordinary meeting took place at the San Francisco Bay Area office of Wadsworth Publishing. I was invited by Wadsworth to meet with 10 members of the Wadsworth staff who publish communications texts for the company. Around a large conference room table, everyone from the company's new president to the editorial assistant for communications participated actively in an intense discussion that lasted more than eight hours. We all shared the same goal—to create the best possible fourth edition of *Media/Impact.*

Just a few months since the previous edition of *Media/Impact* had been published, we were talking about a very ambitious revision, to be accomplished within a year. It seemed an impossibility, but you are holding in your hands the exciting result of a commitment that began with that meeting: the fifth edition of *Media/Impact,* comprehensively explaining today's mass media with the most timely information available, published in a beautifully designed, accessible format.

EXCITING NEW FEATURES THAT MAKE THIS EDITION DIFFERENT

To the strong foundation established in previous editions, I have continued and updated these important features from the last edition:

- *Chapter One: You in the Digital Age,* describes and explains how the new media landscape will affect today's students.

- *Chapter Nine: Digital Media and the Web,* focuses on how the contributions of digital technology and the Internet are transforming traditional media.

- *Chapter Twelve: Mass Media and Social Issues,* contains important information on multiculturalism and the media, plus a discussion of the media's portrayal of alternative lifestyles.

- *Impact/On You,* a special feature in each chapter that highlights information about how the mass media affect people in their everyday lives.

- *Impact/Digital,* 17 new perspectives on the latest trends, including forecasts for the media's digital transformation.

- *Impact/Point of View,* offering provocative short essays throughout the book on contemporary media topics to stimulate critical discussion.

- *Impact/Profiles* throughout the text feature the contributions of significant people—Ida Tarbell, Ernie Pyle, Edward R. Murrow and others—who have shaped the development of the mass media.

- *TimeFrames,* adding context to explain each mass media industry, presented in an innovative format that begins today, and then moves backward in time to uncover each medium's early origins.

- *Working the Web,* offering important website information at the end of each chapter for online media research.

- *InfoTrac Exercises,* offers challenging assignments for students to learn about contemporary media issues with this valuable research tool.

IMPORTANT FEATURES THAT I RETAINED AND IMPROVED

This edition of *Media/Impact* maintains the strongest features of earlier editions, including:

- A contextual basis for historical information to add perspective to today's developments.

- A thematic approach that encourages critical thinking.

- The best current scholarship on mass media topics from contemporary experts.

- All the important statistics that anyone could ever need to keep track of the shifting digital media marketplace.

- A writing style that presents information in a way students can understand and enjoy.

I also have revised and improved many other important features of *Media/Impact* that teachers and students have sought from the first edition, including:

- Nine totally redesigned *Impact/Industry* to vividly portray the key elements of each media business.

- A completely updated *Media Glossary,* including the latest terms to help enhance students' digital vocabulary.

- A comprehensive, revised *Student Resource Guide,* including an alphabetical listing of *100 website resources* for media information, organized for easy reference.

WADSWORTH OFFERS NEW RESOURCES FOR STUDENTS AND TEACHERS

To this exciting new edition, Wadsworth has added important new resources. *InfoTrac College Edition,* a searchable online database with more than half a million full-text articles, allows students to expand their knowledge of media issues with contemporary articles from all the major media, plus video clips from library and network news sources. Also, at the end of each chapter is a valuable list of InfoTrac exercises to help students explore critical media topics and issues. In addition, a series of *CNN Videos,* with video segments keyed to material in the text, is available to professors by arrangement with Wadsworth.

For teachers, author Jan Haag has totally revised the *Instructor's Manual,* including complete lecture outlines, multiple choice and essay test items, suggested student assignments, InfoTrac exercises, and a list of CNN videos available through Wadsworth for classroom use. For more information, instructors can request the *Media/Impact Instructor's Manual* package from their Wadsworth Sales Representative or contact Wadsworth Faculty Support by visiting their website at:

http://communication.wadsworth.com

A comprehensive, multimedia presentation tool, *MediaLink,* accompanies this text. Authored by Richard Caplan, University of Akron, this robust PowerPoint program is available on a cross-platform CD-ROM and includes chapter-by-chapter lecture outlines, content hyperlinks, video clips, and photos. Designed to assist professors, *MediaLink* follows the content organization of *Media/Impact* and provides you with a powerful way to enhance your lectures.

ACKNOWLEDGMENTS

Every detail of this book's format and design is the result of the painstaking care of the Wadsworth team that created this edition of *Media/Impact*. Their names appear on the copyright page.

This fifth edition of *Media/Impact* also reflects the suggestions, contributions, and wisdom of the reviewers, for which I am very grateful. They are as follows: **5th Edition:** David Donnelly, University of Houston; Michael Murray, University of Missouri-St Louis; Debra Merskin, University of Oregon; Bradley Lemonds, Santa Monica College; Marshel Rossow, Minnesota State University, Mankato; and Edgar Trotter, California State University, Fullerton. **4th Edition:** Ed Adams, Angelo State University; Thomas Beell, Iowa State University; Michael Carlebach, University of Miami; Meta G. Carstarphen, University of North Texas; Thomas E. Diamond, Montana State University; Irving Fang, University of Minnesota; Trom Grimes, Kansas State University; Kenneth Hardwood, University of Houston; Jules D'hemecourt, Louisiana State University; Sharon Hollenback, Syracuse University; Steve Jones, Tulsa University; Robert G. Main, California State University, Chico; Maclyn Mcclary, Humboldt State University; Kenneth D. Mcmillen, University of Oklahoma; Jim Mitchell, University of Arizona; Tina Pieraccini, State University of New York, Oswego; Peter Pringle, University of Tennessee, Chattanooga; Marshall Rossow, Menkato State University; Randall R. Scott, University of Memphis;

Linda Steiner, Rutgers University; Lee Thomas, Doane College; Mary Trapp, California State University, Hayward; John Ullman, University of Wisconsin-Eau Claire; Hazel Warlaumont, California State University, Fullerton; Bill Withers, Buena Vista University; and Meriam Zimmermann, College of Notre Dame. **3rd Edition:** Jim Bolick, Colorado State University; Ford Burkhart, University of Arizona; Timothy Meyer, University of Wisconsin-Green Bay; Peter Pringle, University of Tennessee, Chattanooga; and Linda Steiner, Rutgers University. **2nd Updated Edition:** Jim Bolick, Colorado State University; Kenneth Hardwood, University of Houston; Greg Lisby, Georgia State University; Timothy Meyer, University of Wisconsin-Green Bay; Linda Steiner, Rutgers University; David R. Thompson, Southwest Texas State University; and Don Tomlinson, Texas A&M University. **2nd Edition:** Paul H. Anderson, University of Tennessee At Martin; Michael Carlebach, University of Miami; Jack F. Hogate, University of Southern Mississippi; Tom Jacobson, State University of New York, Buffalo; and Richard Alan Nelson, Kansas State University. **1st Updated Edition:** Michael Carlebach, University of Miami; Danae Clark, University of Pittsburgh; William Miller, Ohio University; David Mould, Ohio University; Ray Newton, Northern Arizona University; Patricia Bowie Orman, University of Southern Colorado; Manny Paraschos, Emerson College; Jim Patten, University of Arizona; Peter Pringle, University of Tennessee, Chattanooga; Penny Summers, Northern Kentucky University; Jim Tyman, University of Michigan; and Laura Widmer, Northwest Missouri State University. **1st Edition:** Roy Alden Atwood, University of Idaho; Thomas L. Beell, Iowa State University; Gerald Flannery, University of Southwestern Louisiana; Kenneth Hardwood, University of Houston; James Hoyt, University of Wisconsin, Madison; Seong Lee, Appalachian State University; Alfred Lorenz, Loyola University; Maclyn Mcclary, Humboldt State University; Robert Mcconnell, Ball State University; Daniel G. Mcdonald, Cornell University; Alston Morgan, Oral Roberts University; Marlan D. Nelson, Oklahoma State University; Richard Alan Nelson, University of Houston; John H. Vivian, Winona State University; Donald K. Wright, University of Southern Alabama; and Eugenia Zerbinos, University of Maryland.

PEOPLE WHO ARE CRUCIALLY IMPORTANT

None of this would have been possible, of course, without that spring 1997 meeting. And the spring 1997 meeting would not have happened without the support of Susan Badger, Wadsworth's president, who I believe has been central to this book's success. For her continued interest and belief in *Media/Impact,* I am very grateful.

I also would like to thank the current Wadsworth communication team for their patience with my persistent personality, especially the new Mass Communication Editor Karen Austin; my students, who give me continuing inspiration; all the members of my family, who nurture me with constant humor and great new ideas, and especially Vic Bondi, my favorite statistician.

I hope you have an opportunity to explore all of *Media/Impact*'s features. And please let me know what you think. My e-mail address is:

sbiagi@saclink.csus.edu

Shirley Biagi

About the Author

Shirley Biagi is a professor in the Department of Communication Studies at California State University, Sacramento. She is the author of several Wadsworth communications texts besides *Media/Impact*, including *Media/Reader: Perspectives on Mass Media Industries, Effects and Issues* and *Interviews That Work: A Practical Guide for Journalists.* She is co-author, with Marilyn Kern-Foxworth of Texas A&M University, of *Facing Difference: Race, Gender and Mass Media*, published by Pine Forge Press. She also is editor of the national media history quarterly *American Journalism*, published by the American Journalism Historians Association.

She has served as guest faculty for the Poynter Institute, the American Press Institute, the National Writers Workshop, and the Hearst Fellowship Program at the *Houston Chronicle*. She also has been a project interviewer for the Washington (D.C.) Press Club Foundation's Women in Journalism Oral History Project, which completed 57 oral histories of female pioneers in journalism. Her international experience includes guest lecture appointments at Al Ahram Press Institute in Cairo, Egypt, and Queensland University in Brisbane, Australia.

CHAPTER 11

You in the digital AGE

What has happened already is bound to be very *small* in comparison to what lies *ahead.*

Nathan Myhrvold, digital pioneer

magine an appliance that's as easy to use as the telephone, with pictures and sound, offering a massive choice of information, entertainment, and services whenever you want them. You can use this appliance to:

- Watch your favorite program whenever you want to see it;
- See a first-run movie and have an on-screen dialog with the movie's producer about her latest movie release;
- Order groceries delivered from a local market;
- Play the newest video game online with three people you've never met;
- Conduct research for your college term paper;
- Make airline reservations for a trip home during semester break;
- Transfer funds from your savings account to your checking account to cover checks you wrote today.

With all of these services, you can use them individually or all at the same time, whenever you want.

Futurists call this new machine an "information appliance" or a "teleputer," a combination of *television* and *computer* technology. This information appliance is one of the central elements in what has been called the digital superhighway. "The teleputer will end the [current] decade not as a luxury but as an indispensable appliance," says futurist George Gilder.[1]

The digital superhighway, in fact, is more like an intricate, webbed network of many different types of communications systems. Ideally, this network will be connected to each home, school, library, and business, creating a complex universal pathway for high-speed communication.

The digital highway is receiving a great deal of attention today because government has placed communications on the public agenda. More than ten years ago, Vice President Al Gore (when he was a U.S. senator) coined the term *information highway*. Since then, the road has been upgraded to a *digital* highway.

Today, the term *digital highway* is used to describe an interconnected digital communications system using broadcast, telephone, satellite, cable, and computer technologies to connect everyone in the United States (and eventually around the world) to a variety of services. Ideally, this communications system would be accessible and affordable to everyone. The issue, as futurist George Gilder phrased it, is, "Who will ride the next avalanche of bits on the information superhighway—and who will be buried under it?"[2]

UNDERSTANDING THE COMMUNICATION PROCESS

To understand the digital highway, first it is important to understand the process of communication. Communication is the act of sending ideas and attitudes from one person to another. Writing and talking to each other are only two ways human beings communicate. We also communicate when we gesture, move our bodies, or roll our eyes.

Three terms that scholars use to describe how people communicate are *intrapersonal communication, interpersonal communication,* and *mass communication.* Each communication situation involves different numbers of people in specific ways.

If you are in a grocery store and you silently discuss with yourself whether to buy a package of chocolate chip cookies, you are using what scholars call **intra**personal communication: communication within one person.

To communicate with each other, people use many of the five senses— sight, hearing, touch, smell, and taste. Scholars call this direct sharing of experience between two people **inter**personal communication.

mass communication
communication from one person or group of persons through a transmitting device to large audiences or markets.

Mass communication is communication from one person or group of persons through a transmitting device (a medium) to large audiences or markets. In MEDIA/IMPACT you will study mass communication.

To describe the process of mass communication, scholars draw charts and diagrams to convey what happens when people send messages to one another. This description begins with five easily understood terms: *sender, message, receiver, channel,* and *feedback.* (See Figure 1.1.)

Figure 1.1 Elements of Mass Communication   The process of mass communication: A sender (source) puts a message on a channel, which is the medium that delivers the message to the receiver. Feedback occurs when the receiver responds, and that response changes subsequent messages from the source.

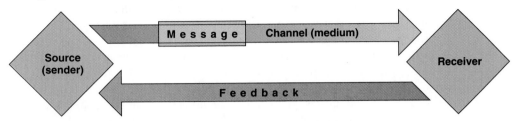

Pretend that you're standing directly in front of someone and you say, "I like your hat." In this simple communication, you are the sender, the message is "I like your hat," and the person in front of you is the receiver (or audience). This example of interpersonal communication involves the sender, the message and the receiver.

In mass communication, the **sender** (or **source**) puts the message on what is called a **channel.** The sender (source) could be your local cable company, for example. The channel delivers the *message.* The channel could be the cable line that hooks into the back of your TV set. A **medium** is the means by which a message reaches an audience. (The plural of the word *medium* is *media;* when scholars discuss more than one medium, they refer to **media.**) Your television set is the medium that delivers the message simultaneously to you (and many other people).

Feedback occurs when the receivers process the message and send a response back to the sender (source). Using a very crude example, say that the cable company (sender/source) sends an advertisement for pizza (the message) over the cable line (channel) into your TV set (medium). If you (the receiver) use the controls on your interactive TV set to order a pizza, the order you place ultimately will bring you a pizza (feedback). This entire loop between sender and receiver, and the resulting response (feedback) of the receiver to the sender, describes the process of mass communication.

Using a very general definition, mass communication today shares three characteristics:

1. A message is sent out on some form of mass media system (such as the Internet, print, or broadcast).

2. The message is delivered rapidly.

3. The message reaches large groups of different kinds of people simultaneously or within a short period of time.[3]

Thus, a telephone conversation between two people would not qualify as mass communication, but a message from the President of the United States, broadcast simultaneously by all of the television networks, would qualify.

Mass media deliver messages to large numbers of people at once. The businesses that produce the mass media in America—newspapers, magazines, radio, television, movies, recordings and books—are the traditional mass media industries. New media are developing to respond to the Internet as a new digital delivery system.

media plural of the word medium.

feedback a response sent back to the sender from the person who receives the communication.

TAKING ADVANTAGE OF THE DIGITAL DELIVERY

The economics of the communications industries make the digital highway an important issue for the United States. All of the industries involved in building and maintaining this interconnected network—broadcast, cable, telephone, computer, software, satellite, and consumer electronics industries—want a piece of the estimated $1 trillion that such a project represents. Leaders of the media industries in the United States believe that the nation is ideally positioned to be the first to develop such a network because many Americans already have most of the tools that such a system needs.

As Figure 1.2 indicates, nearly all of the households in the United States have televisions and telephones, more than three-fourths have VCRs, two-thirds are connected to cable, and half have personal computers. Because the United States already leads the world in so many of the digital highway's necessary elements, people in the media industries believe that it would be logical—and very profitable—for the media industries in this country to develop the technology to package and deliver information worldwide.

One-Way Versus Two-Way Communication

The classic model of mass communication (see p. 3 and Figure 1.1) describes a process that begins with a sender (or source), who puts a message on a channel (a medium); the channel delivers the message to the receiver. This can be described as the equivalent of a one-way road, sender to receiver. The information highway, as envisioned today, begins in the same way. The channel will carry information and entertainment (messages) from many different sources (senders) to many different people (receivers).

The messages that return from the receiver to the sender are called *feedback*. On this new digital highway, messages and feedback can occur instantaneously. The sender and the receiver can communicate with each other at the same time.

To accomplish this, today's delivery system must develop from a communications system that works like an ordinary television (sending messages and programming one-way from the sender to the receiver) to a two-way digital

Figure 1.2 Access to Media Tools

Data from *Communications Daily, The Veronis, Suhler & Associates Communications Industry Forecast* 1999–2003.

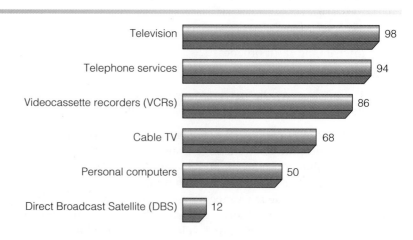

Percentage of U.S. households with access to media tools

system that can send and receive messages simultaneously and that works more like a combination television and computer. This is why some futurists have called this new information appliance a *teleputer.*

"Dumb" Versus "Smart" Communication

The television set is a "dumb" appliance; it can only deliver programming. You can change the channel to receive different programs, but you can't talk back to the people who send the programming to your television set to tell them when you'd like to see a particular program. You can't watch something when you want to watch it, unless you remember ahead of time to tape the program on your VCR. You also can't add anything to the programs on your TV. You can't add your personal commentary about sports programs or replace a bad movie with a good one. This type of mass communication—in which the programs are sent to you on an established schedule and you are a passive receiver (a couch potato) for the program—is *one-way.*

As communications devices, however, telephones are smarter. When you talk on the telephone, the person on the other end of the conversation can listen to you and talk back right away (and, in the case of a teleconference, this can involve several people at the same time). This ability to let you talk back—to receive as well as to transmit messages—makes the telephone **interactive.** Telephone communications are *two-way.*

interactive the ability to receive as well as transmit messages.

To communicate rapidly, telephone communication uses a system of digitized information. When you talk, the telephone system uses electronic signals to transform your voice into a series of digits—ones and zeroes—and then reassembles these digits into an exact reproduction of your voice on the other end of the line. This method of storing and transmitting data is called **digital.**

Like telephone communications, computers also operate using digitized information and they are also interactive. Written words, audio, and video are translated and stored as *bits.* These bits can easily be transmitted, using two-way communication. This is the reason that someone can, for instance, dial up the Internet on a computer and receive and send information. To dial up the Internet, someone uses a device called a *modem,* which connects the computer to a telephone line, making two-way communication possible.

digital information that has been transformed so that it can be transmitted electronically.

Jeff Stahler. Reprinted by Permission of United Features Syndicate, Inc.

And, unlike television and telephones, computers can store information for future use. This ability to store information makes the computer different from broadcast, cable, and telephone communications. "Nearly all of the relevant activity is in the computer industry rather than the television industry," says Gilder. "In the information economy, the best opportunities stem from the exponential rise in the power of computers and computer networks."[4]

HOW THE NEW COMMUNICATIONS NETWORK WILL FUNCTION

The communications network of the future will combine different elements from each of these industries. Today, the broadcast industry can produce content and deliver one-way communication by antenna; the cable industry can deliver one-way communication, and very limited two-way communication, by underground (or overhead) cable; the telephone companies can efficiently deliver digital two-way communication using fiber optics; and the computer industry can create digital storage capability. The network of the future must combine all of these elements: content, two-way digital communication and digital storage. Figure 1.3 shows how this communications network of the future will work.

The Receiver (You, the Subscriber)

The network begins with you, the receiver/subscriber. You choose which services you want. Using a device similar to a TV remote control, but larger, you will turn on your television/computer. The screen will show you a menu of services, much like a computer menu. A **set-top box** sitting on top of your

Figure 1.3   The New Communications Network

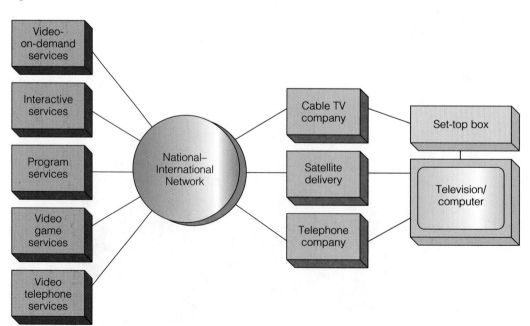

television/computer will be your electronic link to the new communications network. The services will include:

- An online edition of your local newspaper;
- A listing of programs by category (such as comedy, dramas or specials);
- A national video news service;
- A worldwide video news service;
- A library database research service;
- A sports video and information service;
- A family and lifestyle video and information service;
- A travel video and information service;
- A shopping video and information service;
- A music video and information service;
- An online game site;
- A listing of bulletin board discussion group services by topic;
- A video telephone message service, with video messages from the day's callers;
- A first-run movie service.

By clicking your remote control, you can glance through the offerings of each service and then make your choices. Your television/computer will show several screens at once, so that you can use several services at the same time, each on a different screen. For example, you might check your bank balance while you watch a basketball game or check your video phone messages while you watch the news headlines.

The software in the set-top box also will track your usage, detailing the charges for the services you choose. As there is for today's cable users, there will probably be a basic service fee, and then additional charges added as you use premium services.

The Channel (Cable, Telephone, and Satellite Companies)

Delivery will be provided by a cable or satellite company. The cable, telephone, and satellite companies will act as a conduit for all services, gathering them from the national or international network. These companies may choose to offer only specific services; they might package some services together (local, national, and international news services, for example); or they may offer an unlimited menu of all services available, and let you make the choices.

As now envisioned, the cable, telephone, and satellite companies will compete for business in each city. Customers will choose which type of service they want, based on each company's offerings and pricing. Some services will be billed as pay-per-view (there might be a $5 charge to view a first-run movie, for example) or per-minute (to use a library database for research, for example). Billing for these services would arrive monthly or, of course, the company could bill the amount directly to your checking account or your credit card.

The cable, telephone, and satellite companies will be connected to the program services by a national and international network or by a satellite system.

IMPACT

point of view   *The Dawn of Technomania*

By Nathan Myhrvold

It is easy to get caught up in technomania. Those who are most deeply involved with technology want to know more, those who fear it want reassurance, and those who see an opportunity—financial or other—don't want to miss out. *It's gonna change everything. It's gonna be here next Thursday. Watch out or you'll be left behind!*

Even newspaper gossip columns have become technomanical. Suddenly, the geeks who used to ace the math exam are the barons of the information age. If *The Graduate* were to be remade for the late nineties, the single word of advice imparted to Benjamin would be "information."

Such, in any case, is the popular notion, although in the short run it is hopelessly exaggerated. A lot of guys with tool belts will have to shinny up a lot of phone poles before digital television or high-speed Internet gets to your home. Someday, Internet firms will be a major force in the economy. Indeed, someday they will even—dare I predict it!—make a profit. But it will take years before the aggregate sales volume of the Internet industry measures up to that of, say, the pantyhose industry.

In some ways, every attribute of technomania has a parallel in

Karen Moskowitz/CORBIS Outline

the industromania of a hundred years ago. By 1897, large factories had sprouted, creating the notion of "going to work" in urban areas. Previously, cities had been centers of commerce which served the primary source of wealth—the agrarian countryside. Now they became the centers of both population and power. This caused other shifts, as organized labor started to take hold, and a political transformation followed.

Inventions emerged from everywhere—typewriter in 1874, the telephone in 1876, the internal-combustion engine and the phonograph in 1877, electric lights in 1880, the zipper in 1891, and radio in 1895....Few imagined that the industrial revolution

would continue at the same pace for 60 years more....

The twilight of the twentieth century is driven by a mixture of technology and resources very like that which drove nineteenth-century America. This time, it is silicon and software rather than oil and steel. Instead of transcontinental railroads, we have a global communication infrastructure that links us as the railroads did, but at the speed of light. And, once again, this change is being driven by people from around the world, making possible an unprecedented level of economic growth.

Still, we may not be able to gauge the real impact of the information revolution for fifty or sixty years more. Consider our cities, which in many cases have been transformed into artifacts of industrialization. Will large numbers of people begin to telecommute and, in that way, return to a pastoral America? Or will the cities somehow become even more necessary to our lives? Technomania, like its industrial equivalent in 1897, is a reminder that all this lies just beyond our knowing. What has happened already is bound to be very small in comparison to what lies ahead.

The New Yorker, 10/20—27/97, pp. 236—237. Used by permission.

This network and the satellite system are already in place today—the long-distance carrier networks such as AT&T and MCI and satellite services such as USSB. The domestic long-distance networks would probably appear as a basic fee on your television/computer bill; international services would be an additional cost. The **Internet,** an international web of computer networks, will probably become a low-fee backbone of the new network, available to anyone with a television/computer and a cable, satellite, or telephone hookup.

Internet an international web of computer networks.

The Sender (Program Services)

Program services will provide:

1. Video on demand, such as movies.
2. Interactive services, such as banking, shopping, bulletin boards, online newspapers and information research services.
3. Video telephone services.
4. Program services (comedies, game shows, soaps, and sports).
5. Video game services.

Today's broadcast networks and today's cable channels will become program services, so that you could subscribe to NBC and ABC and not CBS, for example. The cable channels, such as MTV and CNN, would provide programming in much the way they do now, and you could select the program services you wanted.

The Message (Content)

All print, audio, and video that is digitized into bits becomes content for a digitized communications system. In this future of networked, rapid, digitized communications, *any* digitized textbook, novel, movie, magazine article, or news story, for example, qualifies as content.

Information and entertainment that has already been produced, stored, and digitized will become the first content. Companies that hold the copyrights on information and entertainment will be able to market quickly and easily the content they own as products, because they won't have to purchase the rights to digitize the content.

Media companies that already produce content, such as newspaper publishers, book publishers, TV program producers, and movie producers, are

Satellite companies such as Direct TV are competing with cable and telephone companies to deliver services to consumers.

Pablo Bartholomew/Gamma Liaison

Digitized video makes information available in many different formats, such as this website for the Radio Advertising Bureau.

busy creating more "inventory," so they will be ready for the online world when it comes. "Movie companies have been increasing production," says *The Wall Street Journal*, "because there is a general feeling that as 'content providers' they will be big winners in the coming age of the information superhighway."[5]

As information and entertainment products are digitized, they will become available in many different formats as quickly as they can be created. For example, a music video of Disney songs could be made available online as soon as the new Disney movie is released; a background story on a well-known musician could be created by a news organization, complete with video and sound, and made available online during the musician's worldwide concert tour; or a publisher could assemble excerpts and photos from a new book, along with an interview with the author, and make it available on the communications network as the book hits bookstores.

HOW THE NEW COMMUNICATIONS NETWORK IS DIFFERENT

Two-way communication on this new network makes it possible for you to receive and send information. You can decide to produce a screenplay, put an ad for your screenplay on a bulletin board, and respond to anyone who wants to see your produced screenplay. Viewers might pay you a fee to receive the video and audio, or you could create a mystery roundtable with authors from different parts of the world contributing to the screenplay. Then you produce the screenplay for the network, complete with music that you could distribute through an online music network.

Computer networks "free individuals from the shackles of corporate bureaucracy and geography and allow them to collaborate and exchange ideas with the best colleague anywhere in the world," says George Gilder.

"Computer networks give every hacker the creative potential of a factory tycoon of the industrial [turn-of-the-century] era and the communications power of a TV magnate of the broadcasting era."[6]

In an interconnected world, the speed and convenience of the network could redefine the mass media industries and erase all previous notions of how mass communication should work.

Creating the Network

The digital highway promises to make all of these services, and many more, available to every single person in the nation, at an affordable price, in the same way that telephone service today is accessible to almost everybody. In 1994, Congress named this new effort to coordinate all of the different senders, channels, and receivers the National Information Infrastructure (NII). In the history of audio and video communication in the United States, the government has always played a regulatory role.

Vice President Al Gore, in proposing the new telecommunications structure, said that three principles would guide its creation:

1. Private industry, not the government, will build the superhighway.

2. Programmers and information providers should be guaranteed access to the superhighway to promote a diversity of consumer choices.

3. Steps should be taken to ensure universal service, so that the highway does not create a society of information "haves" and "have nots."[7]

The NII would be responsible for making sure that all players in the telecommunications arena follow these principles.

Government Regulation

The federal government regulates the new network, and the issue of what will be allowed to be transmitted on the Internet is controversial. In 1996, Congress passed the Telecommunications Act of 1996. Part of that legislation was the Communications Decency Act (CDA), which outlined certain content to be permitted on the Internet. As soon as the act passed, civil liberties organizations challenged the law, and in 1997 the U.S. Supreme Court upheld the concept that the government should not control content on the Internet. (For more information on this legislation, see Chapter 14.)

Copyrights for Intellectual Property

Another reason that the government would supervise the development of the new network is that digitized bits, once they are widely available, could easily be lifted from a television/computer and reproduced for profit. Writers and other creative people who provide the content for the media industries are especially concerned about their ideas being reproduced in several different formats, with no compensation for their property. This issue, the protection of what are called *intellectual property rights*, will be another important part of the design of the new communications network.

It would be possible to capture video from *Dharma and Greg* and join individual bits from that video with bits from an episode of *Saturday Night Live*, putting the two casts together in a newly digitized program. And once these bits could be captured from a network and stored, they would be available to anyone who wanted to manipulate them. This is one of the dilemmas created by digitized

images that can be transmitted to anyone's storage system over an international network. The creative people who contribute this content, and the people who produce and own these programs, are watching carefully that the new laws and regulations will be structured to protect intellectual property rights.

FIVE CHALLENGES FOR THE NEW NETWORK

"Now comes the interesting part," reports *The Wall Street Journal.* "Builders of the information highway have created a media sensation with their plans for wiring America. But to deliver on their promises they will have to meet challenges of unprecedented complexity and size….Like early railroad builders who laid their tracks in different widths more than a century ago, the purveyors of the information highway are using largely incompatible technologies."[8]

For the new communications network to work, five technological developments must take place. These are: (1) improved storage, (2) a coordinated delivery system, (3) a "smart" set-top box, (4) usable menus, and (5) secure ordering and billing systems.

Improved Storage

The main technological advance that makes the new communications network possible is that today's electronic systems can now transform all text, audio, and video communication into digital information. However, no current system can store the digitized information that the new network for text, audio, and video would require.

Researchers are trying to eliminate the need for so many bytes. They are turning to a process called **data compression.** "A single copy of *Jurassic Park,* for example, contains about 100 billion bytes of data. Compression will enable the dinosaur epic to be squeezed down to about 4 billion bytes…But even then, the movie will be big enough to fill the equivalent of 20 personal computers."[9]

When researchers perfect data compression, it will mean that a program service, for example, will need much less storage space to keep movies avail-

data compression a process that squeezes digital information into a smaller electronic space.

able for use. This will help make the movie affordable for a program service to deliver and usable for the customer, who won't need as much data space on the television/computer to view the movie.

Once the data is compressed, it must be stored by the people who will deliver the service. Then researchers must also invent a machine that will grab a selection from the storage area and deliver it to the customer as requested. This *video transfer machine* is often called a **server** because it must be able to serve hundreds of programs to thousands of subscribers, on demand, all at the same time. No one has yet invented a machine that can handle this much volume.

server the equipment that delivers programs from the program source to the program's subscribers.

A Coordinated Delivery System

Today's communication system is a mixture of old and new technologies. For the new communications network, old technology must be replaced with new technology throughout the system

Broadcasters today, for example, send pictures and sounds over airwaves using the same technology they have used since the 1930s, when broadcasting was first introduced. This technology is called **analog.**

Analog technology encodes video and audio information as continuous signals. Then these signals are broadcast through the air on specific airwave frequencies to your TV set, which translates them into pictures and sounds. Analog technology is a very cumbersome way to move information from one place to another because the signal takes up a lot of space on the airwaves. But because the analog signals travel through the air by transmitters, you can receive them free through an antenna. About 20 percent of the homes in the United States still receive only over-the-air broadcasts. They do not subscribe to cable.

analog the original technology that broadcasters used to deliver their signals, using the airwaves to deliver programming.

Cable companies eliminated the need for antennas by using coaxial cable, buried underground or strung from telephone poles. Coaxial cable also uses analog technology. Cable operators capture programming, such as HBO, from satellite systems and put these together with over-the-air analog broadcast signals from your local TV stations and then deliver all of this programming to you, using a combination of coaxial cable, copper wire, and some optical fiber.

Optical fiber is composed of microscopic strands of glass that transmit messages of digitized "bits"—zeros and ones. Each fiber optic strand can carry 250,000 times as much information as one copper wire. It can transmit the entire contents of the *Encyclopaedia Britannica* in one second.[10] A fiber optics communication system is very efficient because digitized information travels easily and quickly from one place to another.

Today's telephone companies have converted almost all of their major communications delivery systems from coaxial cable and copper wire to fiber optics. The incompatibility between analog and digital technology means that all analog signals on non-fiber-optics systems would have to be converted first to digital signals to be able to travel on the information network. Conversion can be very expensive. At today's prices, it would cost about $3,000 to digitize and store one feature-length movie.

The current communications network is a combination of coaxial cable, copper wire, and fiber optics. Digital technology is the most efficient method of delivery, but wiring the whole country with optical fiber is extraordinarily expensive. Satellite delivery of the digital signal directly to the consumer through a cable signal or telephone line may prove to be the most efficient method of delivery.

IMPACT

on you

A Trove of Memorable Moments Goes Online

Time Warner Opens Its Venerable Collection to Rivals, Consumers

By Wendy Bounds
THE WALL STREET JOURNAL

Underneath New York's Rockefeller Center, tucked inside metal cabinets and refrigerated vaults, lie 22 million moments in history.

[In 1999,] much of this archive—Time Inc.'s vast collection of photojournalism and illustrations—[became] available to the public for the first time. Hundreds of thousands of images [went] online for display and licensing via the Internet. The collection, which dates back to the early 1800's, includes such celebrated photos as the sailor and nurse kissing in Times Square on VJ Day, MacArthur wading ashore in the Philippines and Mark McGwire whacking his record-breaking home run.

With this grand photo op, Time Inc., a unit of Time Warner Inc., is riding its stable of magazines—which includes Time, People, Sports Illustrated, and Life—into the race to sell pictures online. Photography is one of the Web's fastest growing businesses, and also one of its most contentious, often pitting photographers and artists, who don't want to lose financial and creative control of their work, against publishers and archives.

In 1995, Bill Gates purchased the Bettmann Archives, one of the world's largest collections of historical photographs with some

Joe Munroe/LIFE Magazine

Some of the pictures available online from the vast Time Inc. archive of published and unpublished images.

Alfred Eisenstaedt/LIFE Magazine/Time Inc.

Margaret Bourke-White/LIFE Magazine/Time Inc.

17 million images, through his privately-owned Corbis Corp. It is now putting the pictures online. Recently, Advance Publications Inc.'s Condé Nast unit bought the Cartoon Bank to chronicle and offer cartoons from The New Yorker magazine electronically.

"Our industry is growing larger and larger, and you need to get maximum exposure of material and return on it," says Ben Chapnick, head of the New York photo agency Black Star. "I'm

very in favor of it because images deteriorate, and moreover, you can find them better electronically."

The Internet is revolutionizing photography for magazines, advertising agencies and book publishers.... Clients once relied on the memories of archivists and musty card catalogs to help them locate images. The Internet lets them search key words and find more photographs, faster.

Visit the Time Warner photo archive at www.thepicturecollection.com.

Article reprinted by permission.

A "Smart" Set-Top Box

Most cable subscribers need a **set-top box**, which translates the various signals so that the TV set can receive the programming and also keep track of the services the subscriber uses. The set-top box sits on top of the TV. For the new national communications network to operate, the set-top box will have to become much smarter than it is now.

The set-top box will be like a switching station, connecting the delivery system coming to the television/computer with your directions for service. This will be the gateway. The set-top box also must be affordable. Some researchers have devised a $3,000 model, but no one yet has invented a successful, affordable set-top box.

> **set-top box** the device that will enable your TV set to receive digitized signals from a variety of sources.

Usable Menus

With all of this programming and all of these services awaiting, the menu will be the way someone navigates the system. Menus "are the software that viewers will see on their screens. It must be simple so technophobes can use it but powerful enough to navigate a mind-numbing assortment of programs."[11] An easy menu system is important, because people who use the system for the first time probably won't be patient enough to figure out something complicated. Researchers say that such a system will require a great deal of consumer testing. "I don't believe we are close to figuring this out," says Arun Netravali, who oversees digital highway technology at AT&T Bell Labs.[12]

Secure Ordering and Billing Systems

Of course, once all of these nice services are available, someone must be billed for the privilege. That's where ordering and billing come in, and developing this process will be challenging. The telephone companies already have a fairly complex system in place that manages to match people with the phone calls they make.

But making sure that your credit card numbers and other personal information are secure from other computer users is more complicated. Software companies must develop systems that will ensure that all the records for interactive transactions are safe. An entirely new industry is being created around the issue of information security.

WHEN WILL THE NEW COMMUNICATIONS NETWORK HAPPEN?

The new communications network, as envisioned by industry and government leaders today, requires that everyone be able to use digitized technology.

Today, broadcasters and cable operators have access to the programming and the services, but they are still using old technology to deliver them. Telephone companies and computer manufacturers are using digital technology, but they don't have access to the programming or the services.

No one yet has created a storage system that can keep the programming and services digitized and ready for you to use on demand. No one yet has created a directory system that would help you find your way through the maze of services and programs that could conceivably be offered on such a system. And no one has devised a secure billing system that could charge everyone accurately for all of the individual services they might choose.

This new communications network, once in place, will have a profound impact on individuals, businesses, and the media industries. For individuals, the new network will affect many everyday activities, such as how people shop, get their news, study, pay bills, even how they socialize with friends. For businesses, national and even global information will be instantly available to more companies at once, making communication much easier, but making competition more intense.

For the media industries, the prospect of a new communications network places every element of each business in transition. Today, owners and managers at the companies that make up the media industries must decide how to invest in equipment, employees, and research and development to protect current income while ensuring that the company will be able to adapt to the demands of the 21st century.

How soon will the new communications network happen? No one can predict. One observer called this a "highway of hype," because so many people are talking about the digital highway even though progress in solving the technological problems seems to be very slow. The changes will probably come gradually, as each challenge to the creation of the new network is solved.

"Computers and television are coming together," says the respected international magazine *The Economist*. "Computers are continuing their relentless march toward greater power at lower cost: that is how microprocessors work. Some giant industries are betting billions on the new TV business: more deals loom. These facts alone guarantee a revolution....Whether it arrives in five years or 15 is almost irrelevant. In the history of communications, 2010 is tomorrow."[13]

UNDERSTANDING THE DIGITAL AGE

When was the last time you spent 24 hours without the media? From the moment you get up in the morning until the time you go to bed at night, the media are waiting to keep you company. Radio news gives you headlines in the shower and traffic reports on the freeway; the newspaper offers you national and local news and helps you keep up with the latest college basketball standings and Garfield's attempts to steal another piece of lasagne; magazines describe new computer software for work, and during your lunch hour they keep you current with the latest fashions; after work, the newest novel competes with your VCR, beckoning you to play a videogame, watch the hottest new video release on DVD, or join an online chat group.

According to industry estimates, the average adult spends more than half of his or her waking life with the media. This is the breakdown of the way Americans divide their time watching, listening and reading:

- About 59 percent of all adults read a daily newspaper; 69 percent of all adults read a newspaper at least once a week.

- Adults spend an average of 80 hours a year reading magazines.

- On weekdays, adults listen to the radio an average of 3 hours and 8 minutes a day.

- Each household leaves the TV set turned on for an average of almost 8 hours a day; adults watch TV an average of 4 hours a day.

- One out of four adults goes to the movies once a month; adults rent an average of one video a week and buy eight videos a year.

- Each American spends an average of $63 per year on recorded music.

- Adults spend an average of 95 hours a year reading books.

- Online households will nearly double to 54 million by 2003.[14]

Some form of mass media touches nearly every American each day—economically, socially, or culturally. The mass media can affect the way you vote and the way you spend your money. It sometimes influences the way you eat, talk, work, study, and relax. This is the *impact* of mass media on American society.

This wide-reaching presence distinguishes American media from the media in other countries. In no other country does the mass media capture so much of people's time and attention. In no other country does the media affect so many aspects of the way people live. And in no other country does the media collect so much money for delivering information and entertainment. The American mass media industries earn about $337 billion a year[15] (see Figure 1.4).

Today's American society has inherited the wisdom and mistakes of the people who work in the mass media and the society that regulates and consumes what the mass media produce. Consider these situations:

- You are a newspaper publisher in a small New England town in the 1700s. You publish an article that angers the local council and they throw you in jail. Yet you want to continue to publish the newspaper. What would you do? (See the discussion of James Franklin and the *New England Courant* in Chapter 2.)

- You have just bought a computer and you want to stay current with new developments in software. You subscribe to *PC World* and *Wired*. How does your choice of magazines reflect the changes in the magazine industry? (See Specialized Magazines Take Over, Chapter 3.)

- You are in a bookstore with $10 to spend. You can't decide whether to buy a novel by Stephen King, a book of poems by Maya Angelou, a travel guide to Mexico or a book by Judy Bloom. What are the economic consequences of these decisions by book buyers for the publishing industry? (See Chapter 4 on consumers' book-buying habits.)

- You download the latest Tori Amos song from the Internet, using MP3 digital technology, which allows you to copy music free. You get the music you want, but are your actions illegal, denying the song's artists the royalties that are due? (See "Music, Tech Giants, Target Cyber Pirates," Chapter 6.)

- You believe you have been misquoted and misrepresented in a major magazine story written by a freelance journalist, so you sue

Figure 1.4 Relative Size of the U.S. Media Industries 2000 (in billions)*

Data from *The Veronis, Suhler & Associates Communications Industry Forecast* 1999–2003.

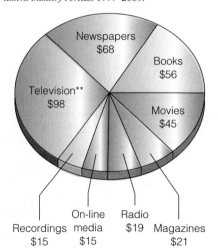

U.S. media industries annual income = $337 billion

*projected

**includes broadcast TV, all cable and direct broadcast satellite (DBS)

the author and the magazine. The case eventually reaches the U.S. Supreme Court. What implications will the court decision have on the media's liability for the stories they print and broadcast? (See *Masson* v. *The New Yorker* magazine, Chapter 14.)

People who work in the media industries and people who watch, listen to, read, and govern what the media offer make choices like these every day. The future of American mass media will be determined by these choices.

UNDERSTANDING THE MASS MEDIA INDUSTRIES: THREE KEY THEMES

This book uses the term **mass media industries** to describe the seven types of traditional American mass media businesses: newspapers, magazines, radio, television, movies, recordings, and books. The use of the word *industries* underscores the major goal of mass media in America—financial success.

But the media are more than businesses: They are key institutions in our society. They affect our culture, our buying habits, and our politics, and they are affected in turn by changes in our beliefs, tastes, interests, and behavior. To help organize your thinking about mass media and their impact, this section introduces three key themes that will recur in the chapters to come: (1) Media are profit-centered businesses; (2) Technology changes the media; and (3) Media both reflect and affect the political, social, and cultural institutions in which they operate.

The Media as Businesses

What you see, read, and hear in the American mass media may cajole, entertain, inform, persuade, provoke, and even perplex you. But to understand the American media, the first concept to understand is that the central

Movies such as *Star Wars*, available to large groups of different kinds of people simultaneously, represent one form of mass communication.

force driving the media in America is the desire to make money: *American media are businesses, vast businesses.* The products of these businesses are information and entertainment.

Other motives shape the media in America, of course: the desire to fulfill the public's need for information, to influence the country's governance, to disseminate the country's culture, to offer entertainment, and to provide an outlet for artistic expression. But American media, above all, are profit-centered.

Who Owns the Media? To understand the media, it is important to know who owns these important channels of communication. In America, all of media is privately owned except the Public Broadcasting Service and National Public Radio, which survive on government support and private donations. The annual budget for public broadcasting, however, is less than 3 percent of the amount advertisers pay every year to support America's commercial media.

Some family-owned media properties still exist in the United States, but today the trend in the media industries, as in other American industries, is for media companies to cluster together in groups. The top ten newspaper chains, for example, own *one-fifth* of the nation's daily newspapers. This trend is called **concentration of ownership** and this concentration takes five different forms.

concentration of ownership the trend of media companies today to consolidate.

1. *Chains.* Benjamin Franklin established America's first newspaper chain. This tradition was expanded by William Randolph Hearst in the 1930s. At their peak, Hearst newspapers accounted for nearly 14 percent of total national daily circulation and nearly 25 percent of Sunday circulation. Today's U.S. newspaper chain giant is Gannett, with 74 daily newspapers, including *USA Today.*

2. *Networks.* A network operates similar to a newspaper chain. It is a collection of radio or television stations that offers programs, usually simultaneously throughout the country, during designated program times. Broadcast companies own groups of stations, called networks, and the **Federal Communications Commission (FCC)** regulates broadcast ownership.

FCC Federal Communications Commission

The four major networks are ABC (American Broadcasting Company), NBC (National Broadcasting Company), CBS (Columbia Broadcasting System), and Fox Broadcasting. NBC, the oldest network, was founded in the 1920s. This network and the two other old ones (CBS and ABC) were established to deliver radio programming across the country, and the network concept continued with the invention of television. Networks can have as many **affiliates** as they want, but no network can have two affiliates in the same broadcast area. (Affiliates are stations that use network programming but are owned by companies other than the networks.)

affiliates stations that use network programming but are owned by companies other than the networks.

Fox is among the youngest networks, founded in 1986, and serves only television. Time Warner and Paramount Communications launched fifth and sixth television networks in 1995, WB (Warner Brothers) and UPN (United Paramount Network).

3. *Cross-Media Ownership.* Many media companies own more than one type of media property: newspapers, magazines, radio and TV stations, for example. Gannett, which owns the largest chain of newspapers, also owns television and radio stations. The merger of Capital Cities/ABC with Disney joined the programming power of Disney with the distribution system of the ABC television network. Rupert Murdoch's News Corporation owns newspapers, television stations, magazines, 20th Century-Fox Film, and Fox Broadcasting.

4. *Conglomerates.* When you go to the movies to watch a Columbia picture, you might not realize that Sony owns the film company. Sony is a *conglomerate*—a company that owns media companies as well as companies unrelated to the media business. Media properties can be attractive investments, but some conglomerate owners are unfamiliar with the idiosyncrasies of the media industries.

5. *Vertical Integration.* The most noticeable trend among today's media companies is **vertical integration**—an attempt by one company to control several related aspects of the media business at once, each part helping the other. For example, besides publishing magazines and books, AOL/Time Warner owns Home Box Office (HBO), Warner movie studios, various cable TV systems throughout the United States and CNN. Seagram's (a company also known for its distilled liquor business) owns Universal Studios and MCA Records. Viacom owns the CBS network, TV stations, movie theaters, and cable networks.

> **vertical integration** an attempt by one company to control several related aspects of the media business at once.

To describe the financial status of today's media is also to talk about acquisitions. The media are buying and selling each other in unprecedented numbers and forming media groups to position themselves in the marketplace to maintain and increase their profits. Since 1986, all three original TV networks—NBC, CBS and ABC—have been bought by new owners.

Media acquisitions have skyrocketed for two reasons. The first is that most conglomerates today are publicly traded companies, which means that their stock is traded on one of the nation's stock exchanges. This makes acquisitions relatively easy.

A media company that wants to buy a publicly owned company can buy that company's stock when the stock becomes available. The open availability

American movies are very popular overseas, representing substantial income for U.S. companies.

AP/Wide World Photos

of stock in these companies means that anybody with enough money can invest in the American media industries, which is exactly how Rupert Murdoch joined the media business.

The second reason for the increase in media alliances is that, beginning in 1980, the Federal Communications Commission (FCC) gradually deregulated the broadcast media. Before 1980, for example, the FCC allowed one company to own only five TV stations, five AM radio stations, and five FM radio stations; companies also were required to hold onto a station for three years before the station could be sold. The post-1980 FCC eliminated the three-year rule and raised the number of broadcast holdings allowed for one owner. This trend of media acquisitions continued throughout the 1990s, as changing technology expanded the market for media products.

The issue of media ownership is important. If only a few corporations direct the media industries in this country, the outlets for differing political viewpoints and innovative ideas could be limited.

Who Pays for the Mass Media? Most of the $337 billion a year in income that the American mass media industries collect comes directly from advertisers. Advertising directly supports newspapers, radio, and television. (Subscribers pay only a small part of the cost of producing a newspaper.) Magazines receive more than half of their income from advertising and the other portion from subscriptions. Income for movies, recordings, and books, of course, comes from direct purchases and ticket sales.

This means that most of the information and entertainment you receive from television, radio, newspapers, and magazines in America is paid for by people who want to sell you products. You support the media industries *indirectly* by buying the products that advertisers sell.

Advertising pays most of the bills. One full-page black-and-white ad in *The Wall Street Journal,* for example, costs about $120,000. To place a full-page color ad in *Rolling Stone* magazine costs about $50,000. A 30-second television commercial in prime time (8 P.M. to 11 P.M.) costs about $100,000. Multiply the prices for all of these ads in all media, and you can understand how easily American media industries accumulate the $337 billion they collect annually.[16]

You also pay for the media *directly* when you buy a book or a compact disc or go to a movie. This money buys equipment, underwrites company research and expansion, and pays stock dividends. Advertisers and consumers are the financial foundation for American media industries. (See Figure 1.5.)

How Does Each Media Industry Work? Books, newspapers and magazines were America's only mass media for 250 years after the first American book was published in 1640. The first half of the twentieth century brought four new media—movies, radio, recordings and television—in less than 50 years.

To understand how this happened and where each medium fits in the mass media industries today, it is important to examine the individual characteristics of each medium. (For a pie chart showing income in the media industries, see Figure 1.4 on page 17.)

Newspapers. There are about 1,500 daily newspapers in the United States. Newspapers are evenly divided between morning and evening delivery, but the number of evening papers is declining. Papers that come out in the morning are growing in circulation, and papers that come out in the afternoon are shrinking. The number of weekly newspapers is also declining. Advertising

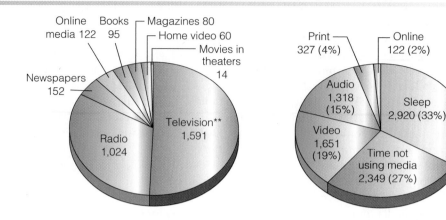

Figure 1.5 Yearly Time Each Person Spends Using Media, 2000*

*projected

Source: Data from *The Veronis, Suhler & Associates Communications Industry Forecast, 1999—2003.*

Online media 122 — Books 95 — Magazines 80 — Home video 60 — Movies in theaters 14

Newspapers 152

Radio 1,024

Television** 1,591

Average estimated number of hours each person spends using media

**includes cable TV

Print 327 (4%) — Online 122 (2%)

Audio 1,318 (15%)

Sleep 2,920 (33%)

Video 1,651 (19%)

Time not using media 2,349 (27%)

Total hours in a year = 8,760
Total hours using media = 3,491
(59% of total waking hours)

makes up about two-thirds of the printed space in daily newspapers. Newspaper income is expected to grow slightly over the next decade.

Magazines. According to the Magazine Publishers of America, about 11,000 magazines are published in the United States. This number is remaining steady. To maintain and increase profits, magazines are raising their subscription and single-copy prices and fighting to maintain their advertising income. The number of magazines people buy by subscription is going up, but newsstand sales are going down. Magazine income is expected to decline slightly in the next decade.

Book Publishing. Publishers issue about 60,000 titles a year in the United States, although some of these are reprints and new editions of old titles. Retail bookstores in the United States account for one-third of all money earned from book sales. The rest of the income comes from books that are sold through book clubs, in college stores, to libraries and to school districts for use in elementary and high schools. Book publishing income is expected to grow slightly.

Radio. About 13,000 radio stations broadcast programming in the United States, evenly divided between AM and FM stations. About 1,800 of these stations are noncommercial, most of them FM. The average American household owns five radios. Radio revenues are expected to grow slightly in the next decade.

Recordings. Most recordings are bought by people who are under 30. Compact discs account for 80 percent of recording industry income. The rest comes from cassettes, vinyls and music videos. The industry is expected to grow slightly, boosted by sales of CD singles.

Television. About 1,500 television stations are operating in the United States; one out of four stations is noncommercial. Many of the stations are affiliated with a network—NBC, CBS, ABC, Fox, UPN, or WB—although an increasing number of stations, called *independents,* are not affiliated with any network.

Ted Turner launched Cable News Network (CNN) in 1980 to serve cable companies. Nearly 66 percent of the homes in the United States are wired for cable, and half of the nation's viewers receive 30 or more channels. The average cable subscriber pays $27 a month. Network income is declining, while income to independents and cable operators is going up. Total industry revenue is projected to grow slightly in the next decade.

Movies. Nearly 34,000 theater screens exist in the United States. The major and independent studios combined make about 400 pictures a year. The industry is collecting more money because of higher ticket prices, but the number of people who go to the movies is declining.

The major increase in income to the movie industry in the past decade came from video sales. The year 1986 marked the first time that the number of videotape rentals was higher than the number of movie ticket purchases. Industry income is expected to increase slightly.

Online Media. The newest media industry is also growing the fastest. Economists predict that the number of consumers online will double between 1998 and 2003 and that the amount of money spent for online advertising will rise more than 400 percent—from $1.9 billion in 1998 to $8.2 billion by the year 2003. Online media are being redefined as a new mass medium as well as an integral part of traditional print, audio, and video mass media.

Overall, media industries in the United States are prospering. The division of profits is shifting, however, as different media industries expand and contract in the marketplace to respond to the audience. For example, if the population's interest shifts away from print media to video entertainment, fewer people will buy newspapers, magazines, and books, which means that these industries could suffer. (For recent trends in consumers' media spending, see Figure 1.6 on page 24.) Understanding the implications of these changes is central to understanding the media as businesses.

The Media and Communications Technology

The second theme that you will encounter throughout this book is *the effect of technological change on the mass media.* The development of communications technology directly affects the speed with which a society evolves. An entire country with only one telephone or one radio may be impossible for people in the United States to imagine, but there are still many countries today in which ten families share a single telephone and people consider a television set to be a luxury.

In the United States and other countries such as Japan that have encouraged technological advancements, communication changes are moving faster than ever before. For the media industries, this means increasing costs to replace old equipment. For consumers, this means a confusing array of products that seem to be replaced as soon as they are marketed—DVDs overcoming VCRs, for example.

By today's standards, the earliest communications obstacles seem unbelievably simple: for instance, how to transmit a single message to several people at the same time, and how to share information inexpensively. Yet it has taken nearly 5,500 years to achieve the capability for instant communication that we enjoy today.

Figure 1.6   How People Will Spend Their Media Dollars, 2000–2003*   Amount each **person** in the United States will spend each year for audio media, print media and video media, including online services.

*projected

Source: Data from *The Veronis, Suhler & Associates Communications Industry Forecast*, 1999–2003.

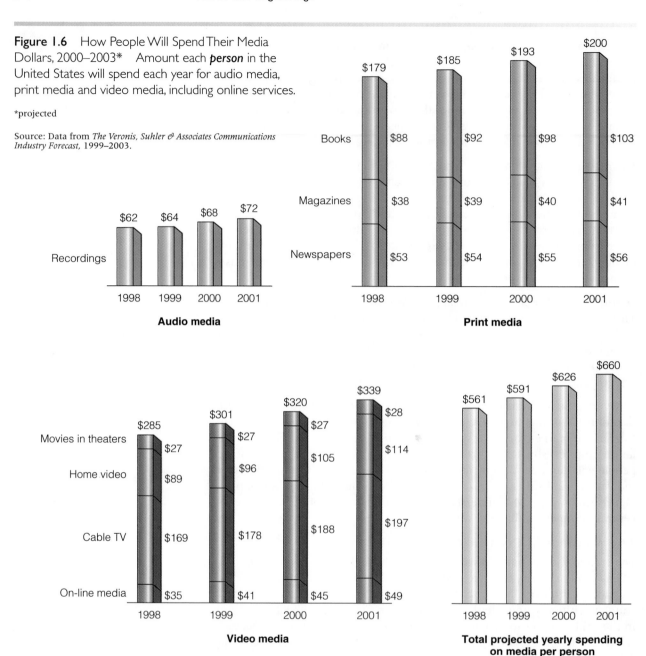

Three Information Communications Revolutions

The channels of communication have changed dramatically over the centuries, but the idea that a society will pay to stay informed and entertained is not new. In imperial Rome, people who wanted to know the news paid professional speakers a coin (a *gazet*) for the privilege of listening to the speaker announce the day's events. Many early newspapers were called gazettes to reflect this heritage.

The first attempt at written communication began modestly with pictographs. A pictograph is a symbol of an object that is used to convey an idea. If you have ever drawn a heart with an arrow through it, you understand

Used by permission of Cartoonists
& Writers Syndicate.

SIGNE
PHILADELPHIA DAILY NEWS
Philadelphia
USA

what a pictograph is. The first known pictographs were carved in stone by the
Sumerians of Mesopotamia in about 3500 B.C.

The stone in which these early pictographic messages were carved served
as a medium—a device to transmit messages. Eventually, messages were
imprinted in clay and stored in a primitive version of today's library. These
messages weren't very portable, however. Clay tablets didn't slip easily into
someone's pocket.

The First Information Communications Revolution. Pictographs as a
method of communication developed into phonetic writing in about 3500
B.C., using symbols for sounds. Instead of drawing a representation of a dog
to convey the idea of a dog, scholars could represent the sounds d-o-g with
phonetic writing. The invention of phonetic writing has been called the *first
information communications revolution.* "After being stored in written form,
information could now reach a new kind of audience, remote from the source
and uncontrolled by it," writes media scholar Anthony Smith. "Writing transformed knowledge into information."[17]

The Greek philosopher Socrates anticipated the changes that widespread
literacy would bring. He argued that knowledge should remain among the
privileged classes. Writing threatened the exclusive use of information, he
said: "Once a thing is put in writing, the composition, whatever it may be,
drifts all over the place, getting into the hands not only of those who understand it, but equally of those who have no business with it."[18]

In about 2500 B.C., the Egyptians invented papyrus, a type of paper made
from a grasslike plant called sedge. The Greeks perfected parchment, made of
goat and sheep skins, in about 200 B.C. By about 100 A.D., before the use of
parchment spread throughout Europe, the Chinese had invented paper,
which was much cheaper to produce than parchment, but Europeans didn't

TIMEFRAME

Today to 3500 B.C.: Three information communications revolutions form the basis for today's digital media

TODAY Electronic information delivery is the standard for all media.

A.D. 1951 Digital computers are developed to process, store, and retrieve information. **(The Third Information Communications Revolution)**

A.D. 1455 Johannes Gutenberg invents movable type and publishes the Gutenberg Bible. **(The Second Information Communications Revolution)**

A.D. 1255 The Chinese invent the copper press.

A.D. 100 The Chinese invent paper.

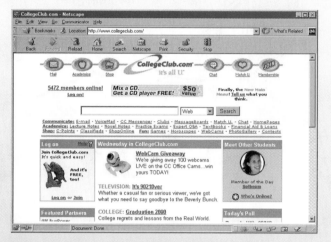

200 B.C. Parchment is perfected by the Greeks.

2500 B.C. The Egyptians invent papyrus.

3500 B.C. Phonetic writing is developed. **(The First Information Communications Revolution)**

start to use paper until more than a thousand years later, in about A.D. 1300. The discovery of parchment and then paper meant that storing information became cheaper and easier.

As Socrates predicted, when more people learned to write, wider communication became possible because people in many different societies could share information among themselves and with people in other parts of the world. But scholars still had to copy painstakingly the information they wanted to keep, or pay a scribe to copy for them. In the 14th century, for example, the library of the Italian poet Petrarch contained more than 100 manuscripts that he had copied individually himself.[19]

In Petrarch's day, literate people were either monks or members of the privileged classes. Wealthy people could afford tutoring, and they could also afford to buy the handwritten manuscripts copied by the monks. Knowledge—and the power it brings—belonged to very few people.

The Second Information Communications Revolution. As societies grew more literate, the demand for manuscripts flourished, but a scribe could produce only one copy at a time. What has been called the *second information communications revolution* began in Germany in 1455, when Johannes Gutenberg printed a Bible on a press that used movable type.

More than 200 years before Gutenberg, the Chinese had invented a printing press that used wood type, and the Chinese also are credited with perfecting a copper press in 1445. But Gutenberg's innovation was to line up individual metal letters that he could ink and then press with paper to produce copies. Unlike the wood or copper presses, the metal letters could be reused to produce new pages of text, which made the process much cheaper. The Gutenberg Bible, a duplicate of the Latin original, is considered the first book printed by movable type (47 copies survive).

As other countries adopted Gutenberg's press, the price for Bibles plummeted. In 1470, the cost of a French mechanically printed Bible was one-fifth the cost of a hand-printed Bible.[20] This second revolution—printing—meant that knowledge, which had belonged to the privileged few, would one day be accessible to everyone. This key development was one of the essential conditions for the rise of modern governments, as well as an important element of scientific and technological progress.

Before the Gutenberg press, a scholar who wanted special information had to travel to the place where it was kept. But once information could be duplicated easily, it could travel to people beyond the society that created it. The use of paper instead of the scribes' bulky parchment also meant that books could be stacked end to end. For the first time, knowledge was portable and storable. Libraries now could store vast amounts of information in a small space. And because these smaller, lighter books could be carried easily, classical works could be read simultaneously in many cities by all different kinds of people. Another benefit of the development of printing was that societies could more easily keep information to share with future generations.

This effort to communicate—first through spoken messages, then through pictographs, then through the written word and finally through printed words—demonstrates people's innate desire to share information with one another. **Storability**, **portability**, and **accessibility** of information are essential to today's concept of mass communication. By definition, mass communication is information that is available to a large audience quickly.

The Third Information Communications Revolution. Today's age of communication has been called the *third information communications revolution* because computers have become the storehouses and transmitters of vast amounts of information that previously relied on the written word. Computer technology, which processes and transmits information much more efficiently than mechanical devices, is driving the majority of changes affecting today's media. This has become possible with the development of digital computers, beginning around 1951. This means that changes in today's media industries happen much faster than in the past. Satellite broadcasts, digital recordings and the international computer network called the Internet are just three examples of the third information communications revolution.

Although each medium has its own history and economic structure, today all of the media industries compete for consumers' attention. Satellite and microchip technology will transform the media business more than we can foresee—enabling faster transmission of more information to more people than ever before.

I M P A C T

profile   *Jeff Bezos: Online Media Mogul*

The Inner Bizos

Chip Bayers

Amazon.com's founder figures out how to sell books on the Web, and now he wants to sell you everything else. Simple, right? So why is he so far ahead of the pack?

Thirty-five-year-old Jeff Bezos, founder, chair, and CEO of Amazon.com, makes Amazon.com, to this point little more than a convenient place to shop for a limited range of goods, the kind of environment that lures men, women, and children in from vast distances, then seduces them into acts of acquisition.

As Internet commerce matures from the exotic to the everyday, as it becomes less about exploiting a position on the frontiers of technology and more about mastering the art of sales and merchandising, the challenges Bezos faces have become exactly those that confronted the great retailers who invented the mass market for consumer goods in the United States a century ago.

To reach historical heights—to become as important to 21st-century culture as Richard W. Sears, Macy's Isidor Straus, and John Wanamaker were to the culture of the late 19th and early 20th centuries, when they fundamentally changed not only the experience of shopping but also the essential nature of American life—Bezos will need to deliver on the second promise in the oft-repeated goal he sets for his staff: "to build a valuable and *lasting* company."...

Karen Moskowitz/CORBIS Outline

The goal is within reach. Bezos's vision has always been about taking advantage of a new platform and new tools to change shopping itself. Long before he launched the company, he had dreams of making Amazon.com "broader than books and music"—a point reinforced... by his... move into gift sales and by his move to offer Amazon.com customers goods from other retailers.

Analysts who had projected $190 million in revenue for the company during the fourth-quarter holiday period were flabbergasted when Amazon.com registered sales of approximately $250 million, news that helped send the company's stock as high as $350 per share by early January (shortly before a three-for-one stock split)—just shy of the $400 per share CIBC Oppenheimer foresees by 2002.

If Jeff Bezos's vision comes true, here's how you'll shop in 2020.

The vast bulk of store-bought goods—food staples, paper products, cleaning supplies, and the like—you will order electroni-

cally. Some physical storefronts will survive, but they'll have to offer at least one of two things: entertainment value or immediate convenience.

Successful "shoptainers" will be like the Gap, with its environment of music and youth culture, or Nordstrom, with its tinkling pianist and distinctive face-to-face service. They may be even more amplified, with personal service and showmanship turning every shopping trip into a Super Bowl-style destination event. "That experience is what you get when you go to movie theaters, and why you don't always rent movies, right?" Bezos notes.

Convenience specialists will also have contemporary antecedents—the 7-eleven chain, say, or Walgreen's, where you can get a quart of milk or NyQuil geltabs at 10 p.m.—but these, too, will evolve: open 24/7, for example, so that you can take care of the last mile of delivery yourself at any time.

The consultants at the Global Business Network even sketch out a scenario where, within a generation or two, vans carrying inventories of more popular necessities, such as toilet paper or diapers, may be constantly circling neighborhoods, ready to drop off an order within moments of receiving it....

"Strip malls," Bezos predicts, "are history."

Computer technology, shown here by a farmer with his notebook computer, represents the *third information communications revolution.*

Joe Sohm/The Stock Market

The Media and Political, Social, and Cultural Institutions

The media industries provide information and entertainment. But media also can affect political, social, and cultural institutions.

This is the third theme of this book—the *impact* of mass media on the society in which they operate. Although the media can actively influence society, they also mirror it, and scholars constantly strive to delineate the differences.

When the advertising industry suddenly marched to patriotic themes by using flags and other patriotic logos in ads following the United States' claim to victory in the 1991 Gulf War, was the industry pandering, or were advertisers proudly reflecting genuine American sentiment, or both? Did the spread of patriotic themes silence those who felt that the United States had overreacted in the Persian Gulf? If you were a scholar, how would you prove your arguments?

This is an example of the difficulty that scholars face when analyzing the media's political, social, and cultural effects. Early media studies analyzed the message in the belief that, once a message was sent, it would be received by everyone the same way. Then studies proved that different people process messages differently—a phenomenon described as **selective perception.** This occurs because everyone brings many variables—family background, interests and education, for example—to each message.

Complicating the study of the media's political, social, and cultural effects is the recent proliferation of media outlets. The multiplying sources for information and entertainment mean that, today, very few people share identical mass media environments. This makes it much more difficult for scholars to determine the specific or cumulative effects of mass media on the general population.

Still, scholars' attempts to describe media's political, social, and cultural roles in society are important because, once identified, the effects can be observed. The questions should be posed so we do not become complacent about media in our lives, so we do not become immune to the possibility that our society may be cumulatively affected by the media in ways we cannot yet define.

Once you understand the media separately, you can consider their collective effects. After you understand how each type of media business works, you can examine why people who work in the media make the decisions they do. Then, you can evaluate the impact of these decisions on you and on society.

selective perception the concept that each person processes messages differently.

IMPACT

digital — *Living Dorm Life in the Camera's Eye*

Students Put Themselves in Focus on the Internet 24 Hours a Day

By Mary Beth Marklein
USA TODAY

For tech-savvy, trend-setting college students, the place to see and be seen...is through the eye of a Webcam.

Through the wonders of this tennis-ball-size piece of technology that hooks to a personal computer, just about any student can capture his or her image live, 24 hours a day, seven days a week, and upload it to the Internet for all the world to behold.

Who, besides Mom and Dad, would care?

You might be surprised.

At Bradley University in Peoria, Ill., a Web site broadcasting the minute-by-minute goings-on of sophomore Jim Crone got so many hits one night in February that he crashed the campus computer system. This spring, a camera trained on a popular street corner midway between Amherst College and the University of Massachusetts' Amherst campus became one of the most visited sites at MassLive, a local commercial Web site.

And this fall, a Pennsylvania State University professor plans to require first-year students to check out an interactive site featuring students to study interpersonal communications.

"It's weird and voyeuristic and different and stupid. And it's fun and funny to watch," says Green-

field (Ill.) College junior Ben Miller, 20, who set up a Webcam in November as the host of a college-oriented Web site for about.com.

This year, he is living off campus, so Jason Davis, his former roommate, offered to operate a camera with his laptop. As a bonus, the school just went wireless, so the camera is no longer tethered to a dorm-based personal computer.

In the past year or so, pockets of students like Miller were independently installing Webcams, video cameras that, when hooked up to computers, transmit images in intervals ranging from seconds to minutes to hours. But as word spreads, costs drops and the inevitable commercialization takes hold, the phenomenon appears ready to explode.

Online all the time: The Webcam is used to send images of college students live on the Internet 24 hours a day, seven days a week. Those students include Melissa Gaunt, below, in San Antonio.

Top photo by Todd Rosenberg; Above photo © 2000 Chris Covatta.

- The digital highway is likely to be more like an intricate webbed network of many different types of communications systems.

- The new information network is likely to be an interconnected communications system using broadcast, telephone, cable, and computer technology.

- The United States is ideally situated to be the first to develop a new information network because many Americans have the tools that such a system needs to get started—television, telephone, VCRs, cable TV, and computers.

- Today's delivery system for information and entertainment is primarily a one-way system. The new communications network will be a two-way system.

- The ability to talk back—to receive as well as transmit messages—makes the telephone interactive. The new communications network must also be interactive.

- The network of the future needs content, two-way digital communication and digital storage.

- A cable company or a telephone company would deliver services on the network.

- Information and entertainment that has already been produced, stored, and digitized will become the first content on the new network.

- In 1994, Congress named the National Information Infrastructure (NII) to coordinate all of the different senders, channels, and receivers. Universal service and copyrights for intellectual property are two important issues to be considered in the development of the NII.

- In 1996, Congress passed the Communications Decency Act (CDA), which contained provisions that attempt to control content on the Internet. So far, the courts have ruled that the government cannot regulate content on the Internet, but the issue is still unresolved.

- The five technological challenges for the new network are improved storage, a coordinated delivery system, a "smart" set-top box, usable menus, and a secure system for ordering and billing.

- Technological changes probably will come gradually, as each challenge to the creation of the new network is solved.

- According to industry estimates, the average adult spends more than half of his or her waking life with the media.

- The mass media industries in the United States earn about $337 billion a year.

- Communication is the act of sending ideas and attitudes from one person to another. Intrapersonal communication means communication within one person. Interpersonal communication means communication between two people. Mass communication is communication from one person or group of persons through a transmitting device (a medium) to large audiences or markets.

- Many motives shape the American media, including the desire to fulfill the public's need for information, to influence the country's governance, to disseminate the country's culture, to offer entertainment, and to provide an outlet for creative expression. Above all, the major goal of the American media is to make money.

Three key themes can be used to study American media:

1. American media operate as profit-centered businesses.

2. The media are greatly affected by technological changes.

3. The mass media are political, social, and cultural institutions that both reflect and affect the society in which they operate.

Although many media businesses are still family-owned, the main trend in the United States today is for media companies to cluster together in groups. This trend is called concentration of ownership and can take five forms: chains, networks, cross-media ownership, conglomerates, and vertical integration.

■ Media acquisitions in the United States have skyrocketed because most conglomerates today are publicly traded companies and because, beginning in 1980, the federal government deregulated the broadcast industry. This trend is expected to continue through the 21st century as changing technology expands the market for media products.

■ U.S. media industries continue to prosper, but the share of profits is shifting among the industries; different media expand and contract in the marketplace to respond to the audience.

■ The communications revolution occurred in three stages. The invention of phonetic writing was considered the first information communications revolution, the invention of movable type marked the second information communications revolution, and the invention of computers ushered in the third information communications revolution.

■ *Storability*, *portability*, and *accessibility* of information are essential to today's concept of mass communication. By definition, mass communication is information that is available to a large audience quickly.

WORKING THE WEB www

■ **All Media E-mail Directory**
   (e-mail addresses for key editors, columnists, correspondents, and executives in magazines, newspapers, radio, TV and news syndicates across the U.S. and Canada)
   www.owt.com/dircon

■ **Communications Topics Website**
   www.syr.edu/-befought

■ **Dilbert (Scott Adam's comic)**
   www.unitedmedia.com/comics/dilbert

■ **ESPN Sportzone**
   www.sportzone.com

■ **Media History Project on the Web**
   www.mediahistory.com

■ **Newslink to Most Major Newspapers, Magazines and Broadcasts**
   www.newslink.org

■ **U.S. Government Documents Online**

www.access.gpo.gov/su_docs/

INFOTRAC COLLEGE EDITION EXERCISES

Using InfoTrac College Edition, a fully searchable online database of articles and abstracts, do the following exercises as directed by your instructor.

1. Type in the keywords "information superhighway" on InfoTrac College Edition and read at least three articles on the challenges of an information-glutted society. Print the articles and either:

   a. write a brief paper on your findings, or

   b. bring the articles to class for a small-group discussion.

2. Type in the keywords "Telecommunications Act of 1996" and read at least three articles on the impact of the act on a specific part of electronic media in the last two years. You could consider, for example, the act's effect on local radio, or on FCC regulation, or on the deregulation of telecommunications. Print the articles and either:

   a. write a brief paper on your findings, or

   b. bring the articles to class for a small-group discussion.

3. How will intellectual property rights be resolved in cyberspace? That's one of the major questions about the Internet. Type in the keywords "intellectual property rights" and find three articles that discuss the issues surrounding the use of people's words, music and/or images on the web. Print the articles and either:

   a. write a brief paper on your findings, or

   b. bring the articles to class for a small-group discussion.

4. Read "Impact on You: A Trove of Memorable Moments Goes Online" in Chapter 1. Then use InfoTrac to look up other examples of the way the Internet is revolutionizing photographic databases. Print the articles and either:

   a. write a brief paper on your findings, or

   b. bring the articles to class for a small-group discussion.

5. Read "Jeff Bezos: Online Media Mogul" about Amazon.com founder Jeffrey Bezos, then search InfoTrac for other articles about Bezos. What has made Bezos's approach to an online business so remarkable? Print the articles and either:

   a. write a brief paper on your findings, or

   b. bring the articles to class for a small-group discussion.

Newspapers

BIZARRO   By DAN PIRARO

SCIENTISTS ESTIMATE THAT BY THE YEAR 2015, THE SUNDAY EDITION OF THE NEW YORK TIMES WILL BE ROUGHLY THE SIZE OF A HUMPBACK WHALE.

n 1882, Harrison Gray Otis bought a 25 percent share of *The Los Angeles Times* for $6,000. In 2000, the Chandler family, Otis' descendants, sold the *Los Angeles Times*, *Newsday*, the *Baltimore Sun* newspapers, the *Hartford Courant*, and other newspapers and media properties to the Tribune Company, based in Chicago. The sale was valued at $6 billion.

The success of Times Mirror demonstrates the rapid growth of newspapers since their beginnings in the United States more than three centuries ago. American newspapers began as one-page sheets in colonial America that consisted primarily of announcements of ship arrivals and departures and old news from Europe. Today's large urban newspapers such as the *Los Angeles Times* rely on satellite-fed information, and these papers often run to 500 pages on Sunday. (The record for the largest single-day's newspaper is held by *The New York Times*. On November 13, 1987, the *Times* published a 1,612-page edition that weighed in at 12 pounds.)[1]

Times Mirror, like all of today's top ten American newspaper chains, has invested in other media properties but continues to devote most of its attention to "newspapering." The huge earnings of these newspaper chains, and their expanding ownership of the nation's smaller newspapers, are a significant theme in the economic evolution of American newspapers.

A second theme in this chapter is how technology changed the role that newspapers play in the delivery of news. For 230 years, newspapers were the only way for large numbers of people to get the same news simultaneously. There was no competition. The invention of broadcasting in the early twentieth century changed the exclusive access to news; broadcasting offered instant access to information. Yet, despite increasing competition for its audience, the newspaper industry today continues to prosper.

A third theme in this chapter is the important part that the newspaper industry historically played in defining the cultural concept of an independent press, based on the belief that the press must remain independent from government to fulfill its responsibility to keep the public informed. Newspapers were the only mass medium for the timely delivery of news from 1690 until the introduction of radio in 1920. Debates about what the public should know, when they should know it, and who should decide what the public needs to know happened during a time when newspapers were the main focus of these discussions.

TOWARD AN INDEPENDENT PRESS

The issue of government control of newspapers surfaced early in the history of the colonies. At first, newspapers were the mouthpieces of the British government and news was subject to British approval. Many colonial newspapers were subsidized by the British government, and publishers actually printed "Published by Authority" on the first page to demonstrate government approval.

The first colonial newspaper angered the local authorities so much that the newspaper issued only one edition. This newspaper, *Publick Occurrences*, which was published in Boston on September 25, 1690, is often identified as America's first newspaper.

The first and only edition of *Publick Occurrences* was just two pages, each the size of a sheet of today's binder paper (then called a half-sheet), and was printed on three sides. Publisher Benjamin Harris left the fourth side blank so that the people could jot down the latest news before they gave the paper to friends. Harris made the mistake of reporting in his first issue that the French king was "in much trouble" for sleeping with his son's wife. Harris' journalism was too candid for the governor and council of the Massachusetts Bay Colony, who stopped the publication four days after the newspaper appeared.

The nation's first consecutively issued (published more than once) newspaper was the *Boston News-Letter*, which appeared in 1704. It was one half-sheet printed on two sides. In the first issue, editor John Campbell reprinted the queen's latest speech, some maritime news, and one advertisement telling people how to put an ad in his paper. Like many subsequent colonial publishers, Campbell reprinted several items from the London papers.

The next challenge to British control came when James Franklin started his own newspaper in Boston in 1721. His *New England Courant* was the first American newspaper to appear without the crown's "By Authority" sanction. *Thus, James Franklin began the tradition of an independent press in this country.*

Today to 1690: Newspapers adapt to maintain their audience share

TODAY Newspapers use color, graphics, and creative information design to grab readers' attention, and many newspapers offer online editions.

1982 Gannett creates *USA Today,* using a splashy format and color throughout the paper.

1950 Newspaper readership begins to decline following the introduction of television.

1900 One-third of the nation's newspapers follow the popular trend toward yellow journalism.

Michael Newman/Photo Edit

1827 John B. Russwurm and the Reverend Samuel Cornish launch *Freedom's Journal,* the nation's first black newspaper.

1734 John Peter Zenger is charged with sedition. While he is in jail, his wife, Anna Zenger, continues to publish *The New York Weekly Journal,* making her America's first woman publisher.

1704 *The Boston News-Letter,* America's first continuously published newspaper, begins publication.

1690 *Publick Occurrences,* America's first newspaper, is published.

James Franklin argued in print with the local clergy and accused regional authorities of not doing enough to combat pirates. In 1722, the town council charged him with contempt and threw him in jail. When he was released, the council forbade James to publish his newspaper, so James named his brother, Ben, as publisher.

In 1729, Ben Franklin moved to Philadelphia and bought the *Pennsylvania Gazette* to compete with the only other newspaper in town, the *American Weekly Mercury,* published by Andrew Bradford. The *Pennsylvania Gazette* became the most influential and most financially successful of all the colonial newspapers.

In the same printshop that printed the *Gazette,* Franklin published *Poor Richard's Almanack* in 1732, an annual that sold about 10,000 copies a year for the next 25 years. *Benjamin Franklin proved that a printer could make money without government sanctions or support.*

The first New York paper, the *New York Gazette,* was founded by William Bradford (Andrew Bradford's father) in 1725. Bradford's title was "King's Printer to the Province of New York," for which he received a British salary.

The second New York newspaper was the *New-York Weekly Journal,* begun in 1733 by John Peter Zenger. The *Journal* continually attacked Governor William Cosby for incompetence, and on November 17, 1734, Zenger was arrested and jailed, charged with printing false and seditious writing. (**Seditious language** is writing that authorities believe could incite rebellion

seditious language writing that authorities believe could incite rebellion against the government.

against the government.) While Zenger was in jail, his wife, Anna, continued to publish the paper.

Truth Versus Libel: The Zenger Trial

Zenger's trial began on August 4, 1735, nine months after his arrest. His defense attorney argued that truth was a defense against libel, and that if Zenger's words were true, they could not be libelous. (A **libelous statement** is one that damages a person by questioning that person's character or reputation.) Referring to Britain's power over the colonies, the defense attorney told the crowded courtroom and the jury:

> *Power may justly be compared to a great River, while kept within its due Bounds, its both Beautiful and Useful; but when it overflows its Banks, it is then too impetuous to be stemm'd, it bears down all before it, and brings Destruction and Desolation wherever it comes....*[2]

The trial established a *landmark precedent for freedom of the press in America— the concept that truth is the best defense for libel.* If what someone publishes is true, the information cannot be considered libelous. (The issue of libel is discussed in Chapter 14.)

Women's Early Role as Publishers

Colonial women were not encouraged to work outside the home at all. Therefore, those women who published newspapers during the colonial period are especially notable because they are among the few examples of women who managed businesses early in the country's history.

Early colonial women printers, such as Anna Zenger, usually belonged to printing families that trained wives and daughters to work in the printshops. By the time the American Revolution began, at least 14 women had been printers in the colonies.[3] One of these family-trained printers was the first woman publisher.

Elizabeth Timothy became editor of the weekly *South Carolina Gazette* in Charleston when her husband, Lewis, died unexpectedly, and their son, Peter, was only 13. Elizabeth Timothy published her first edition on January 4, 1737, under her son's name. Her first editorial appealed to the community to continue to support the "poor afflicted Widow and six small Children." Mother and son ran the paper together until 1746, when Peter formally took over the business.[4]

Birth of the Partisan Press

As dissatisfaction with British rule grew in the colonies, newspapers became political tools that fostered the debate that eventually led to the colonies' independence. By 1750, 14 weekly newspapers were being published in the colonies.[5]

The Stamp Act. Opposition to the British Stamp Act in 1765 signaled the beginning of the revolutionary period. The Stamp Act taxed publishers a half-penny for each issue that was a half-sheet or less and one penny for a full sheet. Each advertisement was taxed two shillings. All the colonial newspapers, even those loyal to the crown, fought the act.

Many newspapers threatened to stop publication, but only a few of them did. Most editors published editions that mocked the tax. William Bradford III issued the famous tombstone edition of the *Pennsylvania Journal* on

---

libelous statement language that damages a person by questioning that person's character or reputation.

October 31, 1765. The front page, bordered in black, was printed with a skull and crossbones where the official stamp should have been.

The Stamp Act Congress met in New York in October 1765, and adopted the now-familiar slogan, "No taxation without representation." Parliament, facing united opposition from all the colonial publishers, repealed the Stamp Act on March 18, 1766.

The Alien and Sedition Laws. During the early part of the country's history, newspapers often were an outlet for journalists opposed to the new government. The Alien and Sedition Laws, passed by Congress in 1798, were the federal government's first attempt to control its critics. Congress said that anyone who "shall write, print, or publish…false, scandalous and malicious writing or writings against the government of the United States, or either house of the Congress of the United States, or the President of the United States," could be fined up to $2,000 and jailed for two years.

Several people went to jail. A Boston publisher spent 30 days in jail for libeling the Massachusetts legislature. A New York editor was fined $100 and jailed for four months. By 1800, the angry rhetoric had dissipated. The Alien and Sedition Laws expired after two years and were not renewed. However, *throughout American press history, the tradition of an independent press, established by James Franklin in 1721, continued to confront the government's desire to restrain criticism.*

TAKING ADVANTAGE OF 19TH-CENTURY TECHNOLOGY: NEWSPAPERS DIVERSIFY

The technological advances of the 19th century—such as cheaper newsprint, mechanized printing, and the telegraph—meant that newspapers could reach a wider audience faster than before. Confined to Eastern cities and highly educated urban audiences during the 1700s, newspaper publishers in the 1800s sought new readers—from the frontier, from among the nation's growing

BOSTONIANS READING THE STAMP ACT.

Furious colonists reacted to the Stamp Act in 1765 by threatening to stop publication and by printing editions that mocked the tax. The Stamp Act was repealed a year later.

The Granger Collection

Elias Boudinot published the first Native American newspaper, the *Cherokee Phoenix*, from 1828 to 1832.

number of immigrants, and from within the shrinking Native American population. This expansion resulted in three additions to American newspapers: frontier journalism, ethnic and cultural newspapers, and the alternative press.

Frontier Journalism

Gold, silver, and adventure lured people west, and when the people arrived they needed newspapers. The *Indiana Gazette*, the *Texas Gazette*, the *Oregon Spectator*, the *Weekly Arizonian*, and Colorado's *Rocky Mountain News* met that need, aided by the telegraph, which moved news easily from coast to coast.

The wide-open land beckoned many journalists. The most celebrated journalist to chronicle the frontier was Samuel Clemens, who traveled to Nevada in 1861, prospecting for silver. Clemens didn't find any silver, but a year later the Virginia City *Territorial Enterprise*—the area's largest paper—hired him for $25 a week. Clemens first signed his name as Mark Twain on a humorous travel letter written for the *Enterprise*.

Ethnic and Native American Newspapers

English-language newspapers did not satisfy everyone's needs. In the first half of the 19th century, many newspapers sought to succeed by catering to ethnic and cultural interests. In the early 1800s, Spanish-speaking people in Georgia could read *El Misisipi*. Herman Ridder's German newspaper, *New Yorker Staats-Zeitung*, founded in 1845, was the most successful foreign-language newspaper in the United States. It formed the financial basis for today's Knight-Ridder chain. People outside the mainstream of society, such as Spanish and German immigrants, used newspapers to create a sense of community and ethnic identity.

In the 1800s, Native Americans who had been displaced by the settlers also felt a need to express their culture through a newspaper. As a nonmainstream group, they especially felt the need to voice their complaints. On February 21, 1828, the nation's first Native American newspaper appeared. The *Cherokee Phoenix* was edited by Elias Boudinot, a Native American who had been educated at a northern seminary. The Cherokee nation held exclusive control over the four-page paper, which was printed half in English and half in an 86-character alphabet that represented the Cherokee language. (Authorities shut down the press in 1832 because they felt that Boudinot was arousing antigovernment sentiment.)

Dissident Voices: The Early Alternative Press

Two strong social movements, emancipation and women's suffrage, brought new voices to the American Press. This **alternative press** movement signaled the beginning of a significant American journalistic tradition. Newspapers became an outlet for the voices of social protest, a tradition that continues today. (The alternative press is also called the **dissident press**.)

Five early advocates of domestic change who used the press to advance their causes—the abolition of slavery and suffrage for women—were John B. Russwurm, the Reverend Samuel Cornish, Frederick Douglass, Jane Grey Swisshelm, and Ida B. Wells.

Russwurm and Cornish, who were African-American, started *Freedom's Journal* in 1827 in New York City with very little money. They started their newspaper to respond to racist attacks in several local newspapers. *Freedom's Journal* lasted for two years and reached only a few readers, but it was the

dissident press media that present **alternative** viewpoints that challenge the mainstream press.

INDUSTRY
IMPACT

Newspapers

*K*ey trends in the newspaper industry today: the majority of daily newspapers are online and newspapers are also trying to increase readership in the 18–34 age group.

Nearly two out of three daily newspapers have created online editions.

Total number of dailies: 1,500

Number of dailies on the Internet: 950

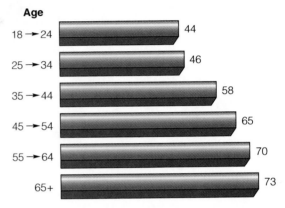

Age

18 → 24	44
25 → 34	46
35 → 44	58
45 → 54	65
55 → 64	70
65+	73

Percentage of people who say they read a newspaper every day

Who reads newspapers? Although newspaper circulation is holding steady, daily readership is declining—especially among young adults.

Source: The Veronis, Suhler & Associates Communications Industry Forecast, 1999–2003.

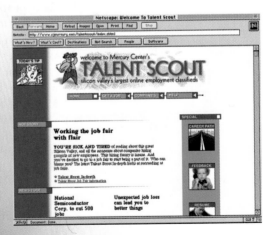

To expand their readership, many newspapers have created online editions, such as "Mercury Center," created by California's *San Jose Mercury*.

Journalists learned to improvise. This press operation, assembled to publish New Mexico's first newspaper, was set up under a juniper tree near Kingston, New Mexico.

Bettmann/CORBIS

beginning of an African-American press tradition that eventually created more than 2,700 newspapers, magazines, and quarterly journals.[6]

What has often been called the most important African-American pre–Civil War newspaper was Frederick Douglass' weekly *North Star*. "Right is of no Sex—Truth is of no Color—God is the Father of us all, and we are all Brethren" read the masthead. Beginning in 1847, Douglass struggled to support the *North Star* by giving lectures. The newspaper eventually reached 3,000 subscribers in the United States and abroad with its emancipation message.

Like Douglass, Jane Grey Swisshelm campaigned for civil rights. Her first byline appeared in 1844 in the *Spirit of Liberty*, published in Pittsburgh. Four years later she began her own abolitionist publication, the *Pittsburgh Saturday Visiter*, which also promoted women's rights.

As a correspondent for Horace Greeley's *New York Tribune* in Washington, D.C., Swisshelm convinced Vice President Millard Fillmore to let her report from the Senate press gallery. The gallery had been open to male journalists for 55 years, and on May 21, 1850, Swisshelm became the first female journalist to sit in the gallery.

Ida B. Wells didn't start out to be a journalist, but the cause of emancipation drew her to the profession. In 1878, both of Wells' parents and her infant sister died in a yellow fever epidemic, and so 16-year-old Wells took responsibility for her six brothers and sisters, attended Rust College, and then moved the family to Memphis and became a teacher.

A Baptist minister, who was an editor of the Negro Press Association, hired Wells to write for his paper. She wrote under the pseudonym Iola. Soon she became part-owner of the Memphis *Free Speech* and *Headlight*. She traveled throughout the Delta soliciting subscriptions and circulation rose from 1,500 to 4,000 under her management.[7]

In 1892, Wells wrote a story about three African-American men who had been kidnapped from a Memphis jail and killed. "The city of Memphis has demonstrated that neither character nor standing avails the Negro, if he dares to protect himself against the white man or become his rival," she wrote. "We are out-numbered and without arms." [8] While in New York, she read in the *New York Sun* that a mob had sacked the *Free Speech* office.

Wells decided not to return to Memphis. She worked in New York and lectured in Europe and then settled in Chicago, where she married a lawyer, Ferdinand Lee Barnett. Ida Wells-Barnett and her husband actively campaigned for African-American rights in Chicago, and she continued to write until she died at age 69 in 1931.

These pioneers—Russwurm, Cornish, Douglass, Swisshelm, and Wells—had used newspapers to lobby for social change. These dissident newspapers offered a forum for protest, which is an important cultural role for an independent press.

MAKING NEWSPAPERS PROFITABLE

The voices of social protest reached a limited, committed audience, but most people could not afford to subscribe to a daily newspaper. Newspapers were sold by advance yearly subscription for $6 to $10 at a time when most skilled workers earned less than $750 annually. Then, in 1833, Benjamin Day demonstrated that he could profitably appeal to a mass audience by dropping the price of a newspaper to a penny and selling the paper on the street every day.

Toward Mass Readership: The Penny Press

Day's *New York Sun* published sensational news and feature stories to interest the working class. He was able to lower the price to a penny by filling the paper

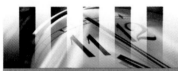

T I M E F R A M E

1889 to 1690: 19th-century alternative newspapers evolve to serve a multicultural audience

1889 Ida B. Wells becomes part-owner of the *Memphis Free-Speech and Headlight,* and begins her anti-lynching campaign.

1848 Jane Grey Swisshelm publishes the first issue of the abolitionist newspaper, the *Pittsburgh Saturday Visiter,* which also promoted women's rights.

1847 Frederick Douglass introduces the weekly *North Star,* considered America's most important African-American pre-Civil War newspaper.

1827 John B. Russwurm and the Reverend Samuel Cornish launch *Freedom's Journal,* the nation's first black newspaper.

1821 The *Cherokee Phoenix* is launched by Elias Boudinot.

1808 *El Misisipi,* America's first Spanish-language newspaper, begins publication in Georgia.

1690 *Publick Occurrences,* America's first newspaper, is published.

Ida B. Wells, part-owner of the *Memphis Free Speech and Headlight,* wrote under the pseudonym Iola.
The Granger Collection

penny paper newspapers that sold for a penny.

with advertising and by hiring newsboys to sell the paper on street corners. The first successful **penny paper** reported local gossip, sensationalized police news, and carried a page and a half of advertising in a four-page paper. Newsboys bought 100 papers for 67 cents and tried to sell them all each day to make a profit. Even *The New York Times*, founded by Henry J. Raymond in 1851, was a penny paper when it began. The legacy of the penny paper continues in today's gossip columns and crime reporting. Newspapers and broadcast stations sometimes report sensationalized stories in an effort to attract an audience.

Cooperative and For-Profit News Gathering

The invention of the telegraph by Samuel F. B. Morse in 1844 meant that news that once took weeks to reach publication could be transmitted in minutes. In 1848, six newspapers in New York City decided to share the cost of gathering foreign news by telegraph from Boston. Henry Raymond drew up the agreement among the papers to pay $100 for 3,000 words of telegraph news.[9]

cooperative news gathering member news organizations that share the expense of getting the news.

Soon known as the New York Associated Press, this organization was the country's first **cooperative news gathering** association. This meant that the member organizations shared the expense to get the news, returning any profits to the members. Today's Associated Press is the result of this early partnership, as newspapers joined together in a cooperative, with several members sharing the cost of gathering the news, domestic and foreign.

A different way of sharing information was devised by the United Press, founded in 1882 to compete with the Associated Press. The United Press was established not as cooperative but as a privately owned, for-profit wire service. (Today, these wire services are called news services.)

ACCREDITATION AND PHOTOJOURNALISM: THE CIVIL WAR YEARS

In the 1860s, interest in the emotional issues of the Civil War sent many reporters to the battlefront. Hundreds of correspondents roamed freely among the soldiers, reporting for the North and the South. Two important results of Civil War reporting were the accreditation of reporters and the introduction of photographs to enhance written reports.

Government Accreditation of Journalists

The issue of government interests versus press freedom surfaced early in the Civil War. In 1861, Union General Winfield Scott forbade telegraph companies from transmitting military information because he was afraid that some stories would help the South.

At the Battle of Bull Run in July 1861, The *New York Times* editor, Henry Raymond, reporting the war from the front, mistakenly telegraphed a story that said the North had won. When he followed up with the correct story, military censors blocked the news, arguing that the information should be kept secret. Then General William T. Sherman ordered *New York Herald* correspondent Thomas E. Knox arrested and held as a spy for sending sensitive military information.

accreditation the process by which the government certifies members of the press to cover news events.

President Lincoln intervened to compromise the needs of the press with the needs of the nation through a process called **accreditation**. This meant that members of the press would be certified by the government to cover the war. Accredited journalists were required to carry press passes issued by the military. The practice of accreditation continues to be the government's method of certifying war-reporting journalists. (See Chapter 14 for further discussion of the press in wartime.)

The Birth of Photojournalism

Also at the Battle of Bull Run was photographer Mathew Brady, who convinced President Lincoln that a complete photographic record of the war should be made. Until the Civil War, photography had been confined primarily to studio portraits because of the cumbersome equipment and slow chemical processing.

Brady photographed the battles of Antietam and Fredericksburg and sent photographic teams to other battles. Newspapers did not yet have a method to reproduce the photographs, but Brady's pictures were published in magazines, making Brady the nation's first news photographer. His 3,500 photographs demonstrated the practicality and effectiveness of using photographs to help report a news story, although newspaper photographs did not become widely used until the early 1900s. The marriage of photographs and text to tell a better story than either text or photographs could tell alone formed the beginnings of today's concept of **photojournalism**.

photojournalism using photographs, as well as text, to tell a story.

NEWSPAPERS DOMINATE THE COUNTRY

For the first 30 years of the 20th century—before radio and television—newspapers dominated the country. Newspapers were the nation's single source of daily dialogue about political, cultural, and social issues. This was also the era of the greatest newspaper competition.

Competition Breeds Sensationalism

In large cities such as New York, as many as ten newspapers competed for readers at once, so the publishers looked for new ways to expand their audience. Two New York publishers—Pulitzer and Hearst—revived and refined the penny press sensationalism that had begun in 1833 with Benjamin Day's *New York Sun*. Like Day, Pulitzer and Hearst proved that newspapers could reap enormous fortunes for their owners. They also demonstrated that credible, serious reporting is not all that people want in a newspaper. Pulitzer and Hearst promoted giveaways and fabricated stories.

An ambitious man who knew how to grab his readers' interest, Joseph Pulitzer published the first newspaper comics and sponsored journalist Nellie Bly on an around-the-world balloon trip to try to beat the fictional record in the popular book, *Around the World in 80 Days*. Bly finished the trip in 72 days, 6 hours, and 11 minutes, and the stunt brought Pulitzer the circulation he craved.

In San Francisco, young William Randolph Hearst, the new editor of the *San Francisco Examiner*, sent a reporter to cover Bly's arrival.[10] In 1887, Hearst convinced his father, who owned the *Examiner*, to let him run the paper. Hearst tagged the *Examiner* "The Monarch of the Dailies," added a lovelorn column, and attacked several of his father's influential friends in the newspaper. He spent money wildly, buying talent from competing papers and staging showy promotional events.

The Birth of Yellow Journalism: Hearst's Role in the Spanish-American War

In New York, Hearst hired Pulitzer's entire Sunday staff and cut the *Journal's* price to a penny, so Pulitzer dropped his price to match it. Hearst bought a

Mathew Brady was the nation's first photojournalist, documenting the Civil War.

Bettmann/CORBIS

color press and printed color comics. Then he stole Pulitzer's popular comic, "Hogan's Alley," which included a character named the Yellow Kid.

Hearst relished the battle, as the *Journal* screamed attention-grabbing headlines such as "Thigh of the Body Found," and the paper offered $1,000 for information that would convict the murderer. Critics named this sensationalism **yellow journalism** after the Yellow Kid, an epithet still bestowed on highly emotional, exaggerated, or inaccurate reporting that emphasizes crime, sex, and violence. By 1900, about one-third of the metropolitan dailies were following the trend toward yellow journalism.[11]

Beginning in 1898, the Spanish-American War provided the battlefield for Pulitzer and Hearst truly to act out their newspaper war. For three years, the two newspapers unrelentingly overplayed events in the Cuban struggle for independence from Spain, each trying to beat the other with irresponsible, exaggerated stories, many of them manufactured.

The overplaying of events that resulted from the sensational competition between Pulitzer and Hearst showed that newspapers could have a significant effect on political attitudes. The Spanish-American War began a few months after the sinking of the U.S. battleship *Maine* in Havana harbor, which killed 266 men. The cause of the explosion that sank the ship was never determined. But Pulitzer's and Hearst's newspapers blamed the Spanish. Hearst dubbed the event "the *Journal*'s War," but in fact Hearst and Pulitzer shared responsibility, because both men had inflamed the public unnecessarily about events in Cuba. The serious consequences of their yellow journalism directly demonstrated the importance of press responsibility.

Tabloid Journalism: Sex and Violence Sell

The journalistic legacy of Day, Pulitzer and Hearst surfaced again in the **tabloid journalism** of the 1920s, often called **jazz journalism**. In 1919, the publishers of the *New York Daily News* sponsored a beauty contest to inaugurate the nation's first tabloid. A **tabloid** is a small-format newspaper, usually 11 inches by 14 inches, featuring illustrations and sensational stories.

The *Daily News* merged pictures and screaming headlines with reports about crime, sex, and violence to exceed anything that had appeared before.

yellow journalism news that emphasizes crime, sex and violence; also called **jazz journalism** and **tabloid journalism**.

Joseph Pulitzer (right) and William Randolph Hearst (left), whose New York newspaper war spawned the term *yellow journalism*.

Left and Right: Bettmann/CORBIS

It ran full-page pictures with short, punchy text. Love affairs soon became big news, and so did murders. In the ultimate example of tabloid journalism, a *Daily News* reporter strapped a camera to his ankle in 1928 and took a picture of Ruth Snyder, who had conspired to kill her husband, as she was electrocuted at Sing Sing. The picture covered the front page, and the caption stated, "This is perhaps the most remarkable exclusive picture in the history of criminology." Photojournalism had taken a sensational turn, very different from what Mathew Brady had envisioned when he documented the Civil War. Today, jazz journalism successors are the supermarket tabloids, such as the *National Enquirer*, which feature large photographs and stories about sex, violence, and celebrities.

UNIONIZATION ENCOURAGES PROFESSIONALISM

The first half of the 20th century brought the unionization of newspaper employees, which standardized wages at many of the nation's largest newspapers.

Labor unions were first established at newspapers in 1800, and the International Typographical Union went national in the mid-1850s. Other unions formed to represent production workers at newspapers: the International Stereotypers and Electrotypers' Union, the International Photo-Engravers' Union, and the International Printing Pressmen and Assistants' Union. But reporters didn't have a union until 1933, when *New York World-Telegram* reporter Heywood Broun called on his colleagues to organize.

The Newspaper Guild held its first meeting in early 1934 and elected Broun its president. Broun remained president until he died in 1939 at age 51. Today, the Guild continues to cover employees at many of America's large newspapers. Unions represent roughly one in five newspaper employees.

With the rise of unions, employee contracts, which once had been negotiated in private, became public agreements. In general, salaries for reporters at union newspapers rose, and this eventually led to a sense of professionalism, including codes of ethics.

Left: This 1928 photo of Ruth Snyder's execution exemplifies the screaming headlines and large photographs that still prosper in today's tabloid journalism. Left: The *New York Daily News*. Right: AP/World Wide Photos

NEWSPAPERS IN THE TELEVISION ERA

The advent of television affected the newspaper industry dramatically. Newspaper publishers already had learned how to live with only one other 20th-century news industry—radio. In the 1920s, when radio had first become popular, newspapers had refused to carry advertising or time logs for the programs, but eventually newspapers conceded the space to radio.

In the 1950s, however, television posed a larger threat: television offered moving images of the news, in addition to entertainment. The spread of television demonstrated how interrelated the media were. The newspaper industry relinquished its supremacy as the major news medium, and was forced to share the news audience with broadcasting. And over time, television's influence changed both the look and the content of many newspapers.

The Revival of the Alternative Press

The social movements of the 1960s briefly revived one portion of the newspaper industry—the alternative press. Like their 1800s predecessors in the abolitionist and emancipation movements, people who supported the revival of the alternative press in the 1960s felt that the mainstream press was avoiding important issues, such as the anti–Vietnam War movement, the civil rights movement, and the gay rights movement.

In 1964, as a way to pass along news about the antiwar movement, the *Los Angeles Free Press* became the first underground paper to publish regularly. The *Barb* in Berkeley, California, *Kaleidoscope* in Chicago, and *Quicksilver Times* in Washington, D.C., soon followed. In 1965, Jim Michaels launched the nation's first gay newspaper, the Los Angeles *Advocate*.

What the 1960s underground press proved had already been proven in the 19th century—in America, causes need a voice, and if those voices are not represented in the mainstream press, publications emerge to support alternative views.

Declining Readership

Since the 1970s, the overall number of newspapers has declined. Many afternoon papers died when TV took over the evening news. Other afternoon papers changed to morning papers. Then, newspaper publishers realized that television could provide the news headlines, but newspapers could offer the background that television news could not.

Newspaper publishers also began to see that they could play on the popularity of television personalities, who became news items. Eventually, advertisers realized that viewers cannot clip coupons out of their television sets or retrieve copies of yesterday's TV ads, so advertisers began to use newspapers to complement television advertising campaigns.

Today, the majority of small dailies are part of a chain, and most cities have only one newspaper. And in an attempt to match television's visual displays, newspapers have introduced advanced graphics and vivid color. The newspaper industry still earns more every year than any other media industry.

WORKING FOR NEWSPAPERS

Many colonial publishers handled all of the tasks of putting out a newspaper single-handed, but today's typical newspaper operation is organized into two separate departments; the editorial side and the business side. The *editorial* side handles everything that you read in the paper—the news and feature

profile

Ernie Pyle: The War Correspondent Who Hated War

*Ernie Pyle worked for Scripps Howard. This reflection on his work was written by **Dan Thomasson**, the editor of Scripps Howard News Service, to accompany a collection of Pyle's dispatches that was published in 1986. The Pyle story about Captain Waskow cited here is a fine example of war correspondence.*

The other day while going through some old files in our library, I came upon a yellowed and tattered dispatch.

It made me cry.

It told about the death of a Capt. Waskow during the Italian campaign of 1944. And it probably is the most powerful treatise on war and death and the human spirit I have ever read.

I took it out and had it treated and framed and I hung it in the office in a prominent position where now and then one of the younger reporters will come by and read it and try to hide the inevitable tear.

The man who wrote it, Ernest Taylor Pyle, is but a memory as distant as the war he covered so eloquently and ultimately died in.

But unlike so many who perished beside him, Pyle's contribution to what Studs Terkel calls "the last good war" remains with us in his work—thousands of words that will forever memorialize brave men and debunk the "glory" of war.

The column that says it best perhaps is the one drafted for the end of the fighting in Europe. It was found in his

War correspondent Ernie Pyle (1890–1945) died during the last days of World War II on the Japanese island of Ie Shima.

Bettmann/CORBIS

pocket by the foot soldiers who had risked their lives to retrieve his body on the Japanese island of Ie Shima in 1945.

"Those who were gone would not wish themselves to be a millstone of gloom around our necks.

"But there are many of the living who have burned into their brains forever the unnatural sight of cold dead men scattered over the hillsides and in the ditches along the high rows of hedge throughout the world.

"Dead men by mass production—in one country after another—month after month and year after year. Dead men in winter and dead men in summer.

"Dead men in such familiar promiscuity that they become monotonous.

"Dead men in such infinity that you come almost to hate them."

...When I was a kid starting out in this business, the trade magazines were full of job-seeking ads by those who claimed they could "write like Ernie Pyle." This was 10 years after his death and he was still everyone's model....

Here is some of what he wrote about the death of Capt. Waskow...

"Then a soldier came and stood beside the officer [a captain], and bent over, and he too spoke to his dead captain, not a whisper but awfully tenderly, and he said:

"'I sure am sorry, sir.'

"Then the first man squatted down, and he reached down and took the dead hand, and he sat there for a full five minutes, holding the dead hand in his own and looking intently into the dead face and he never uttered a sound all the time he sat there.

"And finally he put the hand down, and then reached up and gently straightened the points of the captain's shirt collar, and then he sort of rearranged the tattered edges of his uniform around the wound. And then he got up and walked away down the road in the moonlight, all alone."

"Why They Still Write Ernie Pyle Books," *Honolulu Advertiser,* June 20, 1986, p. A-11. Reprinted by permission of Scripps Howard News Service.

stories, editorials, cartoons and photographs. The *business* side handles everything else—production, advertising, distribution, and administration.

On the editorial side at a medium-size daily, different *editors*—a news editor, a sports editor, a features editor, and a business editor, for example—handle different parts of the paper. The managing editor oversees these news departments. A copyeditor checks the reporters' stories before they are set in type, and a layout editor positions the stories. Editorial writers and cartoonists usually work for an editorial page editor. All these people report to the *editor-in-chief* or the *publisher* or both.

A *business manager* and his or her staff run the business side of the paper: getting the paper out to subscribers, selling advertising, and making sure the paper gets printed every day. These people also ultimately report to the editor-in-chief or the publisher. Sometimes the publisher is also the owner of the paper. If a corporation owns the paper, the publisher reports to its board of directors.

Technology has strongly affected the way newspapers are published. The history of newspapers, like that of all media, is the history of technological advances. In their book, *The Press and America*, Edwin and Michael Emery describe the clumsiness of colonial printing:

> *The bed of the press is rolled out by means of a wheel and pulley arrangement. The type, all set by hand, is locked tight in the form and is placed on the bed. A young apprentice, or "devil," applies the homemade ink to the type, using a doeskin dauber on a stick for this purpose.*
>
> *The paper is then moistened in a trough so that it will take a better impression. It is placed carefully over the type. The bed is rolled back under the press.*
>
> *The "platen," or upper pressure plate, is then pressed against the type by means of a screw or lever device. The platen is released; the bed is wheeled out; the sheet is hung on a wire to dry before it is ready for its second "run" for the reverse side.[12]*

THE BUSINESS OF NEWSPAPERS

Today, newspapers sell 60 million copies daily, and six out of ten adults read a newspaper every day. Big-city newspapers are losing readers as people move to the suburbs, and suburban newspapers are growing, as are suburban editions of big-city papers. Newspapers depend primarily on advertising for support. Subscriptions and newsstand sales account for only a small percentage of newspaper income.

Newspaper companies in the 1980s, looking for new ways to make money, rediscovered and expanded on some old ideas. Many newspapers introduced online editions. Gannett introduced a new national newspaper. The news services streamlined their operations. And more newspaper organizations joined the syndication business.

Online Newspapers

Most newspaper publishing companies have launched electronic delivery of news and newspapers to capture new audiences for the information they gather. Newspapers arriving on-screen at computers is just part of the reader-friendly future, according to many industry analysts.

More than 1,000 regional and national daily newspapers, including newspapers in New York; Atlanta; Washington, D.C.; Chicago; Fort Worth; St.

IMPACT

on you   *Dailies Offer More "News You Can Use"*

By David Armstong

If you've noticed more news you can use and special sections on subjects like career development and personal finance, it's no accident. Dailies are becoming more like magazines and weeklies, packaging information to save time for readers who have precious little time.

They're providing context for people bombarded with fragmented, often frantic news-squibbs in the electronic media and wrapping practical information in themed advertising packages that are changing the way newspapers look and read. Things are changing for people who produce newspapers, too.

Time was when the wall between church and state—i.e., editorial and business—was expected to be absolute. Reporters wrote and editors assigned, in theory, without reference to advertising concerns, but in accord with what they felt the

Renee Lynn/Photo Researchers

public needed to know. Finding ads to drop in around the stories was an afterthought. Not our department.

But the advertising recession of the early '90s plus a downsized staff and shrinking newshole has changed much of that. These days, editors who want more

space for stories are often expected to come up with a content package—or at least a theme—that the advertising department can sell. The industry as a whole is more dependent on advertising than ever.

San Francisco Examiner, Nov. 23, 1997, B-1. Used by permission.

Louis; San Jose; Los Angeles; and Albuquerque offer online services. Newspapers are trying to generate some income from home computer users and information services are also becoming easier to use.

The *Albuquerque Tribune's Electronic Trib* offers public-record databases, restaurant reviews, a movie guide, and a calendar of events. *Chicago Online* offers news, weather, and sports headlines, as well as movie and restaurant reviews and listings of local events.

Online editions publish shorter highlights of the day's news, as well as special features that don't appear in the daily newspaper. Bulletin boards offer subscribers the chance to discuss the newspaper's movie reviews, for example, or to get more information on subjects that appear in the online edition. This is just one way that newspapers are trying to retain their audience using a new delivery system.

National Newspapers

Of all the nation's group owners, the Gannett newspaper chain has been the biggest gambler. In 1982, Gannett created *USA Today*, which it calls "The Nation's Newspaper," to compete with the country's only other major national newspaper, *The Wall Street Journal*. Dubbing it "McPaper" with only "McNuggets" of news, critics said the slim publication was the fast-food approach to newspapers. It features expensive color graphics, a detailed national weather report, comprehensive sports coverage, and news stories that rarely run longer than 600 words.

USA Today went after a different audience than the *Journal* did—people who don't want to spend a lot of time reading but who like to know the headlines. Someone in an airport or someone who wants something to read on a coffee break, Gannett argued, may not need a paper the size of *The Wall Street Journal* or a large metropolitan daily. Gannett's innovations also have influenced many other newspapers, which have added graphics and color and have shortened the average length of stories.

USA Today and the *Journal* both publish regional editions by satellite so that a local bank, for example, can place an ad. Each area's regional edition is distributed in a defined geographic area, so a local advertiser (such as the bank) pays a lower price than someone who advertises nationwide.

USA Today and the *Journal* are today's two leaders in the competition to become the nation's most successful national newspaper. Each paper has about 2 million daily readers.

News Services

news services the modern name for the original *wire* services.

Using satellites and computer terminals instead of the original telegraph machines, cooperative and for-profit news gathering has grown faster and more efficient. Today the wire services prefer to be called **news services**. Most American newspapers subscribe to at least one news service, such as the Associated Press. Many other news services send stories and broadcasts worldwide: Agence France-Presse (France), Reuters (Great Britain), the Russian Information Telegraph Agency—RITA (Commonwealth of Independent States), Agenzia Nationale Stampa Associate (Italy), Deutsche Presse Agentur (Germany), and Xinhua (China).

The news services especially help small newspapers (and broadcast stations) that can't afford overseas correspondents. Large dailies with their own correspondents around the world still rely on news services when they can't get to a story quickly.

The Associated Press is still a cooperative, as it was when it began in New York in 1848, Scripps Howard sold the financially struggling UPI in 1982, and since then UPI has had several owners and continues to struggle financially.

Some newspaper organizations in the United States—*The New York Times*, *The Washington Post*, *The Los Angeles Times*, and Knight-Ridder—have started their own news services. Newspapers that subscribe can publish each other's news service stories. For many newspapers, these stories fill space at a relatively low cost because the newspaper doesn't need as many staff reporters.

Syndicates

syndicates news agencies that sell articles for publication to a number of newspapers simultaneously.

Newspapers also can add to their content without having to send their own reporters to stories by using **syndicates**, which are news agencies that sell articles for publication to a number of newspapers simultaneously. The first syndicated column was a fashion letter distributed in 1857. Today, more newspapers are syndicating their columns and features to try to add income. Syndicates mainly provide columnists and comics—Dave Barry, Molly Ivins, and William Raspberry, as well as *Dilbert* and *Cathy,* for example. The price of syndicated copy for each newspaper is based on the newspaper's circulation. A large newspaper pays more for syndicated cartoons than a small newspaper.

TECHNOLOGY AND THE FUTURE

Since their colonial beginnings, newspapers have shown their ability to appeal to changing audiences, adapt to growing competition, and continue to attract advertisers. The Newspaper Association of America and other newspaper analysts project these advances in the future:

- Reporters in the field will send most of their stories from portable computers through cellular telephones in their cars, without needing a telephone line for their computer hookup. Photographers will use video and digital cameras, sending their pictures to the newsroom electronically. Several manufacturers have developed systems that can reproduce still pictures for newspapers from video images.

- Newspapers will expand profits by selling more of the information they gather. Once a story is in a computer, the information can be sold to people who want that information: lawyers, researchers, and home computer users.

- Satellite publishing will bring more customized newspapers in regional editions, and advertisers will be able to choose their audiences more selectively. Cheaper production methods could mean that the cost of starting a newspaper will decrease, which could increase the number of alternative and small community weeklies.

- Lower costs for information systems will mean that more newspapers will be able to afford more computer technology.

- The offset process may be replaced by a new system called *flexography*, which uses less paper and replaces expensive, toxic oil-based inks with water-based inks.

Three other emerging trends that will affect the future of the newspaper industry are the growing challenges by publishers to newspaper unions; as in all media, the intensifying concentration of ownership; and the changing newspaper audience.

Unions Versus Technology

The new technology means that machines are doing work formerly done by people. For newspaper unions, this has meant a consistent effort among newspaper owners to challenge union representation.

Before 1970, newspapers needed typographers to hand-set metal type, and labor unions represented most of these typographers. With the introduction of photocomposition, newspaper management slowly moved to eliminate the typographers' jobs. The unions fought the transition, and many newspaper workers went on strike—notably at the *New York Daily News* in 1990, at the *San Francisco Chronicle* and *San Francisco Examiner* in 1994, and at the *Detroit News* in 1996.

Unionization of newspaper employees began in the 1800s. Workers at the *Detroit News* walk the picket line in 1996.

Reuters/John Hillery/Archive Photos

With the threat of technology eliminating even more jobs in the future, newspaper unions are understandably worried. Membership in the Newspaper Guild (which covers reporters) has remained steady, but most of the other unions have lost members, especially the International Typographers Union, whose membership is half what it was before photocomposition.[13] Forecasts report that union influence at newspapers with circulations above 50,000 will remain strong, but that the effort to diffuse union influence at smaller newspapers will continue.

Chain Power

Newspapers are economically healthy, but overall newspaper circulation remains static. Instead of editors competing locally within a community, like Hearst battling Pulitzer, national chains now compete with one another. Today, chains own three-fourths of America's daily newspapers (see Figure 2.1 and Table 2.1).

This doesn't mean that every newspaper in a chain speaks with the voice of the chain owner. Chains can supply money to improve a newspaper's printing plant and to add more reporters. But critics say that the tendency to form chains can consolidate and limit the sources of information for readers.

According to media scholar Anthony Smith, "It is obvious that in some of the chains…there are clear editorial lines to which editors normally adhere." The majority of Scripps Howard papers, says Smith, "print the editorials sent out to them from the chain's Washington bureau on subjects affecting national and international policy".[14] Critics fear that chain ownership may mean less debate on public issues because the editorial policy for all newspapers in the same chain will become uniform. (See Chapter 13 for further discussion of this issue.)

A Scramble for Readers

Although newspapers still hold power for advertisers, recent studies reveal that younger readers are deserting the medium. "It dawned on us that if we

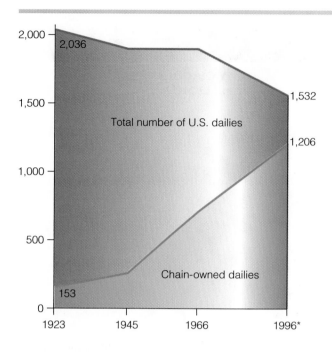

Figure 2.1 The Growth of the Chains   While the total number of U.S. dailies has declined since the 1920s, the number and proportion of dailies owned by chains have increased dramatically.

Source: Data from Christopher H. Sterling and Timothy R. Haight, *The Mass Media: Aspen Institute Guide to Communication Industry Trends* (New York/London; Praeger, 1977), Newspaper Association of America, *Facts about Newspapers*, 1996, and *Editor & Publisher International Yearbook* CD-ROM.

*Last year for which statistics are available.

don't start luring teenagers into the paper and start them reading us now, they may not subscribe in the future," according to Grant Podelco, arts editor of the Syracuse (New York) *Herald-Journal*.[15]

To stop the slide among young readers, many newspapers have added inserts directed to, and sometimes written by, teenagers. *The Wall Street Journal* introduced a high school classroom edition. At the *Chicago Tribune*, five teenage film reviewers appear in the newspaper every Friday with their choices, and a "Preps Plus" section covers high school sports. *The Dallas Morning News* runs a half-sheet called "The Mini Page," subtitled "Especially for Kids and Their Families," which carries puzzles, explanatory stories about current issues, and a teacher's guide.

Women readers also are abandoning newspapers in unprecedented numbers. Karen Jurgenson, editorial page editor of *USA Today*, says that readership surveys show that women today are less likely to be daily newspaper readers than men. "Women across the board are more likely than men to feel that the paper doesn't speak to them,"[16] she says.

To attract more female readers, Jurgenson says that newsroom employees should reflect more closely society's diversity in gender and ethnic origin, and that the newspaper should examine its coverage of issues that concern primarily women. The Charlotte *Observer*, says Jurgenson, has created a daycare beat, and some newspapers are attempting to devote more space to women's sports. Some newspapers are experimenting with a section targeted specifically for women. The *Chicago Tribune*, for example, has launched a section called "WomaNews."

Newspaper executives also blame television for the declining audience, but others say that people's reading habits reflect the changing uses of family time. "That time has been lost to working moms, aerobic classes, and of course TV," according to Jean Gaddy Wilson, executive director of New

T A B L E   2 . 1

Top Ten U.S. Newspaper Chains

		DAILY CIRCULATION (IN MILLIONS)	NUMBER OF DAILIES
1.	Gannett Co., Inc.	6	74
2.	Knight-Ridder, Inc.	3.9	33
3.	Newhouse Newspapers	2.8	23
4.	Times Mirror Co.	2.4	9
5.	Dow Jones &Co., Inc.	2.3	20
6.	The New York Times Co.	2.3	20
7.	MediaNews Group	1.8	51
8.	E.W. Scripps Co.	1.3	20
9.	The Hearst Newspapers	1.3	12
10.	The McClatchy Co.	1.3	11

Data from *Facts About Newspapers 1998;* John Morton, Morton Research, Inc; Audit Bureau of Circulations FAS-FAX; Editor & Publisher.

Directions for News, an independent research group at the University of Missouri School of Journalism, "Many kids today don't even see a paper at home these days. At best, a paper is in a mix of entertainment and news media."[17]

Newspapers are competing to maintain their audience because audiences attract advertisers—and profits. The average daily newspaper is about two–thirds advertising, and in some newspapers advertising runs as high as 70 percent. National advertisers (such as Procter & Gamble) buy television time as much as they buy newspaper space, but for small businesses nothing works as well as local newspapers. Seventy cents for each local advertising dollar goes to newspapers. There may be fewer newspaper owners in the country, but as long as newspapers can maintain their profitability, the survivors will continue comfortably.

IN FOCUS

The issue of government control of newspapers surfaced early in colonial America, when the authorities stopped *Publick Occurrences* in 1690, after a single issue, because the paper angered local officials.

- The tradition of an independent press in this country began when James Franklin published the first newspaper without the heading "By Authority."

- The John Peter Zenger case established an important legal precedent: If what a newspaper reports is true, the paper cannot be sued successfully for libel.

- As dissatisfaction grew over British rule, newspapers became essential political tools in the effort to spread revolutionary ideas, including opposition to the British Stamp Act and to the Alien and Sedition Laws.

- The technological advances of the 19th century, such as cheaper newsprint, mechanized printing, and the telegraph, meant that newspapers could reach a wider audience faster than ever before. This also lowered production costs, which made newspaper publishing companies attractive investments.

- Newspapers spread their reach in the 1800s to include people on the frontier, the growing number of immigrants, and the Native American population.

- The penny press made newspapers affordable for virtually every American.

- The emancipation and suffrage movements found a voice in the dissident press, which marked the beginning of newspapers as a tool for social protest.

- Cooperative news gathering began in 1848 with the formation of the New York Associated Press. The United Press followed. AP is a cooperative; UPI is struggling financially.

- Government interests confronted the issue of press freedom during the Civil War, when the government decided to certify journalists to cover the war through a process called accreditation. This practice continues today.

- Mathew Brady's careful documentation of the Civil War demonstrated that news photography can be practical and effective. This documentary record is the first example of what today is called photojournalism.

- Intense competition bred yellow journalism, which nurtured the sensational coverage of the Spanish-American War in 1898. This newspaper war underscored the importance of press responsibility.

- Unionization at newspapers standardized wages for newspaper employees and increased professionalism.

- Television contributed to a decline in newspaper readership in the 1950s, although the social causes of the 1960s briefly revived the alternative press.

- Although individually owned newspapers still exist in some cities, today chains and conglomerates publish three-fourths of American daily newspapers.

- Newspapers still hold power for advertisers, but recent studies reveal that younger readers are deserting the medium faster than any other age group. Readership among women also has declined. To stop the slide, many newspapers have introduced features and sections targeted toward teenagers and toward women.

- Several newspaper publishing companies have launched online newspapers to capture new audiences for information they gather.

- The future success of newspapers depends on their ability to appeal to a shifting audience, meet growing competition, and continue to attract advertisers.

WORKING THE WEB www

- **Denver Post**
  www.denverpost.com

- **Los Angeles Times**
  www.latimes.com
- **Miami Herald**
  www.miamiherald.com
- **The New York Times**
  www.nytimes.com
- **Newspaper Association of America**
  www.naa.org
- **The San Francisco Chronicle**
  www.sfgate.com
- **San Jose Mercury News**
  www.mercurycenter.com
- **Seattle Post-Intelligencer**
  www.seattlep-i.com
- **USA Today**
  www.usatoday.com
- **The Wall Street Journal Interactive Edition**
  www.wsj.com
- **The Washington Post**
  www.washingtonpost.com

INFOTRAC COLLEGE EDITION EXERCISES

Using InfoTrac College Edition, a fully searchable online database of articles and abstracts, do the following exercises as directed by your instructor.

1. Read Chapter 2 in the textbook and use InfoTrac College Edition to research the following figures in newspaper history:

   - Benjamin Franklin
   - Ida B. Wells
   - John Peter Zenger
   - Frederick Douglass
   - Mark Twain (Samuel Clemens)
   - Mathew Brady

   Print at least one article on three of the historic newspaper figures about his or her involvement with newspapers and/or journalism. Bring the articles to class. Be prepared to speak briefly about the persons you have selected, or find more sources about one of the people and write a longer paper, as directed by your instructor.

2. Look up information on early 20th century newspaper publishers William Randolph Hearst and Joseph Pulitzer on InfoTrac College Edition. Print at least one article about each man and bring the article to class for discussion, or find more sources about one of the publishers and either:

   a. write a brief paper on your findings, or

   b. bring the articles to class for a small-group discussion.

3. Read the Impact Profile: "Ernie Pyle: the War Correspondent Who Hated War" in Chapter 2. Look up more information about Pyle on InfoTrac College Edition and write a brief paper on why Pyle was and is so admired by journalists.

4. Look up the subject heading "newspaper industry" on InfoTrac College Edition and choose three articles on the industry that interest you. Print them and bring them to class for a discussion on the ways the newspaper industry has changed as it enters the 21st century.

5. Using InfoTrac College Edition, select one of the following two options:

Option 1: Look up articles on *The Wall Street Journal* and *USA Today*. See what you can learn about what makes these two national daily newspapers different and why they appeal to different audiences. Print at least two articles about each paper and either:

a. write a brief paper on your findings, or

b. bring the articles to class for a small-group discussion.

Option 2: Look up articles on the two best-known news services, the Associated Press and United Press International. What can you learn about the functions of these news services? Print at least two articles about each news service and either:

a. write a brief paper on your findings, or

b. bring the articles to class for a small-group discussion.

3

Magazines

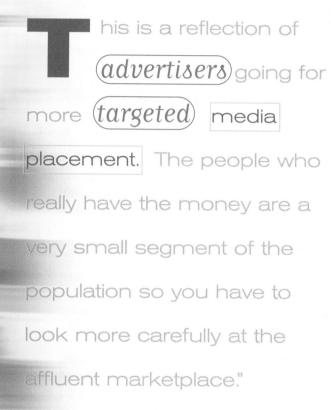

This is a reflection of (*advertisers*) going for more (*targeted*) media placement. The people who really have the money are a very small segment of the population so you have to look more carefully at the affluent marketplace."

Valerie Muller, Media Director for DeWitt Media, which places magazine ads for BMW.

By the early 1950s, magazine mogul Henry Luce's *Time* and *Fortune* were well established. He often traveled with his wife, Ambassador Clare Boothe Luce. Many of the people that Henry Luce met overseas wanted to talk with him about sports instead of asking him questions of international importance.

"Luce knew nothing about sports," says *Los Angeles Times* sports columnist Jim Murray, who in the early 1950s was writing about sports for *Time* magazine. "But every place he'd go, all over the world, the conversation would veer to the World Cup or the British Open or whatever.

"He got fascinated and irritated, I guess, and finally said, 'Why this all-consuming interest in games?' We said, 'Well, that's the way the world is, Henry.' He said, 'Well, maybe we ought to start a sports magazine.'"[1] The result, of course, was *Sports Illustrated,* which today is ranked among the nation's most profitable magazines.

Sports Illustrated was one of the earliest magazines to anticipate today's trend in magazines. Today, successful magazines cater to specialized audiences. You probably have seen a copy of *Sports Illustrated* recently, or perhaps you have read *Glamour, PC World* or *Muscle & Fitness.* All of these publications are ranked among the country's top 200 magazines. They give their readers information that they can't find anywhere else, and their vast readership might surprise you.

Glamour, published by Condé Nast, reaches more than 2 million readers every month and is ranked among the nation's top ten women's magazines. *PC World,* the nation's fastest growing computer magazine, caters primarily to small business and home computer users. Nearly a million people read the magazine every month, and the magazine's readership is very attractive to advertisers. The company that publishes *PC World,* Ziff Communications, also publishes several other computer magazines. *Muscle & Fitness,* following the national fight against flab, advertises products such as exercise equipment and bodybuilding formulas to nearly half a million subscribers.

These examples highlight a significant fact about the history of the magazine industry: *Magazines reflect the surrounding culture and the characteristics of the society.* As readers' needs and lifestyles change, so do magazines. The trend toward specialty and online magazines is the latest chapter in this evolution.

COLONIAL COMPETITORS

In 1741, more than 50 years after the birth of the colonies' first newspaper, magazines entered the American media marketplace. Newspapers covered daily crises for local readers, but magazines could reach beyond the parochial concerns of small communities to carry their cultural, political and social ideas and foster their identity as part of a nation.

The magazine industry began in 1741 in Philadelphia, when Benjamin Franklin and Andrew Bradford raced each other to become America's first magazine publisher. Franklin originated the idea of starting the first American magazine, but Bradford issued his *American Magazine* first, on February 13, 1741. Franklin's first issue of *General Magazine* came out three days later. Neither magazine lasted very long. Bradford published three issues and Franklin published six. But their efforts initiated a rich tradition.

Because they didn't carry advertising, early magazines were expensive and their circulations remained very small, but like colonial newspapers, early magazines provided a means for political expression.

THE FIRST NATIONAL MASS MEDIUM

Newspapers flooded the larger cities by the early 1800s, but they circulated only within each city's boundaries, so national news spread slowly. Colleges were limited to the wealthy, and books were expensive. Magazines became America's only *national* medium, and subscribers depended on them for news, culture and entertainment. The magazine that first reached a large public was *The Saturday Evening Post,* started in 1821.

The *Post* (published every Saturday at a time when there were no Sunday papers) featured news, fiction, poetry, essays, theater reviews and a column called "The Lady's Friend." The early *Post*s cost a nickel each and were only four pages, with no illustrations. One-fourth of the magazine was advertising, and for 40 years it was one of America's most important weeklies.

A sample of 1875 fashions displayed in *Godey's Lady's Book,* edited by Sarah Josepha Hale.

CORBIS/Bettmann

T I M E F R A M E

Today to 1821: Magazines grow as a specialized medium that targets readers

TODAY Magazines are very specialized, targeting narrow groups of readers for advertisers.

1985 Newhouse buys *The New Yorker* for more than $185 million, beginning the era of magazine industry consolidation.

1945 John Johnson launches *Ebony* and then *Jet*.

1923 Henry Luce creates *Time,* the nation's first news magazine, and then *Fortune* and *Life*.

1910 W.E.B. Du Bois and the National Association for the Advancement of Colored People (NAACP) start *The Crisis*.

1893 Samuel A. McClure founds *McClure's Magazine,* the nation's first major showcase for investigative magazine journalism, featuring muckrakers Ida Tarbell and Lincoln Steffens.

1865 *The Nation,* featuring political commentary, appears in Boston.

1830 Louis A. Godey hires Sarah Josepha Hale as the first woman editor of a general circulation women's magazine, *Godey's Lady's Book*.

1821 *The Saturday Evening Post* becomes the first magazine to reach a wide public audience.

Michael Newman/PhotoEdit

REACHING NEW READERS

Magazines like *The Saturday Evening Post* reached a wide readership with their general-interest content. But many other audiences were available to 19th-century publishers, and they spent the century locating their readership. Four enduring subjects that expanded the magazine audience in the 1800s were women's issues, social crusades, literature and the arts and politics.

Women's Issues

Because women were a sizable potential audience, magazines were more open to female contributors than were newspapers. Many early magazines published poetry and stories by women. Although some women wrote under men's names, most used their true names. Two central figures in the history of women's magazines in America were Sarah Josepha Hale and Edward Bok.

In 1830, Louis A. Godey was the first publisher to capitalize on an audience that the *Post* had identified as "The Lady's Friend" column. Women, most of whom had not attended school, sought out *Godey's Lady's Book* and its gifted editor, Sarah Josepha Hale, for advice on morals, manners, literature, fashion, diet and taste.

When her husband died in 1822, Hale sought work to support herself and her five children. As the editor of *Godey's* for 40 years beginning in 1837, she fervently supported higher education and property rights for women. By

1860, *Godey's* had 150,000 subscribers.[2] Hale retired from the magazine when she was 89, a year before she died.

Social Crusades

Magazines also became important instruments for social change. *The Ladies' Home Journal* is credited with leading a crusade against dangerous medicines. Many of the ads in women's magazines in the 1800s were for patent medicines like Faber's Golden Female Pills ("successfully used by prominent ladies for female irregularities") and Ben-Yan, which promised to cure "all nervous debilities."

The Ladies' Home Journal was the first magazine to refuse patent medicine ads. Founded in 1887 by Cyrus Curtis, the *Journal* launched several crusades. It offered columns about women's issues, published popular fiction, and even printed sheet music.

Editor Edward Bok began his crusade against patent medicines in 1892 after he learned that many of them contained more than 40 percent alcohol. Next Bok revealed that a medicine sold to soothe noisy babies contained morphine. Other magazines joined the fight against dangerous ads and, partly because of Bok's crusading investigations, Congress passed the Pure Food and Drug Act of 1906.

The most notable Bok crusade began in 1906, when he published an editorial about venereal disease. Bok believed that women should know about the disease's threat, and he continued articles about the subject even after 75,000 subscribers canceled. Eventually, the readers returned and Bok's crusading made *The Ladies' Home Journal* even more popular.

Fostering a Literary Tradition

In the mid-1800s, American magazines began to seek a literary audience by promoting the nation's writers. Two of today's most important literary magazines—*Harper's* and *The Atlantic Monthly*—began more than a century ago. *Harper's New Monthly Magazine,* known today as *Harper's,* first appeared in 1850. As a monthly, *Harper's* didn't try to compete for the *Post*'s general audience or for Sarah Hale's readers. The magazine earned an early reputation for its attention to science, biography, travel and fiction. By the 1860s, *Harper's* circulation was 200,000.[3] Today, *Harper's* continues to publish essentially the same mix of articles that made it so popular in the 1800s.

The American literary showcase grew when *The Atlantic Monthly* appeared in 1857 in Boston. In 1909, *Atlantic* editor Ellery Sedgwick said the magazine's purpose was "to inoculate the few who influence the many." That formula continues today, with *The Atlantic* still provoking literary and political debate.

Political Commentary

With more time (usually a month between issues) and space than newspapers had to reflect on the country's problems, political magazines provided a forum for public arguments by scholars and critical observers. Three of the nation's progressive political magazines that began in the 19th and early 20th centuries have endured: *The Nation, The New Republic* and *The Crisis.*

The Nation, founded in 1865, is the oldest continuously published opinion journal in the United States, offering critical literary essays and arguments for progressive change. This weekly magazine has survived a succession of owners and financial hardship.

The Crisis, founded by W. E. B. Du Bois in 1910 as the monthly magazine of the National Association for the Advancement of Colored People (NAACP) continues to publish today.

The Crisis

Another outspoken publication, which began challenging the establishment in the early 1900s, is *The New Republic,* founded in 1914. The weekly's circulation has rarely reached 40,000, but its readers enjoy the role it plays in regularly criticizing political leaders. Through a succession of owners and support from sympathetic patrons, the original concept of the magazine has remained, as one of its early editors put it, to start "little insurrections."

An organization that needed a voice at the beginning of the century was the National Association for the Advancement of Colored People (NAACP). For 24 years, beginning in 1910, that voice was W.E.B. Du Bois, who founded and edited the organization's monthly magazine, *The Crisis.*

Du Bois began *The Crisis* as the official monthly magazine of the NAACP. Du Bois attacked discrimination against African-American soldiers during World War I, exposed Ku Klux Klan activities and argued for African-American voting and housing rights. By 1919, circulation was more than 100,000. *The Crisis* continues today to publish monthly.

The Postal Act's Effects

Passage of the Postal Act of 1879 encouraged the growth of magazines. Before passage of the Act, newspapers traveled through the mail freely while magazines had to pay postage.

With the Postal Act of 1879, Congress gave magazines second-class mailing privileges. Congress then instituted a rate of a penny a pound for newspapers and magazines. This meant quick, reasonably priced distribution for magazines, and today magazines still travel on a preferential rate.

Aided by cheaper postal rates, the number of monthly magazines grew from 180 in 1860 to over 1,800 by the turn of the century. However, because magazines travel through the mail, they are vulnerable to censorship (see Chapter 14).

THE MUCKRAKERS: MAGAZINE JOURNALISTS CAMPAIGN FOR CHANGE

The colorful, campaigning journalists just before the turn of the century became known as **muckrakers.** The strongest editor in the first ten years of the 20th century was legendary magazine publisher Samuel S. McClure, who founded *McClure's Magazine* in 1893.

McClure and his magazine were very important to the Progressive era in American politics, which called for an end to the close relationship between government and big business. To reach a large readership, McClure priced his new monthly magazine at 15 cents an issue, while most other magazines sold for 25 or 35 cents.

Ida Tarbell joined *McClure's* in 1894 as associate editor. Her series about Lincoln boosted the magazine's circulation. Subsequently, Tarbell tackled a series about Standard Oil. (See Impact/Profile, "Ida Tarbell Targets John D. Rockefeller" below.)

Tarbell peeled away the veneer of the country's biggest oil trust. Her 19-part series began running in *McClure's* in 1904. Eventually the series became a two-volume book, *History of the Standard Oil Company,* which established Tarbell's reputation as a muckraker.

The muckrakers' targets were big business and corrupt government. President Theodore Roosevelt coined the term *muckraker* in 1906 when he compared

muckrakers investigative magazine journalists who targeted abuses by government and big business.

Magazines

*T*oday's magazines target specific audiences.

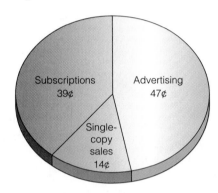

Where the magazine revenue dollar comes from: Most magazines receive more income from single-copy sales and subscriptions than from advertising.

Source: Data from Magazine Publishers of America

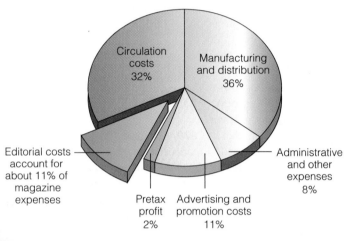

Where the magazine revenue dollar goes: The cost to create the editorial content of a magazine is only 11% of the total cost to produce the magazine.

Source: Data from Magazine Publishers of America

Many magazines, like *U.S. News & World Report,* have introduced on-line versions of their magazines for computer users.

Sources: U.S. News & World Report, Inc. All rights reserved.
http://www.usnews.com

IMPACT

profile Ida Tarbell Targets John D. Rockefeller

When John D. Rockefeller refused to talk with her, Ida Tarbell sat at the back of the room and watched him deliver a Sunday-school sermon. In her autobiography, *All in the Day's Work,* written when she was 80, Tarbell described some of her experiences as she investigated the Standard Oil Company:

"The impression of power deepened when Mr. Rockefeller took off his coat and hat, put on a skullcap, and took a seat commanding the entire room, his back to the wall. It was the head which riveted attention. It was big, great breadth from back to front, high broad forehead, big bumps behind the ears, not a shiny head but with a wet look.

In 1904, muckraker Ida Tarbell targeted oil magnate John D. Rockefeller, who called her "that misguided woman."

Bettmann/CORBIS

The skin was as fresh as that of any healthy man about us. The thin sharp nose was like a thorn. There were no lips; the mouth looked as if the teeth were all shut hard. Deep furrows ran down each side of the mouth from the nose. There were puffs under the little colorless eyes with creases running from them.

"Wonder over the head was almost at once diverted to wonder over the man's uneasiness. His eyes were never quiet but darted from face to face, even peering around the jog at the audience close to the wall....

"My two hours' study of Mr. Rockefeller aroused a feeling I had not expected, which time has intensified. I was sorry for him. I know no companion so terrible as fear. Mr. Rockefeller, for all the conscious power written in face and voice and figure, was afraid, I told myself, afraid of his own kind...."[4]

reformers like Tarbell to the "Man with the Muckrake" who busily dredged up the dirt in John Bunyan's *Pilgrim's Progress.*

An important colleague of Tarbell's at *McClure's* was another muckraker, Lincoln Steffens. His special interest was politics, and for *McClure's* Steffens wrote *Shame of the Cities,* a series about political corruption in major U.S. cities. *McClure's* embodied muckraking at its best. By 1910, many of the reforms sought by the muckrakers had been adopted, and this particular type of magazine journalism declined. The muckrakers often are cited as America's original investigative journalists.

TARGETED VERSUS BROAD READERSHIP: *THE NEW YORKER* AND *TIME* MAGAZINES

Magazines in the first half of the 20th century matured and adapted to absorb the invention of radio and then of television. As with magazines today, magazine publishers had two basic choices: (1) publishers could seek a *definable, targeted loyal audience,* or (2) publishers could seek a *broad, general readership.* These two different types of American publishers in the first half of the 20th century are best exemplified by Harold Ross, founding editor of *The New Yorker,* and Henry Luce, who started Time Inc.

Published since 1925, *The New Yorker* is one of the nation's most successful magazines.

Harold Ross and *The New Yorker*

Harold Ross' *The New Yorker* magazine launched the wittiest group of writers that ever gathered around a table at New York's Algonquin Hotel. The "witcrackers," who met there regularly for lunch throughout the 1920s, included Heywood Broun, Robert Benchley, Dorothy Parker, Alexander Woollcott, James Thurber and Harpo Marx. Because they sat at a large round table in the dining room, the group came to be known as the Algonquin Round Table. Harold Ross persuaded Raoul Fleischmann, whose family money came from the yeast company, to invest half a million dollars in *The New Yorker* before the magazine began making money in 1928, three years after its launch. Ross published some of the country's great commentary, fiction and humor, sprinkled with cartoons that gave *The New Yorker* its charm. Ross edited the magazine until he died in 1951, and he was succeeded by William Shawn.

After one owner—the Fleischmann family—and only two editors in 60 years, *The New Yorker* was sold in 1985 to Advance Publications, owned by the Newhouse family. William Shawn retired in 1987, and today the magazine is edited by Tina Brown, who once edited *Vanity Fair*. Today, *The New Yorker* continues to be the primary showcase for contemporary American writers and artists.

Henry Luce's Empire: *Time*

Henry Luce is the singular giant of 20th-century magazine publishing. Unlike Harold Ross, who sought a sophisticated, wealthy audience, Luce wanted to reach the largest possible audience.

Luce's first creation was *Time* magazine, which he founded in 1923 with his Yale classmate Briton Hadden. Luce and Hadden paid themselves $30 a week and recruited their friends to write for the magazine.

The first issue of *Time* covered the week's events in 28 pages, minus six pages of advertising—half an hour's reading. "It was of course not for people who really wanted to be informed," wrote Luce's biographer W. A. Swanberg. "It was for people willing to spend a half-hour to avoid being entirely uninformed."[5] The brash news magazine became the foundation of a Luce empire that now publishes *Time, Fortune, Life, Sports Illustrated, Money* and *People Weekly*.

Today, Time Inc. is one of the largest magazine publishers in the United States but the magazines are only part of the giant company Time Warner, which includes television stations, book publishing companies and Home Box Office.

Many of Luce's magazines fostered lookalikes. *Look* magazine mimicked *Life.* So did *Ebony,* an African-American magazine introduced in the 1940s by John H. Johnson, whose chain also launched *Jet* magazine. By the 1990s, *Ebony* and *Jet* had a combined readership of 3 million. Johnson is grooming his daughter, Linda Johnson Rice, to assume management of the company.

SPECIALIZED MAGAZINES TAKE OVER

In the 1950s, television began to offer Americans some of the same type of general-interest features that magazines provided. General-interest magazines collapsed. Gradually, readers began to buy magazines for specialized information that they could not get from other sources. These new specialized magazines segmented the market, which meant that more magazines got fewer readers.

Linda Johnson Rice with her father, John H. Johnson, publisher and founder of Johnson Publications. Rice is gradually taking over responsibility for the Johnson company.

AP/Wide World Photos

Very few general-interest magazines survive today. The trend, since television expanded the media marketplace, is for magazines to find a specific audience interested in the information that magazines can deliver. This is called *targeting an audience,* which magazines can do more effectively today than any other media.

Today's magazines can be categorized into three types: (1) consumer publications; (2) trade, technical and professional publications and (3) company publications.

consumer magazines all magazines sold by subscription or at newsstands, supermarkets and bookstores.

You probably are most familiar with **consumer magazines,** which are popularly marketed: *Time, Glamour* and *Wired,* for example. *Rolling Stone* and *Muscle & Fitness* also are considered consumer magazines. In the magazine business, *consumer* magazines are not just those that give buying advice. This term refers to all magazines sold by subscription or at newsstands, supermarkets and bookstores. As a group, consumer magazines make the most money because they have the most readers and carry the most advertising.

Trade, technical and professional magazines are read by people in a particular industry to learn more about their business. *Veterinary Practice Management,* for example, is a trade magazine, published as "a business guide for small animal practitioners." So are the *Columbia Journalism Review* (published by Columbia University) and *American Medical News* (published by the American Medical Association). These magazines are issued by media companies for their subscribers (*Veterinary Practice Management,* for example, is published by Whittle Communications); universities or university-connected organizations for their subscribers (*Columbia Journalism Review,* for example), or professional associations for their members (*American Medical News,* for example). Most trade, technical and professional magazines carry advertising directed at the professions they serve.

Company magazines are produced by businesses for their employees, customers and stockholders. These magazines usually don't carry advertising. Their main purpose is to promote the company. Chevron, for instance, publishes a company magazine called *Chevron USA Odyssey.*

WORKING FOR MAGAZINES

Magazine employees work in one of five divisions: (1) editorial, (2) circulation sales, (3) advertising sales, (4) manufacturing and distribution and (5) administration.

The *editorial* department handles everything regarding the content of the magazine, except the advertisements. This is the department for which magazine editors work, and they decide the subjects for each magazine issue, oversee the people who write the articles and schedule the articles for the magazine. Designers who determine the "look" of the magazine also are considered part of the editorial department. The *circulation* department manages the subscription information. Workers in this department enter new subscriptions and handle address changes and cancellations, for example.

The *advertising* department is responsible for finding companies that would like to advertise in the magazine. Advertising employees often help the companies design their ads to be consistent with the magazine format. *Manufacturing* and *distribution* departments manage the production of the magazine and get it to readers. This often includes contracting with an outside company to print the magazine. Many magazine companies also contract with an outside distribution company rather than deliver the magazines themselves. *Adminis-*

tration, as in any media company, takes care of the organizational details—the paperwork of hiring, paying bills and managing the office, for example.

Because advertisers provide nearly half of a magazine's income, tension often develops between a magazine's advertising staff and its editorial staff. The advertising staff may lobby the editor for favorable stories about potential advertisers, but the editor is responsible to the audience of the magazine. The advertising department might argue with the editor, for example, that a local restaurant will not want to advertise in a magazine that publishes an unfavorable review of the restaurant. If the restaurant is a big advertiser, the editor must decide how to best maintain the magazine's integrity.

Circulation figures for member magazines are verified and published by the Audit Bureau of Circulations, an agency of print media market research. Advertisers use ABC figures to help them decide which magazines to use to reach their audience.

Putting the magazine together and selling it (circulation, advertising, administration, manufacturing and distribution) cost more than organizing the articles and photographs that appear in the magazine (editorial). Often a managing editor coordinates all five departments.

The magazine editor's job is to keep the content interesting so people will continue to read the magazine. Good magazine editors can create a distinctive, useful product by carefully choosing the best articles for the magazine's audience and ensuring that the articles are well written.

Many articles are written by full-time magazine staffers, such as a food editor who creates recipes or a columnist who writes commentary. Nearly half of the country's magazines, however, use articles by **freelancers.** Freelancers do not receive a salary from the magazine; instead, they are paid individually for each of their articles published in the magazine. Many freelancers write for several magazines simultaneously. Some freelancers specialize—just writing travel articles, for example. Other freelancers work just as the tradition of their name implies: They have a pen for hire, and they can write about any subject a magazine editor wants.

The trend toward specialized audience targeting will continue. As the audience becomes more segmented, magazine publishers will seek more specific readership, such as the Latino audience sought by the magazine *Hispanic.*

freelancers writers who are not on the staff of a magazine and are paid for each individual article published.

THE BUSINESS OF MAGAZINES

Today, trends in magazine publishing continue to reflect social and demographic changes, but magazines no longer play the cutting-edge social, political and cultural role they played in the past. Instead, most magazines are seeking a specific audience, and many more magazines are competing for the same readers. *Newsweek* and *U.S. News & World Report* compete with *Time* to serve the reader who wants a weekly news roundup. *Fortune* is no longer alone; it has been joined by magazines like *Business Week, Forbes* and *Nation's Business.* Some new magazines, such as *George,* have been launched successfully to appeal to a younger audience. However, most magazine audiences have grown older and today read magazines like *PC World, Money* and *Better Homes and Gardens.*

Women continue to be the single most lucrative audience for magazines. *Family Circle* and *Woman's Day* are called point-of-purchase magazines because they are sold only at the checkout stands in supermarkets and are only one part of the women's market. *Vogue, Glamour* and *Cosmopolitan* cater to the fashion-conscious, and women's magazines have matured to include the working women's audience with *Savvy, Self* and *Working Woman,* for example. The market is divided still further by magazines like *Essence,* aimed at professional African American women, and the specifically targeted *Today's Chicago Woman* for female executives who live in Chicago.

Segmenting the Audience

The two newest segments of the magazine audience to be targeted by special-interest magazines are owners of personal computers and videocassette recorders. Titles like *PC Magazine, PC World* and *PC Week* already are among the nation's top 500 magazines, and so is *Wired.*

The tendency to specialize has not yet reached the level suggested by one magazine publisher, who joked that soon there might be magazines called *Working Grandmother, Lefthanded Tennis* and *Colonial Homes in Western Vermont.* But magazine publishers are seeking readers with a targeted interest and then selling those readers to the advertisers who want to reach that specific audience—skiers, condominium owners, motorcyclists, toy collectors and so on.

Besides targeting a special audience, such as gourmets or computer hackers, today magazines also can divide their audience further with regional and special editions that offer articles for specific geographic areas along with regional advertising, or webzines, which are online magazines available on the Internet. The news weeklies, for example, can insert advertising for a local bank or a local TV station next to national ads. This gives the local advertiser the prestige of a national magazine, at a lower cost.

One specialization success is *Modern Maturity.* Unlike most other successful specialized magazines, which are published by commercial publishers, *Modern Maturity* is published by an association. People who join the American Association of Retired Persons (AARP) receive the magazine as part of their association membership. With over 22 million readers, this bimonthly magazine provides articles on investments, careers and personal relationships for readers 50 years and older. *Modern Maturity* boasts more readers than any other American magazine.

Modern Maturity's success story is a comment on the current state of the magazine industry. The audience for magazines, as for newspapers, is growing

Japanese-speaking readers can find Japanese translations of popular magazines at a specialty bookstore in New York.

AP/Wide World Photos

older. Younger readers are less likely to read magazines than their parents. In 1990, for the first time, the number of magazines published in the United States stopped growing.

Magazine Start-Ups

Most new magazines "started each year are modest publications, probably designed on someone's kitchen table, produced on a laptop computer and financed by loyal relatives or friends. But the choices of subject often mirror those coming out of the boardrooms of the giant media companies." Sex is the favorite category for new magazines, followed by lifestyle, sports, media personalities and home subjects.[6] In 2000, Oprah Winfrey launched a lifestyles magazine called *O*.

But only a few new magazines succeed. Today, only one in three new magazines will survive more than five years.[7] The reason most magazines fail is that many new companies do not have the money to keep publishing long enough so that they can refine the editorial content, sell advertisers on the idea and gather subscribers: in other words, until the magazine can make a profit. And all magazines are vulnerable to trends in the economy.

The number of magazines people buy each year remains static, but revenues are increasing. Although magazines were once very inexpensive and advertising paid for most of the cost of production, publishers gradually have been charging more, and subscribers are willing to pay more for the magazines they want.

A Valuable Audience

The average magazine reader is a high-school graduate, is married, owns a home and works full-time.[8] This is a very attractive audience for advertisers. Advertisers also like magazines because people often refer to an ad weeks after they first see it.

Many readers say that they read the magazine as much for the ads as they do for the articles. This, of course, is also very appealing to advertisers. The

In 2000, media mogul Oprah Winfrey, seen here on her TV talk show with basketball star Michael Jordan, launched a lifestyles magazine called **O**.

AP/Wide World Photos

I M P A C T

on you

The Beauty World Follows the Money to the Internet

By Nancy Hass

Most fashionable young editors at places like Condé Nast and Hearst might be expected to wrinkle their perfect noses at the thought of anyone—much less themselves—hawking makeup online. But how long can a girl sit back and watch her college classmates, even the ones with no style at all, make a killing on Internet I.P.O.'s [initial public offerings]?

About as long as it takes mascara to dry. [In fall 1999], more than a dozen well-financed Internet start-ups [began] selling cosmetics directly to consumers on the Web. Most of those sites will be shaped by former editors from the top fashion and beauty magazines: places like *Vogue*, *Elle*, and *Mirabelle*.

"It's totally exciting, because you're involved in all these areas that you never even knew existed," said Wendy Schmid, who left her job as beauty editor at *Vogue* earlier this summer to be a co-editor of one of the new sites, Beautyjungle.com. "One minute you're talking about the new eye shadow from Fendi and the next you're using words like 'universal branding' and 'broadband communications.'"

This exodus from the elegant corridors of the magazine world to the rough-and-tumble frontiers of cyberspace may seem reckless, because it's still uncertain whether consumers will actually buy lipstick shades without trying them on. But lured with stock options and creative control, they're taking the risk even if the price may be a loss of status.

"After all these years of being royalty at magazines," said Jean Godfrey-June, a former beauty editor of *Elle* who is now vice president of editorial content at Beautyscene.com,… "it's a little like you don't exist. People say things like, 'She used to be great,' like you're dead."

The new cyber-editors are hoping all that will change after the fall debuts, which in the small world of the beauty industry is the highlight of this season, as eagerly awaited as the fall fashion shows.

"The coming explosion of all these sites is foremost on everyone's mind in the industry," said Kate Sullivan, director of marketing at Nars, which is refurbishing its own Web site…."It's pretty much an obsession."

Traditionally, the so-called "prestige" cosmetics—a $6-billion-a-year business that includes mainstream lines like Clinique and niche brands like Trish McEvoy, Face and Nars—have been available almost exclusively at department store counters. Reports that millions of women did their shopping last Christmas on the Internet has fueled the belief that those same women can be persuaded to buy makeup—considered the ultimate touch-and-feel product—online.

One of the things in the Web's favor, said Sarah Kugelman, the founder of Gloss.com, is what she calls a general dissatisfaction with service at department stores. "There was a time when you got good, personalized service," she said, "but those days are long gone. Now, we're going to be able to give you better, more intimate treatment over the Internet."

By Thanksgiving, the airwaves, bus stops and magazines themselves will be plastered with campaigns for such soundalike sites as Beauty.com, Beautyscene.com, Beautyjungle.com, Ionbeauty.com, and Ibeauty.com.

Hybrids of information and commerce, most of the sites will offer the service journalism found in beauty sections of magazines, but with interactive twist. And E-commerce: their real goal is to sell. Consumers will be able to place instant orders for the products they have just read about online.

The New York Times, on the Web, August 29, 1999. Copyright © 1999 by the New York Times Co. Reprinted by permission.

Magazine Publishers Association reports that people keep a magazine an average of 17 weeks, and that each magazine has at least four adult readers. This magazine sharing is called **pass-along readership.**

pass-along readership
people who share a magazine with the original recipient.

TECHNOLOGY AND THE FUTURE

In 1984, for the first time, the price paid for individual magazine companies and groups of magazines bought and sold in one year reached $1 billion. *U.S. News & World Report* sold for $100 million. *Billboard* sold for $40 million. The Newhouse chain paid $25.5 million for 17 percent of *The New Yorker,* which the company eventually bought for more than $150 million.[9] Like other media industries, magazines are being gathered together under large umbrella organizations, and this trend is continuing.

The trend toward more refined audience targeting by magazines also will continue. As the audience becomes more segmented, magazine publishers envision a time when they will deliver to each reader exactly what he or she wants to read. This means an infinitely defined readership, so that advertisers will be able to reach only the people they want.

Changes in the way that magazines do business in the future will be affected by technology as well as by the shifting economics of the industry. Magazine editors predict these developments:

- Online magazines will expand magazine readership. In 1993, for example, *Newsweek* launched an online edition of its weekly magazine. In 1994, *Business Week* began offering its magazine over a computer online service, including a feature that gives readers access to online conferences with editors and newsmakers, and forums where readers can post messages related to topics covered in each issue of the magazine. Most major consumer magazines today publish online editions.

- More editors will review the final copy on a screen and transmit the full-color product by satellite directly to remote printing plants located for the quickest distribution to subscribers, newsstands, supermarkets, bookstores and other outlets.

- Advertisers will be able to target their audience better because magazines can divide their audiences not only by geography, income and interest but also by zip code.

- Subscribers may be asked to pay as much as half of the cost of producing each magazine. If subscription prices rise substantially, fewer people will be able to afford to buy magazines, thus decreasing the potential audience.

- Desktop publishing is expanding the number of small publishers. Using a personal computer, a scanner, desktop publishing software and image-setting equipment, desktop operations can do everything to get a magazine ready for production.

Magazines survive because they complement the other media and have their own special benefits. Wayne Warner, president of Judd's Inc., which prints more than 77 American magazines as diverse as *The New Republic, Modern Plastics* and *Newsweek,* best describes the advantages of magazines as a medium: "With magazines, we can read *what* we want, *when* we want, and *where* we want. And we can read them again and again at our pace, fold them, spindle them, mutilate them, tear out coupons, ads, or articles that interest us and, in short, do what we damn well please to them because they are 'our' magazines."[10]

IMPACT

on you *Keeping Magazines All in the Family*

Spinoffs Seek Readers and the Advertisers Who Love Them

By Alex Kuczynski

Your newsstand is overflowing. It's stacked to the rafters with *People, Teen People* and *People en Español.* There's *Country Living* and *Country Living Country Gardener* and *Country Living Healthy Living.*

And don't forget *Traditional Home* and *Traditional Home Decorator Showhouse* and *Traditional Home Renovation Style.*

In the last two years, publishers have come to see the spinoffs as the future of magazines. Spinoffs are new magazines that take the title of the original publication and, by adding a subtitle like "For Women," "Finance" or "Gardener," try to attract new readers and provide a new marketplace for advertisers.

The seemingly endless iterations are only accelerating. *Sports Illustrated for Women,* the brainchild of Time Warner's *Sports Illustrated* publishing staff, [joined] its first-born sibling, *Sports Illustrated for Kids,* on the newsstand. And they, in turn, will be joined by the National Geographic Society's *National Geographic Adventure,* the offspring of *National Geographic.* Even Condé Nast, previously reluctant to risk diluting any of its brand names, is participating.

The unit of Advance Publications announced last week that in partnership with Ideas Publishing Group, a Miami company, it would publish *Vogue en Español.*

The pace is picking up faster than you can say *Sports Illustrated for Teen People en Español.*

The New York Times, March 29, 1999, C-1. Copyright ©1999 by the New York Times Co. Reprinted by permission.

Photo by Austin MacRae

Spin City

Many publishers are trying to capitalize on the success of one publication by spinning off magazines that target subsets of readers. Here are a few examples.

AMERICAN EXPRESS PUBLISHING
Publication *Travel & Leisure*
Spinoffs (year) *Travel & Leisure Golf* (1998); *Travel & Leisure Family* (1998, now testing as twice a year)

- - - - - - - - - - - - - - - - - -

HEARST CORPORATION
Publication *Country Living*
Spinoffs (year) *Country Living Healthy Living* (1996); *Country Living Gardener* (1993); plus the occasional special interest publication like *Country Living Home Decorating*

- - - - - - - - - - - - - - - - - -

THE NATIONAL GEOGRAPHIC SOCIETY
Publication *National Geographic*
Spinoffs (year) *National Geographic Traveler* (1984); *National Geographic Adventure* (1999)

MEREDITH CORPORATION
Publication *Better Homes and Gardens*
Spinoffs (year) *Better Homes and Gardens Family Money* (1997); plus more than 45 special interest publications like *Better Homes and Gardens Bedroom and Bath*

- - - - - - - - - - - - - - - - - -

TIME INC.
Publication *People*
Spinoffs (year) *In Style* (1994); *People en Español* (1996); *Teen People* (1998)

- - - - - - - - - - - - - - - - - -

TIME INC.
Publication *Sports Illustrated*
Spinoffs (year) *Sports Illustrated for Kids* (1989); *Sports Illustrated for Women* (1999)

Projects that are in the works

- - - - - - - - - - - - - - - - - -

HEARST CORPORATION
Spinoffs *Cosmopolitan* for young women; *Smart Money's* parenting and finance magazine

- - - - - - - - - - - - - - - - - -

TIME INC.
Spinoffs *In Style's* bridal magazine; *Fortune's* style magazine

- - - - - - - - - - - - - - - - - -

MARIAH MEDIA INC.
Spinoffs *Outside* magazine will introduce *Outside for Women*

Reprinted by permission of The New York Times Co. Copyright ©1999.

IN FOCUS

- American magazines began in 1741 when Andrew Bradford published *American Magazine* and Benjamin Franklin published *General Magazine*. Like colonial newspapers, early magazines provided a means for political expression.

- *The Saturday Evening Post,* first published in 1821, was the nation's first general-interest magazine.

- Magazines widened their audience in the 1800s by catering to women, tackling social crusades, becoming a literary showcase for American writers and encouraging political debate.

- The Postal Act of 1879 encouraged the growth of magazines because it ensured quick, reasonably priced distribution for magazines; today magazines still travel on a preferential rate.

- American investigative reporting was pioneered by *McClure's Magazine* at the turn of the century. *McClure's* published the stories of Lincoln Steffens and Ida Tarbell, who were critical of public officials and American industrialists.

- Magazines in the first half of the 20th century adapted to absorb the invention of radio and television. To adapt, some publishers sought a defined, targeted audience; others tried to attract the widest audience possible. *The New Yorker* and *Time* magazines are media empires that began during this period.

- Magazines in the second half of the 20th century have survived by targeting readers' special interests. Specialization segments an audience for advertisers, making magazines the most specific buy an advertiser can make.

- Magazines can be grouped into three types: (1) consumer publications; (2) trade, technical and professional publications; and (3) company publications.

- Women continue to be the single most lucrative audience for magazines.

- Very few general-interest magazines survive today. Most magazines target a very specific readership.

- The audience for magazines, as for newspapers, is growing older. In 1990, for the first time, the number of magazines published in the country stopped growing.

- Magazine prices will probably rise as each subscriber is asked to pay as much as half of the cost of producing each magazine. This rise in prices may mean that the audience for magazines will become smaller than it is today.

- Online magazines will expand magazine readership and, perhaps, advertising revenue.

- Publishers can capitalize on the success of one publication by *spinning* off magazines that target subsets of readers.

WORKING THE WEB www

- **American Society of Journalists and Authors**
  www.asja.org/cwpage.htm
- **Editing for Magazines**
  www.well.com/user/mmcadams/copy.editing.html

- **Entertainment Weekly Online Magazine**
  cgi.pathfinder.com/ew/
- **People Magazine Online**
  www.people.com
- **Salon Magazine**
  www.salon.com
- **Slate Magazine**
  www.slate.com

INFOTRAC COLLEGE EDITION EXERCISES

Using InfoTrac College Edition, a fully searchable online database of articles and abstracts, do the following exercises as directed by your instructor.

1. Explore the history of Time magazine on InfoTrac College Edition by using the subject heading "Time, Inc." or "Time/Life, Inc." Look particularly at articles about *Time* magazine's 75th anniversary. Print at least three articles on *Time* magazine and either:

   a. write a brief paper on your findings, or

   b. bring the articles to class for a small-group discussion.

2. Look up information on InfoTrac College Edition about two of the following long-published magazines:

   1. *Saturday Evening Post*

   2. *Harper's*

   3. *Ladies' Home Journal*

   4. *New Yorker*

   5. *The Atlantic Monthly*

   6. *Jet*

   Print at least two articles about two different magazines and either:

   a. write a brief paper on your findings, or

   b. bring the articles to class for a small-group discussion.

3. Learn more about the muckrakers of the early 20th century by looking up "muckrakers" on InfoTrac College Edition. You might also search for articles about muckrakers Ida Tarbell and Lincoln Steffens.
   What were their major accomplishments? Either:

   a. write a brief paper on your findings, or

   b. bring the articles to class for a small-group discussion.

4. Magazines, like most other media, thrive through advertising. Read "Impact on You: Keeping Magazines in the Family" in Chapter 3. Then use the keywords "magazine advertising" on InfoTrac College Edition and print at least three related articles on the subject. Either:

   a. write a brief paper on your findings, or

   b. bring the articles to class for a small-group discussion.

5. What do you think is the future of electronic magazines? Using the keywords "electronic periodicals," find at least two articles that interest you about online magazines (not newspapers) or net 'zines. Print the articles, and then come to class and in small groups develop an idea for your own online magazine. Create a title, a focus and a list of articles that might appear in the magazine. Identify the audience for your magazine, and discuss how you might market your magazine to the public and who would advertise in the publication. Then share your creation with the rest of the class.

Books

There are no intelligent, unhappy people in my (books.) I want to be known as a writer of good entertaining narrative. I'm not trying to be taken seriously by the East Coast literary establishment. But I'm taken very seriously by the bankers.

Judith Krantz, author

What's Ahead

'm not sure I can explain how to write a book," said essayist and author E. B. White, who wrote 19 of them, including *Charlotte's Web.* "First you have to *want* to write one very much. Then, you have to know of something that you want to write about. Then, you have to begin. And, once you have started, you have to keep going. That's really all I know about how to write a book."[1]

The process of writing a book is a little more complex than White suggests, but every year in the United States, publishers produce about 60,000 individual titles.[2] This number includes revised editions of previously published books, but most of the titles are new.

The Association of American Publishers offers the following requirements or definitions of a book:

• All hardcover volumes that are not magazines, regardless of how long they are.

- All juvenile titles, hardbound or softbound, regardless of how long they are, except coloring books.

- All softbound volumes that are not magazines and that are more than 48 pages long. (A softbound volume that is less than 48 pages long is called a pamphlet, unless it is a text-related workbook.)

The publishing industry always has been tugged by what publishing scholars Lewis A. Coser, Charles Kadushin and Walter W. Powell call "the culture and commerce of publishing"—the desire to preserve the country's intellectual ideas versus the desire to make money. But a publisher who doesn't make a profit cannot continue to publish books.

Coser and his colleagues describe the four characteristics of book publishing in America today:

1. The industry sells its products—like any commodity—in a market that, in contrast to that for many other products, is fickle and often uncertain.

2. The industry is decentralized among a number of sectors whose operations bear little resemblance to each other.

3. These operations are characterized by a mixture of modern mass-production methods and craftlike procedures.

4. The industry remains perilously poised between the requirements and restraints of commerce and the responsibilities and obligations that it must bear as a prime guardian of the symbolic culture of the nation.[3]

Many new owners of publishing houses try to bring some predictability to the market. Says Coser, "Publishers attempt to reduce…uncertainty…through concentrating on 'sure-fire' blockbusters, through large-scale promotion campaigns or through control over distribution, as in the marketing of paperbacks. In the end, however, publishers rely on sales estimates that may be as unreliable as weather forecasts in Maine." [4]

HOW AMERICAN BOOK PUBLISHING GREW

Today, the book publishing industry divides responsibilities among many people. But when Americans first started publishing books, one person often did all of the work.

Aboard the *Mayflower* in 1620 there were two dogs and 70 adults and only a few books. The Pilgrims were very practical. They brought a map of Virginia and John Smith's *Description of New England,* but the main books they carried were their Bibles.

The first books in the United States were imports, brought by the new settlers or ordered from England after the settlers arrived. In 1638, the colonists set up a press at Cambridge, Massachusetts, and in 1640 they printed America's first book: *The Bay Psalm Book.* As the only book, it became an instant best-seller. There were only about 3,500 families in the colonies at the time, and the book's first printing of 1,750 sold out.[5]

By 1680, Boston had 17 booksellers, but most of the books still came from England. Between 1682 and 1685, Boston's leading bookseller, John Usher, bought 3,421 books. Among the books he ordered were 162 romance novels.

In 1731, Benjamin Franklin decided that Philadelphia needed a library. So he asked 50 subscribers to pay 40 shillings each to a Library Company. The company imported 84 books, which circulated among the subscribers. This circulating library was America's first.

The year after he established the circulating library, Franklin published *Poor Richard's Almanack.* Unlike most printers, who waited for someone to come to them with a manuscript, Franklin wrote his own books. The typical author sought a patron to pay for the book's printing and then sold the book at the printshop where it was published.

REACHING A WIDER AUDIENCE

To expand readership, early publishers sold political pamphlets, novels, poetry and humor. In addition, three events of the 19th century ensured that the book publishing industry would prosper in the 20th century: passage of the International Copyright Law, formation of publishing houses and establishment of compulsory education.

T I M E F R A M E

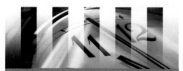

Today to 1620: Books retain their central place as a mass medium

TODAY The majority of books are sold through book chains, but the number of books sold online is growing faster than in-store sales.

1960 Publishing houses begin to consolidate, concentrating power in a few large corporations, and decreasing the role of small presses and independent booksellers.

1948 New American Library begins publishing serious fiction by African American authors, including Richard Wright, James Baldwin and Lorraine Hansberry.

1939 Robert de Graff introduces Pocket Books, America's first series of paperback books.

1926 Book-of-the-Month Club is founded, increasing the audience for books.

1900 Elementary education becomes compulsory, which

means increased literacy and more demand for textbooks.

1891 Congress passes the International Copyright Law of 1891, which required publishing houses to pay royalties to U.S. authors.

1776 Thomas Paine publishes the revolutionary pamphlet *Common Sense.*

1640 America's first book, *The Bay Psalm Book,* is printed at Cambridge, Massachusetts.

1620 Imported books arrive in the colonies on the Mayflower.

Photo by Brandon Carson

Political Pamphlets

The big seller of the 1700s was Thomas Paine's revolutionary pamphlet *Common Sense,* which argued for independence from Great Britain. From January to March 1776, colonial presses published 100,000 copies of Paine's persuasive political argument—one copy for every 25 people in the colonies—a true best-seller. Throughout the Revolutionary War, Paine was America's best-read author.

Novels and Poetry

Political pamphlets became much less important after the new nation was established, and printers turned their attention to other popular reading, especially fiction. Benjamin Franklin is credited with selling *Pamela* by Samuel Richardson in 1744, the first novel published in the United States, although it was a British import that had first appeared in England in 1740.

Like other media industries, book publishing has always faced moral criticism. Novels, for example, didn't start out with a good reputation. One critic said that the novel "pollutes the imaginations." Women wrote one-third of all of the early American novels,[6] and women also bought most of them.

Because there was no International Copyright Law, colonial printers freely reprinted British novels like *Pamela* and *Clarissa* and sold them. It was cheaper than publishing American authors, who could demand royalties.

Especially popular after the Civil War, and before the turn of the century, were dime novels, America's earliest paperbacks. Eventually most of them cost only a nickel, but some early paperbacks were as expensive as 20 cents.

Poetry generally has been difficult to sell, and it is correspondingly difficult for poets to get published. Literary scholar James D. Hart says that, although poetry was never as popular as prose, the mid-1800s was "the great era of poetry....It was more widely read in those years than it has been since."[7]

Humor

Humor has been a durable category in book publishing since the days of humorist Mark Twain. Made famous by his *Celebrated Jumping Frog of Calaveras County,* Twain became a one-man publishing enterprise. One reason his books sold well was that he was the first American author to recognize the importance of advance publicity.

Like most books, Twain's novels were sold door to door. Sales agents took advance orders before the books were published so that the publisher could estimate how many to print. More than three-fourths of the popular books sold in America before 1900 were sold door to door.[8]

International Copyright Law of 1891

Before 1891, publishers were legally required to pay royalties to American authors, but not to foreign authors. As noted previously, this hurt American authors, because books by American authors were more costly to publish.

After the passage of the International Copyright Law of 1891, all authors—foreign and American—had to give permission to publish their works. For the first time, American authors cost publishing houses the same amount as foreign authors. This motivated publishers to look for more American writers. After 1894, of the novels published in the United States, more were written by American writers than by foreign writers.[9]

INDUSTRY
IMPACT

Book Publishing

*L*ike moviemakers, many trade book publishers seek block-buster projects and try to capitalize on the name recognition of their stars—best-selling authors. But this type of publishing is only one aspect of a complex industry.

Trade books and mass market paperbacks represent the glamour of the book industry but less than 25% of all books sold.

Source: The Veronis, Suhler & Associates Communications Industry Forecast, 1997–2001

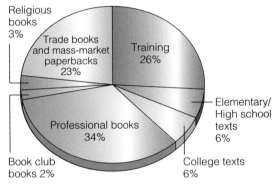

Religious books 3%

Trade books and mass-market paperbacks 23%

Training 26%

Professional books 34%

Elementary/ High school texts 6%

College texts 6%

Book club books 2%

Total $62 billion annually*
*projected for 2000

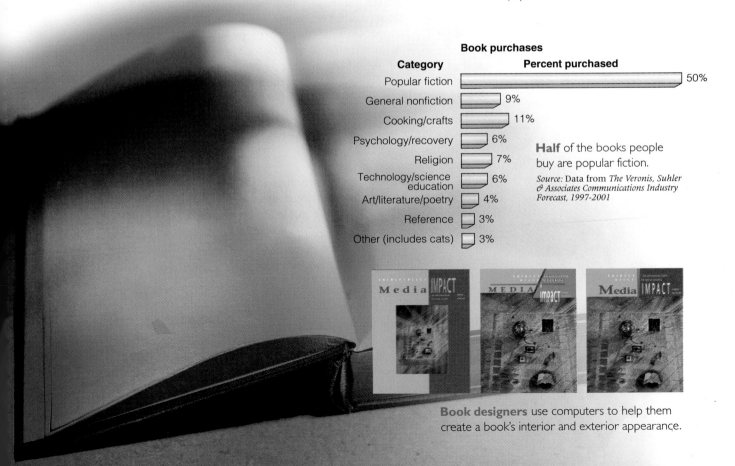

Book purchases

Category	Percent purchased
Popular fiction	50%
General nonfiction	9%
Cooking/crafts	11%
Psychology/recovery	6%
Religion	7%
Technology/science education	6%
Art/literature/poetry	4%
Reference	3%
Other (includes cats)	3%

Half of the books people buy are popular fiction.

Source: Data from The Veronis, Suhler & Associates Communications Industry Forecast, 1997-2001

Book designers use computers to help them create a book's interior and exterior appearance.

"DO YOU REMEMBER THE TIME WHEN PEOPLE USED TO READ BOOKS AT THE BEACH?"

Publishing Houses

Many publishing houses that began in the late 18th century or at some time during the 19th century continued into the 20th century. Nineteenth-century book publishing houses were just that—book publishing houses. They were nothing like today's multimedia corporations. These pioneering companies housed all aspects of publishing under one roof: They sought out authors, reviewed and edited copy, printed and then sold the books.

Compulsory Education

By 1900, 31 states had passed compulsory education laws. This was important to book publishing because schools buy textbooks, and also because education creates more people who read. Widespread public education meant that schools broadened their choices, and that textbook publishing flourished. Expanded public support for education also meant more money for libraries—more good news for the publishing industry.

CREATING A MASS MARKET

The first quarter of the 20th century enabled still more publishing houses, such as Simon & Schuster and McGraw-Hill, to meet the public's needs. Publishers that specialized in paperbacks started in the 1930s and 1940s: Pocket Books (1939), Bantam Books (1946) and New American Library (1948).[10]

As the newspaper industry learned at the beginning of the 20th century with the penny press, if you drop a product's price drastically, sales can explode. That's exactly what happened to book publishing with the introduction of book clubs and paperbacks.

Book Clubs

Book clubs replaced the door-to-door sales agent as a way to reach people who otherwise wouldn't buy books. Book-of-the-Month Club was founded in 1926, and Literary Guild in 1927. By 1946, there were 50 book clubs in America, and the Book-of-the-Month Club was selling nearly 12 million copies a year.[11]

Paperbacks

In 1939, Robert de Graff introduced America's first series of paperback best-sellers, called Pocket Books. Unlike the paperbacks published after the Civil War, which appeared only in paperback, Pocket Books issued titles that had already succeeded as hardbound books. They were inexpensive, and they fit in a pocket or a purse. "Suddenly, a book could reach not hundreds or thousands of readers but millions, many of whom had never owned a book before. Universally priced at 25 cents in its early years, the paperback democratized reading in America."[12]

Other publishers joined Pocket Books: New American Library (NAL), Avon, Popular Library, Signet and Dell. NAL distinguished itself by being the first mass-market reprinter willing to publish serious books by African-American writers—Richard Wright's *Native Son,* Lillian Smith's *Strange Fruit* and Ralph Ellison's *Invisible Man.* Signet's unexpected hit was J. D. Salinger's novel *Catcher in the Rye.*

Grove Press Tests Censorship

Book publishers have always resisted any attempts by the government to limit freedom of expression. One of the first publishers to test those limits was Grove Press.

In 1959, Grove published the sexually explicit *Lady Chatterley's Lover* by D. H. Lawrence (originally published in 1928); in 1961, the company published *Tropic of Cancer* by Henry Miller (originally published in Paris in 1934). Both books had been banned as obscene. The legal fees to defend Miller's book against charges of pornography cost Grove more than $250,000, but eventually the U.S. Supreme Court cleared the book in 1964.[13]

The publisher again challenged conventional publishing in 1965, when it issued in hardback the controversial *Autobiography of Malcolm X,* the story of the leader of the African-American nationalist movement.

BOOK PUBLISHING CONSOLIDATES

Forecasts for growing profits in book publishing in the 1960s made the industry attractive to corporations looking for new places to invest. Before the 1960s, the book publishing industry was composed mainly of independent companies whose only business was books. Then, rising school and college attendance from the post–World War II baby boom made some areas of publishing, especially textbooks, lucrative investments. Beginning in the 1960s, publishing companies began to consolidate. Publishing expert John P. Dessauer said: "Publishing stocks, particularly those of educational companies, became glamour holdings. And conglomerates began to woo every independent publisher whose future promised to throw off even a modest share of the forecast earnings."[14]

IMPACT

on you   *Luring Today's Teen Back to Books*

By Patrick M. Reilly

Books aimed at teenagers, like teen movies and music before them, are increasingly turning R-rated.

Book publishers want to combat the age-old problem they call "the gap." That's the point in their mid-teens when formerly avid readers of series like "Babysitters Club" and "Goosebumps" suddenly drop books for school sports, parties, and homework. Publishers fear the ranks of book dropouts will only swell as teens are assaulted by the growing array of media and Internet alternatives. And they worry that if they lose touch with the sophisticated and jaded teenagers of the late 1990's, these readers may be lost to them for good.

That's why publishers are launching risky campaigns to try to get and keep the attention of teens. They're introducing titles that venture into dark areas of drug use and casual sex. And they're featuring heroes and heroines who are confronting the hard realities of the late 1990s.

In May, Simon & Schuster's Pocket Books will publish *The F—Up*, by Arthur Nersesian, the gritty tale of a slacker on New York's Lower East Side who goes from apartment to apartment and job to job but can't seem to get his life together. After snorting cocaine with a friend, for example, the book's protagonist, who had pretended he was gay, has sex with a female roommate. The book, which will be part of Pocket

Books for teens take on edgier themes.
Source: The Wall Street Journal (3/24/99).

Books' MTV Books series, will be heavily promoted on MTV.

"When you are competing with TV, movies and videos, you have to keep up. And if being slightly provocative is the way to do it, it is probably OK," says Kara Welsh, who oversees the MTV Books line for Pocket Books.

"Teenagers today don't fit neatly into old categories about childhood," adds Marc Aronson, a senior editor at Henry Holt, a unit of Germany's Von Holtzbrinck Group. "They got all of Monica [Lewinsky] and have gone through years of sex and AIDS education."

Holt had a success last year with *Smack*, an unflinching look at British youth on the dole and lost in a world of drugs. Steve Geck, director of children's books for the Barnes & Noble book chain, says

that *Smack*, which won two major fiction awards in the U.K., did "very well," selling roughly what a good hardcover fiction title for adults might. "It was an honest look at that particular experience," he adds….

Book retailers are supporting the new push for teen readers. Barnes & Noble Inc. and other retailers have told publishers they are considering establishing separate teen-books areas within their superstores. Amazon.com Inc., the largest Internet book-seller, plans to unveil a separate teen area with its own bestseller list and featured titles. It will be labeled "teen," not "young adult," a term that publishers have found is a big turnoff for teens.

The Wall Street Journal, March 24, 1999, B-1. Reprinted by permission.

Dessauer acknowledges that the new owners often brought a businesslike approach to an industry that was known for its lack of attention to the bottom line. But, according to Dessauer, another consequence of these large-scale acquisitions was that "in many cases they also placed the power of ultimate decision and policymaking in the hands of people unfamiliar with books, their peculiarities and the markets."[15] The same pace of acquisitions continues today.

WORKING IN BOOK PUBLISHING

When authors get together, they often tell stories about mistakes publishers have made—about manuscripts that 20 or 30 publishers turned down but that some bright-eyed editor eventually discovered and published. The books, of course, then become best-sellers. Some of the stories are true.

But the best publishing decisions are made deliberately, to deliver an awaited book to an eager market. Successful publishing companies must consistently anticipate both their competitors and the market.

Books must not only be written, they must be printed and they must be sold. This whole process usually takes at least 18 months from the time a book is signed by an editor until the book is published, so publishers are always working ahead. The classic publisher's question is, "Will someone pay $25 (or $5 or $10—whatever the projected price of the book is) for this book 18 months from when I sign the author?"

Authors and Agents

Publishers acquire books in many ways. Some authors submit manuscripts "over the transom," which means that they send an unsolicited manuscript to a publishing house, hoping that the publisher will be interested. However, many of the nation's larger publishers refuse to read unsolicited manuscripts and only accept books that are submitted by agents.

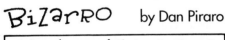

Bizarro©1997 by Dan Piraro. Reprinted with permission of Universal Press Syndicate. All rights reserved.

Agents who represent authors collect fees from the authors they represent. Typically, an agent's fee is 10 to 15 percent of the author's royalty, and a typical author's royalty contract can run anywhere from 10 to 15 percent of the *cover price* of the book. If a publisher priced a book at $20, for example, the author would receive from $2 to $3 per book, depending on the author's agreement with the publisher; the agent would then receive 20 to 45 cents of the author's $2 to $3, depending on the agent's agreement with the author.

Today the author is only one part of publishing a book. Departments at the publishing house called acquisitions, production, design, manufacturing, marketing and fulfillment all participate in the process. At a small publishing house, these jobs are divided among editors who are responsible for all of the steps.

The Publishing Process

The *author* proposes a book to the acquisitions editor, usually with an outline and some sample chapters. Sometimes an agent negotiates the contract for the book, but most authors negotiate their own contracts.

The *acquisitions editor* looks for potential authors and projects and works out an agreement with the author. The acquisitions editor's most important role is to be a liaison among the author, the publishing company, and the book's audience. Acquisitions editors also may represent the company at book auctions and negotiate sales of **subsidiary rights,** which are the rights to market a book for other uses—to make a movie, for example, or to print a character from the book on T-shirts.

The *production editor* manages all of the steps that turn a double-spaced typewritten manuscript into a book. After the manuscript comes in, the production editor sets up a schedule and makes sure that all of the work gets done on time.

The *designer* decides what a book will look like, inside and out. The designer chooses the typefaces for the book and determines how the pictures, boxes, heads and subheads will look and where to use color. The designer also creates a concept—sometimes more than one—for the book's cover.

The *manufacturing supervisor* buys the typesetting, paper and printing for the book. The book usually is sent outside the company to be manufactured.

Marketing, often the most expensive part of creating a book, is handled by several different departments. *Advertising* designs ads for the book. *Promotion* sends the book to reviewers. *Sales representatives* visit bookstores and college campuses to tell book buyers and potential adopters about the book.

Fulfillment makes sure that the books get to the bookstores on time. This department watches inventory so that if the publisher's stock gets low, more books can be printed.

subsidiary rights using the contents of a book to create related products.

THE BUSINESS OF BOOK PUBLISHING

Twenty thousand American companies call themselves book publishers today, but only about 2,000 publishing houses produce more than four titles a year. Most publishing houses are small: 80 percent of all book publishing companies have fewer than 20 employees.[16]

Today, fiction accounts for about half of all books sold. The rest are nonfiction, such as biography, economics and science. (See Impact/Industry, p. 85)

The number of new books and new editions has stabilized, but the per-copy price is going up. Today, paperbacks and hardbacks cost nearly three times what they cost in 1977. Books fall into six major categories. These classifications once described the publishing houses that produced different types of books. A company that was called a textbook publisher produced only textbooks, for example. Today, many houses publish several different kinds of books, although they may have separate divisions for different types of books and markets.

Trade Books

These are books designed for the general public. Usually, they are sold through bookstores and to libraries. Trade books include hardbound books and trade (or "quality") paperbound books for adults and children.

Typical trade books include hardcover fiction, current nonfiction, biography, literary classics, cookbooks, travel books, art books and books on sports, music, poetry and drama. Many college classes use trade books as well as textbooks. Juvenile trade books can be anything from picture books for children who can't read yet to novels for young adults.

Religious Books

Hymnals, Bibles and prayer books fall into this category. Recently, religious publishers have begun to issue books about social issues from a religious point of view, but these books are considered trade books, not religious books.

Professional Books

These are directed to professional people and are specifically related to their work. Professional books fall into three subcategories. *Technical and science books* include the subjects of biological and earth sciences as well as technology. They may be designed for engineers or scientists, for example. *Medical books* are designed for doctors and nurses and other medical professionals. *Business and other professional books* are addressed to business people, librarians, lawyers and other professionals not covered in the first two categories.

Mass-Market Paperbacks

Here, definitions get tricky. These books are defined not by their subjects but by where they are sold. Although they can also be found in bookstores, mass-market paperbacks are mainly distributed through "mass" channels—newsstands, chain stores, drugstores and supermarkets—and usually are "rack-sized." Many are reprints of hardcover trade books; others are originally published as mass-market paperbacks. Generally they're made from cheaper paper and cost less than trade paperbacks.

Textbooks

These books are published for elementary and secondary students (called the "el-hi" market) as well as for college students. Most college texts are paid for by the students but are chosen by their professors.

Very little difference exists between some college texts and some trade books. The only real difference between many textbooks and trade books is that texts include what publishers call *apparatus*—for example, test questions and summaries. The difference may be difficult to discern, so the Association of American Publishers classifies these two types of books (that is, trade books and textbooks) according to where they are sold the most. A book that is sold mainly through college bookstores, for example, is called a textbook.

University Press Books

A small proportion of books are published every year by university presses. These books are defined solely by who publishes them: A university press book is one that is published by a university press. Most university presses are nonprofit and are connected to a university, museum, or research institution. These presses produce mainly scholarly materials in hardcover and softcover. Most university press books are sold through the mail and in college bookstores.

CORPORATIONS DEMAND HIGHER PROFITS

The result of consolidation is that the giants in today's publishing industry are demanding increasingly higher profits. The companies look for extra income in three ways: subsidiary rights, blockbuster books and chain bookstore marketing.

Subsidiary Rights

Trade and mass-market publishers are especially interested in and will pay more for books with the potential for subsidiary-rights sales. The rights to make a CD-ROM version of a book, for example, are subsidiary rights. "In the nineteenth century, a hardcover trade book's profit was determined by the number of copies sold to individual readers. Today, it is usually determined by the sale of subsidiary rights to movie companies, book clubs, foreign publishers, or paperback reprint houses."[17] The same rights govern whether a book character becomes a star on the front of a T-shirt. For some houses, subsidiary-rights sales are the difference between making a profit and going out of business.

Blockbusters

Selling many copies of one book is easier and cheaper than selling a few copies of several books. This is the concept behind publishers' eager search for blockbuster books. Publishers are attracted to best-selling authors because they are usually easy to market. There is a "brand loyalty" among many readers that draws them to buy every book by a favorite author, and so publishers try to capitalize on an author's readership in the same way movie producers seek out stars who have made successful films.

Judith Krantz, who received $3.2 million for her sex-filled *Princess Daisy,* explained the benefits of being a blockbuster author: "I'm no Joan Didion—there are no intelligent, unhappy people in my books. I want to be known as a writer of good, entertaining narrative. I'm not trying to be taken seriously by the East Coast literary establishment. But I'm taken very seriously by the bankers."[18]

Following are some amounts that publishers and moviemakers paid for blockbusters:

- Mystery writer Mary Higgins Clark received $35 million in advance from Simon & Schuster for her next six books. Simon & Schuster says that 22 million copies of Clark's books are in print in the United States.

- Random House paid $6.5 million in advance for General Colin Powell's autobiography, about $1.5 million more than his military colleague General Norman Schwarzkopf received for his autobiography. Powell served as Chairman of the Joint Chiefs of Staff. Both men figured prominently in the Gulf War.

- Michael Crichton, author of *Jurassic Park,* received $2.5 million from Time Warner for the film rights to his next book. This amount tied the record paid for movie rights to John Grisham's *The Client.*
- Tom Clancy, who wrote *The Hunt for Red October* and *Patriot Games,* also received a $2.5 million advance for the film rights to his new novel *Without Remorse.*

Only the big publishing houses can afford such a bidding game. Some publishers have even developed computer models to suggest how high to bid for a book, but these high-priced properties are a very small part of book publishing, perhaps 1 percent. The majority of editors and writers rarely get involved in an argument over seven-figure advances. Many authors would be pleased to see five-figure advances in a contract.

Some critics believe that what has been called a blockbuster complex among publishing houses hurts authors who aren't included in the bidding. One Harper & Row editor told *The Wall Street Journal* that seven-figure advances "divert money away from authors who really need it and center attention on commercial books instead of less-commercial books that may nonetheless be better. God help poetry or criticism."[19]

CHAIN BOOKSTORES

The most significant change in book marketing in the past 30 years has been the growth of book chains. The big chains—B. Dalton, Waldenbooks and Barnes & Noble—account for more than half the bookstore sales of trade books. They have brought mass-marketing techniques to the book industry, offering book buyers an environment that is less like the traditional cozy atmosphere of a one-owner bookstore and more like a department store.

"The large chains are the power behind book publishing today," says Joan M. Ripley, a former president of the American Booksellers Association. "Blockbusters are going to be published anyway, but with a marginal book, like a volume of poetry, a chain's decision about whether to order it can sometimes determine whether the book is published."[20]

Discount chains are another factor in book marketing. Discount chains buy in huge volume, and they buy books only from publishers that grant them big discounts. Books that are published by smaller publishing houses, which usually cannot afford these large discounts, never reach the discount chain buyer. But for the blockbusters, issued by bigger houses, the discount chain is just one more outlet.

Like the resistance to book clubs when they were first introduced, the skepticism among book publishers about chain bookstores has changed into an understanding that chain stores in shopping malls have expanded the book market to people who didn't buy very many books before. But a major unknown factor is what happens when the distribution of an industry's products is controlled by so few companies.

SMALL PRESSES CHALLENGE CORPORATE PUBLISHING

The nation's large publishing houses (those with 100 or more employees) publish 80 percent of the books sold each year. But many of the nation's publishers

IMPACT

profile   *No Longer King*

Stephen King remains a force in the literary world, but he is no longer its top draw. Other authors have enjoyed greater success…more recently and now command a wider following in the publishing world and in the movie industry. Here is how Mr. King stacks up against some of his contemporaries.

The New York Times, November 9, 1998. Copyright ©1998 by the New York Times Co. Reprinted by permission.

Stephen King	Michael Crichton	John Grisham	Tom Clancy
AP/Wide World Photos	AFB/CORBIS	AP/Wide World Photos	AP/Wide World Photos

Estimated Income

$40 million 1998	**$65 million** 1998	**$36 million** 1997*	**$34 million** 1997*

Best-Selling Hardcover Book
Based on number of weeks on *The New York Times* best-seller list

"Firestarter" 1981; **"It"** 1987; **"The Stand"** (complete) 1991 *35 weeks each*	**"Andromeda Strain"** 1970 *30 weeks*	**"The Pelican Brief"** 1993 *49 weeks*	**"Red Storm Rising"** 1987 *50 weeks*

Most Recent Hardcover Book
Number of weeks on *The New York Times* best-seller list

"Bag of Bones" 1998 *5 weeks***	**"The Lost World"** 1996 *24 weeks*	**"The Street Lawyer"** 1998 *26 weeks*	**"Rainbow Six"** 1998 *12 weeks*

Most Successful Movie Adaptation
Based on North-American box-office receipts

"The Shining" 1980 *$75.5 million*	**"Jurassic Park"** 1993 *$356.8 million*	**"The Firm"** 1993 *$158.3 million*	**"Clear and Present Danger"** 1994 *$122.0 million*

*Most recent figure available.   **Currently on the list.

are small operations with fewer than ten employees. These publishers are called *small presses,* and they counterbalance the corporate world of large advances and multimedia subsidiary rights.

Small presses do not have the budgets of the large houses, but their size means that they can specialize in specific topics, such as the environment or bicycling, for example, or specific types of writing that are unattractive to large publishers, such as poetry.

Small presses are, by definition, alternative. Many of them are clustered together in locations outside of the New York City orbit, such as Santa Fe, New Mexico, and Santa Barbara, California. The book titles they publish probably are not familiar: *Bicycle Technology: Technical Aspects of the Modern Bicycle* by Rob Van der Plas, published by Bicycle Books; *Nine-in-One, Grr! Grr!*, a Hmong folktale by Blia Xiong and Cathy Spagnoli, published by Children's Book Press; *Warning! Dating May Be Hazardous to Your Health* by Claudette McShane, published by Mother Courage Press; or *48 Instant Letters You Can Send to Save the Earth* by Write for Action, published by Conari Press.

Still, some small presses and some small press books are quite successful. One example of a small press success is *The Lemon Book* by Ralph Nader and Clarence Ditlow. This step-by-step guide to buying a car, and what to do if you get a bad one, grabbed the attention of the *Larry King Show, Good Morning America*, and more than 50 other local TV and radio programs. The book sold 42,000 copies in its first year. As *The Lemon Book* demonstrates, specialization and targeted marketing are the most important elements of small press success.

TECHNOLOGY AND THE FUTURE

Technology will be a factor in most of the future changes in book publishing. Because books cost so much to publish, any advances in technology that lower production costs benefit the industry. Several changes are coming:

1. Computers already can monitor more closely inventories so that publishers can order a new printing of a book that is running low in stock.

2. Book publishing is becoming an on-screen industry. Publishers can now receive manuscripts from authors over phone lines by computer modem. These manuscripts are edited on a computer screen and then sent into production by computer, the same process which is used now at many newspapers.

3. Electronic graphics will make books more interesting to look at, and some book publishers are using CD-ROM to produce expanded versions of traditional books.

4. Desktop publishing will lower the cost of book production. The result should be more new small presses to publish specialized books for targeted audiences.

5. Writers' organizations in the United States are lobbying for an authors' lending royalty—a computer-assisted system of payment to authors every time someone borrows a book from a library. Lending royalties already are paid to writers in ten countries, including Great Britain. Every time someone checks out a book from a library, the author's account is credited. The money, which would come from federal taxes, would be paid to the author yearly.

6. Although the larger publishers are buying one another, the number of small publishers that issue less than 20 books a year is increasing. New York is still the center of book publishing, but the number of houses based in the East is declining. Seven percent of the country's book publishers are now in California, and that percentage is increasing.[21]

Because book publishing has been in America's culture so long, the contrast between book publishing's simple beginnings and its complicated corporate life

IMPACT digital

Taking on New Forms, Electronic Books Turn a Page

But Don't Try Reading One While Soaking in the Bathtub or Sunbathing on the Beach

By Peter H. Lewis

Let's face it, if the printed book had just been invented, it would probably get three stars out of five in reviews from the computer magazines. A review of Paper Book 1.0 might conclude with the following summary:

"Pros: Lightweight, portable, inexpensive, high resolution, practically unbreakable, available in multiple languages, easily annotated with write-only stylus, requires no batteries. Can be read while sitting in the smallest room of the house.

"Cons: Pages are static rather than dynamic (they cannot be updated once printed); fonts and type sizes are fixed; lack of backlighting makes it difficult to read at night without an external light source; topic selection is limited; paper is inefficient, bulky and subject to mildew and yellowing; paper production is environmentally unfriendly, and content is vulnerable to rampant copyright violations."

"In subsequent versions," the electronic reviewers might write, "we would like to see the Paper Book add interactivity, hyperlinking, a built-in dictionary, animated illustrations, online connections to content repositories, encryption to protect the publisher's copyright and other features we take for granted in electronic books."

Printed books have been popular for five centuries, of course, and have enjoyed great success despite the aforementioned shortcomings. But that hasn't stopped recent generations of science fiction authors, futurists, entrepreneurs, and even politicians from fantasizing about electronic and digital books…

Even the inventors of these first models of electronic books stress that they are not intended to replace the paperback novel. "You can't beat paperbacks. Paperback books are too cheap." Instead, all are trying to win customers among professionals like doctors, lawyers, accountants, engineers and others who need to keep reading updated journals and reference works….

A digital book would have some undeniable advantages. Students would not be bent under bulging backpacks filled with heavy textbooks. Children would not have to read by flashlight under the covers after curfew at night because a button turns on the illumination for the book's display screen (and shuts it off quickly when footsteps approach)….

In theory, an online bookstore could have hundreds of thousands of book titles ready for instant delivery. There would no longer be out-of-print books because once a title was digitized, there would be no cost to "print" another copy, even for one customer. In reality, though, very few books today exist in digital form, so publishers or distributors would have to pay several hundred dollars each to have older books retyped or scanned into a computer.

Establishing electronic royalties for authors and illustrators would be a legal morass. Other than that, because the publisher has no paper, printing and distribution costs, one could expect the cost of a digitally delivered book to be less than that of one tatooed onto dried paste made from dead trees.

From left, The Softbook, Rocketbook and EB Dedicated Reader will offer links to databases

today is especially stark. This may be because Americans maintain a mistaken romantic idea about book publishing's early days:

> *The myth is widespread that book publishing in the nineteenth and twentieth centuries was a gentlemanly trade in which an editor catered to an author's every whim, whereas commercialism and hucksterism have taken over in our day. It is a useful myth, to be sure, for it permits authors to point to a golden past and allows publishers to fashion for themselves a fine pedigree going back to a time when their profession was not sullied by the crass requirements of the marketplace. There once may have been more gentlemen in publishing than there are now, but there were surely sharp operators, hucksters, and pirates galore. In publishing, as in many other spheres of social life, there is very little that is new.* [22]

IN FOCUS

The book publishing industry has always been divided by what publishing scholars call the culture versus the commerce of publishing—the desire to preserve the nation's intellectual ideas versus the desire to make money.

- America's first book was *The Bay Psalm Book,* printed in 1640.

- Early publishers widened their audience by publishing political pamphlets, novels, poetry and humor.

- Many of the nation's major publishing houses were founded in the 19th century; these pioneering companies housed all aspects of publishing under one roof.

- The International Copyright Law of 1891 expanded royalty protection to foreign writers, which also benefited American authors. The formation of publishing houses centralized the process of producing books.

- Compulsory education throughout the United States was good for book publishing because schools buy textbooks and education creates more readers. Expanded support for education also meant more money for libraries.

- Book clubs and the introduction of paperbacks made books available to more people at a lower cost. Book-of-the-Month Club, founded in 1926, was the first book club.

- One of the first publishers to resist government limits on freedom of expression was Grove Press.

- The process of publishing a book usually takes at least 18 months from the time an author is signed until the book is published.

- The six departments at a publishing house are called acquisitions, production, design, manufacturing, marketing and fulfillment.

- American book publishers produce about 40,000 new titles every year. Most of these are nonfiction. The number of new books has stabilized over the years.

- Books can be grouped by six categories: trade books, religious books, professional books, mass-market paperbacks, textbooks and university press books.

- Before the 1960s, the book publishing industry was composed mainly of independent companies, whose only business was books. Publishing company consolidation began in the 1960s, and this pattern of consolidation continues today.

- To reduce their risks, many publishers look for blockbuster books (and best-selling authors), which they can sell through large-scale promotion campaigns. Publishers are especially interested in books with subsidiary-rights potential.

- One significant change in book marketing in the past 30 years has been the growth of book chains.

- Most of the nation's books are published by the large publishing houses, but many of the nation's specialized books are issued by small presses. Small presses are, by definition, alternative.

- Computer technology and desktop publishing are changing the way books are published, lowering the cost, streamlining the process and creating new products, such as CD-ROMs, for book publishers.

- Electronic books will be able to offer digital copies of thousands of titles instantly.

WORKING THE WEB www

- **Amazon.com Online**
  www.amazon.com
- **American Association of University Presses**
  aaup.pupress.princeton.edu:70/
- **Barnes & Noble**
  www.barnesandnoble.com
- **Bookfinder**
  www.bookfinder.com
- **Borders Books and Records**
  www.borders.com
- **Links to American Publishers**
  www.lights.com/publisher/
- **Society for the History of Authorship, Reading and Publishing**
  www.indiana.edu/~sharp

INFOTRAC COLLEGE EDITION EXERCISES

Using InfoTrac College Edition, a fully searchable online database of articles and abstracts, do the following exercises as directed by your instructor.

1. Read "Impact/Profile: No Longer King" in Chapter 4. Look up one of the following popular authors, using InfoTrac College Edition:

   1. Stephen King
   2. Judy Blume
   3. Tom Clancy
   4. Michael Crichton
   5. John Grisham
   6. Amy Tan

Or choose a book author you admire and research for more information on that author using InfoTrac College Edition. Print three articles or book reviews to prepare a brief oral presentation that you can present to the class about either:

a. one of the popular authors listed above, or

b. the author of your choice

2. Read "Impact on You: Luring Today's Teens Back to Books" in Chapter 4. Then using InfoTrac College Edition, look up "young adult literature" and find at least two other articles about what publishing companies are doing to attract teenage readers/buyers. Print them and either:

a. write a brief paper on your findings, or

b. bring the articles to class for a small-group discussion.

3. Using InfoTrac College Edition, research articles on "book publishing" or "Association of American Publishers" to identify at least two major trends in book publishing in recent years. Print the articles that support your point of view, and either:

a. write a brief paper on your findings, or

b. bring the articles to class for a small-group discussion.

4. Using InfoTrac College Edition, look up the names of at least two of the following publishers:

■ Pocket Books, Inc.

■ Bantam Books, Inc.

■ Simon & Schuster

■ McGraw-Hill

Then print articles about each of your two publishers that speak about the publishing industry, and bring them to class for a small-group discussion.

5. Chain bookstores are growing tremendously in America. Using InfoTrac College Edition, look up "chain bookstores" or one particular chain ("Barnes & Noble, Inc.," for example) and print at least two articles about how chain bookstores work today. Then either:

a. write a brief paper on your findings, or

b. bring the articles to class for a small-group discussion.

5

Radio

What's Ahead

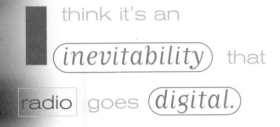

think it's an *(inevitability)* that radio goes *(digital.)*

Gordon Hodge, radio industry analyst

magine that the date is September 8, 1940. War has begun its second year in Europe. You do not have a television set. You are sitting at home in the United States, listening to your radio. CBS announces a special bulletin from journalist Edward R. Murrow, reporting the first bombing of London: 625 German bombers have pounded the city, leaving more than 1,000 people dead and 2,000 people injured. You and your family listen intently in your front room as Murrow describes:

> *men with white scarves around their necks instead of collars…dull-eyed, empty-faced women….Most of them carried little cheap cardboard suitcases and sometimes bulging paper shopping bags. That was all they had left….*
>
> *A row of automobiles with stretchers racked on the roofs like skis, standing outside of bombed buildings. A man pinned under wreckage where a broken gas main sears his arms and face…*
>
> *the courage of the people; the flash and roar of the guns rolling down streets…the stench of air-raid shelters in the poor districts.*[1]

This was radio news reporting at its best. And for 26 years, from 1921 until the advent of television news in 1947, broadcast reporters like Murrow painted pictures with words. Radio reporters described Prohibition and its repeal, the stock market crash, the Depression, the election of Franklin D. Roosevelt, the New Deal, the bombings of London and Pearl Harbor, the Normandy invasion, Roosevelt's funeral and the signing of the armistice that ended World War II.

Today, our memory of events that happened in the quarter-century, beginning in 1921, is keenly tied to radio. Newspapers offered next-day reports and occasional extras, movie theaters offered weekly newsreels, magazines offered long-term perspectives. But radio gave its listeners an immediate record at a time when world events demanded attention.

Radio also gave people entertainment: big bands, Jack Benny, George Burns and Grace Allen, Abbott and Costello, Bob Hope and the original Shadow ("The weed of crime bears bitter fruit. Crime does not pay! The Shadow knows!").

Radio became America's second national mass medium, after magazines. Radio transformed national politics by transmitting the voices of public debate, as well as the words, to the audience. Radio also expanded Americans' access to popular, as well as classical, culture; opera played on the same dial as slapstick comedy.

The legacy of news and music remains on radio today, but the medium that was once the center of attention in everyone's front room has moved into the bedroom, the car, even the shower. Radio wakes you up and puts you to sleep. Radio goes with you when you run on the trail or sit on the beach. Consider these industry statistics about radio today:

- 99 percent of America's homes have radios.

- 95 percent of America's cars have radios, and radio reaches four out of five adults in their cars at least once each week.

- 40 percent of Americans listen to the radio sometime between 6 A.M. and midnight.

- 7 percent of America's bathrooms have radios.[2]

Radio today has become an everyday accessory rather than a necessity.

Stone/Don Smetzer

Although radio is more accessible today, what you hear is not the same as what your parents or grandparents heard. Advertisers, who once sought radio as the only broadcast access to an audience, have many more choices today. For audiences, radio has become an everyday accessory rather than a necessity. No one had envisioned radio's place in today's media mix when radio's pioneers began tinkering just before the turn of the century. All they wanted to do was send information along a wire, not through the air.

RADIO: A TECHNOLOGICAL LEAP

Today, we are so accustomed to sending and receiving messages instantaneously, that it is hard to imagine a time when information took more than a week to travel from place to place. In the early 1800s, the pony express took ten and a half days to go from St. Joseph, Missouri, to San Francisco, California. Stage coaches needed 44 hours to bring news from New York to Washington.[3]

Technological advances brought rapid changes in how quickly information could move throughout the country. First came the invention of the telegraph and the telephone, which depended on electrical lines to deliver their messages, and then wireless telegraphy, which delivers radio signals through the air.

Using perhaps the first version of today's Walkman, a couple on Guglielmo Marconi's yacht *Electra* do the fox trot while sailing to Albany, New York, in 1922.

Library of Congress

In 1835, Samuel F. B. Morse first demonstrated his electromagnetic telegraph system in America. In 1843, he asked Congress to give him $30,000 to string four telegraph lines along the Baltimore & Ohio Railroad right-of-way from Baltimore to Washington. The first official message—"What hath God wrought?"—was sent from Baltimore to Washington, D.C., on May 24, 1844.

Telegraph lines followed the railroads, and for more than 30 years Americans depended on Morse's coded messages printed on tape, sent from one railroad station to another. Then on March 10, 1876, Alexander Graham Bell sent a message by his new invention, the telephone, to his associate Thomas A. Watson in an adjoining room of their Boston laboratory: "Mr. Watson, come here. I want you."

Both Morse's telegraph and Bell's telephone used wires to carry messages. Then in Germany in 1887, the physicist Heinrich Hertz began experimenting with radio waves, which became known as Hertzian waves—the first discovery in a series of refinements that led to the development of radio broadcasting.

Radio's Revolution

Broadcasting was truly a revolutionary media development. Imagine a society in which the only way you can hear music or enjoy a comedy is at a live performance or by listening to tinny noises on a record machine. The only way you can hear a speech is to be in the audience. Movies show action but no sound. Without the inventions of broadcasting's early pioneers such as Heinrich Hertz, you could still be living without the sounds of media that you have come to take for granted. The four pioneers besides Hertz that are credited with advancing early radio broadcasting in America: Guglielmo Marconi, Reginald Aubrey Fessenden, Lee de Forest and David Sarnoff.

Wireless Breakthrough: Marconi. Twenty-year-old Guglielmo Marconi, the son of wealthy Italian parents, used the results of three discoveries by Morse, Bell and Hertz to expand his idea that messages should be able to travel across space without a wire. Marconi became obsessed with the idea, refusing food and working at home in his locked upstairs room.

T I M E F R A M E

Today to 1899: Radio technology and programming chase the audience

TODAY The radio industry is consolidating into large groups of stations and most are programming with standardized formats.

1996 Congress passes the Telecommunications Act of 1996, which encourages consolidation in the radio industry.

1960 The Manhattan Grand Jury indicts disc jockey Alan Freed for payola.

1959 Gordon McLendon introduces format radio at station KABL in San Francisco.

1938 "Mercury Theater on the Air" broadcasts "War of the Worlds," demonstrating how quickly broadcast misinformation can cause a public panic.

Michael Rothwell/FPG International

1936 Edwin H. Armstrong licenses frequency modulation (FM).

1934 Congress establishes the Federal Communications Commission to regulate broadcasting.

1920 Station KDKA in Pittsburgh goes on the air, the nation's first commercial radio station.

1907 Lee de Forest introduces the Audion tube, which improves the clarity of radio signal reception.

1899 Guglielmo Marconi first uses his wireless radio to report the America's Cup Race.

Soon Marconi could ring a bell across the room or downstairs without using a wire. His father sponsored Guglielmo and his mother on a trip to England, where Marconi showed the invention to the chief telegraph engineer in the British Post Office. Their first messages traveled 100 yards. Eventually Marconi was able to broadcast over a distance of nine miles. "The calm of my life ended then," Marconi said later.[4]

The *New York Herald* invited Marconi to the United States to report the America's Cup Race in October 1899. Marconi reported "by wireless!" American business people, intrigued by the military potential of Marconi's invention, invested $10 million to form American Marconi.[5]

Amateur radio operators created clubs to experiment with the new discovery. Two experimenters, Reginald Aubrey Fessenden and Lee de Forest, advanced the Marconi discovery to create today's radio.

Experimental Broadcasts: Fessenden. Reginald Aubrey Fessenden, a Canadian, began wireless experiments in the United States in 1900 when he set up his National Electric Signaling Company to attempt sending voices by radio waves. On Christmas Eve 1906, "ship wireless operators over a wide area of the Atlantic...were startled to hear a woman singing, then a violin playing, then a man reading passages from Luke. It was considered uncanny; wireless rooms were soon crowded with the curious."[6] The noises were coming from Fessenden's experimental station at Brant Rock, Massachusetts. Fessenden's experiment in 1906 is considered the world's first voice and music broadcast.

Detecting Radio Waves: de Forest. Lee de Forest called himself the father of radio because in 1907 he perfected a glass bulb called the Audion that could detect radio waves. "Unwittingly then," wrote de Forest, "had I discovered an invisible Empire of the Air."[7]

Besides being an inventor, de Forest was a good publicist. He began what he called "broadcasts" from New York and then from the Eiffel Tower. In 1910, he broadcast Enrico Caruso singing at the Metropolitan Opera House. Later his mother broadcast an appeal to give women the vote. Gradually, the Audion became the foundation of modern broadcasting.

Radio for the People: Sarnoff. In 1912, 21-year-old wireless operator David Sarnoff relayed news from Nantucket Island, Massachusetts, that he had received a distress call from the *Titanic* on his Marconi Wireless. Four years later, when Sarnoff was working for the Marconi Company in New York, he wrote a visionary memo that predicted radio's future, although in 1916 his ideas were widely ignored:

> *I have in mind a plan of development which would make radio a household utility. The idea is to bring music into the home by wireless. The receiver can be designed in the form of a simple "radio music box," and arranged for several different wave lengths which should be changeable with the throwing of a single switch or the pressing of a single button. The same principle can be extended to numerous other*

David Sarnoff, who began his broadcast career as a wireless operator, eventually became president of RCA (Radio Corporation of America).

Bettmann/CORBIS

fields, as for example, receiving lectures at home which would be perfectly audible. Also, events of national importance can be simultaneously announced and received. Baseball scores can be transmitted in the air. This proposition would be especially interesting to farmers and others living in outlying districts.[8]

Eventually, as commercial manager and then president of RCA, Sarnoff would watch his early vision for radio come true.

FEDERAL GOVERNMENT POLICES THE AIRWAVES

The federal government decided to regulate broadcasting almost as soon as it was invented. *This decision to regulate separated the broadcast media, which were regulated early, from the print media, which are not regulated directly by any federal government agency.*

As amateurs competed with the military for the airwaves, Congress passes the Radio Act of 1912 to license people who wanted to broadcast or receive messages. The federal government decided to license people to transmit signals because *there were only a certain number of frequencies available to carry broadcast signals.* Many amateurs, trying to send signals on the same frequency, were knocking each other off the air. The government intervened to try to keep the operators out of each other's way.

Then, during World War I, the federal government ordered all amateurs off the air and took control of all privately owned stations, and the military took over radio broadcasting. After the war, with the freeze lifted, the navy argued that it should maintain the monopoly over the airwaves that it had enjoyed during the war.

Faced with strong arguments by the amateurs that they should be able to return to the airwaves, Congress decided against a navy monopoly. Instead, the government sanctioned a private monopoly formed by General Electric, Westinghouse, AT&T, Western Electric Company and United Fruit Company. General Electric bought out American Marconi and its patents, and in 1919 these five sympathetic interests pooled the patents they controlled to form Radio Corporation of America (RCA).

Each company owned a percentage of RCA and the right to membership on the RCA board. David Sarnoff became RCA's general manager in 1921. Because of this early monopoly, RCA dominated early radio development, but eventually smaller operations formed all over the country as radio fever spread from coast to coast.

EXPERIMENTAL STATIONS MULTIPLY

A plaque in San Jose, California, celebrates the 1909 founding of the experimental station FN: "On this site in 1909, Charles D. Herrold founded a voice radio station which opened the door to electronic mass communication. He conceived the idea of 'broadcasting' to the public, and his station, the world's first, has now served Northern California for half a century." Today, that station is San Francisco's KCBS.

Various other stations claim that they were among the earliest radio pioneers. Station 9XM broadcast music and weather reports from Madison, Wisconsin; 6ADZ broadcast concerts from Hollywood; 4XD sent phonograph music from a chicken coop in Charlotte, North Carolina; and 8MK in Detroit, operated by *Detroit News* publisher William E. Scripps, transmitted election returns.

These radio operators broadcast messages to each other and their friends, but not to the general public. These amateur radio operators were early examples of broadcast entrepreneurs. They were tinkerers, fascinated with an invention that could carry sounds through the air. One of these tinkerers, Frank Conrad, is credited with creating the beginnings of the nation's first commercial radio station.

KDKA LAUNCHES COMMERCIAL BROADCASTING

An ad in the September 29, 1920, *Pittsburgh Sun* changed broadcasting from an exclusive hobby to an easy-to-use medium that soon was available to everyone. The ad described a 20-minute evening concert broadcast from the home of Frank Conrad, a "wireless enthusiast" who worked for Westinghouse.

Conrad often broadcast concerts from his garage on his station 8XK. But his boss at Westinghouse, Harry P. Davis, had an idea: Why not improve the broadcasts so more people would want to buy radios? Davis talked Conrad into setting up a more powerful transmitter at the Westinghouse plant by November 2, so that Conrad could broadcast election returns.

Conrad directed the construction of a 100-watt transmitter, and the *Pittsburgh Post* agreed to telephone election returns to the station. On October 27, 1920, using the powers of the 1912 Radio Act, the U.S. Department of Commerce licensed station KDKA as the nation's first *commercial* station. The broadcast began at 8 P.M. on November 2, 1920, and continued past midnight, reporting that Warren G. Harding was the nation's next president. KDKA immediately began a daily one-hour evening schedule, 8:30–9:30 P.M.

THE RADIO AUDIENCE EXPANDS QUICKLY

The crude KDKA broadcasts proved that regular programming could attract a loyal audience. KDKA was just the beginning of what eventually became radio networks. The radio craze led almost immediately to a period of rapid expansion as entrepreneurs and advertisers began to grasp the potential of the new medium. Almost as quickly, government was compelled to step in to expand its regulation of radio broadcasting.

In 1922, Americans spent $60 million on receivers; amateurs built the remaining sets. Amateurs also rushed to put stations on the air—more than 500 stations began broadcasting in 1922.[9] Radio's potential as a moneymaker for its owners incited competition for the airwaves. Three important developments for radio's future were the blanket licensing agreement, the decision that radio would accept commercial sponsors and the Radio Act of 1927.

Blanket Licensing

At first, stations played phonograph records; then they invited artists to perform live in their studios. Some of the nation's best talent sought the publicity that radio could give them, but eventually, the performers asked to be paid.

In 1923, the American Society of Composers, Authors and Publishers (ASCAP) sued several stations for payment, claiming that broadcasting

Radio

*R*adio today sells itself as the "go-anywhere" medium that reaches listeners while they drive, work, shop and jog. Advertisers like radio's ability to reach targeted audiences.

Listeners prefer FM to AM by a margin of 4 to 1.

Source: The Veronis, Suhler & Associates Communications Industry Forecast, 1999–2003.

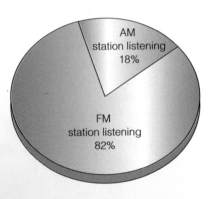

AM station listening 18%

FM station listening 82%

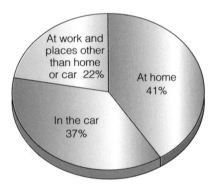

At work and places other than home or car 22%

At home 41%

In the car 37%

Radio listeners tune in everywhere.

Source: The Veronis, Suhler & Associates Communications Industry Forecast, 1999–2003.

Classical 2%
Religious 2%
Middle-of-the-Road (MOR) 3%
Jazz/Alternative 3%
Classic Rock 5%
Oldies 6%
Spanish 6%
Album-oriented Rock (AOR) 7%

News & News/Talk 17%
Adult contemporary 14%
Country 10%
Top 40 9%
All other formats 8%
Urban 8%

Country, Rock, News and News/Talk are the most popular formats for radio listeners. Prepackaged formats such as these allow a radio station to use a proven formula to target a specific audience.

Source: Arbitron, Fall 1998.*

* Last year for which statistics are available

ASCAP-licensed music on the radio meant that people would buy less sheet music. Station owners argued that playing the songs on their stations would publicize the sheet music.

Eventually the stations agreed to pay ASCAP royalties through a blanket licensing agreement, which meant that the stations paid ASCAP a fee ($250 a year at first). In exchange, the stations could use all ASCAP-licensed music on the air. (ASCAP licenses its music to stations the same way today. Eventually another licensing organization, Broadcast Music, Inc., would also collect broadcast royalties; see page 136.)

Commercial Sponsorship

Once station owners agreed to pay for their programs, they had to figure out where they would get the money. AT&T had the answer with an idea they pioneered at their station WEAF in New York. WEAF inaugurated the policy of selling time. Its first sponsored program cost $100 for ten minutes.

The success of commercial sponsorship, as a way to support radio, settled the issue of who would pay the cost of airing the programs. Advertisers paid for the programs through their advertising; the American public paid for the programs indirectly by supporting the advertisers who supported radio.

CONGRESS REGULATES RADIO

As more stations began to crowd the air, their signals interfered with one another. With only so many good frequencies available, the provisions of the Radio Act of 1912 (see page 106) began to seem inadequate. Congress passed the Radio Act of 1927, which formed the Federal Radio Commission under the jurisdiction of the Department of Commerce. The commission's five members were appointed by the president, with the approval of the Senate.

The limitations on air space required that broadcasting in the United States would operate under a type of government regulation unknown to newspaper and magazine publishers. Stations were licensed for three years and were required by the commission to operate *"as a public convenience, interest or necessity requires."*

The commission, created to protect the stations by allocating frequencies, also became the license holder. The stations could operate only with the government's approval, and stations could be sold or transferred only if the commission approved. The Radio Act of 1927, including the concept that broadcasters would operate in the *"**public interest, convenience and necessity**," became the foundation for all broadcast regulation in the United States.*

In 1934, Congress established the Federal Communications Commission (FCC) to regulate the expanding wireless medium, making the FCC a separate agency of government and no longer a part of the Department of Commerce. It is important to remember that the commission's original purpose was to allocate the spectrum so that station broadcasts would not interfere with one another. The FCC was not originally envisioned to oversee broadcast content.

The FCC began work on July 11, 1934, with seven commissioners appointed by the president, with Senate approval. This same basic structure and purpose govern the commission's actions today, but now there are only five commissioners. The establishment of the FCC in 1934 also set the precedent for the regulation of television later.

THE NATION TUNES IN

By 1924, many radio program lineups included entertainment with names like the Ipana Troubadours, the Schrafft's Tearoom Orchestra and the Wanamaker Organ Concert. The sponsors—Ipana toothpaste, Schrafft's candy and Wanamaker's Department Store—didn't simply pay for commercial time on the shows. They produced the programs themselves and gave them to the radio stations. "Sponsors were, in effect, being encouraged to take charge of the air."[10] Most stations mixed entertainment, culture, and public service.

Radio permitted a new kind of collective national experience. Since the days of George Washington, only those few thousand people, who were actually present at a presidential inauguration, could hear the oath of office administered and the president-elect's address. But when Calvin Coolidge was reelected president, radio covered his inauguration on March 4, 1925, with an estimated audience of 15 million.[11]

Radio in the 1930s and 1940s became a powerful cultural and political force. Radio gave multitudes of people a new, inexpensive source of information and entertainment. The commercialization of American broadcasting also gave advertisers access to this audience at home. Radio's massive audience sat enraptured with sponsored programming of many types: comedy, music, serials, drama and news. Eventually, all of these types of programming migrated to television.

"WAR OF THE WORLDS" CHALLENGES RADIO'S CREDIBILITY

On Halloween Eve, October 30, 1938, the Mercury Theater on the Air broadcast a play based on the H. G. Wells story "War of the Worlds." The live 8 P.M. broadcast played opposite the very popular Edgar Bergen Program on NBC, and rarely had even 4 percent of the audience. Very few people heard at the beginning of the program the announcement that the Mercury Theater was performing a version of the Wells story.

The program began with the announcer introducing some band music. A second voice then said, "Ladies and gentlemen, we interrupt our program of dance music to bring you a special bulletin. At 20 minutes before 8 o'clock Central Time, Professor Farrell of Mount Jennings Observatory, Chicago, reports observing several explosions of incandescent gas occurring at regular intervals on the planet Mars."

More dance music followed, and then more bulletins about the Martians, with the startling news that 1,500 people near Princeton, New Jersey, had died when they were hit by a meteor. Then the announcer said it was not a meteor but a spaceship carrying Martians armed with death rays.

Two professors from the Princeton geology department actually set out to locate the "meteors." In Newark, more than 20 families rushed out of their homes, covering their faces with wet handkerchiefs to protect themselves from the "gas." After a burst of horrified calls, CBS began repeating the announcement that the program was just a play.

The episode demonstrated how easily alarming information could be innocently misinterpreted, especially because the listeners had no other source to check the reliability of what they were hearing. Radio listeners truly were a captive audience.

RADIO NETWORKS EXPAND

The formation of the networks as a source of programming and revenue is a crucial development in the history of American radio. A **network** is a collection of stations (radio or television) that offers programs, usually simultaneously, throughout the country, during designated times. As the networks stretched across the country, they provided a dependable source of programming. Most stations found it easier to affiliate with a network and receive its programming than to develop local programs.

network a collection of stations (radio or TV) that offers programs, usually simultaneously, throughout the country.

David Sarnoff Launches NBC

NBC grew out of the government's original agreement with RCA. RCA, GE and Westinghouse formed the National Broadcasting Company in 1926. By January 1927, NBC, headed by David Sarnoff, had formed two networks: the Red network (fed from WEAF) and the Blue Network (originating from station WJZ in Newark). Station engineers drew the planned hookups of the two networks with red and blue colored pencils—hence their names.

RCA faced criticism about its broad control over the airwaves because RCA continued as the world's largest distributor of radios, which were made by Westinghouse and General Electric.

William S. Paley Starts CBS

Twenty-six-year-old William S. Paley, heir to a tobacco fortune, bought the financially struggling Columbia Phonograph Company in 1929. He changed the name to Columbia Broadcasting System. He put the CBS network on the air with 25 stations. Programming originated from WABC in New York. Paley became the nemesis of NBC, then controlled by David Sarnoff, and this early competition between Sarnoff and Paley shaped the development of American broadcasting.

Edward Noble Buys ABC

In 1941, the FCC ordered RCA to divest itself of one of its networks. In 1943, RCA sold NBC-Blue to Edward J. Noble (who had made his fortune as head of the company that produced LifeSavers). Noble paid $8 million for the network that became the American Broadcasting Company, giving the country a three-network radio system.

Radio networks prospered until the 1980s, when NBC sold its radio network and CBS and ABC (who also own television properties) gave more attention to their television holdings.

RADIO IN THE TV ERA

Initially, it seemed that television would cause the death of radio. As soon as television proved itself, advertisers abandoned radio, said comedian Fred Allen, "like the bones at a barbecue."[12] The talent fled, too—Bob Hope, Milton Berle, Jackie Gleason, even Burns and Allen. Public affairs programs like *Meet the Press* made the move to TV, as did Edward R. Murrow's *Hear It Now*, which became *See It Now*.

Four developments in the 1940s and 1950s changed the medium of radio and guaranteed its survival alongside television: the FCC's licensing of FM; a new source of recorded music for broadcast; the introduction of radio formats; and the introduction of reliable clock and car radios.

Edwin H. Armstrong's invention of FM made radio signals clearer.

Photo courtesy Antique Wireless Association Electronic Communication Museum

The FCC Recognizes FM: Edwin H. Armstrong

After working for more than a decade to eliminate static from radio broadcasts, engineer Edwin H. Armstrong applied to the FCC in 1936 to broadcast using his new technique, frequency modulation (FM). Because of the way FM signals travel through the air, FM offered truer transmission with much less static. Armstrong faced difficult opposition from David Sarnoff, who had been an early Armstrong sponsor.

The FCC received 150 applications for FM licenses in 1939, but then froze licensing during World War II. After the war, Armstrong again faced Sarnoff, and this time Armstrong lost. RCA, which was using Armstrong's frequency modulation in its TV and FM sets, refused to pay him royalties. Armstrong sued RCA.

RCA fought the suit for four years, saying that RCA had been among the early developers of FM, citing RCA's sponsorship of Armstrong's beginning experiments. In 1953, Armstrong became ill and suffered a stroke.

> *One day, neatly dressed, he stepped out of a window of his thirteenth-floor East Side apartment. He was found on the third-floor extension. Shortly afterward, RCA made a million-dollar settlement with the estate. Litigation with other companies continued for thirteen years. All suits were won by the Armstrong estate.*[13]

FM eventually became the spectrum of choice for music lovers, far surpassing the broadcast quality of AM.

Licensed Recordings Launch Disc Jockeys

Early radio station owners avoided playing records because they would have had to pay royalties. The FCC also required stations that played records to remind their audiences every half-hour that they were listening to recorded music, not a live orchestra. This discouraged record-spinning.

In 1935, newscaster Martin Block at New York's independent station WNEW began playing records in between his newscasts, and then he started a program called *Make Believe Ballroom*. He is generally considered America's first disc jockey. Then, in 1940, the FCC ruled that once stations bought a record, they could play it on the air whenever they liked, without the half-hour announcements.

To counteract ASCAP's insistence on royalties, broadcasters formed a cooperative music licensing organization called Broadcast Music, Inc. Most rhythm and blues, country and rock 'n' roll artists eventually signed with BMI, which charged stations less for recording artists than ASCAP. With an inexpensive source of music available, a new media personality was created—the DJ.

Gordon McLendon Introduces Format Radio

How would the stations know which mix of records to use? The answer came from Gordon McLendon, the father of format radio. McLendon first became known as a play-by-play baseball announcer on KLIF in Dallas in 1948. He also outfitted KLIF news cars to search for local news. McLendon targeted local people for interviews on national subjects. He beat television, which was burdened with heavy camera equipment. KLIF's innovative news coverage gave rise to McLendon's first idea for a successful format: all-news radio.

Then McLendon combined music and news in a predictable rotation of 20-minute segments, and eventually, KLIF grew very popular. Next he refined the music by creating the Top-40 format. Top 40 played the top-selling hits continually, interrupted only by a disc jockey or a newscast.

By 1959, McLendon launched the beautiful-music format at KABL in San Francisco. In 1964, McLendon used a 24-hour news format for Chicago's WNUS, using three news vans with a "telesign" that showed news on the roof in lights as the van drove around town. Formats meant that stations could now share standardized programs that stations previously had to produce individually. Eventually, the idea of formatted programming spread, making network programming and the networks themselves less important to individual stations.

Clock and Car Radios Make Radio Portable

Two technological innovations helped ensure radio's survival by making it an everyday accessory. Transistor radios, first sold in 1948 for $40, were more reliable and cheaper than tube radios. Clock radios woke people up and caused them to rely on radio for the first news of the day.

The car radio was invented in 1928 by William Lear, who designed the Lear jet. Early car radios were enormous, with spotty reception, but the technology that was developed during World War II helped refine them. In 1946, 9 million cars had car radios. By 1963, the number was 50 million.[14] **Drive-time audiences** (who listened from 6–9 A.M. and 4–7 P.M.) were growing at the time that radio station owner Gerald Bartell coined the term in 1957.

drive-time audience people who listen to the radio in their cars from 6–9 A.M. and 4–7 P.M.

A Columbia University report, commissioned by NBC in 1954, defined radio's new role. "Radio was the one medium that could accompany almost every type of activity....Where radio once had been a leisure-time 'reward' after a day's work, television was now occupying that role. Radio had come to be viewed less as a treat than as a kind of 'companion' to some other activity."[15] Like magazines, radio survived in part because the medium adapted to fill a different need for its audience.

Alan Freed and the Payola Scandals

The rise of rock 'n' roll coincided with the development of transistor and portable radios, which meant that radio played a central role in the rock revolution. "Rock and radio were made for each other. The relationship between record companies and radio stations became mutually beneficial. By providing the latest hits, record companies kept stations' operating costs low. The stations, in turn, provided the record companies with the equivalent of free advertising."[16]

Eventually this relationship would prove too close. On February 8, 1960, Congress began hearings into charges that disc jockeys and program directors had accepted cash to play specific recordings on the air. The term **payola** was coined to describe this practice, combining pay and Victrola (the name of a popular record player).

payola the practice of accepting payment to play specific recordings on the air.

In May 1960, the Manhattan grand jury charged eight men with commercial bribery for accepting more than $100,000 in payoffs for playing records. The most prominent among them was Alan Freed, who had worked in Cleveland (where he was credited with coining the term rock 'n' roll) and at New York's WABC. He was charged with 26 counts of accepting payoffs when he went on trial in February 1962. He pleaded guilty to two counts, paid a $300 fine, and received six months' probation. Then Freed was found guilty of income tax evasion. He died in 1965 while awaiting trial, at age 43. In September 1960, Congress amended the Federal Communications Act to prohibit the payment of cash or gifts in exchange for air play.[17]

WORKING IN RADIO

About 12,000 radio stations are on the air in the United States. They are about evenly divided between FM and AM.

In radio today, network programming plays a much smaller role than when radio began. National Public Radio (NPR) is the only major noncommercial network. Many commercial stations today use *program services*, which provide satellite as well as formatted programming.

Country singers like Leann Rimes have made country music radio's number one format.

Paul S. Howell/Gamma Liaison

Some stations are part of a *group*, which means they are owned by a company that owns more than one station in more than one broadcast market. Other stations are part of a *combination AM/FM* (a *"combo"*), which means that one company owns both an AM and an FM station in the same market. Many stations remain family-owned, single operations that run just like any other small business.

The *general manager* runs the radio station. The *program manager* oversees what goes on the air, including the news programs, the station's format and any on-air people. Salespeople who are called *account executives* sell the advertising for programs.

Traffic people schedule the commercials, make sure they run correctly and bill the clients. *Production people* help with local programming and produce commercials for the station. *Engineers* keep the station on the air. *Administrative people* pay the bills, answer the phones and order the paper clips. At a small station, as few as five people will handle all of these jobs.

THE BUSINESS OF RADIO

Instead of dying after the spread of television, radio managed to thrive by adapting to an audience that sought the portability and immediacy that radio offers. Nothing can beat radio for quick news bulletins or the latest hits. Radio also delivers a targeted audience much better than television because the radio station you prefer defines you to an advertiser much better than the television station you watch.

The advertising potential for an intimate medium like radio is attracting entrepreneurs who have never owned a station and group owners who want to expand their holdings, given the FCC's deregulation. When you listen to the radio in your car or through earphones while you jog, for instance, radio is not competing with any other medium for your attention. Advertisers like this exclusive access to an audience. Four important issues for people in radio today are the rise of FM over AM, deregulation, ratings and formats.

FM Beats AM

The way that FM signals travel makes them better carriers for stereo sound than AM. So in most markets, FM is more attractive to advertisers than AM.

"Although radio is prospering, AM stations are losing listeners at an alarming rate," reports the *Wall Street Journal*. In 1970, two out of three listeners regularly tuned to AM. By 1991, FM had captured three-fourths of the audience.[18]

AM typically fares best with news, sports, local information and call-in shows. This type of programming attracts a more loyal audience than the audience for music, which tends to be fickle, switching the dial to hear favorite songs. Today, radio as a mass medium has receded into the background. However, radio still generates enough money to make it an attractive investment.

The Telecommunications Act of 1996 Overhauls Radio

The Telecommunications Act of 1996 was the first major overhaul of broadcast regulation since the Federal Communications Commission was established in 1934. The Act continues a deregulation policy of commercial radio that began in the 1980s.

Before the Act was passed, the FCC limited the number of radio stations that one company could own nationwide. The Telecommunications Act removes the limit on the number of radio stations a company can own and,

IMPACT

on you   *Radio's Brave New World*

The Coolest Stations on the Web

By Jeff Salamon

Back in the sixties, radio was a wide-open space where regional hits could grow into national chart-busters and stoned FM DJs could play all of Side One of the Grateful Dead's *Anthem of the Sun* without getting fired.

Nowadays, with media consolidation rampant, the only place you'll find that sort of freedom is on the left end of the dial, where low-watt college and community stations spin everything from Bulgarian folk music to hardcore punk. But if you're out of their modest broadcast range, you're out of luck—unless you're hooked up to the Internet, in which case you have it better than the hippies ever did.

There's already some consolidation going on in Web radio—Broadcast.com and ImagineRadio have grouped together large numbers of stations on their Web Sites—but the nature of the medium ensures that alternatives will always be available. Here's a sample of the best—or at least the oddest.

Rapweek Now that even your mom knows who Lauryn Hill is, you might want to start exploring hip-hop's underground, which is every bit as ornery and vital as the punk underground of the Eighties. This weekly show, beamed out of New York, is a good place to start.

Hosts Eddie Ill and DL throw in a few familiar names, but for every act you know (the Roots, KRS-One, Nas), they mix in ten you don't (Polyrhthym Addicts, Slum Village, Cloudkickers featuring Yeshua, J-Tred's, Pumpkinhead). Along with some uncontestable wit ("I don't like Oprah/She's just corny/Medi-okra"), you get fresh bears, déjà vu-inducing samples, and some virtuoso scratching and mixing—although I wish Eddie and DL would let Rasco's majestic "How Many Times" play out a bit longer. **www.rapweek.com**

Radio Free Kansas Fortysomething Steve Taaffe is a bit older than most Webcasters, and it shows—his heartland site is split between his collection of vintage-radio airchecks ("Rockin' Radio WCIF/FM, Carbondale!") and his deep library of grog rock. Among his archival treasures are shows spotlighting Norwegian metal and the late-Sixties Canterbury scene.

On one particularly nice prairie afternoon, Taaffe moved his equipment outside and shared his bandwidth with the local wildlife. "It's a beautiful, sunny day," he solemnly announced as birds chirped and a stream burbled. "A good day to play Italian progressive music." But hey—what day isn't? **www.tafcommedia.net**

Underground Radio 3WK: 24/7, this year-old Web site is the FM radio station of your dreams. In one typical set, the popular bumps up against the obscure, moving

DL (left) and Eddie Ill spin everything from the Roots to Pumpkinhead on rapweek.com.

Photo by Len Irish

from the white-boy funk of Fun Lovin' Criminals' "Korean Bodega" to the shoe-gazer revivalism of All Natural Lemon and Lime Flavors' "In Between and After."

The downside of all this variety is a distinct lack of flow (if I never hear Built to Spill's "Sidewalk" segue into Whale's "Hobo Humpin' Slobo Babe" again, it'll be too soon), but the upside is getting a sneak preview of what the Rhino compilation *That's a Pretty Nice Haircut: Alternarock Hits of the Nineties* will sound like. **www.yuk.com**

in each local market, the number of stations that one owner can hold depends on the size of the market. (For a complete discussion of the Telecommunications Act, see Chapter 14).

The larger the radio market, the more stations that one company is allowed to own within it. In a market with 45 or more commercial radio stations, for example, a broadcaster may own eight stations, but no more than five of one kind (AM or FM). In markets with 30 to 44 stations, a broadcaster may own seven in total, but no more than four of one kind. In markets with 15 to 29 stations, one broadcaster may own six stations, but no more than four of one kind. In markets with 14 or fewer stations, one broadcaster may own three stations of one kind, but no more than half the stations in the market.

The Telecommunications Act also allows **cross-ownership**, which means that companies can own radio and TV stations in the same market, and broadcast and cable outlets in the same market.

cross-ownership the practice of one company owning radio and TV stations in the same broadcast market.

As soon as the Act passed in February 1996, radio stations sales began to soar. In radio's largest merger, Westinghouse bought Infinity Broadcasting in a deal valued at $3.9 billion. This combination made Westinghouse the nation's largest radio broadcast company, with 83 radio stations and 32 percent of the nation's top radio markets. Westinghouse now owns six stations in New York City alone, with a stable of on-air personalities as different as Charles Osgood, Don Imus and Howard Stern.

The Telecommunications Act encourages this type of consolidation, with one forecaster saying that there will soon be many companies with 100 stations or more. Supporters of the changes say that radio will become more competitive because these larger companies will be able to give the stations better support than small, single owners. Opponents point out that consolidation in the radio industry could lead to less program variety for consumers.

Are Radio Ratings Accurate?

Radio station owners depend on ratings to set adverting rates, and the stations with the most listeners command the highest ad rates. A company called

Today's radio stations are highly automated. Often the on-air talent simultaneously runs the equipment.

AP/Wide World Photos

Arbitron provides the radio business with its ratings. To find out what radio stations people are listening to, Arbitron requests that selected listeners complete and return diaries, which the company initially sends them.

Arbitron uses four measures of radio listening: average quarter-hour "cume," ratings and share.

1. *Average quarter-hour* means the average number of people listening to a station in any given 15-minute period.

2. *"Cume"* stands for the cumulative audience—the estimated number of people listening to a station for five minutes or more in any given 15-minute time period.

3. *Ratings* is the percentage of the total population that a station is reaching.

4. *Share* stands for the percentage of people listening to the radio that a station is reaching.

Arbitron often is criticized because minorities, non–English-speaking listeners and people ages 18 to 24 don't return the diaries in the same proportion as the other people who are surveyed. Arbitron acknowledges the problems and has tried filling out diaries for people over the phone and adding bilingual interviewers. Still, questions persist.

"Arbitron critics contend that its ratings hurt the different rock and ethnic formats, while aiding the middle-of-the-road, news, and talk formats, whose audiences are older and more responsive to the diaries."[19] Yet no other major competing radio ratings service exists, and stations are very dependent on ratings to set their rates for advertising.

Radio Depends on Ready-Made Formats

Today's radio station owners, looking for an audience, can use one of several ready-made formats. By adjusting their formats, radio managers can test the markets until they find a formula that works to deliver their audience to advertisers. If you were a radio station manager today, and you wanted to program your station, you could choose from several popular formats listed here according to the number of stations currently using them:

Country. The Grand Ole Opry first broadcast country music on WSM in Nashville in 1925, and this radio format is the most popular, aimed at 25- to 45-year-olds in urban as well as rural areas. About 2,400 stations use this format.

Adult Contemporary. This program format includes adult rock and light rock music by artists such as Kenny G and Anita Baker. It aims to reach 25- to 40-year-olds in all types of markets. About 1,400 stations use this format.

News/Talk. A station with this format devotes most of its air time to different types of talk shows, which can include call-in features, where listeners question on-the-air guests. Its typical audience is 35 and older, and you can hear this format on about 1,275 stations nationwide.

Religious. "Here's the news of today and the promise of tomorrow," begins one station with religious programming. Although some denominations own stations and broadcast their points of view, many stations have adopted religious programming purely as a way to make a profit. These stations offer inspirational music, news, weather, sports and drama. About 970 stations broadcast a religious format.

Middle of the Road (MOR). "Not too hard, not too soft" is the phrase most often used to describe this format. You could also add "not too loud, not too fast, not too slow, not too lush, not too new." The audience is 25 to 35 years old, and the music may include the Beatles, James Taylor, the Supremes and Stevie Wonder. About 400 stations use this format.

Spanish. Spanish stations are the fastest-growing foreign-language format, as radio owners target the nation's expanding Latino population. Spanish-language radio usually features news, music and talk. Most Spanish-language stations are AMs that recently have been converted from less-profitable formats. About 350 U.S. stations offer Spanish-language programming.

Contemporary Hit/Top 40. Playing songs on *Billboard*'s current hits list, a Top-40 station closely follows trends among listeners, especially teenagers. About 320 stations use this format.

Album-Oriented Rock (AOR). Directed toward 18- to 24-year-olds, this format delivers contemporary hits, like Top 40, but with songs from a longer span of time—from within the past two years, for example, instead of the past month. About 170 stations broadcast AOR.

News. It is difficult for a radio station to survive on news alone, so most stations are in big cities because of the continuing source of news stories. The news stations with the largest total weekly audience in the country, WINS in New York, advertises that it gives "all the news all the time." Seventy times an hour, for example, WINS tells listeners what time it is. About 65 stations broadcast all-news.

Two of the fastest-growing formats are News/Talk and Spanish-language radio. The number of stations using a News/Talk format has doubled from 1993 to 1998. Larry King, Rush Limbaugh and Howard Stern are the most notable "personalities" who have profited from the expanding audiences for the News/Talk phenomenon.

News/Talk radio is very popular in Los Angeles, but the most-listened-to radio station in the Los Angeles area is a Spanish-language station. The popularity of the station in an area with an expanding Spanish-language population shows how cultural changes in urban areas can quickly affect the economics of radio in that area.

The number of radio stations using a News/Talk format doubled from 1993 to 1998. Larry King (shown here), Rush Limbaugh and Howard Stern are the most notable "personalities" who have profited from this format.

Stations can divide these traditional formats into even more subcategories: AOR is splitting into modern rock and oldies; some adult contemporary stations play only love songs. The use of taped program formats means that a station can specialize its programming simply by changing the tapes or discs.

This makes disc jockeys as personalities much less important than they once were. Many stations operate without disc jockeys altogether, or limit personality programming to morning and evening drive-time. The rest of the day and evening these stations can rely on an engineer and an announcer to carry the programming.

Today, networks, which once dominated radio programming, mainly provide national news to their affiliates. Station managers can program their own stations, mixing local news, music and announcements. Stations also can get programming from syndicated and satellite program services. Syndicates provide prepackaged program formats. Satellites make program distribution easier; satellite networks, such as Satellite Music Network, promise the broadcaster original, up-to-date programming without a large, local staff.

TECHNOLOGY AND THE FUTURE

The most significant trend in radio is the move toward more segmentation of the audience, similar to the division of audiences in the magazine industry. Identifying a specific audience segment and programming for it is called **narrowcasting**. "With narrowcasting, advertising efficiency goes way up as overall costs go down….We are approaching the unstated goal of all radio programmers: to create a station aimed so perfectly that the listener will no longer have to wait, ever, for the song that he wants to hear." [20]

narrowcasting segmenting the radio audience.

Demand programming is a new term that describes radio's future possibilities. In the ultimate form of narrowcasting, a listener would be able to order up any particular selection at any time—do-it-yourself request radio.

demand programming allows the listener to order up any selection at any time.

In an *Esquire* magazine article "Radio Lives!" Eric Zorn predicted:

Listeners of the future, instead of having access to just 30 or 40 stations (many playing the same music and aimed at the same mainstream audiences), will be able to hook into hundreds of channels—blues stations, business-news stations, Czech-language stations, even full-time stations for the blind, anything you can't hear now because the audience for it is too small and scattered for even the biggest cities to support. [21]

Zorn's production may become possible before the next century begins, through a new technology known as **digital audio broadcast** (DAB). Digital audio can send music and information in the form of zeroes and ones, as in a computer code. This eliminates all of the static and hiss of current broadcast signals, and could mean infinite program choices for consumers.

digital audio broadcast a new form of audio transmission that eliminates all static and makes more program choices possible.

Discussions have even begun about global radio, using DAB as the standard, combining transmission from satellites and land-based towers on a single radio digital dial that would no longer distinguish among AM, FM, satellite or other programming. You would simply dial up a number for the signal, and the receiver could translate the programming using digital codes.

As radio technology grows more complex, and new formats and different program delivery systems are tested, the competition for your ear expands the choices that advertisers can make to reach you. The more stations there are competing for customers, the harder every station must compete for each advertising dollar. This means less revenue for each station because each station's potential audience becomes smaller. In the 1950s, radio learned how to compete with television. Now it must learn how to compete with itself.

IN FOCUS

- Radio was America's second national medium, after magazines. Radio transformed national politics and also expanded Americans' access to popular, as well as classical, culture.

- Radio technology began with Samuel F. B. Morse's invention of the telegraph, first demonstrated in 1835; Alexander Graham Bell's invention of the telephone, demonstrated in 1876; and Heinrich Hertz's description of radio waves in 1887.

- Guglielmo Marconi's promotion of wireless radio wave transmission began in 1897. Reginald Fessenden advanced wireless technology, but Lee de Forest called himself the father of radio because he invented the Audion tube to detect radio waves. David Sarnoff made radio broadcasting a visible business in the United States.

- The federal government intervened to regulate broadcasting almost as soon as it was invented. This early regulation separated the broadcast media from the print media, which are not regulated directly by the federal government.

- Two important developments in the 1920s were blanket licensing and commercial sponsorship. Blanket licensing meant that radio owners could use recorded music inexpensively. Commercial sponsorship established the practice of advertisers underwriting the cost of American broadcasting.

- The Radio Act of 1927 established the concept that the government would regulate broadcasting "as a public convenience, interest or necessity requires." The 1927 act is the foundation for all broadcast regulation in the United States, including the establishment of the Federal Communications Commission in 1934.

- Radio in the 1930s and 1940s became a powerful cultural and political force. Radio programming expanded to include comedy, music, serials, drama and news. Radio also indirectly created a collective national experience that had not existed before.

- A broadcast of "War of the Worlds" by the *Mercury Theater on the Air* demonstrated the vulnerability of a captive audience.

- Originally, the three radio networks (NBC, CBS and ABC) provided most radio programming. Today, most stations program themselves using a variety of sources.

- Clock and car radios expanded radio's audience, but the role of radio changed with the advent of TV, which could offer visual entertainment and news.

IMPACT

digital   *Digital Opens Doors for Radio Revolution*

By Kalpana Srinivasan

A stereo that reveals the title and artist on a digital screen as the song plays. Disc jockeys promoting products on-air—then sending electronic coupons for the items to listeners over personal computing devices. A car radio that display real-time traffic reports and stock quotes as they are streamed over the airwaves.

After decades of minimal fine-tuning, the world of radio is finally headed for a makeover.

Companies behind the digital revolution say they are on the way to making a long-sought vision a reality: CD-quality sound for FM listeners, less interference for AM listeners and prospects for a whole host of new data services.

"Here is an industry that has not seen any technological change since the 1940s, when FM was introduced," said Suren Pai, president of Lucent Digital Radio, one of several companies vying to develop technology that would allow for a seamless transition between the current analog service and the new digital system. "Consumers were looking for innovation in the radio space."

Using the language of computers—0s and 1s—to transmit information, the digital signal is less susceptible to interference and more efficient. Radio airwaves have enough bandwidth to carry large volumes of digital data—more than existing wireless technology. That opens the door for a new breed of radios that can give listeners much more than sound.

The goal is for broadcasters to transmit quality encoded music or data at the same time that they send out regular AM or FM service. That means traditional radios would continue to work, even as listeners started to replace them with the digital models.

"The first order of business is to do no harm to analog radio," said Robert Struble, president of USA Digital Radio, which has the backing of some of the nation's top radio groups for its bid to create the standard for digital radio technology.

The company is running trials of digital radio in a number of markets—even driving buses under bridges and in wooded areas to make sure the signal can be picked up in hard-to-reach places.

But the industry expects it will be another 12 to 18 months before consumers can sample the high-quality sound.

First, regulators must adopt a technical standard for digital radio....

Manufacturers also must roll out new radios that can receive the signal.

"I think it's an inevitability that radio goes digital," said Gordon Hodge, a radio industry analyst

- Edwin H. Armstrong is responsible for the invention of FM radio. Today, FM stations are three times as popular as AM stations.

- Arbitron is the primary ratings service for radio. Stations use ratings to set their rates for advertising.

- The most significant trend in radio today is the move towards more segmentation of the audience, similar to the division of audiences in the magazine industry.

- The Telecommunications Act of 1996 removed the limit one company can own on the number of radio stations and, in each local market, the number of stations that one owner can hold depends on the size of the market. The larger the radio market, the more stations that one company is allowed to own within it.

with Thomas Weisel Partners in San Francisco. "Really, what it boils down to is cost."

Analysts expect that digital radios will be cheap enough to entice consumers to switch. Some industry estimates put the cost of new receivers at 15 percent to 30 percent more than current high-quality radios....

A specially equipped clock radio could receive continual weather reports over the digital signal from a broadcasting service, even while remaining in sleep mode. Then, if an emergency arose, instructions sent over the air could turn the radio on and display the relevant information on a nearby screen.

Home entertainment systems also lend themselves to the technology: A television screen could be used to tell consumers how to order the latest Mariah Carey album as her song plays on the stereo.

"The ultimate capabilities will depend on the creativity of the software providers or broadcast-ers," said Bob Law, vice president of Kenwood USA, which expects to manufacture digital car radios by the spring of 2001....

It may take several years of experimentation with the emerging technology before broadcasters discern what consumers want, said Dennis Wharton of the National Association of Broadcasters.

"The possibilities are endless," Wharton said. "I don't think anybody has a real business plan yet."

Reprinted by permission of the Associated Press.

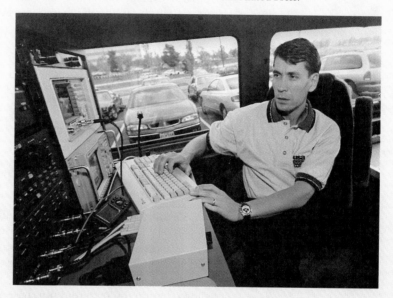

USA Digital Radio head Robert Struble sat in a tech van in Columbia, Md.

AP/World Wide Photos

■ Demand programming and digital audio broadcast may soon offer even more program choices for listeners, another challenge to the radio industry's growing competition within itself.

WORKING THE WEB www

■ **Canadian Broadcasting Corporation (CBC) Radio (audio and text)**
   www.radio.cbc.ca/radio/programs/news/headline-news
■ **Inside Radio**
   www.insideradio.com

- **National Public Radio**
  www.realaudio.com/contentp/nrp.html
- **The Radio Archive**
  www.oldradio.com
- **Radio History**
  home.luna.nl/~arjan-muil/radio/history.html
- **Surfing the Aether: Radio and Broadcasting Technology History**
  www.northernnet.com/bchris/home.html

INFOTRAC COLLEGE EDITION EXERCISES

Using InfoTrac College Edition, a fully searchable online database of articles and abstracts, do the following exercises as directed by your instructor.

1. Using InfoTrac College Edition, look up at least two of the following radio broadcasting pioneers:

   - David Sarnoff
   - Edwin Armstrong
   - Orson Welles ("War of the Worlds")
   - Bob Hope
     Then print at least two articles about two of the pioneers and either:

   a. Write a brief paper on your findings, or

   b. bring the articles to class for a small-group discussion

2. "Pirate radio" is a controversial and illegal use of radio airwaves by amateur broadcasters. Search the term "pirate radio" on InfoTrac College Edition and print at least three articles about it. Bring them to class and break into small groups to discuss the concept of pirate radio. Be prepared to debate both sides of the issue—why pirate radio should be allowed and why it should not, based on your findings.

3. Talk radio can be controversial. Look up "talk radio" on InfoTrac College Edition and pick a particular kind of talk radio you'd like to learn more about—sports talk, celebrity interview, shock jocks or a certain host/hostess who intrigues you (Larry King, Rush Limbaugh or Howard Stern, for example). Print at least three articles about the category or person you're interested in, and either:

   a. write a brief paper on your findings, or

   b. bring the articles to class and be prepared to do a brief talk about your subject.

4. Read "Impact on You: Radio's Brave New World" in Chapter 5, and then look up "web radio" or "Internet radio" on InfoTrac College Edition. Read and print at least three articles on web radio and reach some conclusions about the subject that you can share in class in a small-group discussion.

5. Read "Digital Impact: Digital Opens Doors for Revolution in Radio" in Chapter 5. Then look up "digital radio" or "digital audio broadcasting" on InfoTrac College Edition. Print at least two articles and either:

   a. write a brief paper on your findings, or

   b. bring the articles to class and be prepared to discuss them.

6

Recordings

What's Ahead

The information highway could be bad news if we [recording companies] don't control the right of distribution and receive fair remuneration.... I want my hands on the wheel.

*James Fifield, President
EMI Music*

Popular music is like a unicorn," writes R. Serge Denisoff in his book *Solid Gold*. "Everyone knows what it is supposed to look like, but no one has ever seen it." [1] More than half of the recordings sold every year in the United States are categorized as popular music.

If the average person buys four recordings a year, as the Recording Industry Association reports, popular music is recorded on two of them. Other types of music—country, gospel, classical, show tunes, jazz and children's recordings—make up the other half, but most of the big profits and losses in the recording business result from the mercurial fury of popular music.

Like the radio and television industries, the recording industry is challenged by rapidly changing technology. Like the movie industry during the first half of this century, the recording industry is at the center of recent debates over the protection of free artistic expression versus the industry's perceived effect on moral values.

FROM EDISON'S AMAZING TALKING MACHINE TO 33 ¹/₃ RPM RECORDS

Today's recording industry would not exist without Thomas Edison's invention, more than a century ago, of what he called a phonograph (which means "sound writer"). In 1877, *Scientific American* reported Thomas Edison's first demonstration of his phonograph. Edison's chief mechanic had constructed the machine from an Edison sketch that came with a note reading, "build this."

In 1887, Emile Berliner developed the gramophone, which replaced Edison's cylinder with flat discs. Berliner and Eldrige Johnson formed the Victor Talking Machine Company (later to become RCA Victor) and sold recordings of opera star Enrico Caruso. Edison and Victor proposed competing technologies as the standard for the industry, and eventually the Victor disc won. Early players required large horns to amplify the sound. Later the horn was housed in a cabinet below the actual player, which made the machine a large piece of furniture.

In 1925, Joseph Maxfield perfected the equipment to eliminate the tinny sound of early recordings. The first jukeboxes were manufactured in 1927 and brought music into restaurants and nightclubs.

By the end of World War II, 78 rpm (revolutions per minute) records were standard. Each song was on a separate recording, and "albums" in today's sense did not exist. An album in the 1940s consisted of a bound set of ten envelopes

Today's complex recording equipment is a direct descendant of turn-of-the-century inventions.

Mike Hashimoto/CORBIS Bettmann

about the size of a photo album. Each record, with one song recorded on each side, fit in one envelope. (This is how today's collected recordings got the title "album" even though they are no longer assembled in this cumbersome way.) Each shellac hard disc recording ran three minutes. Peter Goldmark, working for Columbia Records (which was owned by CBS), changed that.

Peter Goldmark Perfects Long-Playing Records

In 1947, Goldmark was listening with friends to Brahms' Second Piano Concerto played by pianist Vladimir Horowitz and led by the world-famous conductor Arturo Toscanini. The lengthy concerto had been recorded on six records, 12 sides. Goldmark hated the interruptions in the music every time a record had to be turned over. He also winced at the eight sound defects he detected.

"He asked his friends to play the records again," reports Robert Metz in his book *CBS: Reflections in a Bloodshot Eye*, "and while they did so, he sat gritting his teeth and racking his brain. Finally he produced a ruler and started calculating, counting 80 grooves to the inch, and he began pondering the principle of the phonograph....He concluded that he could get more mileage by slowing the turntable speed while crowding significantly more grooves onto a disk."[2] The result, after several refinements and the approval of CBS's William Paley, was the long-playing (LP) record, which could play for 23 minutes.

Paley Battles Sarnoff for Record Format

Paley realized that he was taking a big risk by introducing this product when most people didn't own a record player that could play the bigger 33¹/₃ rpm LP records at the slower speed. While the LP record was being developed, Paley decided to contact RCA executive David Sarnoff, since RCA made record players, to convince Sarnoff to form a partnership with CBS to manufacture LPs. Sarnoff refused.

Stubbornly, Sarnoff introduced his 7-inch, 45 rpm records in 1948. Forty-fives had a quarter-size hole in the middle and required a different record player, which RCA started to manufacture.

The smooth sound of today's recording artists such as Lauryn Hill is the direct result of the development of sophisticated technology that began with CBS Records' introduction of long-playing records (LPs) in the 1940s.

AP/World Wide Photos

T I M E F R A M E

Today to 1877: The recording industry caters to a young audience

TODAY The recording industry earns more than half its revenue from people under 34, but the only revenue growth is in online sales.

1985 The recording industry begins to consolidate into six major international corporations. Only one of these companies is based in the United States.

1979 Sony introduces the Walkman as a personal stereo.

1958 Motown introduces the "Detroit Sound" of African-American Artists, popularizing rock' n' roll.

1956 Stereo arrives.

1947 Peter Goldmark develops the long-playing record.

1943 Ampex develops tape recorders and Minnesota Mining and Manufacturing perfects plastic recording tape.

1877 Thomas Edison first demonstrates the phonograph.

Forty-fives were a perfect size for jukeboxes, but record sales slowed as the public tried to figure out what was happening. "General Sarnoff was foolish to refuse Paley's offer of a license [to manufacture LPs]," says Robert Metz. "When Sarnoff decided to fight against Columbia's superior system, he was guilty—and not for the first time—of allowing pride to triumph over good sense."[3]

Eventually Toscanini convinced Sarnoff to manufacture LPs and to include the 33⅓ speed on RCA record players to accommodate classical-length recordings. CBS, in turn, agreed to use 45s for its popular songs. Later, players were developed that could play all three speeds (33⅓, 45 and 78 rpm).

HI-FI AND STEREO ROCK IN

The introduction of rock 'n' roll redefined the concept of popular music in the 1950s. Contributing to the success of popular entertainers like Elvis Presley were the improvements in recorded sound quality that originated with the recording industry.

First came *high fidelity*, developed by London Records, a subsidiary of Decca. "The hi-fi collector preferred good recordings of boat whistles, passing trains, or even geese in flight to the muddy music of the old 78s."[4]

Tape recorders grew out of German experiments during World War II. Ampex Corporation built a high-quality tape recorder, and Minnesota Mining and Manufacturing (3M) perfected the plastic tape. Tape meant that recordings could be edited and refined, something that couldn't be done on discs.

Stereo arrived in 1956, and soon afterward came groups like the Supremes with the Motown sound, which featured the music of African-American blues and rock 'n' roll artists. At the same time, the FCC approved "multiplex" radio broadcasts so that monaural and stereo could be heard on the same stations. The development of condenser microphones helped bring truer sound.

In the 1960s, miniaturization resulted from the transistor. Eventually the market was overwhelmed with tape players smaller than a deck of playing

Improvements in recorded sound quality—hi-fi and stereo—contributed to the success of popular entertainers like Elvis Presley.

©Archive Photos

cards. Quadraphonic (four-track) and eight-track tapes seemed ready to become the standard in the 1970s, but cassette tapes proved more adaptable and less expensive. In 1979, Sony introduced the Walkman as a personal stereo. (The company is Japanese, but the name Sony comes from the Latin *sonus* for sound and *sunny* for optimism.) Walkmans were an ironic throwback to the early radio crystal sets, which also required earphones.

Today's compact discs (CDs) promise crystal sound, transforming music into digital code on a 4.7-inch plastic and aluminum disc read by lasers. Discs last longer than records and cassettes, and they can play for as long as 74 minutes. "It took VCRs seven years to get to the point where we got in just two years," said Leslie Rosen, executive director of the Compact Disc Group.[5] Music videos and the cable TV music channel MTV expanded the audience and the potential income for featured artists.

WORKING IN THE RECORDING INDUSTRY

Recordings, like books, are supported primarily by direct purchases. But a recording company involves five separate levels of responsibility before the public hears a sound: artists and repertoire, operations, marketing and promotion, distribution and administration.

Artists and repertoire, or A&R, functions like an editorial department in book publishing—to develop and coordinate talent. Employees of this division are the true talent scouts.

Operations manages the technical aspects of the recording, overseeing the sound technicians, musicians, even the people who copy the discs. This work centers on creating the master recording, from which all other recordings are made. Before stereophonic recording was developed in 1956, a recording session meant gathering all the musicians in one room, setting up a group of microphones, and recording a song in one take. Today, artists on the same song—vocals, drums, bass, horns, guitars—are recorded individually, and then the separate performances are mixed for the best sound.

The producer, who works within the operations group, can be on the staff of a recording company or an independent freelancer. Producers coordinate the artist with the music, the arrangement and the engineers.

Marketing and promotion decides the best way to sell the record. These employees oversee the cover design and the copy on the cover (jacket or sleeve). They also organize giveaways to retailers and to reviewers to find an audience for their product. Marketing and promotion might decide that the artist should tour or that the record needs a music video to succeed. Recording companies often use promoters to help guarantee radio play for their artists. This has led to abuses such as payola (See Chapter 5, pp. 113–114.)

Distribution gets the record into the stores. There are two kinds of distributors: independents and branches. Independents contract separately with different companies to deliver their recordings. But independents, usually responsible for discovering a record that is outside of the mainstream, are disappearing as the big studios handle distribution through their own companies, called branches. Because branches are connected with the major companies, they typically can offer the retailer better discounts.

Administration, as in all industries, handles the bills. Accounting tracks sales and royalties. Legal departments handle wrangles over contracts.

All of these steps are important in the creation of a recording, but if no one hears the recording, no one will buy it. This makes record promotion particularly important.

A new type of promotional partnership, between a recording company and a television show, was introduced in 1992. Giant Records, which produced the sound track for the television program *Beverly Hills, 90210,* ran videoclips from the album during the closing credits of the 1992–1993 season of the television show. After the first video—"Saving Forever for You," featuring *90210* star Brian Austin Green—played during the closing credits of a November episode, the song reached number 8 on the *Billboard* Hot 100 Singles Chart in two weeks.[6]

THE RECORDING BUSINESS

About 5,000 companies in the United States produce tapes and CDs. These companies sell over one billion records, cassettes and compact discs each year. The biggest recording-industry profits are divided among the five major companies: Sony (formerly CBS Records), Time Warner, EMI, Bertelsmann (RCA) and Seagram (MCA and Polygram)(see Table 6.1, p. 134). The main recording centers are Los Angeles, New York and Nashville, but most large cities have at least one recording studio to handle local productions.

The recording industry, primarily concentrated in large corporations, generally chooses to record what has succeeded before. "Increasingly, the big

INDUSTRY IMPACT

Recordings

*F*rom cylinders to cassettes to CDs and music videos, the recording industry has always been a volatile, technology-driven business. Not only the format changes—consumers' tastes change, too, with each new wave of youthful listeners.

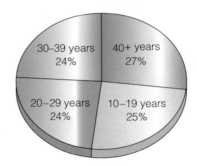

The recording industry's average consumer is younger than consumers in any other media industry. People under 30 account for about half the industry's revenues.

Source: The Veronis, Suhler & Associates Communications Industry Forecast, 1999-2003.

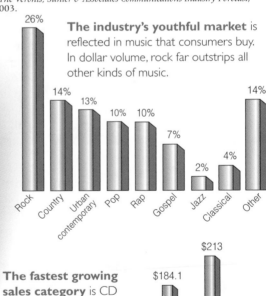

The industry's youthful market is reflected in music that consumers buy. In dollar volume, rock far outstrips all other kinds of music.

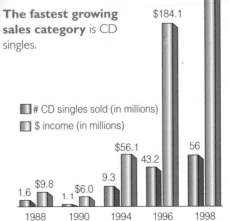

The fastest growing sales category is CD singles.

- ■ # CD singles sold (in millions)
- ■ $ income (in millions)

IMPACT

on you   Free Tunes for Everyone!

MP3 Music Moves into the High School Mainstream

By Lee Gomes

Picture high school kids hanging out at the local record store, flipping through the racks, looking for cool new tunes. That's how teenagers got their music in ancient times, before the Internet.

To see how kids these days keep up with the latest bands, enter the dark but tidy bedroom of an Oakland, Calif., high school senior named Brendan, who is expanding his already considerable music collection courtesy of an Internet technology known as MP3.

"Let's see if we can find some Korn," says Brendan as he sits down at his desk on a recent Saturday morning. "Not that I really

like them. I don't go for that sort of angry, show-how-loud-we-can-scream-at-you, blaring guitars kind of music. But still, they are pretty popular."

Brendan logs on to the World Wide Web, heads to a search engine called scour.net, and types in "Korn." Seconds later, his screen fills up with a list of Korn songs available for downloading. "Let's see," Brendan muses. "How about 'Lost'?" He clicks on the song and, sure enough, the sounds of angry, screaming, blaring guitars soon fill the room.

It was barely a year ago that the world first heard tales of computer-science students at the nation's elite technical colleges sharing MP3 files over their high-speed networking connections. But MP3s, one of the fastest-growing phenomena in the history of

the Web, are moving rapidly down in the age ladder. During the past few months, they have made the jump from the college quad to the high school cafeteria.

"At my school, almost everyone who has an Internet connection has MP3s," says Brendan, who himself has $1\frac{1}{2}$ giga-bytes of MP3 music, the equivalent of several hundred singles.

The MP3 explosion is driving the recording industry nuts, since many of the MP3 files cluttering the Web are pirated, in violation of copyright law. (*The Wall Street Journal* is identifying the young pirates by first names only.)

Converting a track on a music CD into an MP3 file requires just a PC and some free software. Hundreds of thousands of MP3 files are posted all over the Internet, thanks to students like Brendan and just

record companies are concentrating their resources behind fewer acts," reports *The Wall Street Journal*, "believing that it is easier to succeed with a handful of blockbuster hits than with a slew of moderate sellers. One result is that fewer records are produced."[7]

TABLE 6.1

The Music Industry's Big Five	
COMPANY	**COUNTRY**
Bertelsmann (RCA)	Germany
Seagram (MCA and Polygram)	Canada
Sony	Japan
EMI	United Kingdom
Time Warner	United States

Most radio formats today depend on popular music, and these recordings depend on radio to succeed. The main measurement of what is popular is *Billboard,* the music industry's leading trade magazine. *Billboard* began printing a list of the most popular vaudeville songs and the best-selling sheet music in 1913. In 1940, the magazine began publishing a list of the country's top-selling records.

Today, *Billboard* offers more than two dozen charts that measure, for example, air play and album sales as well as the sale of singles. Elvis Presley has had 149 recordings on the charts, for example, and 20 Beatles hits reached No. 1. Radio, governed by ratings and what the public demands, tends to play proven artists.

Tuning into MP3s

1 Get a player.
The many programs that play MP3 music include Winamp, Sonique, Audio Catalyst, MusicMatch and Real Jukebox.
You can find them at numerous Web sites, including www.emusic.com or www.mp3.com.

2 Get music.
There are legal MP3s at the emusic and mp3 sites and on many bands' sites. As long as you don't share the music with other people, it is pefectly legal to make MP3 versions of your own private CD collection.
The net is also teeming with illegal MP3s. Special search engines, such as www.scour.net, www.audiogalaxy.com, www.filequest.com, mp3.lycos.com and www.oth.net prowl for links to MP3 files of all legal persuasions.
(Caution: Many of these links won't exist any more by the time you find them.)

"Buying a CD just isn't very useful anymore," says David, a sophomore at Mountain View High School in the heart of Silicon Valley. "I can get any CD I want on the Internet."

Debra Gable, the librarian at Mountain View High, says downloading Internet music is one of the most popular uses of the cluster of high-speed PCs in the library. "There are kids doing it all day," she says. "It's especially popular at lunchtime."

Brendan says he spends several hours a week downloading songs. He plays them in lieu of a radio station. While doing his homework, Brendan has MP3 versions of the Red Hot Chili Peppers, Sheryl Crow, Lenny Kravitz, and many others to keep him company. "If you see a video you like on MTV, and then go type in the name of the song, you'll get it," he says.

A prime use of MP3s is to get the one hit song from an album without spending $15 for the entire CD. "Here's an example of a song I like from an album I would never buy," says Brendan, as he searches through his computer and plays "Kiss Me," by Sixpence None the Richer. "Talk about a one-hit wonder."

Brendan also uses his considerable knowledge of the intricacies of the MP3 world in the services of other time-honored adolescent pursuits—like getting dates. He has shared MP3 lore "with a couple of cheerleaders at my school," he says, smiling.

The Wall Street Journal, 6/15/99, B-1. Reprinted with permission.

about every other music fan with a PC. Downloading takes a few minutes with a regular modem and only a few seconds with a high-speed Internet connection, like DSL or cable modems.

Where the Money Is: Sales and Licensing

The industry collects income from direct sales and from music licensing.

Direct Sales. The promotional tour was once the major way a company sold records. But in the 1980s, music videos became a very visible form of promotion for an artist. This shift changed the industry's economics. The Fugees and Celine Dion are attractive to record companies because they are recording artists who also can perform well in videos.

> *It is now virtually impossible for an LP to succeed without the exposure that a video can generate. So promoting a record these days requires not only the extra expense of producing a video but also the complications of battling others for air time on the cable channel Music Television (MTV) and on other video-oriented programs over network and cable TV.*[8]

Music Licensing: ASCAP versus BMI. For the first 30 years of commercial radio, one of the reasons broadcasters used live entertainment was to avoid paying royalties to the recording companies. Today, two licensing agencies handle the rights to play music for broadcast: the American Society of Composers, Authors and Publishers (ASCAP) and Broadcast Music, Inc. (BMI).

ASCAP, founded in 1914, was the first licensing organization. As noted in Chapter 5, ASCAP sued radio stations in the 1920s that were playing recorded music. Eventually some radio stations agreed to pay ASCAP royalties through a blanket licensing agreement, which meant that each station that paid ASCAP's fee could play any music that ASCAP licensed.

Throughout the 1930s, many stations refused to pay ASCAP because they didn't have enough money. These stations agreed to explore the idea of forming a separate organization so that they could license the music themselves.

In 1939, the broadcasters came together to establish a fund to build their own music collection through BMI. ASCAP and BMI became competitors— ASCAP as a privately owned organization and BMI as an industry-approved cooperative. BMI used the same blanket licensing agreement, collecting payments from broadcasters and dividing royalties among its artists. ASCAP licensed the majority of older hits, but rhythm and blues and rock 'n' roll gravitated toward BMI.

Today, most broadcasters subscribe to both BMI and ASCAP. They also agree to play only licensed artists, which makes getting on the air more difficult for new talent. BMI and ASCAP, in turn, pay the authors, recording artists, producers, sometimes even the recording companies—whoever owns the rights to use the music.

Recording industry income has received a boost from the higher prices that consumers pay for CDs; prices of cassettes also have been edging upward. Growth in the actual number of recordings sold is much slower.

CHALLENGES TO INCOME AND CONTENT

Three issues face today's recording industry: piracy, attempts to control the content of recordings and the authenticity of artists' performances.

Pirates Steal Industry Revenue

The recording industry loses substantial income when people make their own tapes. The Japan Phonograph Record Association estimates that cassette-recorder owners make 8 billion illegal copies of tapes and CDs every year.[9] The Recording Industry Association of America (RIAA) has even proposed royalties for music that is digitally transmitted on cable.

A more threatening type of piracy for the industry is overseas copying of prerecorded cassettes that are then sold in the United States. Pirates control 18 percent of tape and album sales; the recording industry estimates that this represents $300 million a year in lost income.[10]

Content of Recordings

In 1985, the Parents Music Resource Center (PMRC) called for recording companies to label their records for explicit content. The new group was made up primarily of the wives of several national political leaders, notably Susan Baker, wife of then-Treasury Secretary James A. Baker III, and Tipper Gore, wife of then-Senator Al Gore.

Saying that records come under the umbrella of consumer protection, the PMRC approached the National Association of Broadcasters and the Federal

Figure 6.1   U.S. Recorded Music Sales, 1985–2003.

Data from *The Veronis, Suhler & Associates Communications Industry Forecast*, 1999–2003.

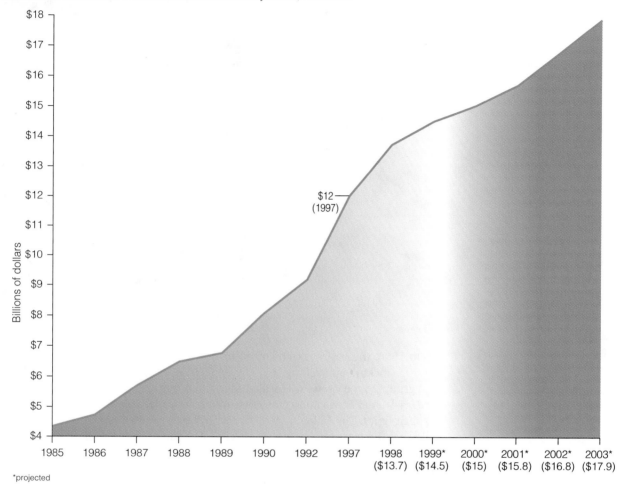

*projected

Communications Commission with their complaints. "After equating rock music with the evils of 'broken homes' and 'abusive parents,' and labeling it a 'contributing factor' in teen pregnancy and suicide, they single[d] out Madonna, Michael Jackson, Mötley Crüe, Prince, Sheena Easton, Twisted Sister, and Cyndi Lauper for their 'destructive influence' on children," reported Louis P. Sheinfeld, who teaches journalism law at New York University.[11]

The result was that beginning in January 1986, the Recording Industry Association (whose member record companies account for 95 percent of U.S. record sales) officially urged its members either to provide a warning label or to print lyrics on record albums that have potentially offensive content. Cassettes and CDs must carry the words "See LP for Lyrics." As with the movie industry when it adopted its own ratings system (see Chapter 8), the recording industry favored self-regulation rather than government intervention.

CDs have become the leading format for recordings, boosting industry income because CDs cost more than tapes.

STONE/David R. Frazier

In 1990, the nation's two largest record retailers ordered all of their outlets to stop stocking and selling sexually explicit recordings by the controversial rap group 2 Live Crew. A Florida judge ruled that the group's album *As Nasty as They Wanna Be* was obscene, even though it carried a warning about explicit lyrics. The Luke Skywalker record label, which produced the album, said that the controversy increased sales, but the ban meant that more than 1,000 stores nationwide refused to sell the record. Eventually, the decision was overturned, but sales of the album already had plummeted.

AUTHENTICITY OF PERFORMANCES

In 1990, a new controversy arose in the recording industry when the Grammy-winning duo Milli Vanilli admitted that they did not sing a note on the album that won them the award. (The album had sold more than 10 million copies worldwide.) The National Academy of Recording Arts and Sciences, which awards the Grammys, asked the group to return the prize. No artist in the Grammys' history had been charged with similar allegations.

The two Milli Vanilli singers (Robert Pilatus and Fab Morvan) were hired as front men for the actual singers, appearing on the album cover and in promotional materials and to lip-synchronize for music videos.

"Technology is helping a growing number of performers expand truth as it never has been expanded before," wrote *Los Angeles Times* columnist Robert Epstein. Epstein described recent technological changes in the industry that contributed to the problem: (1) singers use body microphones, which amplify their voices; (2) recordings—pop and classical—are dubbed and enhanced to a degree "only dreamed of by mere human performers"; and (3) most of the video industry seems based on lip-synchronized and computer-engineered performances.[12]

IMPACT

profile

Capturing Ears on the Internet

Musicians Love Him. Labels Are Skeptical

By Alce Foege

"Hell's Bells," a raucous anthem by the rock group AC/DC, blared from loudspeakers as Michael Robertson, the chief executive of MP3.com, walked to the podium. It seemed an unlikely introduction at last month's New York Music and Internet Expo for a man who wore a conservative camel hair sports jacket—and who had an evangelical Christian background.

Yet after his keynote speech, Mr. Robertson, a 32-year-old entrepreneur with blond surfer looks, received warm handshakes from teenagers with nose rings and hip-hop artists in baggy jeans. In the 16 months since he started his San Diego-based business, which distributes music over the Internet with a digital compression technology known as MP3, Mr. Robertson has been embraced by struggling musicians as a fellow revolutionary.

Even though he says he really isn't.

"I'm no revolutionary, I'm a pure-bred capitalist," Mr. Robertson said later. "I'm just talking about a new way of delivering music."

Still, Mr. Robertson is hoping that his outsider reputation will be a plus. When he introduced his service, which enables musicians to distribute their music cheaply over the Internet, he was virtually ignored by top labels. But now that MP3.com offers free music

Michael Robertson, chief executive of MP3.com, is hailed by some musicians as a revolutionary because of his distribution of music on the Internet.

Robert Burroughs/*The New York Times*

from 7,000 artists and gets 250,000 visitors a day, the labels, as well as investors, are noticing....

Mr. Robertson says he doesn't worry much about competition, even if it's Microsoft. Over take-out chicken and French fries in his New York hotel room, he asserted that in the Internet world, timing and instincts could be as valuable as capital. It is a lesson he says he learned observing his idol, Steven P. Jobs.

"He did it with Apple; he did it with Pixar," Mr. Robertson said.

"I've got a lot of respect for him because he zigged when everybody else zagged, and that's what we're doing."

MP3.com began two-and-a-half years ago as the Z Company, a Yahoo-style search engine founded by Mr. Robertson. In October 1997, Greg Flores, now MP3.com's director of sales, showed the MP3 software to Mr. Robertson, who was impressed enough to buy the rights to the MP3.com domain name and to rename his company.

At that point, MP3.com had four employees, including Mr. Robertson, working out of their homes. Last summer, it expanded into a 1,000-square-foot loft. "We had this sign up for new employees," he recalled. "It was the steps you had to do to join the company: Order chair. Put chair together. Order desk. Put desk together." The business has since moved to a larger office and employs about 35 people.

For now, Mr. Robertson's gamble appears to have paid off. In January, Sequoia Capital, a venture capital firm, invested $10 million in the company. Then Tom Petty posted a new song on MP3.com to promote an album.

At the end of March, Theodore W. Waitt, chief executive of Gateway, signed on to MP3.com's board. The computer mainstream has, in effect, signaled that Michael Robertson is the leader in his field.

Recording-industry executives claimed that the Milli Vanilli incident was an isolated event. Ironically, the technology that contributed to the quality of today's recordings also made the Milli Vanilli hoax possible.

TECHNOLOGY AND THE FUTURE

From the beginning, profits in the recording industry have been tied to technology. Ever since William Paley and David Sarnoff decided to produce LPs and 45s, the consumer has tracked the equipment manufacturers, looking for better, more convenient sound.

Today, recording companies worry that music pirates will copy digitized music, which can be sent over the Internet. Online subscribers can now browse through online music catalogs, downloading samples of music they like. But once digitized, the music is available to anyone and can be sent over the Internet around the world. The challenge for music company executives is to develop a way to protect this new technology with an even newer technology that will make copying impossible. "The information highway could be bad news if we don't control the right of distribution and receive fair renumeration," says James Fifield, president of EMI Music. "I want my hands on the wheel."[13]

The expansion of MP3 digital technology in 1999 signaled a new era for music lovers, making music available on the Internet. MP3 software allows any computer user with an Internet connection to download the latest music.

Singer Tori Amos is among the first performers to offer live performances on a website devoted to MP3 music.

Ebet Roberts

IMPACT

digital   *Music, Tech Giants Target Cyber Pirates*

By Clint Swett
THE SACRAMENTO BEE

Heavyweights in the music and technology industries announced [in1998] that they are joining forces to thwart music pirating on the Internet while, at the same time, encouraging the distribution of their artists over the Web.

They are calling their effort Secure Digital Music Initiative (SDMI), in which they envision all technologies will be compatible so consumers can download music with a wide variety of hardware and software.

Hilary Rosen, president and chief executive officer of the Recording Industry Association of American (RIAA), said the technology should be as standard as the common compact disc.

"Every consumer knows that when they go into a store to buy a CD, it will work on every CD player in the world. That's what has allowed the marketplace to flourish," she said.

Downplayed at the press conference but hovering in the background was the specter of MP3, a popular format for posting and downloading music on the Web. In the past, industry executives have complained bitterly that people are taking music from commercial CDs and violating copyright laws by distributing the music over the Web via MP3 without paying royalties to the artists or record labels.

The industry has had a difficult time combating piracy because of

Hilary Rosen (second from left), CEO of the Recording Industry Association of America, appeared at a news conference in New York to support technology that will combat music piracy.

AP/Wide World Photos

the ease with which violators can establish or shut down Web sites with pirated music.

Recording executives declined... to speculate how much they are losing to online pirating.

Few record companies voluntarily put their music online via MP3 because there is currently no way to keep it from being pirated. But with new security technology, the major labels would be more inclined to put their music on the Web.

Not everyone in the music industry is against MP3. Some artists are posting samples of their songs online using that format to bypass the major record labels and market directly to consumers.

Larry Iser, a lawyer in Los Angeles specializing in the music industry and intellectual property, said SDMI has been spurred by Rio, a $200 Walkman-size device that can play MP3 music downloaded from the Internet with CD-quality sound. The RIAA unsuccessfully sued to bar Rio from the market, saying it encouraged music pirating.

"Here comes a means for downloading music and putting it on a device where you can hear real sound quality," Iser said. "The music industry has seen that and now they want to jump in."

The Sacramento Bee, December 16, 1998, E-1. Used by permission.

Recording artists, such as Tori Amos and Alanis Morissette, have posted original new songs on the Internet to promote their albums, but MP3 allows users to transfer and send any song, which has vast copyright implications for recording artists and recording companies.

Aware of the potential damage to record company income, officials of the Recording Industry Association of America (RIAA) announced that they were going to crack down on Internet pirates, people who download copyrighted music on the Internet, but policing the Internet for music pirates is difficult. The economic implications for the recording industry could be substantial if people are able to easily access the songs they want for free.

As an alternative, rock star David Bowie decided to sell his 1999 album *Hours* online two weeks before the album was available in stores. "Just as color television broadcasts and film content on home videotapes required first steps to cause their industries to expand to consumer use," said Bowie, "I am hopeful that this small step will lead to larger leaps by myself and others."[14]

Portable MP3 players, Walkman-like minicomputer devices about the size of pagers, allow users to download music to a computer chip-based player. Priced at about $150, the players were introduced in 1999. Because they have no moving parts and use a computer chip, they are easier on batteries than portable tape and CD players. The price is expected to drop quickly as sales of MP3 players increase. "They are the hottest new thing in portable audio players," said Amy Hill, spokesperson for the Consumer Electronics Manufacturing Association. "Every teenager I know wants one of these things."[15]

When Thomas Edison demonstrated his phonograph for the editors of *Scientific American* in 1877, the magazine reported that

> *Mr. Thomas Edison recently came into this office, placed a little machine on our desk, turned a crank, and the machine inquired as to our health, asked how we liked the phonograph, informed us that it was very well, and bid us a cordial good night. These remarks were not only perfectly audible to ourselves, but to a dozen or more persons gathered around.[16]*

None of the discoveries by Edison's successors has been a new invention, only a refinement. Berliner flattened the cylinder; Goldmark and Sarnoff slowed down the speed; hi-fi, stereo and quadraphonic sound increased the fidelity; and cassettes, compact discs, digital recorders, and MP3 refined the sound further. But the basic discovery of the foundation for today's recording all began in 1877 with Thomas Edison.

Reflecting on the movie version of Edison's life, Robert Metz discusses the importance of Edison's development of the phonograph:

> *[A] tinkerer employed in the Edison labs... was shown playing with a makeshift device consisting of a rotating piece of metal with a pointed piece of metal scratching its surface. The device was full of sound and fury—and signified a great deal. Edison seized upon the idea and labored to construct a better device. Eventually he was seen speaking into a metal diaphragm whose vibrations in turn wiggled a needle pressed against a rotating cylinder of wax. And thus, supposedly through idle play, came the first permanent "record" of ephemeral sound. By any measure, it was an invention of genius. [17]*

IN FOCUS

- Rapidly changing technology affects the recording industry more quickly than some media industries.

- Thomas Edison first demonstrated his phonograph in 1877. Emile Berliner developed the gramophone in 1887. Berliner and Eldrige Johnson formed the Victor Talking Machine Company (later RCA Victor) to sell recordings. Joseph Maxfield perfected recording equipment to eliminate the tinny sound.

- The first standard records were 78 rpm. The long-playing record ($33^1/_3$ rpm) was developed by Peter Goldmark, working for William Paley. The 45 rpm record was developed by David Sarnoff's staff at RCA. Eventually, record players were sold that could play all three record speeds.

- High fidelity became popular in the early 1950s, and eventually stereo and quadraphonic sound followed.

- The recording industry efforts to improve recorded sound quality contributed to the success of rock 'n' roll entertainers like Elvis Presley.

- A recording company is divided into artists and repertoire, operations, marketing and promotion, distribution and administration.

- About 5,000 companies produce recordings in the United States. These companies sell over one billion records, cassettes and compact discs a year. The industry collects income from direct sales, music licensing and music videos, but recording-industry income today is flat.

- Three issues facing today's recording industry are piracy, attempts to control the content of recordings, and the authenticity of artists' performances.

- The recording industry, like the movie industry, responded to threats of government regulation of music lyrics by adopting its own standards for record labeling.

- Technology is changing the industry very quickly. Advances in recording technology contributed to the possibility of inauthentic performances being sold as authentic. Digital audiotape (DAT) recorders could replace today's current technologies. Other promising projects include: recordable compact discs; compact discs that provide audio, video and computer information; digital audio on television; a credit card–sized audio disc; and MP3 players.

WORKING THE WEB www

- **CD Now (CD Sales)**
  www.cdnow.txt

- **Grateful Dead Concerts Online**
  www.deadradio.com

- **MP3**

  www.mp3.com

- **Real Networks (audio on the Internet)**

  www.real.com

- **Recording Industry Association of America**

  www.riaa.com

- **Sony**

  www.sony.com

- **Virtual Recordings**

  www.virtualrecordings.com/mp3.htm

INFOTRAC COLLEGE EDITION EXERCISES

Using InfoTrac College Edition, a fully searchable online database of articles and abstracts, do the following exercises as directed by your instructor.

1. Choose one of your favorite recording artists or groups and research him/her/them on InfoTrac College Edition. Read and print at least three articles (profiles and/or reviews) about the artist or group. Then either:

   a. write a brief paper on your findings, or

   b. bring the articles to class and be prepared to do a brief talk about your subject.

2. Look up "sound recording industry" on InfoTrac College Edition and find three articles that interest you about the industry—what the industry is doing to increase sales or create new formats, for example. Be specific and narrow your interest to a specific industry issue. Then either:

   a. write a brief paper on your findings, or

   b. bring the articles to class and be prepared to discuss them.

3. Thomas Alva Edison not only invented the phonograph, but he also held patents for more than 1,000 inventions. Look up "Thomas Edison" on InfoTrac College Edition and learn more about him, his inventions and where people can go to see Edison's archives. Print at least three articles. Then either:

   a. write a brief paper on your findings, or

   b. bring the articles to class and be prepared to discuss them.

4. Read "Impact on You: Free Tunes for Everyone" and "Impact/Profile: Capturing Ears on the Internet" in Chapter 6. Then look up "MP3" on InfoTrac College Edition and research at least three articles on this new technology. In a three-page paper, explain what MP3 is and how it's changing the recording industry.

5. Read "Digital/Impact: Music, Tech Giants Target Cyber Pirates" in Chapter 6. Then look up "music piracy" on InfoTrac College Edition and find at least two articles on the issue. Cite specific examples of piracy that have occurred in the recording industry and either:

a. write a brief paper on your findings, or

b. bring the articles to class and be prepared to discuss them.

CHAPTER 7

Television

A new generation now has the chance to put the *vision* back into tele*vision,* and to travel from the wasteland to the promised land

Newton Minow, former chairman, Federal Communications Commission

"Television is the pervasive American pastime," writes media observer Jeff Greenfield. "Cutting through geographic, ethnic, class and cultural diversity, it is the single binding thread of this country, the one experience that touches young and old, rich and poor, learned and illiterate. A country too big for homogeneity, filled by people from all over the globe, without any set of core values, America never had a central unifying bond. Now we do. Now it is possible to answer the question, *'What does America do?'* We watch television."[1]

Americans, on average, watch nearly eight hours of television a day, according to the A. C. Nielsen Company, which monitors television usage for advertisers. (See Figure 7.1, p. 148.) Even though *you* may not watch TV this much, the percentage of the population that watches television more than seven hours counterbalances the time that you spend with your television set.

It's not surprising that the effects of such a pervasive medium have attracted so much attention from parents, educators, social scientists, religious leaders,

Figure 7.1 Average Daily Per-Household Hours of Television Use in the United States, 1950–1998

Data from Christopher H. Sterling and Timothy R. Haight, *The Mass Market: Aspen Institute Guide to Communication Industry Trends*, New York/London: Praeger, 1977, p. 366; Radio Advertising Bureau, Nielsen Media Research; Veronis Suhler & Associates, *Communications Industry Forecast*, 1999–2003.

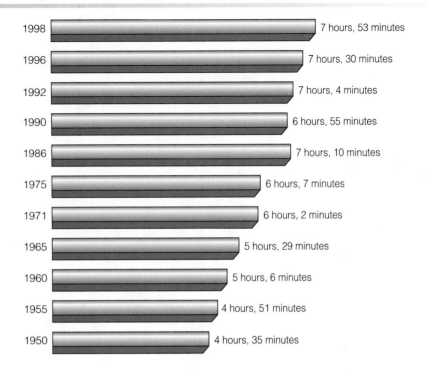

Year	Hours
1998	7 hours, 53 minutes
1996	7 hours, 30 minutes
1992	7 hours, 4 minutes
1990	6 hours, 55 minutes
1986	7 hours, 10 minutes
1975	6 hours, 7 minutes
1971	6 hours, 2 minutes
1965	5 hours, 29 minutes
1960	5 hours, 6 minutes
1955	4 hours, 51 minutes
1950	4 hours, 35 minutes

public officials and anyone else who is concerned with society's habits and values. TV has been blamed for everything from declines in literacy to rises in violent crime to the trivialization of national politics. Every once in a while it is praised, too, for giving viewers instant access to world events and uniting audiences in times of national crisis.

An industry with this much presence in American life is bound to affect the way we live. Someone who is watching television is not doing other things: playing basketball, visiting a museum or looking through a telescope at the stars, for instance. Television, however, can bring you to a museum you might never visit, or to a basketball game you cannot attend or closer to the solar system than you could see through a telescope.

The technology of television, adding pictures to the sounds of radio, truly transformed Americans' living and learning patterns. The word *television*, which once meant programs delivered by antennas through over-the-air signals, now means a *television screen*, where a variety of delivery systems brings viewers a diversity of programs.

The programs Americans watch today are delivered by antennas, cables and satellites, but they all appear on the same television screen, and, as a viewer, you can't tell how the program arrived at your television set and probably don't care. What you do know is that television gives you access to all types of programs—drama, comedy, sports, news, game shows and talk shows. You can see all kinds of people—murderers, public officials, foreign leaders, reporters, soldiers, entertainers, athletes, detectives, doctors. The television screen is truly, as scholar Erik Barnouw observed, a "tube of plenty."

About 1,500 television stations operate in the United States. Three out of four of these are commercial stations and the others are noncommercial stations. More than half of the commercial stations are affiliated with a network.

Commentator Jeff Greenfield writes:

The most common misconception most people have about television concerns its product. To the viewer, the product is the programming. To the television executive, the product is the audience.

Strictly speaking, television networks and stations do not make any money by producing a program that audiences want to watch. The money comes from selling advertisers the right to broadcast a message to that audience. The programs exist to capture the biggest possible audiences.[2]

To understand why we get the programming we do, it is important to remember that *commercial television exists primarily as an advertising medium.* Programming surrounds the advertising, but it is the advertising that is being delivered to the audience. Commercial television, from its inception, was created to deliver audiences to advertisers.

Because television can deliver a larger audience faster than any other medium, television can charge the highest rates of any medium for its advertising—which makes TV stations rich investments. A 30-second ad during a network television program, for example, costs an average of $120,000, but during a widely watched program like the Super Bowl (with an estimated audience of half the U.S. population), a 30-second ad costs nearly $2 million.

Today, even the smallest television station is a multimillion-dollar operation. The television era began much more humbly, and with very little excitement, near the turn of the century.

The most profitable type of TV programming today is sports. Here NY Yankees pitcher David Cone celebrates after the final out in his 1999 no-hitter against the Montreal Expos.

AP/World Wide Photos

TELEVISION TECHNOLOGY: BEGINNINGS

The word *television* first appeared in the June 1907 issue of *Scientific American*.[3] Before then, experiments in image transmission had been called "visual wireless," "visual radio" and "electric vision."

Alexander Graham Bell's telephone and Samuel F. B. Morse's telegraph contributed to the idea of sending electrical impulses over long distances. The first major technological discovery to suggest that pictures also could travel was the *Nipkow disk*. Twenty-four-year-old Paul Nipkow patented his "electrical telescope" in Germany in 1884. This disk, which formed the basis for television's development through the 1920s, was about the size of a phonograph record, perforated with a spiral of tiny holes.

Also crucial in television's (and radio's) development were Guglielmo Marconi and Lee de Forest (see Chapter 5). Marconi eliminated sound's dependence on wires and put sound on airwaves. De Forest contributed the Audion tube, which amplified radio waves so that people could hear the sound clearly.

In 1927, Secretary of Commerce Herbert Hoover appeared on a 2-inch screen by wire in an experimental AT&T broadcast. On September 11, 1928, General Electric broadcast the first dramatic production, *The Queen's Messenger*—the sound came over station WGY, Schenectady, and the picture came from experimental television station W2XAD. All of the pictures were close-ups, and their quality could best be described as primitive.

Two researchers, one working for a company and one working alone, brought television into the electronic age. Then the same man who was responsible for radio's original popularity, RCA's **David Sarnoff**, became television's biggest promoter.

Vladimir Zworykin was working for Westinghouse when he developed an all-electronic system to transform a visual image into an electronic signal. Zworykin's electronic signal traveled through the air. When the signal reached the television receiver, the signal was transformed again into a visual image for the viewer.

MIKE SMITH Reprinted by permission of United Feature Syndicate, Inc.

TIMEFRAME

Today to 1884: Television becomes the nation's major medium for news and entertainment

TODAY Television programming is delivered on more than 200 different channels by over-the-air broadcast, cable, fiber optics and satellite.

1979 Ted Turner starts Cable News Network (CNN).

1973 The television networks present live broadcasts of the Watergate Hearings.

1963 Network television provides nonstop coverage of the assassination and funeral of President John F. Kennedy. Public Television begins broadcasting as National Educational Television (NET).

1951 CBS launches *I Love Lucy,* a situation comedy, which proved to be TV's most durable type of entertainment program.

1947 NBC and CBS begin broadcasting television news on the *Camel News Caravan* (NBC) and *Television News* with Douglas Edwards (CBS).

1939 NBC debuts at the World's Fair in New York City with a broadcast that includes President Franklin D. Roosevelt, who becomes the first U.S. president to appear on television.

1884 Paul Nipkow patents the "electrical telescope" in Germany, which formed the basis for TV's development through the 1920s.

CBS Photo Archive

Philo T. Farnsworth, working alone in California, developed the cathode ray tube (which he called a dissector tube). Farnsworth's cathode ray tube used an electronic scanner to reproduce the electronic image much more clearly than Nipkow's earlier mechanical scanning device. In 1930, 24-year-old Farnsworth patented his electronic scanner.

NBC television's commercial debut was at the 1939 World's Fair in New York City at the Hall of Television. On April 30, 1939, President Franklin D. Roosevelt formally opened the fair and became the first president to appear on television. Sarnoff also spoke, and RCA displayed its 5-inch and 9-inch sets, priced from $199.50 to $600.[4]

NBC and CBS were the original TV networks. As explained in Chapter 5, a network is a collection of radio or television stations that offers programs, usually simultaneously, throughout the country, during designated program times. Chapter 5 also describes how the third major network, ABC, developed from the old Blue network of NBC in 1943. ABC labored from its earliest days to equal the other two networks but didn't have as many affiliates as NBC and CBS. The two leading networks already had secured the more powerful, well-established broadcast outlets for themselves. David Sarnoff and **William Paley** controlled the network game.

TELEVISION TAKES OVER RADIO

When the FCC resumed television licensing in 1945, ten television stations were on the air in the United States.

> *By the late 1940s, television began its conquest of America. In 1949, the year began with radio drawing 81 percent of all broadcast audiences. By the year's end, television was grabbing 41 percent of the broadcast market. When audiences began experiencing the heady thrill of actually seeing as well as hearing events as they occurred, the superiority of television was established beyond doubt.[5]*

Black-and-white television replaced radio so quickly as the nation's major advertising medium that it would be easy to believe that television erupted suddenly in a surprise move to kill radio. But remember that the two major corporate executives who developed television—Sarnoff and Paley—also held the country's largest interest in radio. They used their profits from radio to develop television, foreseeing that television eventually would expand their audience and their income.

A New Kind of News

Broadcast news, pioneered by radio, adapted awkwardly at first to the new broadcast medium—television. According to **David Brinkley**, a broadcast news pioneer who began at NBC,

> *When television came along in about 1947–48, the bigtime newsmen of that day—H. V. Kaltenborn, Lowell Thomas—did not want to do television. It was a lot of work, they weren't used to it, they were doing very well in radio, making lots of money. They didn't want to fool with it. So I was told to do it by the news manager. I was a young kid and, as I say, the older, more established people didn't want to do it. Somebody had to.[6]*

In 1947, CBS initiated *Television News with Douglas Edwards* and NBC broadcast *Camel News Caravan* (sponsored by Camel cigarettes) with John Cameron Swayze. Eventually, David Brinkley joined Swayze for NBC's 15-minute national newscast. He recalls:

> *The first broadcasts were extremely primitive by today's standards. It was mainly just sitting at a desk and talking. We didn't have any pictures at first. Later we began to get a little simple news film, but it wasn't much.*
>
> *In the beginning, people would call after a program and say in tones of amazement that they had seen you. "I'm out here in Bethesda, and the picture's wonderful." They weren't interested in anything you said. They were just interested in the fact that you had been on their screen in their house.[7]*

At first, network TV news reached only the East Coast because the necessary web of national hookups wasn't in place to deliver television across the country. By 1948, AT&T's coaxial cable linked Philadelphia with New York and Washington. The 1948 political conventions were held in Philadelphia and broadcast to the 13 Eastern states. When the 1952 conventions were broadcast, AT&T's national coaxial hookups joined 108 stations across the country.

Television

*T*oday's television audience is
fragmented with six networks,
cable, VCRs and satellite systems.

Although many homes have cable, the
cable audience is fragmented by the number
of program offerings. As a result, national
advertisers still find broadcast TV the most
efficient way to reach masses of viewers.

Source: Data from *The Veronis, Suhler & Associates Communications Industry Forecast,* 1997-2001.

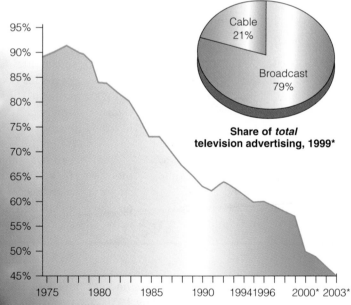

Cable
37%

Network-
affiliated
stations
44%

Basic cable
7%

Independent
stations
12%

**Share of *total*
television viewing, 1999***

*projected

Cable
21%

Broadcast
79%

**Share of *total*
television advertising, 1999***

95%
90%
85%
80%
75%
70%
65%
60%
55%
50%
45%

1975   1980   1985   1990   19941996   2000* 2003*

**Network's share of prime-time audience (includes Fox beginning in
1987, UPN and WB beginning in 1995).**

*projected

The prime-time audience for the television networks
(ABC, CBS, NBC, Fox, UPN and WB) is declining because of
increased competition from satellite and cable programming.

Source: Data from *The Veronis, Suhler & Associates Communications Industry
Forecast,* 1997-2001.

IMPACT

profile Edward R. Murrow (1908–1965)

*Edward R. Murrow had established a reputation for excellence as a CBS radio news broadcaster when he migrated to television news in 1951. In this profile, veteran journalist **Theodore H. White** outlines Murrow's broadcast career and its impact on television audiences.*

It is so difficult to recapture the real Ed Murrow from the haze that now shrouds the mythical Ed Murrow of history.

Where other men may baffle friends with the infinite complexity of their natures, Ed was baffling otherwise. He was so straightforward, he would completely baffle the writers who now unravel the neuroses of today's demigods of television. When Ed was angry, he bristled; when he gave friendship, it came without withholding.

He could walk with prime ministers and movie stars, GIs and generals, as natural in rumpled GI suntans as in his diplomatic homburg. But jaunty or somber, to those of us who knew him he was just plain old Ed. In his shabby office at CBS cluttered with awards, you could loosen

Edward R. Murrow set a very High standard for TV news in the 1950s.
Bettmann/CORBIS

your necktie, put your feet up and yarn away. The dark, overhanging eyebrows would arch as he punctured pretension with a jab, the mouth would twist quizzically as he questioned. And then there were his poker games, as Ed sat master of the table, a cigarette dangling always from his lips—he smoked 60 or 70 a day—and called the bets.

Then—I can hear him now—there was the voice. Ed's deep and rhythmic voice was compelling, not only for its range, halfway between bass and baritone, but for

the words that rolled from it. He wrote for the ear—with a cadence of pauses and clipped, full sentences. His was an aural art but, in Ed, the art was natural—his inner ear composed a picture and, long before TV, the imagination of his listeners caught the sound and made with it their own picture.

We remember the voice. But there was so much more to Ed. He had not only a sense of the news but a sense of how the news fit into history. And this sense of the relation of news to history is what, in retrospect, made him the great pioneer of television journalism.

...He is very large now, for it was he who set the news system of television on its tracks, holding it, and his descendants, to the sense of history that give it still, in the schlock-storm of today, its sense of honor. Of Ed Murrow it may be said that he made all of us who clung to him, and cling to his memory still, feel larger than we really were.

"When He Used the Power of TV, He Could Rouse Thunder," *TV Guide* 34, no. 3 (Jan. 18, 1986): 13–14. Reprinted by permission of the Julian Bach Literary Agency, Inc. © 1986 by Theodore H. White.

CBS had developed a strong group of radio reporters during World War II, and by 1950 many of them had moved to the new medium. CBS News also made a practice, more than the other networks, of using the same reporters for radio and television. The major early news figure at CBS was Edward R. Murrow, who, along with David Brinkley at NBC, created the early standards for broadcast news. (See Impact/Profile, Edward R. Murrow, above.)

Public affairs programs like *See It Now* continued to grow along with network news, and in 1956 NBC teamed David Brinkley with Chet Huntley to cover the political conventions. The chemistry worked, and after the convention NBC put

Huntley and Brinkley together to do the evening news, *The Huntley-Brinkley Report.* Brinkley often called himself "the other side of the hyphen."

Entertainment Programming

Early television was like late radio with pictures: It offered variety shows, situation comedies, drama, Westerns, detective stories, Hollywood movies, soap operas and quiz shows. The only type of show that television offered that radio did not (besides movies, of course) was the talk show. (Ironically, today's radio has created call-in programs, its own version of the talk show.)

Quiz Show Scandals. CBS's *$64,000 Question* premiered June 7, 1955, and was sponsored by Revlon. Contestants answered questions from a glass "isolation booth." Successful contestants returned in succeeding weeks to increase their winnings, and Revlon advertised its Living Lipstick. By September, the program was drawing 85 percent of the audience, and Revlon had substituted an ad for another product; its factory supply of Living Lipstick had completely sold out.

The $64,000 Question engendered imitation: *Treasure Hunt, Giant Step,* and *Twenty-One.* Winnings grew beyond the $64,000 limit; Charles Van Doren won $129,000 on *Twenty-One.* In the fall of 1955, CBS replaced Murrow's *See It Now* with a quiz program.

Many network quiz shows like *The $64,000 Question* were produced by sponsors for the networks, and these programs often carried the sponsor's name. In the 1958–59 quiz show scandals, Revlon was implicated when a congressional subcommittee investigated charges that the quiz shows were rigged to enhance the ratings.

Charles Van Doren admitted before the congressional subcommittee that he had been fed the answers by *Twenty-One*'s producer. Staff members from other quiz shows added to Van Doren's testimony.

The scandals caused the networks to reexamine the relationship between advertisers and programs. Before the scandals, one-quarter to one-third of network programming was produced by advertisers and their agencies. The networks began to look to other sources.

Charles Van Doren, shown here, won $129,000 on the quiz show *Twenty-One.* Eventually, Van Doren admitted that he had been fed the answers by the show's producers. He became a central figure in the 1950s quiz show scandals.

Bettmann/CORBIS

By the late 1960s, advertisers provided less than 3 percent of network programming, and soon advertisers provided no network shows. The networks programmed themselves. They used the newly acquired studio movies to replace the quiz shows, but quiz shows have resurfaced today with *Wheel of Fortune*, *Family Feud* and *Jeopardy*.

Variety Shows. The best radio stars jumped to the new medium. Three big variety-show successes were Milton Berle's *Texaco Star Theater*, *The Admiral Broadway Revue* (later *Your Show of Shows*) with Imogene Coca and Sid Caesar and Ed Sullivan's *Toast of the Town* (later *The Ed Sullivan Show*). These weekly shows featured comedy sketches and appearances by popular entertainers. *The Ed Sullivan Show*, for example, is where most Americans got their first glimpse of Elvis Presley and the Beatles. All of the shows were done live.

The time slot in which these programs were broadcast, 7–11 P.M., is known as **prime time**. Prime time simply means that more people watch television during this period than any other, so advertising during this period costs more. Berle's 8 P.M. program during prime time on Tuesday nights often gathered 85 percent of the audience. *Texaco Star Theater* became so popular that one laundromat installed a TV set and advertised "Watch Berle while your clothes twirl."

> **prime time** the TV time period from 7 to 11 P.M. when more people watch TV than at any other time.

Situation Comedies. Along with drama, the **situation comedy** (sitcom) proved to be one of TV's most durable types of programs. The situation comedy established a fixed set of characters in either a home or work situation. *I Love Lucy*, starring Lucille Ball and Desi Arnaz, originated from Los Angeles because the actors wanted to live on the West Coast. In 1951, Ball began a career as a weekly performer on CBS that lasted for 23 years. *Friends, Frasier* and *Everybody Loves Raymond* are examples of more contemporary situation comedy successes.

> **situation comedy** a TV program that establishes a fixed set of characters in a home or work situation.

Drama. *The Loretta Young Show* offered noontime drama—broadcast live—every day in the 1950s. *The Hallmark Hall of Fame* established a tradition for high-quality dramatic, live presentations. For many years, TV dramas were limited to 1- or 2-hour programs. But in the 1970s, encouraged by the success of Alex Haley's *Roots*, which dramatized Haley's search for the story of his

I Love Lucy is an example of one of TV's most durable types of prime-time programming—the situation comedy.

The Kobal Collection/Paul Drinkwater

African ancestry, television began to broadcast as many as 14 hours of a single drama over several nights.

Westerns. TV went Western in 1954, when Jack Warner of Warner Bros. signed an agreement with ABC to provide the network with a program called *Cheyenne.* The outspoken Warner had openly criticized TV's effect on the movie business, but when ABC asked Warner to produce programs for them, Warner Bros. became the first movie company to realize that the studios could profit from television.

Detective Stories. *Dragnet*, with Sergeant Friday, was an early TV experiment with detectives. The genre became a TV staple: *Dragnet's* successor in the 1990s is a program like *Law and Order.*

Movies. The movie industry initially resisted the competition from TV, but then realized that there was money to be made in selling old movies to TV. In 1957, RKO sold 740 pre-1948 movies to television for $25 million. The other studios followed. Through various distribution agreements, movie reruns and movies produced specifically for television were added to television's program lineup.

Soap Operas. Borrowed from radio serials, soap operas filled morning television programming. Today, game shows and reruns are more popular choices, but programs like *The Young and the Restless* survive. Soap operas have their own magazines, and some newspapers carry weekly summaries of plot development.

The Talk Show. Sylvester "Pat" Weaver (actress Sigourney Weaver's father) created and produced television's single original contribution to programming: the talk show. Weaver's *Tonight Show* (originally *Jerry Lester's Broadway Open House*) first appeared in 1954. Through a succession of hosts from Lester to Steve Allen to Jack Paar to Johnny Carson and Jay Leno, *The Tonight Show* has lasted longer than any other talk show on television. Modern-day imitators include David Letterman and Conan O'Brien.

Ratings Target the Audience

After the quiz show scandals, the major criticism of the networks was that they were motivated only by ratings. Ratings provide sponsors with information about the audience they're reaching with their advertising—what advertisers are getting for their money. By the late 1950s the A. C. Nielsen Company dominated the television ratings business. The national Nielsen ratings describe the audience to advertisers; based on the Nielsens, advertisers pay for the commercial time to reach the audiences they want.

Today, Nielsen provides two sets of numbers, known as rating and share. The **rating** is a percentage of the total number of households with television sets. If there are 95 million homes with TV sets, for example, the rating shows the percentage of those sets that were tuned in to a specific program.

The **share** (an abbreviation for *share-of-audience*) compares the audience for one show with the audience for another. *Share* means the percentage of the audience with TV sets turned on that is watching each program. If TV sets in 50 million homes were turned on at 8 P.M. on Friday night, and 25 million homes were tuned to program A, that program would have a rating of 26 (25 million divided by 95 million, expressed as a percentage) and a share of 50 (see Figure 7.2).

rating a percentage of the *total* number of households with TV sets.

share the percentage of the audience *with TV sets turned on* that is watching each program.

IMPACT

on you   *Viewers Identify with TV Characters*

By Eileen Kinsella

Who cares about juicy plots and cool explosions? TV viewers want to see shows with cast members similar to themselves.

That's the conclusion of a recent study of television-viewer habits conducted by the Yale School of Management....

The Yale study found that viewers' preference for characters like themselves can outweigh such show attributes as the level of comedy or action. A woman who lives with her family is 45 percent more likely to watch a show centered on a family than one that is not, and a Generation X woman living alone most likely will choose *Caroline in the City* over *Home Improvement*, a show about a baby boomer and his family.

But some industry insiders dispute the findings. "*Third Rock From the Sun* is one of the most popular shows on TV, and none of us are aliens," says Richard Kurlander, a spokesman for Petry Television, which sells commercial time and gives programming advice. He also cites *MASH* and *Golden Girls*, which had many fans who didn't serve in Korea and weren't over 60, living in Florida.

Anne Elliot, a spokeswoman for Nielsen Media Research, doesn't doubt the study's findings but argues that viewer data can be interpreted in many ways. "Every day within the television industry, networks can find information that will portray what they want," she

says. She also notes that *Friends* is a favorite of hers, but she isn't single, no longer lives in the city and is past her 20s. "Do I watch *Friends* because I'm like them? No. I simply think the show is funny."

The study's author, Ron Shachar, responds that the networks can use his findings to maximize their audiences. He argues that they should air sitcoms after 10 P.M. when there are no competing shows.

Mr. Kurlander doesn't disagree but maintains there is already such a high failure rate for such shows that a later time slot won't guarantee success. "It's difficult to pull off a hit no matter how you look at it," he says.

The Wall Street Journal, March 31, 1997, B-1.

Third Rock From the Sun is meant to appeal to an under-30 audience, which is an important age group for the networks.

Courtesy of Carsey-Werner

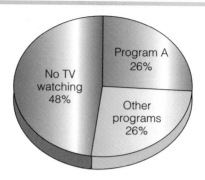
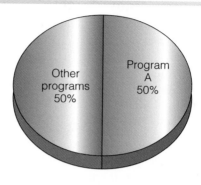

Rating =
TV households tuned
to Program A
(25 million)
——————————
Total TV households
(95 million)

Share =
TV households
watching Program A
(25 million)
——————————
TV households
watching TV
(50 million)

Figure 7.2 Measuring the Audience: What TV Ratings Mean Suppose that at 8 P.M. on Friday, TVs are on in 50 million out of 95 million TV households and that 25 million households are tuned to program A. Program A's *rating* is 26, meaning 26 percent of the total TV households are tuned to Program A. Program A's *share* is 50, meaning 50 percent of the total number of TV households watching TV are watching Program A.

The most concentrated ratings periods for local stations are "sweeps" months—February, May and November. (Ratings are taken in July, too, but the numbers are not considered accurate because so many people are on vacation.) The sweeps provide an estimate of the local TV audience, and advertisers use that information when they decide where to place their commercials.

Sweeps are the months when the ratings services gather their most important ratings, so the networks and local stations often use these important months to showcase their best programs. This is when you are most likely to see a special one-hour episode of a popular series, for example, or a very expensively produced made-for-TV movie.

Today's Nielsen ratings work essentially the same as they did in the 1950s, except that the Nielsen's now deliver very specific information on **demographics** —age, occupation and income, for instance. Advertisers use this information to target their most likely consumers. Nike shoes might choose to create a new advertising campaign for the NBA playoffs, for instance, and Nielsen could tell Nike, from judging previous championships, all about the people the company will reach with its ads.

Criticism about the ratings persists. The main flaw in the ratings today, critics contend, is the way the ratings are religiously followed and used by the broadcast community to determine programming.

sweeps the months when TV ratings services gather their most important ratings—February, May and November.

demographics personal characteristics of the audience, such as age, occupation and income.

TV DOMINATES THE AIRWAVES

The 1950s were a trial period for television, as the networks and advertisers tested audience interest in various types of programming. Captured by the miracle that television offered, audiences initially seemed insatiable; they would watch almost anything that TV delivered. But in the 1960s, audiences became more discriminating and began to question how well the medium of television was serving the public.

Newton Minow Targets TV as a "Vast Wasteland"

With television established even in the smaller cities, the medium needed a public conscience. That public conscience was Newton Minow.

An unassuming soothsayer, Minow was named chairman of the FCC in 1961 by newly elected President John F. Kennedy.

On May 9, 1961, speaking to the National Association of Broadcasters in his first public address since his appointment, Minow articulated what he felt were the broadcasters' responsibilities to the public.

> *Your license lets you use the public's airwaves as trustees for 180 million Americans. The public is your beneficiary. If you want to stay on as trustees, you must deliver a decent return to the public—not only to your stockholders....*
>
> *Your industry possesses the most powerful voice in America. It has an inescapable duty to make that voice ring with intelligence and with leadership. In a few years this exciting industry has grown from a novelty to an instrument of overwhelming impact on the American people. It should be making ready for the kind of leadership that newspapers and magazines assumed years ago, to make our people aware of their world.*
>
> *Ours has been called the jet age, the atomic age, the space age. It is also, I submit, the television age. And just as history will decide whether the leaders of today's world employed the atom to destroy the world or rebuild it for mankind's benefit, so will history decide whether today's broadcasters employed their powerful voice to enrich the people or debase them.*[8]

Minow then asked his audience of broadcast station owners and managers to watch their own programs. He said that they would find a "vast wasteland," a phrase that resurfaces today during any critical discussion of television.

PUBLIC TELEVISION FINDS AN AUDIENCE

The concept of educational television has been alive since the 1950s, when a few noncommercial stations succeeded in regularly presenting public service programs without advertisements. But the shows were low-budget and little national programming was done.

The educational network NET (National Educational Television) emerged in 1963 to provide some national programming (about ten hours a week), sponsored mainly by foundations, with some federal support. Then in 1967, the Ford Foundation agreed to help pay for several hours of live evening programming.

Also in 1967, the Carnegie Commission on Educational Television released its report *Public Television: A Program for Action*, which included a proposal to create the Corporation for Public Broadcasting. CPB would collect money from many sources—including the enhanced federal funds that the Carnegie report suggested—and disburse the money to the stations.

The Johnson administration and several foundations added money to CPB's budget. The Public Broadcasting Service (PBS) was created to distribute programs. The extra money underwrote the creation of programs like *Sesame Street* and *The French Chef*. PBS also began to buy successful British television programs, which were broadcast on *Masterpiece Theater*. PBS programs actually started to show up in the ratings.

Today, the Corporation for Public Broadcasting, which oversees public television, receives most of its funding from the federal government. Local funding supplements this government underwriting, but within the past ten years, donations to public television have been declining.

PBS has provided many memorable programs like *Sesame Street*, yet PBS commonly attracts less than 5 percent of the national audience. In 1995, members of Congress were calling for the "privatization" of public television.

Photofest

This decline in funding has led public broadcasters to seek underwriting from more corporate donors. But companies accustomed to advertising on commercial networks are reluctant to advertise on a network that commonly attracts less than 5 percent of the national audience. This means that, for the first time, public television is beginning to pay attention to ratings.

This attention to an audience of consumers means that the pressure is building on public television executives to make each program segment profitable. The FCC began "liberalizing" its rules for commercial announcements on public television in 1981. Now, corporate sponsors often make 10-second announcements, including graphics, at the beginning and the end of PBS-produced programs. These announcements often resemble advertisements on commercial television.

Critics of this "commercialization" of public television are calling for more government funding, but Congress has seemed unwilling to expand its underwriting. Today, public television is struggling to reinvent itself, but it still remains commercial television's stepchild.

SATELLITES BRING TECHNOLOGICAL BREAKTHROUGH

By 1965, all three networks were broadcasting in color. Television demonstrated its technological sophistication in December 1968 with its live broadcast from the *Apollo* spacecraft while the spacecraft circled the moon, and seven months later television showed Neil Armstrong stepping onto the moon.

On July 10, 1962, Telstar I sent the first trans-Atlantic satellite broadcast. Before Telstar, copper cable linked the continents, film footage from overseas traveled only by plane, and in most homes a long-distance telephone call was a special event.

Today, Telstar's descendants orbit at a distance of more than 22,000 miles. A single modern communication satellite can carry 30,000 telephone calls and three television channels. Modern satellites made CNN, Rupert Murdoch's Sky TV and DirecTV possible.

TV NEWS DOCUMENTS CONFLICT AND TRAGEDY

Just as radio matured, first as an entertainment medium and expanded to cover important news events, television first established itself with entertainment and then developed a serious news presence. Just as Franklin D. Roosevelt had been the first president to understand and use radio, John F. Kennedy became the country's first television president. Kennedy's predecessors had appeared on television, but he instinctively knew how to *use* television.

Observers credited Kennedy's 1960 presidential victory partly because of his success in the televised debates with Richard Nixon. Kennedy was the first president to hold live televised news conferences. In July 1962, he oversaw the launch of the first communications satellite, Telstar I. So it was fitting that he would be the first president to play Cold War brinks-manship on television, when TV grew to become a part of politics, not just a chronicler of political events.

TV and the Cold War

President Kennedy asked all three networks to clear him time on Monday, October 22, 1962 at 7 P.M. Eastern time. The president had learned that missile sites were being built in Cuba with Russian help.

Kennedy used television to deliver his ultimatum to dismantle the missile bases. "Using the word 'nuclear' eleven times, Kennedy drew a panorama of devastation enveloping the whole hemisphere. The moves that had made such things possible, said Kennedy, could not be accepted by the United States 'if our courage and our commitments are ever to be trusted again by either friend or foe.'"[9]

Kennedy admonished Russian Premier Nikita Khrushchev and urged him to stop the ships that the Soviet Union was sending to Cuba to help build the missile sites. Faced with such a visible challenge, the Soviet Union turned its ships around in the Atlantic and sent conciliatory messages in order to reach a settlement. The Cuban missile "crisis" had in fact been a carefully constructed live television drama, in which Kennedy performed well.

TV Covers the Kennedy Assassination

In 1963, television was forced into an unexpected role as it conveyed a sense of collective national experience following a presidential assassination. For four days beginning at 1:30 P.M. Eastern time on Friday, November 22, 1963, the country witnessed the aftermath of the assassination of President John F. Kennedy. Lyndon Johnson was sworn in as president. On Saturday, TV viewers watched the world's diplomats arrive for the funeral. On Sunday, they watched the first murder ever broadcast live on television, as Jack Ruby killed suspect Lee Harvey Oswald. Then, on Monday came the president's funeral.

As many as nine out of ten television sets were turned on during the marathon events surrounding President John Kennedy's funeral. The networks canceled all commercials. "Some television employees had slept as little as six hours in three nights. They went on, almost welcoming the absorption in the task at hand."[10]

They were called television's finest four days. "On the whole, television had won a degree of acceptance that must have exceeded the dreams of Sarnoff," writes Erik Barnouw. "For most people it had become their window on the world. The view it offered seemed to be *the* world. They trusted its validity and completeness."[11]

The Vietnam War

Soon after Kennedy's assassination, the longest-running protest program in the nation's history began appearing on television news, as anti-Vietnam War marchers showed up on camera daily. During live coverage of the Chicago Democratic Convention in 1968, demonstrators faced police in a march toward the convention hall. Television covered the resulting violence, which caused injuries to hundreds of protesters and to 21 reporters and photographers.

> *When the war in Vietnam began to escalate in 1965, it was the television networks, covering the war with few official restrictions, that brought to American homes pictures of the face of war that had never been shown before: not friendly troops welcomed by the populace, but troops setting fire to villages with cigarette lighters; troops cutting off the ears of dead combat foes; allies spending American tax money for personal gain.* [12]

Candid reporting from the war itself shook viewers as previous war reporting never had.

TELEVISION CHANGES NATIONAL POLITICS

Television received credit for uniting the nation, but it also was blamed for dividing it. President Lyndon Johnson, beleaguered by an unpopular war, used television to announce in 1968 that he would not run for a second term. His successor, President Richard Nixon, had always been uncomfortable with the press and, under the Nixon administration, the press was attacked for presenting perspectives on world affairs that the Nixon administration did not like. Upset with the messages being presented, the Nixon administration battled the messenger, sparking a bitter public debate about the role of a free press (especially television) in a democratic society.

Ironically, television's next live marathon broadcast would chronicle an investigation of the Nixon presidency—Watergate. The Watergate scandal began when burglars broke into the offices of the Democratic party's national headquarters in the Watergate complex in Washington, D.C., on June 17, 1972. Some of the burglars had ties to President Nixon's reelection committee as well as to other questionable activities originating in the White House. In the following months, the president and his assistants sought to squelch the resulting investigation. Although Nixon denied knowledge of the break-in and the cover-up, the Senate hearings on the scandal, televised live across the country, created a national sensation.

> *Running from May through August 1973, and chaired by North Carolina's crusty Sam Ervin, these hearings were a fascinating live exposition of the political process in America, and were "must" television watching as a parade of witnesses told—or evaded telling—what they knew of the broad conspiracy to assure the reelection of Nixon and then to cover up the conspiracy itself.* [13]

For more than a year the political drama continued to unfold on television's nightly news. Ultimately the Judiciary Committee of the House of Representatives began a televised debate on whether to impeach the president. For the first time in its history, the nation faced the prospect of seeing a president brought to trial live on national television. On August 8, 1974, President Nixon brought the crisis to an end by announcing his resignation—on television.

In 1987, television repeated its marathon coverage of an important national investigation with the Iran-contra hearings, a congressional investigation of the Reagan administration's role in providing weapons illegally to Nicaraguan rebels, called contras.

In 1997, TV became an international window on grief when the networks carried nonstop coverage of the events surrounding the death and funeral of Diana, Princess of Wales.

Television news has matured from its early beginnings as a 15-minute newscast to today's access to 24-hour coverage of significant news events. Today, network television news continues to play an important role in setting the agenda for discussion of public issues.

WORKING IN TELEVISION

A typical television station has eight departments: sales, programming (which includes news as well as entertainment), production, engineering, traffic, promotion, public affairs and administration.

People in the *sales* department sell the commercial slots for the programs. Advertising is divided into *national* and *local* sales. Advertising agencies, usually based on the East Coast, buy national ads for the products they handle.

Ford Motor Company, for instance, may buy time on a network for a TV ad that will run simultaneously all over the country. But the local Ford dealers, who want you to shop at their showrooms, buy their ads directly from the local station. These ads are called local (or spot) ads. For these sales, salespeople (called account executives) at each station negotiate packages of ads based on their station's rates. These rates are a direct reflection of that station's position in the ratings.

In 1997, television became an international window on grief when the networks broadcast the live coverage of the funeral of Diana, Princess of Whales.

Agence France Presse/CORBIS Bettmann

The *programming* department selects the shows that you will see and develops the station's schedule. Network-owned stations, located in big cities (KNBC in Los Angeles, for example), are called **O & Os,** which stands for owned and operated. Stations that carry network programming but that are not owned by the networks are called affiliates (see Chapter 1).

O & Os automatically carry network programming, but affiliates are paid by the network to carry its programming, for which the network sells most of the ads and keeps the money. The affiliate is allowed to insert into the network programming a specific number of local ads, for which the affiliate keeps the money.

Because affiliates can make money on network programming, and don't have to pay for it, many stations choose to affiliate themselves with a network. When they aren't running what the network provides, affiliates run their own programs and keep all of the advertising money they collect from them.

More than one-third of the nation's commercial TV stations operate as independents. Independent stations must buy and program all of their own shows, but independents also can keep all of the money they make on advertising. They run some individually produced programs and old movies, but most of their programming consists of reruns that once ran on the networks. Independents buy these reruns from program services called **syndicators.**

Syndicators also sell independently produced programs such as *The Oprah Winfrey Show* and *Wheel of Fortune.* These programs are created and sold either by nonnetwork stations or by independent producers. Stations pay for these first-run syndication programs individually; the price is based on the size of the station's market.

Local news usually makes up the largest percentage of a station's locally produced programming. In some large markets, such as Los Angeles, local news programming runs as long as three hours.

The *production* department manages the programs that the station creates in-house. This department also produces local commercials for the station.

The *engineering* department makes sure that all of the technical aspects of a broadcast operation are working: antennas, transmitters, cameras and any other broadcast equipment.

The *traffic* department integrates the advertising with the programming, making sure that all of the ads that are sold are aired when they're supposed to be. Traffic also handles billing for the ads.

The *promotion* department advertises the station—on the station itself, on billboards, on radio and in the local newspaper. These people also create contests to keep the station visible in the community.

The *public affairs* department often helps organize public events, such as a fun run to raise money for the local hospital.

Administration handles the paperwork for the station—paychecks and expense accounts, for example.

O & Os TV stations that are owned and operated by the networks.

syndicators services that sell programming to broadcast stations and cable.

THE BUSINESS OF TELEVISION

Today's most-watched television programs are situation comedies, sports and feature movies. More than 100 million households tuned in for the final episode of the situation comedy *Cheers* in 1993, making it the highest-rated television program ever. Super Bowls generally grab nearly half of the homes in the United States.

Five developments promise to affect the development of the television industry over the next decade: station ownership changes, the shrinking

IMPACT

point of view

Why TV Networks Are Still Worth Buying

Micheal J. Wolf
THE WALL STREET JOURNAL

When Viacom announced its plans to merge with CBS, the big entertainment company was tipping its hat to the tremendous value that still exists in network television. Yes, network audiences are declining, even as the numbers of TV households rises. Yes, a lot of highly targeted networks have emerged with the help of cable and satellite television. And yes, the Internet is creating new channels and vast entertainment alternatives, all competing for viewers' limited attention.

But rather than spelling the end of network television, these trends have made the mass audiences and big-event buzz that CBS, NBC, ABC, and Fox can deliver to advertisers more valuable than ever.

Declining Audiences

At first glance, the numbers suggest the opposite. When NBC aired its final *Seinfeld* episode last year, 76.3 million viewers tuned in. Yet when *M*A*S*H* said goodbye in 1983, it grabbed a tube-burning audience of 106 million.

The final episode of *Cheers*, with 80.5 million viewers, also beat *Seinfeld*. This drop-off in network audiences took place even as the number of TV households grew to 99 million last year from 83.3 million in 1983. The combined audience share of NBC, CBS, and ABC stands below 40 percent today; it was 56 percent in 1990. Cable now captures 40 percent of the overall TV audience.

Yet the three networks still bring in almost double the total advertising revenue of cable. Why? A fragmenting media market has made mass audiences harder and harder to reach, and

Mel Karmazin and Sumner Redstone: The CBS-Viacom merger is the latest sign that big media companies know only networks can reach a mass audience.

© Ismael Roldan

role of the networks, the accuracy of ratings, the growth of cable and changing technology.

Station Ownership Changes and Mergers

The Telecommunications Act of 1996 (see Chapter 14) uses a station's potential audience to measure ownership limits. The Act allows one company to own TV stations that reach up to 35 percent of the nation's homes. Broadcasters also are no longer required, as they once were, to hold a station for three years before selling it. Today, stations may be sold as soon as they are purchased.

In 1999, the FCC adopted new regulations that allow media companies to own two TV stations in the market, as long as eight separately owned TV stations continue to operate in that market after the merger. The four top-rated stations in one market cannot be combined, but a station that is among the top-rated four could combine with one that is not in the top four.

the networks offer an unparalleled platform to reach those audiences through their prime-time programming. At the same time, big television events—the Olympics, the Academy Awards, the Super Bowl, network movie premieres like *Titanic*—are very hard to replicate. They generate a level of excitement that brings a cachet to brands well beyond mere audience share.

The price of a 30-second Super Bowl spot has climbed 60 percent, to $1.6 million, since 1995, and there are certain advertisers we see again and again, such as Pepsi, General Motors, Budweiser, and Visa. Network television remains squarely at the center of the pitched battle for consumers' attention.

While the mass market is becoming more valuable, so are targeted audiences. This can be seen in the tremendous shareholder value and new audiences that specialized cable and satellite networks are creating. The ability to reach teenagers, women or Wall Street investors is crucial to many advertisers. A quick glance at the media plans of many major advertisers make this abundantly clear. CNBC, TV Food Network, CNN, Nickelodeon, Lifetime, MTV, ESPN—all reach potentially lucrative groups of consumers in an efficient way. The amount advertisers are willing to pay for these outlets is growing even faster than network ad rates are increasing.

The answer for the big media and entertainment companies is a mix of both mass-market and targeted vehicles, as well as the integration of these operations with their affiliated stations and Web outlets. A good example of this is the model created by NBC and its sister cable-news networks, CNBC and MSNBC. Combine this with the ability to marry integrated distribution—including, today, the all-important Internet—with valuable programming, and you have a formidable combination. Recently announced deals to trade advertising inventory for stakes in Web portals further highlight this point.

Players in the media and entertainment world know that their industry is fraught with risk—and so is network television. While the big-event programming that networks provide is winning greater and greater premiums from advertisers, this cannot go on forever.

And unless the entertainment companies that own major broadcast networks continue to assemble a powerful collection of targeted cable networks, as well as effective Internet distribution, they will fail to take full advantage of the broadcast networks' greatest assets.

Wolf is the senior partner of the Media and Entertainment Group at Booz-Allen & Hamilton and author of The Entertainment Economy: How Mega-Media Forces Are Transforming Our Lives *(Times Books, 1999).*

The Wall Street Journal, September 8, 1999, A-26. Reprinted by Permission.

About 100 of the nation's TV markets have eight or more separately owned stations. "I think [the rule change] is going to change television," said USA Networks Chairman Barry Diller, whose company owns 13 stations. "It opens up so many options...from buying to partnering to selling to combining."[14]

The relaxation of these ownership rules means that the major characteristics of the television business today are changing and merging ownerships. Television is *concentrating* ownership, but it is also *shifting* ownership, as stations are bought and sold at an unprecedented rate. This has introduced instability and change to an industry that until 1980 witnessed very few ownership turnovers.

The Networks' Shrinking Role

Advertisers always have provided the economic support for television, so in 1986 the networks were disturbed to see the first decline in revenues in 15 years. New and continuing developments—such as cable, satellite broadcast and VCRs—have turned the television set into a smorgasbord of choices. The audience—and advertisers—are deserting the networks, and network ratings are declining as a result. Because there are so many new sources of information and entertainment for the audience, advertisers are looking for new ways to capture viewers.

The network share of the *prime-time audience* has gone from 90 percent in 1978 to about 58 percent today, reflecting the continued growth of independent TV stations, syndicated programming, satellite and cable systems. The networks' share of the audience for the evening news also is shrinking.

The story is a familiar one, paralleling radio in the late 1940s when it first was supplanted by television and then began competing with itself. More stations and more sources of programming mean that the networks will have to redefine their audience and give the audience what it cannot get elsewhere.

How Accurate Are TV Ratings?

People meters, first used in 1987 by the A. C. Nielsen Company to record television viewing, gather data through a 4-inch by 10-inch box that sits on the television set in metered homes. People meters monitor the nation's Nielsen families (about 4,000 of them), and the results of these recorded viewing patterns (which Nielsen says reflect a cross section of American viewers) sets the basis for television advertising rates.

Nielsen family members each punch in an assigned button on top of the set when they begin to watch television. The system's central computer, linked to the home by telephone lines, correlates each viewer's number with information about that person stored in its memory. Network ratings have plunged since people meters were introduced as a ratings system, and the networks have complained that the new measuring device underestimates viewership.

In 1994, frustrated with the slowness of the Nielsen company to deliver a new measurement system, NBC, ABC and CBS set up their own experimental ratings system, announcing a plan to establish a separate ratings service by the year 2000.

Cable Challenges Broadcast

Today's cable giants, ESPN (Entertainment & Sports Programming Network) and TNT (Turner Network Television), are descendants of America's first cable TV system, which was established in Pennsylvania and Oregon to bring TV signals to rural areas that couldn't receive an over-the-air signal. Soon, this community-antenna television (CATV) system spread to remote areas all over the country where TV reception was poor.

By 1970, there were 2,500 CATV systems in the United States, and commercial broadcasters were getting nervous about what they called wired TV. Cable operators were required by the FCC to carry all local broadcast programming, and programs often were duplicated on several channels. The FCC also limited the programs that cable could carry. One FCC ruling, for example, said that movies on cable had to be at least ten years old.

Believing that cable should be able to offer its own programming, Home Box Office (owned by Time Warner) started operating in Manhattan in 1972, offering a modest set of programs. Ted Turner's TNT first relayed programs by

Fees paid by the TV networks fund most of the cost of professional sports in the United States.

AP/World Wide Photos

satellite in 1976, and in 1979 Turner started Cable News Network (CNN). Today, more than 200 different program services, ranging from the frantic sounds of Music Television (MTV) to classic 1930s and 1940s movies on Arts & Entertainment (A&E), are available by satellite. About 60 percent of the homes in America have basic cable.

Cable television as an alternative to the traditional networks moved to the center of the national news agenda in 1991 when CNN offered 24-hour coverage of the Gulf War in Iraq. CNN's fast response to world events underlined the new global role that CNN, and many other cable companies, will play in future television developments.

TV Changes Professional Sports

The single most profitable type of television programming is sports. In 1964, CBS paid $28 million for television rights to the 1964–65 National Football League (NFL) games. In 1990, the price paid for rights to broadcast NFL football totaled $3.6 billion.[15]

Television fees fund most of the cost of organized sports. Televised sports has become spectacularly complex entertainment packaging, turning athletes as well as sports commentators into media stars. The expansion of sports programming beyond the networks to cable channels such as ESPN means even more sports programming choices for viewers, and more money for American sports teams.

IMPACT

digital

So What Exactly Is Digital Television?

**By Bryan Gruley
and Kyle Pope**

Circuit City salesman shows a captivated crowd advantages of digital TV.

Carlos Avila Gonzalez/San Francisco Chronicle

With the federal government about to issue the country's first licenses for digital television, the question is: Should consumers care?

Digital TVs, hailed as the biggest thing to hit broadcasting since color TV, will offer movie-quality pictures and the sharp sound of compact disks. But so far, consumers have reacted with a yawn.... Here's what consumers may want to know.

What's Different about Digital TV?

Broadcasters will be able to send more data over the airwaves using a digital signal that can handle more information. That produces a more detailed picture, with clearer images, brighter colors and sharper sound. The sets themselves will be flatter, like the screens at movie theaters....

Sports fans especially will appreciate the wider angle and zippier images of high-definition TV. Imagine, for instance, a close-up of a quarterback that includes a much wider view of the field around him and the coaches on the sidelines....

A basketball game, for instance, could be accompanied by a stream of data containing team statistics and player bios, called up at a viewer's whim.

How Much Will Digital Sets Cost?

TV makers estimate the earliest sets will be available...at a starting price of about $2,500, making them a likely purchase only for gadget freaks and videophiles. But digital-set prices are expected to tumble as more people buy sets and makers cut manufacturing costs....

Must I Buy a New TV Set?

Not for a long time. Local stations will continue to broadcast their current analog signals for as long as another decade while they launch the digital service. While current TVs can't receive a digital signal, you will be able to buy a converter box, which will cost $100 to $200 and look like the boxes provided by cable operators....

Will I Still Be Able to Get Cable or Satellite-Dish Service?

Yes, without any noticeable difference. Digital TV sets will enhance reception for satellite customers, because satellite carriers already broadcast in digital.

That will also be true for cable customers as the cable industry converts to a digital feed over the next several years.

Will I Still Be Able to Watch My Favorite Old Programs?

Yes, all the programs in the networks' current libraries will be reformatted for the digital standard. Some shows, like movies and some filmed dramas shot in high-quality film, already work digitally.

Production of other programs, though, will have to be completely revamped to comply with the digital standard. News and sports programming, for instance, will require new sets, new cameras and even new makeup to look right on a sharper digital screen.

TECHNOLOGY AND THE FUTURE

When technological developments move like a rocket, as they have in the past decade, program delivery becomes easier and less expensive. New technologies have brought more competition.

Significant Technological Developments

Several new delivery systems have been developed to bring increasingly more choices to consumers. Some of the most important recent technological developments are described here.

Digital Video Recorders (DVRs). DVRs can download programming, using a device called a "set-top box" (which looks much like today's cable boxes and sits on or near the TV).

Scheduled to be introduced in fall 1999, DVRs use hard-drive computer storage to receive information from any program service (including the broadcast networks, satellite and cable programmers) to send viewers up-to-date information about what's on TV. DVRs transfer the information to an on-screen program guide, where viewers can decide what to watch and when, a practice called **time-shifting**. One of the biggest features of a DVR is that it allows viewers to hit the "pause" button for a show they're watching, leave the TV set on, and then start up the program again when they return, or fast-forward through the recorded portion.

Because DVRs could change viewers' control over which programming they watch (and, most importantly, which commercials), all of the major TV networks have invested in the companies that are producing this technology. The networks want to be able to influence what consumers can record and when, but the value of total viewer control is one of DVRs' most attractive features for consumers.

Web Television. The first adaptation of traditional TV sets as a consumer appliance for using the Internet was announced in 1997 as Web TV. This service allows a consumer to use an existing TV set like a computer by connecting through telephone lines. Then, using an expanded keypad similar to a remote control, the user can direct the Internet activity from across the room. The remote control works through a set-up box, which translates the computer signal so it can be viewed on the TV screen.

Enhanced Television. Another development using traditional broadcast television technology to give consumers online access is enhanced television, announced late in 1997. Enhanced television merges information from the World Wide Web and television programs on one screen. This technology allows someone to watch a football game as it's happening and, at the same time, follow a discussion about the game taking place in a web-based chat session on a separate portion of the screen. To use the new technology, consumers will have to buy a decoder device that attaches to the TV set.

High-Definition Television (HDTV). A normal television picture scans 525 lines across the screen. **High-definition television (HDTV)** scans 1,125 lines. CBS first demonstrated HDTV in the United States in 1982. HDTV, which would mean a wider, sharper picture and better sound, is waiting for a practical method to transmit the higher-resolution picture, because it requires more spectrum space than conventional television signals. HDTV is already in

time-shifting recording a television program on a DVR or VCR to watch at a more convenient time.

high-definition television (HDTV) a type of television that provides a picture with a clearer resolution than on normal TV sets.

use in Japan but has not been very successful, mainly because HDTV sets are priced at the equivalent of $3,000.

Direct Broadcast Satellites. The FCC authorized DBS in 1982, making direct-to-home satellite broadcasts possible. In 1994, two companies called DirecTV and DSS (Digital Satellite System) began offering services directly to the home by satellite. Subscribers pay about $300 for a miniaturized 18-inch dish, and, for a monthly fee, DirecTV provides access to 70 different *worldwide* channels, with a promise of 150 channels in the future. The monthly fee is about the same cost as, or cheaper than, a monthly cable bill. The main advantages are access to worldwide programming at a reasonable cost and the elimination of the set-top box. The main disadvantage is that this satellite service offers only national and global programming; local stations are not on the satellite service yet. So subscribers who want to receive local channels must use a separate antenna.

Forecasting the Future: A *Telepresence?*

Forecasts for the future of television parallel the forecasts for radio—a menu board of hundreds of programs and services available to viewers at the touch of a remote-control button. In the 1990s, several regional telephone companies (called **telcos**) rushed to merge with cable TV companies to form giant telecommunications delivery systems. "Cable TV companies and telephone companies are joining forces because each has something valuable that the other wants," reports the *Los Angeles Times*.

> **telcos** an abbreviation for telephone companies.

"Telephone companies have wired virtually every household in their service area and want to deliver the wide variety of program and information services controlled by the cable companies," says the *Times*. "The cable operators, on the other hand, want to use their cable TV wires to go into the phone business, delivering voice, data and video over...fiber-optic lines."[16]

The result of these mergers will be that some new financial media powerhouses will have the ability to invest large sums of money in research and expansion for developing technologies with vast potential, such as fiber optics.

Fiber optics, which allows the transmission of huge amounts of data using clear glass strands as thin as a human hair, forms the basis for many of today's cable systems, and fiber optics could change television dramatically.

Imagine your television as an artificial reality machine. This machine, says *The Wall Street Journal*, would use "remarkably crisp pictures and sound to 'deliver' a viewer to a pristine tropical beach, to a big football game or to a quiet mountaintop retreat. Japanese researchers envision golfers practicing their swings in front of three-dimensional simulations of courses."[17]

The definition of television today is expanding faster than our ability to chronicle the changes. Lanny Smoot, an executive at Bell Communications Research, calls the future of television a *telepresence*. "This," he says, "is a wave that is not possible to stop."[18]

IN FOCUS

■ The word *television*, which once meant programs delivered by antennas through over-the-air signals, today means a television screen, where a variety of delivery systems brings viewers a diversity of programs.

■ About 1,500 television stations operate in the United States. Three out of four of these are commercial stations and more than half of U.S. stations are affiliated with a network.

■ More than any other media industry today, commercial television exists primarily as an advertising medium.

■ Guglielmo Marconi put sound on airwaves. Lee de Forest invented the Audion tube. Vladimir Zworykin turned an electronic signal into a visual image. Philo T. Farnsworth added the electronic scanner.

■ The rivalry between David Sarnoff (RCA) and William S. Paley (CBS) is central to the early history of television. The ABC network was formed when the FCC ordered Sarnoff to sell one of his two networks (Red and Blue). The Blue network became ABC.

■ The first television news broadcasts were primitive compared to today's broadcasts. At that time, television news, like radio news, developed its own standard of excellence, led by news pioneers David Brinkley and Edward R. Murrow.

■ Most of television entertainment programming was derived from radio. The only type of program that didn't come from radio was the talk show. The situation comedy proved to be one of television's most durable types of programming.

■ The 1950s quiz show scandals caused the networks to eliminate advertiser-produced programming.

■ In the 1960s, audiences grew more discriminating and began to question how well the medium of television was serving the public. An influential spokesperson for these views was FCC Chairman Newton Minow, who coined the phrase "vast wasteland" to describe television.

■ As TV's news capability matured, it helped create national experiences, but TV also drew criticism for the way it was perceived to influence politics and the dialogue about national issues.

■ Many groups are concerned that, because of its pervasiveness, television influences the nation's values, habits and behavior.

■ The Nielsen ratings determine the price that TV advertisers pay to air their commercials. Nielsen introduced people meters in 1987. The company promises passive audience measurement before the year 2000.

■ Deregulation, with relaxed ownership rules, means that instability, mergers, and change have become a major characteristic of the television industry today.

■ Today, traditional network audiences are shrinking, as more stations are licensed to broadcast and as rapidly changing technology competes for TV audiences.

■ More than 200 program services now offer alternatives to network programming.

■ Televised sports are television's second biggest moneymaker after prime-time programming, and television fees fund most of the cost of the nation's organized sports.

■ Several technological developments are changing the way programs are delivered to consumers: digital video recorders (DVRs), web television, enhanced television, high-definition television (HDTV), and direct broad-cast satellites (DBS).

■ In the 1990s, telephone companies joined cable TV companies to form giant telecommunications delivery systems. The result will be some new financial powerhouses with the ability to invest large sums of money in research and expansion for fiber optics. One researcher has defined the new world of television as a *telepresence*.

■ Digital television offers better pictures, clearer sound and a flatter screen than traditional TV. Digital TV will make it easier for manufacturers to combine the functions of TV and the functions of a computer in the same TV set.

WORKING THE WEB www

■ **CNN Audioselect (audio tracks of all CNN channels)**
www.cnn.com/audioselect/

■ **David Letterman**
www.cbs.com/lateshow

■ **PBS**
www/pbs.org/Welcome.html

■ **The Tonight Show**
www.nbctonightshow.com

■ **Vernon Stone's University of Missouri Broadcasting Employment Website**
web.missouri.edu/~jourvs/indix.html

INFOTRAC COLLEGE EDITION EXERCISES

Using InfoTrac College Edition, a fully searchable online database of articles and abstracts, do the following exercises as directed by your instructor.

1. Read "Digital/Impact Technology: So What Exactly is Digital TV?" in Chapter 7. Then using the key words "HDTV" or "digital TV," choose one article from the list of citations on InfoTrac College Edition. Write a brief summary of the article (no more than 300 words) and include some discussion of whether you think HDTV will gain popu-lar support. Be sure to sum up the article's major points or conclu-sions in your overview.

2 Choose two or three other students in class to make up a small group. Then choose one of the following TV personalities:

    1. Edward R. Murrow

    2. Lucille Ball (or "I Love Lucy")

    3. David Brinkley

    4. Flip Wilson

    5. Milton Berle

    6. Ed Sullivan

    7. David Sarnoff

    8. Bill Cosby

Using InfoTrac College Edition, look up information on your group's TV personality. Prepare a three-page report on your group's personality and present it to the class.

3. Read "Impact on You: Viewers Identify With TV Characters" in Chapter 7 and then search for articles on InfoTrac College Edition using the key words "Television-comedies" or the name of one of your favorite TV shows—"Television-Third Rock" or "Television-Friends," for example. Either:

   a. write a brief paper on your findings, or

   b. give a brief presentation in class.

4. Look up the key words "Nielsen Media Research" on InfoTrac College Edition and read at least three articles to get a sense of the current issues facing the ratings service. Then print at least one article and bring it to class for discussion.

5. Look up the key words "Public Television" using InfoTrac College Edition and find articles about PBS's ongoing struggle with issues of government funding and seeking funding from corporate donors. Then break into small groups to discuss the pros and cons of having more corporate donors making 10-second announcements before and after programs. Consider: Does this "commercialization" dilute the quality or credibility of public television? Each group should share its conclusions with the class.

Movies

GODZILLA
BULWORTH
QUEST FOR CAMELOT
DEEP IMPACT
GODZILLA   PG 13
CLOCKWATCHERS   PG 13
HORSE WHISPERER   PG 13

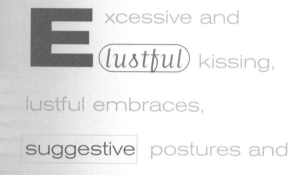

E xcessive and (*lustful*) kissing, lustful embraces, suggestive postures and gestures are not to be shown.

Motion Picture Production Code, 1930

"I n no other business is a single example of product fully created at an investment of millions of dollars with no real assurance that the public will buy it. In no other business does the public 'use' the product and then take away with them...merely the memory of it. In the truest sense, it's an industry based on dreams."[1]

It would be easy to assume that the movie industry is one of the biggest media industries because the publicity surrounding movie celebrities captures a great deal of attention. It is often surprising to learn that the movie industry accounts for a smaller amount of media industries income than newspapers, television or books.

Movies and movie stars need the public's attention because the audience determines whether or not movies succeed. Movies are very costly investments, and most movies lose money. Investors, therefore, often favor "bankable" talent that will bring a following to a movie, rather than new talent that is untested. Yet even movies featuring established talent can fail; no one in the movie industry can accurately predict which movies will be hits.

Writes film scholar Jason E. Squire:

> *At its simplest, the feature film is the shuffling of light images to win hearts in dark rooms. At its most complex, it is a massive venture of commerce, a vast creative enterprise requiring the logistical discipline of the military, the financial foreshadowing of the Federal Reserve, and the psychological tolerance of the clergy, all harnessed in private hands on behalf of the telling of a story. In the commercial movie industry, the idea is to make movies that attract vast audiences who cumulatively pay enough money for the privilege so that all the costs involved in making that movie are recouped, with enough left over to make more movies. The profit motive is at work here, but the formula that attracts audiences is as elusive as can be.[2]*

Movies mirror the society that creates them. Some movies offer an underlying political message. Other movies reflect changing social values. Still other movies are just good entertainment. But all movies need an audience to succeed.

Like other media industries, the movie industry has had to adapt to changing technology. Before the invention of television, movies were the nation's primary form of visual entertainment. Today, the use of special effects—something you seldom get from television—is one way the movie industry competes with television for your attention and dollars. But special effects don't fit every movie, and they are very expensive. Today, the economics of moviemaking is very important.

CAPTURING MOTION ON FILM: HOW MOVIES BEGAN

Movies were invented at a time when American industry welcomed any new gadget, and inventors wildly sought patents on appliances and electrical devices. The motion picture camera and projector were two of the Industrial Revolution's new gadgets.

Early Inventors Nurture the Movie Industry

Movies were not the invention of one person. First, a device to photograph moving objects had to be invented and then a device to project those pictures. This process involved six people: Étienne Jules Marey, Eadweard Muybridge, Thomas Edison, William K. L. Dickson, and Auguste and Louis Lumière.

Marey and Muybridge. Étienne Jules Marey, a scientist working in Paris, sought to record an animal's movement by individual actions—one at a time—to compare one animal to another. He charted a horse's movements on graphs and published the information in a book, *Animal Mechanism*.

Unknown to Marey, photographer Eadweard Muybridge was hired by railroad millionaire and horse breeder Leland Stanford to settle a $25,000 bet. Stanford had bet that during a trot, all four of a horse's feet simultaneously leave the ground. In 1877, Muybridge and Stanford built a special track in Palo Alto, California, with 12 cameras precisely placed to take pictures of a horse as it moved around the track. The horse tripped a series of equidistant wires as it ran, which in turn tripped the cameras' shutters. Stanford won his $25,000—one photograph showed that all four of the horse's feet did leave the ground—and the photographic series provided an excellent study of motion.

This woman in motion is one of the early images photographed by Eadweard Muybridge.

Bettmann/CORBIS

Muybridge expanded to 24 cameras, photographed other animals, and then took pictures of people moving. He traveled throughout Europe showing his photographs. Eventually, Muybridge and Marey met. In 1882, Marey perfected a photographic gun camera that could take 12 photographs on one plate—the first motion picture camera. [3]

Thomas Edison. Thomas Edison bought some of Muybridge's pictures in 1888 and showed them to his assistant, William K. L. Dickson. Edison then met with Marey in Europe, where Marey had invented a projector that showed pictures on a continuous strip of film. But the strip film moved unevenly across the projector lens, so the pictures jumped.

William K. L. Dickson. Back in America, Dickson perforated the edges of the film so that, as the film moved through the camera, sprockets inside the camera grabbed the perforations and locked the film in place, minimizing the jumps. Dickson looped the strip over a lamp and a magnifying lens in a box 2 feet wide and 4 feet tall. The box stood on the floor with a peephole in the top so people could look inside. Edison named this device the kinetoscope.

On April 11, 1894, America's first kinetoscope parlor opened in New York City. For 25 cents, people could see ten different 90-second black-and-white films, including "Trapeze," "Horse Shoeing," "Wrestlers," and "Roosters."

Auguste and Louis Lumière. In France, the Lumière brothers, Auguste and Louis, developed an improved camera and a projector that could show film on a large screen. The first public Lumière showing was on December 28, 1895: ten short subjects with such riveting titles as "Lunch Hour at the Lumière Factory," which showed workers leaving the building, and "Arrival of a Train at a Station." Admission was 1 franc and the Lumières collected 35 francs.[4]

Edison Launches American Movies

Four months after the Lumière premiere in France, Edison organized the first American motion picture premiere with an improved camera developed by independent inventor Thomas Armat. Edison dubbed the new machine the Vitascope, and America's first public showing of the motion picture was on April 23, 1896, at Koster and Bial's theater in New York. Edison sat in a box seat and Armat ran the projector from the balcony.

At first, movies were a sideshow. Penny arcade owners showed movies behind a black screen at the rear of the arcade for an extra *nickel*. But soon the movies were more popular than the rest of the attractions, and the arcades were renamed *nickel*odeons.

T I M E F R A M E

Today to 1877: Movies mature as a popular medium

TODAY   Movie theaters collect about one billion tickets a year, but more people see movies on video than in a movie theater.

1994   Steven Spielberg, Jeffrey Katzenberg and David Geffen launched DreamWorks SKG, the first new movie studio created in the United States since United Artists.

1966   The Motion Picture Producers Association (MPPA) introduces a voluntary content ratings system for the movies.

1948   The U.S. Supreme Court breaks up the large studios' control of Hollywood by deciding in the case of *United States* v. *Paramount* that the studios are a monopoly.

1947   The Hollywood Ten are called to testify before the House Un-American Activities Committee.

1930   The Motion Picture Producers and Distributors Association (MPPDA) adopts a production code to control movie content.

1927   *The Jazz Singer* opens in New York, the first feature-length motion picture with sound.

1916   Brothers Noble and George Johnson launch Lincoln Films, the first company to produce serious narrative movies for African-American audiences, which are called race films.

1915   Director D. W. Griffith introduces the concept of the movie spectacular with *The Birth of a Nation*.

1877   Eadweard Muybridge catches motion on film when he uses 12 cameras to photograph a horse's movements for Leland Stanford in Palo Alto, California.

Decorative Oscar statues delivered to the Dorothy Chandler Pavilion in Los Angeles for the Academy Award ceremonies.

AP/Wide World Photos

In 1900, there were more than 600 nickelodeons in New York City, with more than 300,000 daily admissions.[5] Each show lasted about 20 minutes. The programs ran from noon until late evening, and many theaters blared music outside to bring in business.

By 1907, Edison had contracted with most of the nation's movie producers, as well as the Lumière brothers and the innovative French producer Georges Méliès, to provide movies for the theaters. Licensed Edison theaters used licensed Edison projectors and rented Edison's licensed movies, many of which Edison produced at his own studio.

The important exception to Edison's licensing plan was his rival, the American Biograph and Mutoscope Company, commonly called Biograph. Biograph manufactured a better motion picture camera than Edison's, and Edison was losing business. In 1908, Biograph signed an agreement with Edison, forming the Motion Picture Patents Company (MPPC).

Licensed exhibitors paid $2 a week to MPPC, and any distributor or exhibitor who violated the agreement by handling independent films was banned from the MPPC. The MPPC collected more than $1 million the first year, with Edison receiving most of the royalties.[6] Thomas Edison thus established the first motion picture trust, which gave him a virtual monopoly on the movie business.

Novelty Becomes Art

All of the early films were black-and-white silents. Sound was not introduced to the movies until the 1920s, and color experiments did not begin until the 1930s. Two innovative filmmakers are credited with turning the novelty of movies into art: Georges Méliès and Edwin S. Porter.

Georges Méliès. French filmmaker Georges Méliès added fantasy to the movies. Before Méliès, moviemakers photographed theatrical scenes or events from everyday life. But Méliès, who was a magician and a caricaturist before he became a filmmaker, used camera tricks to make people disappear and reappear and to make characters grow and then shrink. His 1902 film, *A Trip to the Moon,* was the first outer-space movie adventure, complete with fantasy creatures. When his films, which became known as trick films, were shown in the United States, American moviemakers stole his ideas.

Edwin S. Porter. Edison hired projectionist/electrician Edwin S. Porter in 1899, and in the next decade Porter became America's most important filmmaker. Until Porter, most American films were trick films or short documentary-style movies that showed newsworthy events (although some filmmakers used titillating subjects in movies such as *Pajama Girl* and *Corset Girl* to cater to men, who were the movies' biggest fans). In 1903, Porter produced *The Great Train Robbery,* an action movie with bandits attacking a speeding train.

Instead of using a single location like most other moviemakers, Porter shot 12 different scenes. He also introduced the use of dissolves between shots, instead of abrupt splices. Porter's film techniques—action and changing locations—foreshadowed the classic storytelling tradition of American movies.

The Studio System Is Born

None of the players in the early movies received screen credit, but then fans began to write letters to Biograph star Florence Lawrence addressed to "The Biograph Girl." In 1909, Carl Laemmle formed an independent production company, stole Florence Lawrence from Biograph and gave her screen credit. She became America's first movie star.

Biograph was the first company to make movies using the studio system. The **studio system** meant that a studio hired a stable of stars and production people who were paid a regular salary. These people were then under con-tract to that studio and could not work for any other studio without their employer's permission.

In 1910, Laemmle lured Mary Pickford away from Biograph by doubling her salary. He discovered, says film scholar Robert Sklar, "that stars sold pictures as nothing else could. As long as theaters changed their programs daily—and the practice persisted in neighborhood theaters and small towns until the early 1920s—building up audience recognition of star names was almost the only effective form of audience publicity." [7]

The star system, which promoted popular movie personalities to lure audiences, was nurtured by the independents. This helped broaden the movies' appeal beyond the working class. Movie houses began to show up in

George Méliès created these fanciful creatures for his 1902 movie, *A Trip to the Moon,* introducing fantasy to motion pictures.

Courtesy of the Academy of Motion Picture Arts and Sciences

studio system an early method of hiring a stable of salaried stars and production people under exclusive contracts.

the suburbs. In 1914, President Woodrow Wilson and his family watched a popular movie at the White House. From 1908 to 1914, movie attendance doubled.[8]

D. W. Griffith Introduces the Spectacular

In 1915, the first real titan of the silent movies, director D. W. Griffith, introduced the concept of spectacular entertainment. His movies were so ambitious, so immense, that no one could ignore them.

Most early movies were two reels long, 25 minutes. At first Griffith made two-reelers, but then he expanded his movies to four reels and longer, pioneering the feature-length film.

Griffith's best-known epic was as controversial as it was spectacular. In *The Birth of a Nation* (1915), the Southern-born Griffith presented a dramatic view of the Civil War and Reconstruction, portraying racial stereotypes and touching on the subject of sexual intermingling of the races. It was an ambitious film on a bitter, controversial topic, shown to an audience that had not reconciled the war's divisions. The movie's cost—about $110,000—was five times more than that of any American film until that time.[9]

With this and his subsequent epics, Griffith showed the potential that movies had as a mass medium for gathering large audiences. He also proved that people would pay more than a nickel or a dime to see a motion picture. Films had moved from the crowded nickelodeon to respectability.

New production companies quickly formed to feed what seemed to be the public's unquenchable desire for movies. The biggest companies were First National, Famous Players-Lasky, Metro, Loew's, Fox and Paramount. In 1918, Paramount distributed 220 features, more in one year than any single company before or since.[10]

THE MOVIES BECOME BIG BUSINESS

The movie business was changing quickly. Five important events in the 1920s transformed it: the industry's move to California, the adoption of block booking, the formation of United Artists, the efforts at self-regulation and the introduction of sound.

The Movies Go to Hollywood

During the first decade of the 20th century, the major movie companies were based in New York, the theater capital. Film companies sometimes traveled to Florida or Cuba to chase the sunshine because it was easier to build sets outdoors to take advantage of the light. But this soon changed.

In 1903, Harry Chandler owned the *Los Angeles Times*, but he also invested in Los Angeles real estate. Chandler and his friends courted the movie business, offering cheap land, moderate weather and inexpensive labor. The moviemakers moved to Hollywood.

Block Booking

People who owned theater chains soon decided to make movies, and moviemakers discovered that they could make more money if they owned theaters, so production companies began to build theaters to exhibit their own pictures. The connection between production, distribution and exhibition grew, led by Paramount's Adolph Zukor who devised a system called **block booking**.

Block booking meant that a company, such as Paramount, would sign up one of its licensed theaters for as many as 104 pictures at a time. The movie

block booking the practice of requiring theaters to take a package of movies instead of showing the movies individually.

package contained a few "name" pictures with stars, but the majority of the movies in the block were lightweight features with no stars. Because movie bills changed twice a week, the exhibitors were desperate for something to put on the screen. Often, without knowing which movies they were getting in the block, exhibitors accepted the packages and paid the distributors' prices.

United Artists Champions the Independents

In 1919, the nation's five biggest movie names—cowboy star William S. Hart, Mary Pickford, Charlie Chaplin, Douglas Fairbanks and D. W. Griffith—decided it was time to rebel against the strict studio system of distribution.

On January 15, 1919, the stars announced:

A new combination of motion picture stars and producers was formed yesterday, and we, the undersigned, in furtherance of the artistic welfare of the moving picture industry, believing we can better serve the great and growing industry of picture productions, have decided to unite our work into one association, and at the finish of existing contracts, which are now rapidly drawing to a close, to release our combined productions through our own organization.[11]

Eventually Hart withdrew from the agreement, but the remaining partners formed a company called United Artists. They eliminated block booking and became a distributor for independently produced pictures, including their own.

In its first six years, UA delivered many movies that today are still considered classics: *The Mark of Zorro*, *The Three Musketeers*, *Robin Hood* and *The Gold Rush*. These movies succeeded despite the fact that UA worked outside of the traditional studio system, proving that it was possible to distribute films to audiences without using a major studio.

Moviemakers Use Self-Regulation to Respond to Scandals

In the 1920s, the movie industry faced two new crises: scandals involving movie stars, and criticism that movie content was growing too provocative. As a result, the moviemakers decided to regulate themselves.

The star scandals began when comedian Roscoe "Fatty" Arbuckle hosted a marathon party in San Francisco over Labor Day weekend in 1921. As the party was ending, model Virginia Rappe was rushed to the hospital with stomach pains. She died at the hospital, and Arbuckle was charged with murder. Eventually the cause of death was listed as peritonitis from a ruptured bladder, and the murder charge was reduced to manslaughter. After three trials, two of which resulted in hung juries, Arbuckle was acquitted.

Then director William Desmond Taylor was found murdered in his home. Mabel Normand, a friend of Arbuckle's, was identified as the last person who had seen Taylor alive. Normand eventually was cleared, but then it was revealed that "Taylor" was not the director's real name and there were suggestions that he was involved in the drug business.

Hollywood's moguls and business people were aghast. The Catholic Legion of Decency announced a movie boycott. Quick to protect themselves, Los Angeles business leaders met and decided that Hollywood should police itself.

The *Los Angeles Times'* Harry Chandler worked with movie leaders to bring in ex–Postmaster General and former Republican party chairman Will Hays to respond to these and other scandals in the movie business. Hays' job was to lead a moral refurbishing of the industry.

In March 1922, Hays became the first president of the Motion Picture Producers and Distributors Association (MPPDA), at a salary of $100,000 a year.

Movies

*T*oday's moviemaking is a high-stakes business dominated by the major studios, which frequently target youthful audiences. However, movie makers receive most of their income from video sales and rentals.

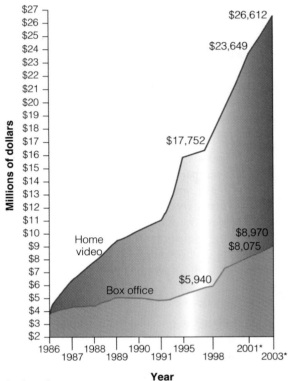

*projected

Who's Who in Hollywood: The Big Six Movie Studios

STUDIO	PARENT COMPANY	COUNTRY
MCA/Universal	Seagram	Canada
Sony Pictures Entertainment	Sony	Japan
20th Century-Fox	News Corp.	Australia
Walt Disney	Disney	U.S.
Warner Bros.	Time Warner	U.S.
Viacom/Paramount	Viacom	U.S.

Source: Data from *Standard & Poor's Industry Surveys*; Value Line, Inc., Value Line Publishing, 1993.

Who Goes to the Movies? The American moviegoing audience is considerably younger than the population as a whole.

Source: The Veronis, Suhler & Associates Communications Industry Forecast, 1999-2003.

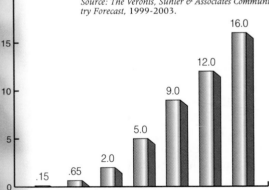

Source: The Veronis, Suhler & Associates Communications Industry Forecast, 1999-2003.

(Left) Left to right: Douglas Fairbanks, Mary Pickford, Charlie Chaplin, and D. W. Griffith, who founded United Artists in 1919. (Right) In 1994, Steven Spielberg, Jeffrey Katzenberg, and David Geffen launched Dreamworks SKG, the first new major studio created in the United States since United Artists in 1919.

(Left) AP/Wide World Photos (Right) Bettmann/CORBIS

A month later, even though Arbuckle had been acquitted, Hays suspended all of Fatty Arbuckle's films.

Besides overseeing the stars' personal behavior, Hays decided that his office also should oversee movie content. The MPPDA, referred to as the Hays Office, wrote a code of conduct to govern the industry.

On February 17, 1930, the MPPDA adopted a production code, which began by stating three general principles:

1. No picture shall be produced which will lower the moral standards of those who see it. Hence the sympathy of the audience shall never be thrown to the side of crime, wrongdoing, evil or sin

2. Correct standards of life, subject only to the requirements of drama and entertainment, shall be presented.

3. Laws, natural or human, shall not be ridiculed, nor shall sympathy be created for its violation.[12]

The code then divided its rules into 12 categories of wrongdoing, including:

- Murder: "The technique of murder must be presented in a way that will not inspire imitation."

- Sex: "Excessive and lustful kissing, lustful embraces, suggestive postures and gestures are not to be shown."

- Obscenity: "Obscenity in word, gesture, reference, song, joke, or by suggestion (even when likely to be understood only by part of the audience) is forbidden."

- Costumes: "Dancing costumes intended to permit undue exposure or indecent movements in the dance are forbidden."[13]

An acceptable movie displayed a PCA seal of approval in the titles at the beginning of the picture. Producers balked at the interference, but most of them, afraid of censorship from outside the industry, complied with the monitoring. Although standards have relaxed, the self-regulation of content still operates in the motion picture industry today.

New Technology Brings the Talkies

By the mid-1920s, silent movies were an established part of American entertainment, but technology soon pushed the industry into an even more vibrant era—the era of the talkies. MPPDA President Will Hays was the first person to appear on screen in the public premiere of talking pictures on August 6, 1926, in New York City. Warner Bros. and Western Electric had developed the sound experiment, which consisted of seven short subjects, including a concert by the New York Philharmonic and a vaudeville comedy skit. Together, the short subjects were called *The Vitaphone Preludes*.

The Warner brothers—Sam, Harry, Jack and Albert—were ambitious, upstart businessmen who beat their competitors to sound movies. On October 6, 1927, *The Jazz Singer*, starring Al Jolson, opened at the Warners' Theater in New York, the first feature-length motion picture with sound. The movie was not an all-talkie, but instead contained two sections with synchronized sound.

The success of *The Jazz Singer* convinced Warners' competitors not to wait any longer to adopt sound. By July 1, 1930, 22 percent of theaters still showed silent films; by 1933, only 0.5 percent of the movies shown in theaters were silents.[14]

RISE OF THE MOGULS: THE STUDIO SYSTEM FLOURISHES

In the 1930s, the movie business was dominated by the Big Five: Warner Bros., Metro-Goldwyn-Mayer, Paramount, RKO and 20th Century-Fox. The Big Five collected more than two-thirds of the nation's box office receipts.[15] United Artists remained solely a distribution company for independent producers.

The Big Five all were vertically integrated: They produced movies, distributed them worldwide and owned theater chains, which guaranteed their pictures a showing. The studios maintained stables of stars, directors, producers, writers and technical staff. Film scholar Tino Balio calls the studios at this point in their history a "mature oligopoly"—a group of companies with so much control over an industry that any change in one of the companies directly affected the future of the industry.

In the 1930s, Walt Disney became the only major successful Hollywood newcomer. He had released *Steamboat Willie* as "the first animated sound cartoon" in 1928. Disney was 26 years old, and he sold his car to finance the cartoon's sound track.

After some more short-animated-feature successes, Disney announced in 1934 that his studio would produce its first feature-length animated film, *Snow White and the Seven Dwarfs*. The film eventually cost Disney $2.25 million, more than MGM usually spent on a good musical. *Snow White* premiered December 21, 1937, at the Cathay Circle Theater in Hollywood.

Box office receipts sagged in the 1930s as the Depression settled into every aspect of America's economy. Facing bankruptcy, several theaters tried to buoy their profits by adding Bingo games and cut-rate admissions. The one innovation that survived the 1930s was the double feature: two movies for the price of one.

The Depression introduced one more factor into motion picture budgets: labor unions. Before the 1930s, most aspects of the movie business were not governed by union agreements. But in 1937, the National Labor Relations

IMPACT

profile *Lighting Up a Black Screen*

By Teresa Moore

The halcyon age for African Americans on the big screen was the period between 1910 and 1950, when blacks—and some whites—produced more than 500 "race movies," showcasing all-black casts in a variety of genres, including Westerns, mysteries, romances and melodrama.

Although most of these movies have disintegrated into silver nitrate stardust, a few dozen of these early films—silents and talkies—are available on video.

"I think it is great that they are available for people to look at, to get an idea of the cultural history of blacks in film, for better or for worse," said Albert Johnson, professor of cinema in the African American studies program of cinema at the University of California at Berkeley.

While most of the surviving films are grainy and crackly, with uneven casts and jagged storyline, they offer a wide range of black characters that subsequent films have yet to match. In the naturally sepia-toned world of race movies, African Americans could—and did—do just about anything.

There were black millionaires and black detectives, black sweethearts and socialites. Black heroines who swooned—tender, wilting ladies who never swept a broom or donned a do-rag. Black heroes who could be gentle and genteel, tough and smart. Black villains of both genders, out to

Paul Robeson and Josephine Baker were important stars who appeared in early "race movies," showcasing African American casts.

Top: UPI-Bettmann/CORBIS
Right: Bettmann/CORBIS

separate black damsels and grandees from their virtue or fortune.

Race movies were so called because they were made for black Southern audiences barred from white-owned theaters. The films were shown either in the black-owned movie palaces of the urban North and Midwest or in "midnight rambles"—special midnight-to-2-A.M. screenings in rented halls or segregated theaters of the South.

Under segregation, the moviemakers created an onscreen world that not only reflected the accomplishments of the rising black middle class but also transformed reality into a realm where race was no impediment to love, power or success.

"They wanted to get away from anything dealing with poverty or slavery—this was dealt with in commercial films where whites in blackface played vaudevillian stereotypes," Johnson said. "They showed black people in nice homes with refined culture. They wanted to establish a respectable black image."

The leading directors and producers, Oscar Micheaux and the brother team of Noble and George Johnson, wanted to uplift African Americans. Besides presenting black images more appealing to black audiences, they also offered black perspectives on racial injustice.

"In some ways these filmmakers were more free because they were making the movies for themselves," said Michael Thompson, a professor of African American history at Stanford.

©San Francisco Chronicle. Reprinted by permission.

Board held an election that designated the Screen Actors Guild to bargain for wages, working conditions and overtime. The Screen Writers Guild was certified in 1938 and the Screen Directors Guild soon afterward.

Unionization limited the moguls' power over the people who worked for them, but union agreements were approved in the late 1930s. The Depression ended, and the studios once again prospered.

MOVIES GLITTER DURING THE GOLDEN AGE

With glamorous stars and exciting screenplays, supported by an eager pool of gifted directors, producers and technical talent, plus an insatiable audience the movie industry reached its apex in the late 1930s and early 1940s. The most successful studio in Hollywood was MGM, which attracted the best writers, directors and actors. MGM concentrated on blockbusters, such as *The Great Ziegfeld*, *The Wizard of Oz* and *Gone with the Wind*. Not only did *Gone with the Wind*'s phenomenal success demonstrate the epic character that movies could provide, but also the movie was a technological breakthrough, with its magnificent use of color.

The movie business was so rich that even MGM's dominance didn't scare away the competition.

Challenges from Congress and the Courts

Before television arrived throughout the country in 1948, two other events of the late 1940s helped reverse the prosperous movie bonanza that began in mid-1930: the hearings of the House Un-American Activities Committee and the 1948 U.S. Supreme Court decision in *United States* v. *Paramount Pictures, Inc., et al.*

The Hollywood Ten. In October 1947, America was entering the Cold War. This was an era in which many public officials, government employees and private citizens seemed preoccupied with the threat of communism and peo-

In the late 1930s and early 1940s, spectaculars such as *The Wizard of Oz* helped to make MGM the most successful studio in Hollywood.

The Kobal Collection

ple identified as "subversives." The House of Representatives Committee on Un-American Activities, chaired by J. Parnell Thomas, summoned ten "unfriendly" witnesses from Hollywood to testify about their communist connections. (Unfriendly witnesses were people whom the committee classified as having participated at some time in the past in "un-American activities." This usually meant that the witness had been a member of a left-wing organization in the decade before World War II.) These eight screenwriters and two directors came to be known as the Hollywood Ten.

The Ten's strategy was to appear before the committee as a group and to avoid answering the direct question "Are you now or have you ever been a member of the Communist party?" Instead, the Ten tried to make statements that questioned the committee's authority to challenge their political beliefs.

In a rancorous series of hearings, the committee rejected the Ten's testimony; the witnesses found themselves facing trial for contempt. All of them were sentenced to jail, and some were fined. By the end of November 1947, all of the Hollywood Ten had lost their jobs. Many more movie people would follow.

In an article for the *Hollywood Review*, Hollywood Ten member Adrian Scott reported that 214 movie employees eventually were blacklisted, which meant that many studio owners refused to hire people who were suspected of taking part in subversive activities. The movie people who were not hired because of their political beliefs included 106 writers, 36 actors and 11 directors.[16] This effectively gutted Hollywood of some of its best talent.

United States v. Paramount Pictures. The U.S. Justice Department began another antitrust suit against the studios in 1938. In 1940, the studios came to an agreement with the government, while admitting no guilt. They agreed to:

1. Limit block booking to five films.

2. Stop **blind booking** (the practice of renting films to exhibitors without letting them see the films first).

3. Stop requiring theaters to rent short films as a condition of acquiring features.

4. Stop buying theaters.

blind booking the practice of renting films to exhibitors without letting them see the film first.

After this agreement, the Justice Department dropped its suit with the stipulation that the department could reinstitute the suit again at any time.

By 1944, the government was still unhappy with studio control over the theaters, so it reactivated the suit. In 1948, *United States v. Paramount Pictures* reached the Supreme Court. Associate Justice William O. Douglas argued that, *although the five major studios*—Paramount, Warner Bros., MGM-Loew's, RKO and 20th Century-Fox—*owned only 17 percent of all theaters in the United States*, these studios did *hold a monopoly over first-run exhibition in the large cities*.

As a result of the Supreme Court decision, by 1954 the five major production firms had divested themselves of ownership or control of all of their theaters. Production and exhibition were now split; vertical integration was crumbling.

When the movie companies abandoned the exhibition business, banks grew reluctant to finance film projects because the companies could not guarantee an audience—on paper. Soon the studios decided to leave the production business to the independents and became primarily distributors of other peoples' pictures. The result was the end of the studio system.

The Hollywood Ten, targeted by the House Committee on Un-American Activities, eventually went to jail for refusing to answer questions before the committee about their political beliefs.

The Kobal Collection

TRANSFORMATIONS IN THE MOVIE INDUSTRY

In the 1950 Paramount movie *Sunset Boulevard*, aging silent screen star Norma Desmond (played by Gloria Swanson) romances an ambitious young screenwriter (played by William Holden) by promising him Hollywood connections.

"You're Norma Desmond. You used to be in silent pictures. You used to be big," says the screenwriter.

"I *am* big," says Desmond. "It's the pictures that got small."

Desmond could have been talking about the picture business itself, which got much smaller after 1948, when nationwide television began to offer home-delivered entertainment.

The House hearings and the consent decrees in the Paramount case foretold change in the movie business, but television truly transformed Hollywood forever. In the 1950s the number of television sets grew by 400 percent, while the number of people who went to the movies fell by 45 percent.[17]

Theaters tried to make up for the loss by raising their admission prices, but more than 4,000 theaters closed from 1946 to 1956.[18] Attendance has leveled off or risen briefly a few times since the 1950s, but the trend of declining movie attendance continues today. The movie industry has tried several methods to counteract this downward trend.

Wide-Screen and 3-D Movies

Stunned by television's popularity, the movie business tried technological gimmicks in the 1950s to lure its audience back. First came 3-D movies, using special effects to create the illusion of three-dimensional action. Rocks, for example, seemed to fly off the screen and into the audience. To see the 3-D movies, people wore special plastic glasses. The novelty was fun, but the

3-D movie plots were weak, and most people didn't come back to see a second 3-D movie.

Next came Cinerama, Cinemascope, VistaVision and Panavision—widescreen color movies with stereophonic sound. All of these techniques tried to give the audience a "you are there" feeling—something they couldn't get from television.

Changes in Censorship

On May 26, 1952, the Supreme Court announced in *Burstyn* v. *Wilson* that motion pictures were "a significant medium for the communication of ideas," which were designed "to entertain as well as to inform." The effect of this decision was to protect movies under the First Amendment. The result was fewer legal restrictions on what a movie could show.

In 1953, Otto Preminger challenged the movies' self-regulating agency, the Production Code Administration. United Artists agreed to release Preminger's movie *The Moon Is Blue,* even though the PCA denied the movie a certificate of approval because it contained such risqué words as *virgin* and *mistress*. Then, in 1956, United Artists released Preminger's *Man with the Golden Arm*, a film about drug addiction, and the PCA restrictions were forever broken.

Buoyed by the Burstyn decision and the United Artists test, moviemakers tried sex and violence to attract audiences away from television. In the 1950s, Marilyn Monroe and Jane Russell offered generously proportioned examples of the new trend. Foreign films also became popular because some of them offered explicit dialogue and love scenes.

Spectaculars

One by one the studio moguls retired, and they were replaced by a new generation of moviemakers. "They [the second generation] inherited a situation where fewer and fewer pictures were being made, and fewer still made money," says Robert Sklar, "but those that captured the box office earned enormous sums. It was as if the rules of baseball had been changed so that the only hit that mattered was a home run."[19]

Spectaculars like *The Sound of Music* (1965) and *The Godfather* (1971) and its sequels rewarded the rush for big money. But then a few majestic flops taught the studios that nothing can demolish a studio's profits like one big bomb.

Movie Ratings

In 1966, Jack Valenti, former presidential adviser to Lyndon Johnson, became president of the Motion Picture Producers Association and renamed the Motion Picture Association of America (MPAA). One of Valenti's first acts was to respond to continuing public criticism about shocking movie content.

The MPAA began a rating system modeled on Great Britain's: G for general audiences, M (later changed to PG) for mature audiences, R for restricted (people under 17 admitted only with an adult), and X for no one under 18 admitted. Valenti still heads the MPAA as the lobbyist for the nation's major studios. The PG-13 rating—special parental guidance advised for children under 13—has been added, and the X rating has been changed to NC-17X.

Standards for the R rating have eased since the ratings system began, further blurring the effectiveness of the ratings system for the public.

THE BUSINESS OF MOVIES

In today's system of moviemaking, each of the six major studios (Columbia, Paramount, 20th Century-Fox, MCA/Universal, Time Warner and Walt Disney) usually makes less than 20 movies a year. The rest come from independent producers, with production, investment, distribution and exhibition each handled by different companies. Most of these independently produced movies are distributed by one of the six large studios.

Today, the dream merchants aim at youthful buyers. Nearly half of the people who go to the movies today are under 30. So the biggest box office successes are movies that appeal to this younger audience, like *George of the Jungle*. Adult films such as *The English Patient* sometimes succeed, but films that chase the under-30 audience usually top the box office list.

Today's movies are created by one group (the writers and producers) funded by another group (the investors), sold by a third group (the distributors) and shown by a fourth group (the exhibitors). No other mass media industry is so fragmented.

Losing Money: Ticket Sales Drop

In 1946, the movies' best year, American theaters collected more than 4 billion tickets. Today, as more people watch more movies on video, the number of theater admissions has dropped to about 1 billion.[20] Exhibitors feel that if they raise their admission prices, they'll lose more of their patrons. This is why exhibitors charge so much for refreshments, which is where they make 10 to 20 percent of their income.[21]

With declining audiences and fewer successful movies, the studios complain that they lose money on *most* of the pictures they underwrite. Producers say the studios make exorbitant profits on the movies they distribute, which raises the cost of making movies for producers.

Today, movies, like many other media, are part of corporate ownership, which means that stockholder loyalty comes first. Studios tend to choose safer projects and seek proven audience-pleasing ideas rather than take many risks.

One way the movie industry collects predictable income is to make movies for television. Half of the movies produced every year are made for television and are underwritten by the networks. Video sales and rentals also bring reliable revenues.

Two important factors for the future funding of the movie industry are the sale of ancillary rights and the advances of new technology.

Calvin and Hobbes   by Bill Watterson

Making Money: Selling Ancillary Rights

In 1950, a ticket to a movie cost about 50 cents. Today you can still see a movie for 50 cents if you rent a video for $2 and invite three friends to join you at home to watch it. The explosion of video rentals and sales since the VCR was first marketed in 1976 had a powerful effect on how the movie business operates today (see Figure 8.1). The sale of movies for video is part of the **ancillary rights** market.

The median cost to make a theatrical movie (as opposed to a made-for-television movie) is $78 million,[22] and only two out of ten theatrical movies make money. [23] "Some pictures make a lot of money," says David V. Picker, "and a lot of pictures make no money."[24] Before a theatrical movie starts shooting, the investors want to be sure they'll make their money back. They may look to ancillary rights to secure a return on their investment. Ancillary rights can include:

- Pay television rights
- Network television rights
- Syndication rights (sales to independent TV stations)
- Airline rights for in-flight movies
- Military rights (to show films on military bases)
- College rights (to show films on college campuses)
- Song rights for soundtrack albums
- Book publishing rights (for original screenplays that can be rewritten and sold as books)[25]

Movies also have been getting more commercialized in the sense that they are tied to products. Products are another way of advertising a movie. A movie that can be exploited as a package of ancillary rights, with commercial appeal, is much more attractive to an investor than a movie with limited potential.

ancillary rights marketing opportunities related to a movie, besides direct income from the movie itself.

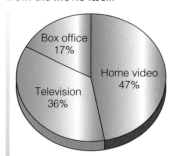

Figure 8.1 Shares of Worldwide Movie Revenues 2000* Movie industry revenue comes from three major sources: home video, box office tickets, and movies made for television.

*projected

Source: The Veronis Suhler & Associates *Communications Industry Forecast* 1999–2003.

George Lucas capitalized on ancillary rights for *Star Wars*, creating the most successful ancillary marketing campaign in movie history.

AP/Wide World Photos

Often the only choice for a filmmaker who wants to make a film that doesn't have substantial ancillary-rights potential is to settle for a low budget. Once the film is made, the independent filmmaker must then find a way to distribute the movie. This severely limits the number of independent films that make it to the box office.

WORKING IN THE MOVIES

Today the center of the movie industry is movie production. Most of the movies that are distributed by the major studios and exhibited at your local theater result from independent companies that produce movies under agreements with individual studios.

Although these production companies work independently, and each company is organized differently, jobs in movie production fall mainly into the following categories: screenwriters, producers, directors, actors, production, marketing and administration.

The beginning for each movie is a story idea, and these ideas come from *screenwriters*. Screenwriters work independently, marketing their story ideas through agents, who promote their clients' scripts to the studios and to independent producers.

Typically, *producers* are the people who help gather the funding to create a movie project. Financing can come from banks or from individuals who want to invest in a specific movie. Once the funding for the story is in place, a director is assigned to organize all of the tasks necessary to turn the script into a movie. The director oversees the movie's budget.

Obviously, *actors* are important to any movie project. Sometimes the producer and director approach particular stars for a project even before they seek funding, to attract interest from the investors and also to help assure the investors that the movie will have some box office appeal.

Production includes all of the people who actually create the movie—camera operators, set designers, film editors, script supervisors and costumers, for example. Once the movie is made, the *marketing* people seek publicity for the project. They also design a plan to advertise and promote the movie to the public. As in any media industry, people who work in *administration* help

IMPACT

digital

Moviemakers Shudder As Illegal Copies of Hot Films Spread on the Internet

The same technology that allows for the spread of bootlegged music over the Internet is now threatening the movie industry. Film filchers have begun distributing copies of hot flicks like *The Matrix* using a data format similar to the so-called MP3 files that are being used to spread free music across cyberspace.

While the data files containing full-length movies are too big for the average home computer user to conveniently download, college students with high-speed hookups in their dorm rooms are doing it and the movie industry is shuddering.

"It's very nice. I get to sit here in the comfort of my own room and watch a new movie without going to the theater and spending $7.50," said a 19-year-old sophomore at the University of California, Santa Cruz, who asked that his name be withheld.

It's not very nice, said Jack Valenti, president of the Motion Picture Association of America. "The theft of copyrighted material in any format cannot be left unapprised. There is no exception in the case of Internet copyright theft. We won't condone it, and we will pursue those who steal

film product and illegally transmit it via the Internet."

The movies can be found on public Web forums, including those run by America Online, and on Internet message boards. The movies are frequently distributed by students at colleges around the country—including Stanford University, UC Berkeley and Virginia Polytechnic Institute.

The quality varies. *Cruel Intentions*, Sony's new release about a pair of evil teens, looked vivid and sounded clear on a standard desktop computer in one cramped dorm room at Santa Cruz. However, *The Matrix*, the surreal sci-fi film, looked somewhat dark and shady, and the musical soundtrack was missing.

Here's how the copying works: The originals usually come from either a mixing studio employee who steals a copy of a yet-to-be released movie, or a projectionist who brings a camcorder into the reel booth and makes a copy.

The video is then transferred digitally into a file, which is recorded into a computer. Once that computer file is distributed onto the Internet, it can be widely available.

The drawback is the size of the file. While a song in MP3 format can be downloaded in a few minutes, it would take hours or even days to download a movie using a typical telephone connection to the Web.

Internet analyst Mark Mooradian, who tracks the proliferation of music on the Web for the research firm Jupiter communications in New York, said the large files are going to limit the widespread use of movies online until the technology improves. "It's just not going to be practical for most people," he said.

But many college students and offices have access to networks with speedy computer lines and vast memory space. With these systems, an entire movie can be downloaded in about 20 minutes.

"It gives me a sense of satisfaction, like I found something and here's the proof that I have it," said one self-described "stereotypical computer-jockey-hacker" who distributes movies campuswide at Santa Cruz.

Associated Press on America Online (AOL), April 22, 1999. Reprinted with Permission.

keep all of the records necessary to pay salaries and track the employees' expenses, as well as keep track of the paperwork involved in organizing any other business.

TECHNOLOGY AND THE FUTURE

Technology affects three aspects of the movie business: production, distribution and exhibition.

Production. Smaller portable cameras mean that a camera operator can move more easily throughout a crowd. New types of film mean that filmmakers can shoot more scenes at night and in dark places with less artificial lighting.

Most directors videotape scenes as they film them and immediately play back the videotape to make sure they have the shot they want. Computer technology offers exciting special-effects possibilities. Filmmakers also are experimenting with the holograph, which uses lasers to make a computer-generated three-dimensional image from a flat picture.

The ability to digitize color, using computers, also means that the images in movies can be intensified, adjusted and even totally transformed after the movie is shot, in a way that was impossible even ten years ago.

Distribution. Reproducing copies of films to send to theaters and guaranteeing their arrival is one of the costliest aspects of moviemaking. In the future, companies will probably send their movies by satellite to satellite dishes on top of each theater. Live performances, such as a symphony concert or a major sports event, could be available regularly by satellite at your local theater, or even in your home.

The theater industry is poised to replace the traditional film projector, invented more than 100 years ago, with digital projectors, which can show movies that are sent by satellite or recorded on optical discs. Digital movies would be cheaper to distribute, and could be shown on more screens, or removed quickly from distribution, depending on audience demand.

The Internet allows new moviemakers to produce movies inexpensively and transfer them to the Internet for downloading. As computer video technology gets faster and more accessible, independent moviemakers may devise a whole new distribution system, based on digital movie downloads delivered directly to consumers (See Impact/On You, "If Only DeMille Had Owned a Desktop," p. 198).

Exhibition. Theaters are turning to the picture-palace environment that enchanted moviegoers in the 1930s. "The movie theatre will have to become an arena; a palace to experience the full grandeur and potential of the theatrical motion picture," says futurist and electronic technology consultant Martin Polon.[26]

In 1994, the nation's largest theater chain, United Artists, announced that it would begin to offer "motion simulation" in some of its theaters. Specially controlled seats will move in conjunction with a "ridefilm" to give the feeling of space travel or other adventures.

"We're looking to marry the moviegoing experience to different kinds of technological experiences, thereby enhancing the attractiveness of the whole complex," said United Artists chairman Stewart Blair.[27]

INTERNATIONAL MARKETS AND CONCENTRATED POWER

Today's movie industry is undergoing two major changes. One recent trend in the movie business is global ownership and global marketing. The second trend is the merging of the movie industry with the television industry.

Global Influence. Foreign companies own half of the major studios (Sony owns Columbia Pictures, for example, and Rupert Murdoch's News Corporation owns 20th Century-Fox). These foreign acquisitions occurred throughout the late 1980s and the first half of the 1990s. This percentage of foreign ownership is higher in the movie industry than in any other American media business.

Foreign ownership means easier access to foreign markets. American motion pictures are one of America's strongest exports, and income from foreign sales accounts for more than one-third of the movie industry's profits. "If Hollywood has learned anything the past few years," says *Business Week*, "it's that the whole world is hungry for the latest it has to offer."[28]

Concentrating Media Power. Today, people in the television business are buying pieces of the movie business and people in the movie business want to align themselves with television companies. In 1993 the Federal Communications Commission voted to allow the TV networks to make and syndicate their own programs. This opens the door for TV networks to enter the movie business.

The result *could* be consolidated companies that would finance movies, make movies and show those movies in their own theaters, on their own television stations and on video. By controlling all aspects of the business, a company would have a better chance to collect a profit on the movies it makes. Sound familiar? The studios held this type of controlling interest in their movies before the courts dismantled the studio system with the 1948 consent decrees (see page 189). Today's major studios are trying to become again what they once were: a mature oligopoly in the business of dreams.

IN FOCUS

- Eadweard Muybridge and Thomas Edison were the two Americans who contributed the most to the creation of the movies. Muybridge demonstrated how to photograph motion and Edison developed a projector, the kinetoscope. Edison also organized the Motion Picture Patents Company (MPPC) to control movie distribution.

- French filmmaker Georges Méliès envisioned movies as a medium of fantasy. Edwin S. Porter assembled scenes to tell a story. D. W. Griffith mastered the full-length movie.

- The practice of block booking, led by Adolph Zukor, obligated movie houses to accept several movies at once, usually without previewing them first.

- Biograph became the first studio to make movies using what was called the studio system. This system put the studio's stars under exclusive contract, and the contract could not be broken without an employer's permission.

- The formation of United Artists by Mary Pickford, Charlie Chaplin, Douglas Fairbanks and D. W. Griffith was a rebellion against the big studios; UA distributed films for independent filmmakers.

- In the 1920s, the movie industry faced two new crises: scandals involving movie stars and criticism that movie content was growing too explicit. The movie industry responded by forming the Motion Picture Producers and Distributors Association (MPPDA), under the direction of Will Hays.

- As the studio system developed, the five largest Hollywood studios were able to control production, distribution and exhibition. In the 1930s, labor unions challenged studio control and won some concessions.

IMPACT

on you   *If Only DeMille Had Owned a Desktop*

The camera glides in on a tableau: Jesus and his apostles gathered solemnly at a long table, each frozen in painterly poses familiar from *The Last Supper*. Then Jesus suddenly comes to life, and in a flurry of special effects that owes more to Dali than da Vinci, he miraculously provides a banquet of breads, crackers and grapes from thin air and transforms water into a blood-red wine cooler called New Testament. Along the way, he transforms himself into a robed pitch man for the new bottled beverage.

This scene was not created by a major Hollywood studio or a high-priced special-effects company like Industrial Light and Magic. Instead, this sequence, part of a five-minute award-winning parody of American advertising excess called *New Testament*, is the work of a two-person production house called Swankytown. Thanks to a tide of new digital technology for filmmakers, Swankytown's founders say, they were able to complete the entire project with an ordinary 16-millimeter camera, two Power Macs and some off-the-shelf software at a cost of $1,700.

There's nothing new these days about digital technology's marriage with the movies. Moviegoers have been getting an eyeful of digital wonders on the big screen, from *Titanic* to *A Bug's Life*. But those displays of digital wizardry were managed by filmmakers with tens of millions of dollars at their disposal for the tedious tasks involved. The flip side of the digital revolution, one that is just starting to make its presence felt, is the democratizing effect that cheap and easier-to-use technology is having on control over the moving image.

In living rooms, basements and makeshift studios, people are taking advantage of powerful home computers stuffed with extra RAM and pumped up with gigabytes of hard drive memory to add sound and motion to digital images. Some are transferring film to video, where images, once digitized, can be cut with editing software and enhanced with easy-to-use animation programs. Others use digital video camcorders—small, relatively inexpensive cameras that can load their already digitized images onto computer hard drives—to breathe cinematic life into what had once flickered only in their imaginations, then transfer the result to film. Some moviemakers have given up film altogether, choosing instead to shoot, edit and, in some cases, distribute their work digitally.

Digital technology has led to a new, decentralized approach to making movies: desktop filmmaking. Computer technology can transform a process that has been mostly mechanical and chemical, labor-intensive and very expensive into a mostly electronic process. So cinematic visions can now be realized by manipulating digital code, lines of ones and zeros.

"A couple of years ago, with the same talent we have now,

- The movies' golden age was the 1930s and the 1940s, supported by the studio system and an eager audience.

- Three factors caused Hollywood's crash in the 1950s: the House Un-American Activities Committee hearings, the U.S. Justice Department's antitrust action against the studios and television.

- Hollywood tried to lure audiences back with technological gimmicks and sultry starlets, but these efforts did not work very well. Today, the number of

we didn't have these kinds of tools available to us," said Philip Pelletier, who with his partner, Verne Lindner, created Swankytown Productions in Hollywood in 1997. "Back then, *New Testament* would have been impossible." Mr. Pelletier, a composer by training, and Ms. Lindner, an illustrator who taught herself computer animation and special effects, estimate that with traditional filming, editing and special effects techniques, their movie would have cost closer to $400,000.

The New York Times, Thursday, January 7, 1999. Copyright ©1999 by The New York Times Co. Reprinted by permission.

Philip Pelletier and Verne Lindner, founders of the Swankytown production house, are among the growing ranks of digital filmmakers who are using off-the-shelf software and home computers to make quality movies.

Marissa Roth for *The New York Times*

moviegoers continues to decline, although video sales and rentals have added to movie industry income; nearly half of the movie-goers are under 30.

- Today's movie ratings system began in 1966, supervised by the Motion Picture Association of America (MPAA). Very few movies actually receive the most explicit (NC-17X) rating.

- The median cost to make a movie today is $36 million, and two out of ten theatrical movies make money. Most movies are funded in part by ancillary rights sales. Thus, most movies are sold as packages, with all of their potential media outlets underwriting a movie before it goes into production. This makes independent filmmaking difficult.

■ Foreign corporations own half of the major movie studios. This is a higher percentage of foreign ownership than in any other media industry.

■ American movies are a major U.S. export; foreign sales account for more than one-third of movie industry income.

■ In 1993, the Federal Communications Commission voted to allow the TV networks to make and syndicate their own programs. This means that, in the future, the movie industry and the television industry may align themselves more closely, which eventually would mean that one company could control all aspects of moviemaking.

■ Dreamworks SKG, launched in 1994 by Steven Spielberg, Jeffrey Katzenberg and David Geffen, is the first major movie studio created in the United States since United Artists was formed in 1919.

■ The biggest technological changes in moviemaking are the result of digital technology. Independent moviemakers can use computers to create movies inexpensively and distribute them on the Internet. Digital projectors will allow theaters to receive movies by satellite and videodisc, which makes movie distribution cheaper and faster.

WORKING THE WEB www

■ **Digital Entertainment Network**
www.den.net
■ **Entertaindom (Time Warner)**
Entertaindom.com
■ **Market Guide to the Motion Picture Industry**
www.marketguide.com/MGI/INDUSTRY/movies.htm
■ **Internet Movie Database**
us.imdb.org/Movies/credits.html
■ **Motion Picture Industry: Behind the Scenes**
library.advanced.org/10015
■ **Motion Picture Industry Book**
www.studentcenter.com/where/industry/IN7822.htm
■ **Women in Film**
www.cinema.ucla.edu/women

INFOTRAC COLLEGE EDITION EXERCISES

Using InfoTrac College Edition, a fully searchable online database of articles and abstracts, do the following exercises as directed by your instructor.

1. Using their names as keywords, look up two of the following historical film people:
   ■ D. W. Griffith
   ■ Mary Pickford

- Thomas Edison
- Charlie Chaplin

Then print at least two articles about each person and bring them to class. Be prepared to share what you learned about your two film personalities with the class.

2. Enter the keywords "motion picture actors and actresses" and read at least two articles about an actor or actress—a current person or a historic one—of you choice. Then either:

   a. write a brief paper on your findings, or

   b. bring the articles to class and be prepared to discuss them.

3. Choose one of your favorite movies and, using InfoTrac College Edition keywords, see if there are any articles about a particular movie. Print at least two articles about the movie—either profiles of people involved with the movie or movie reviews. Then either:

   a. write a brief paper on your findings, or

   b. bring the articles to class and be prepared to discuss them.

4. Read "Impact/Profile: Lighting Up a Black Screen" in Chapter 8 and, using InfoTrac College Edition, look up more information on "race films," "Paul Robeson" or "Josephine Baker." Print at least three articles on the emergence of race films and film stars and bring the articles to class. Be prepared to share what you've learned about the subject in a small-group discussion.

5. Read "Impact/Digital: Moviemakers Shudder As Illegal Copies of Hot Films Spread on the Internet" in Chapter 8. Then, using InfoTrac College Edition keywords, look up "Internet movies," "web motion pictures" or "motion picture piracy." Read at least three articles about the problem of pirated films. Print the articles and either write a brief paper on your findings, or bring the articles to class and be prepared to discuss them, as directed by your instructor.

9

Digital Media and the Web

Nobody ever designed the (Web.) There are no rules, no laws.

Craig McKie, Department of Sociology and Anthropology, Carleton University, Ottawa, Canada, who maintains his own Web site.

What's Ahead

"The Internet is the new frontier of American life, the electronic equivalent of the Wild West," writes David Shaw, media critic of the Los Angeles Times. "About the only point on which even the pioneers in this still primitive digital culture seem to agree is that virtually everything being done now…will either have to change radically or fail."[1]

The Internet is actually a combination of thousands of computer networks sending and receiving data from all over the world—competing interests joined together by a common purpose, but no common owner. "No government or commercial entity owns the Net or directly profits from its operation," notes information designer Roger Fidler. "It has no president, chief executive officer, or central headquarters."[2]

In its global size and absence of central control, the Internet is completely different from traditional media. Originally developed to aid communication among researchers and educators (see Chapter 1), the Internet has "evolved in a way no one planned or expected," says Fidler. "Important scientific data and scholarly thoughts have continued to account for much of the traffic [on the Internet], but it is the relationships among people that have shaped the medium. What has mattered most to Internet users is the free exchange of ideas and discussion of values."[3]

Digital media simultaneously are frustrating and invigorating. They are based on old and new technology, with a terminology all their own. Digital media also are the fastest growing type of media and, because of their rapid growth, digital media promise to become the biggest factor in the future development of the mass-media industries.

Economists predict that the number of consumers online will more than double between 1996 and the year 2001, and the amount of money spent for online advertising will rise 1200 percent.[4]

WHAT ARE DIGITAL MEDIA?

Digital media could be described simply as what are clearly not old media. Old media would be defined as the seven traditional media—Print (newspapers, magazines and books); Audio (radio and recordings); and Video (television and movies) that are discussed in Chapters 2 through 8.

digital media all emerging communications media that combine text, graphics, sound and video, using computer technology.

multimedia any media that combine text, graphics, sound and video.

The term **digital media** is used to describe all forms of emerging communications media. Digital media combine text, graphics, sound and video, using computer technology to create a product that is similar to, but clearly different from, traditional media.

The term **multimedia** is used to describe any media that combine text, graphics, sound and video. Video games, the most familiar early form of multimedia, combined text, graphics, sound and video to create games that could be played on a TV set. The latest video games, which can be played on a computer and also online, are a form of multimedia that have developed into digital media.

Emerging Forms of Digital Media Technologies

Since the definition of digital media is so broad, the term is thrown around very easily by people hoping to get attention and financial support for new products. Emerging forms of new media are being developed every day by people who are experimenting with the process.

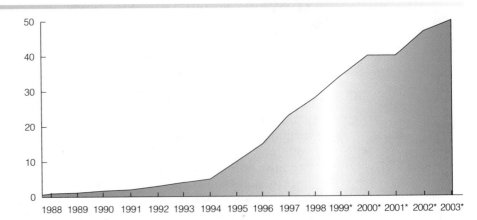

Figure 9.1
U.S. Consumers Online

Sources: Veronis, Suhler & Associates, Wilkofsky Gruen Associates, Electronic Industries Association, U.S. Bureau of the Census, Odyssey Ventures, Find/SVP.

% of U.S. consumer households that are online

*projected

As you know from learning the history of traditional media, some digital media inventions will succeed, some will be transition products that will help to develop new products, and many will fail. Until the digital media landscape is clearer, however, it is important to follow emerging developments because no one can predict exactly where digital media, now in their infancy, are headed.

Some examples of currently emerging digital media technologies are:

Digital Subscriber Line (DSL). Available now in larger cities, DSL provides Internet access that is up to 50 times faster than a dial-up modem. DSL is always on, which means subscribers don't have to dial their Internet service provider each time they want to use the Web. DSL also provides much better delivery of audio and video signals than a standard telephone line.

Immersive Virtual Reality Systems. In the 1960s, computer flight simulators began to be used to train military pilots. These simulators were predecessors of today's virtual reality systems. By the 1980s, this technology was called "artificial reality."

Today, virtual reality systems have been refined to present a remote experience that is even closer to the real thing. The 1995 movie *Disclosure* showed an example of an immersive virtual reality system, when the lead characters in the film "walked" through a database that made them look as if they were inside the New York Public Library.

Virtual reality (VR) systems can give people the experience of being somewhere by creating the reality of that place around them, but require special equipment (a helmet and/or special eyeglasses, for example). These systems, which have been popularized for their entertainment value, actually could have important future applications, allowing a doctor to examine a patient from a distance, for example, and give advice to the attending physician.

Holographic Theaters. A hologram is a three-dimensional image, created on a flat surface, but viewed without special equipment. A holographic theater would allow you to attend a live music concert at your local theater, performed by your favorite rock group at another location. What you would see at your local theater would be a holographic image of the group, projected into the theater, transmitted from the original location. The holographic image could be projected simultaneously to locations throughout the world.

Personal Channels. This technology would allow you to create your own personal set of programs and services to be delivered either on your television set, your computer or both. "By using an on-screen guide…viewers could select the programs they regularly watch and the movies they may want to see, then have their VCR, or digital successor, automatically record the programs as they are broadcast and sequence them to match their schedule,"[5] says Roger Fidler.

Personal channels are similar to today's practice of recording a favorite program for viewing later, but with a personal channel, you would be able to record a collection of programs whenever they were available and then view them whenever you wanted.

Intelligent Video Agents. Once you decided which programs you wanted to watch on your personal channel, an intelligent video agent would be able to track the history of the choices you've made, and would then be able to "learn" your interests, hunt for programs for you and keep them waiting for you to watch at your leisure.

Digital Paper. Researchers at MIT are working on an entirely new type of paper. This paper would look and feel like high-quality paper, but it would be

IMPACT digital

How Bad Was the Hotmail Disaster?

Taking Stock of the Worst Security Breach in Internet History

By Lev Grossman

"For those who use the web-based HotMail free e-mail service, the following code will save you several minutes each day." With these innocent words, posted to the newsgroup comp.lang.javascript on January 4, [1999] a well-meaning computer programmer is believed to have set in motion the worst privacy disaster in the short history of the Internet....

A Swedish newspaper called *Expressen* published the programmer's work, a simple utility designed to save time by allowing Hotmail users to circumvent that pesky password verification process when logging into their accounts. The result? As many as 50 million Hotmail accounts were made fully accessible to the public. Now that the damage has been done, what have we learned?

It wasn't until the lines of code appeared in *Expressen* that people realized how vulnerable Hotmail really was. The utility allowed anybody who wanted to to create a Web page that would allow them [to] log into any Hotmail account.

Once the word was out, dozens of pages...were created to take advantage of the security hole. Unfortunate programmers at Microsoft, which owns Hotmail, were rousted out of bed at 2 A.M. Pacific time to address the problem. By 9 A.M. Hotmail was offline...[H]ackers reported that the security breach had briefly reopened, but by the end of the day it had been closed for good, according to a statement posted by Hotmail on its site.

What will the consequences be? Nobody has yet come forward to state that they suffered any serious damage—financial, personal, or otherwise—as a result of the security breach. Any intrusions that did take place were probably overwhelmingly of a playful nature—for example,

one Web surfer snuck into a friend's account and sent her a screen shot of her in-box, just to prove he could do it.

Microsoft, of course, has learned enough to close the security breach, one of a series that has plagued the company's products over the past six months. Hackers recently discovered a serious security problem related to a Microsoft instant messaging client, and yesterday News.com reported on a Java applet that could allow hackers to take control of a PC running Windows, through the Internet Explorer Web browser. Microsoft has since issued a patch that will repair the problem.

But will the Hotmail disaster ultimately make the Internet a safer place, by forcing Microsoft to make its ubiquitous products more secure? Only if consumers make it clear that they demand better security, and they haven't done that yet.

Time Digital, *http://www.time.com*, August 31, 1999. Reprinted by permission.

totally erasable. Digital paper pages would be bound like a book, and could be turned to read like a book, but the pages would be blank.

Digital images could be "printed" on the digital paper and viewed, then the pages could be "erased," to be replaced by brand new material. MIT researchers suggest that this technology could be used to create the world's first one-volume library. A book that was *Moby Dick* one day could become *The Iliad* the next."[6]

Portable Tablets. These palm-size devices, such as the Palm VII, developed by several companies, provide digital readouts of information, delivered by cellular or other technologies.

Some of today's mobile digital pagers provide a version of this technology, with running news bulletins and sports scores on the pager's small screen. Portable tablets receive, but also send information that is written with an

T I M E F R A M E

Today to 1978: Digital media bring the world to your desktop

TODAY The Internet is causing an explosion of digital media development.

1998 One in four U.S. households is online.

1997 Roger Fidler invents the term "mediamorphosis" to describe the changes taking place in every media industry simultaneously.

1996 Online advertising reaches $200 million.

1995 The movie *Disclosure* popularizes the concept of virtual reality.

1994 Marc Andreessen and his colleagues at the University of Illinois introduce Mosaic, a browser that allows people to combine pictures and text in the same online document. (Netscape is today's most popular browser.)

1989 Tim Berners-Lee develops programming languages that allow people to share all types of information online and the first browser, which allows people to search online for the information they want.

1988 Only 1 percent of U.S. households is online.

1978 Nicholas Negroponte at the Massachusetts Institute of Technology first uses the term "convergence" to describe the intersection of the media industries.

electronic pen or typed on the tablet, using a small keypad about the size of today's TV remote control.

Larger, Clearer TV Screens. A common TV screen size is 32 inches to 36 inches, but some of today's new home theater systems include 125-inch TV screens. Current TV screens cannot deliver the picture quality that high-definition television (HDTV) and Web TV (see p. 170) demand.

Current broadcast TV images are created from 550 horizontal lines that run across the screen. Pictures and text that appear on screens larger than 36 inches are hard to read, but new technology called **line doublers** and **line quadruplers** can actually double and quadruple the number of lines scanning the screen to make the picture sharper.

Doubler technology receives the 550-line broadcast image, changes it into a digital signal and doubles or quadruples the number of lines to as high as 2,200. The result is a much clearer picture. (The clarity of the picture is called **resolution**.)

line doublers and line quadruplers devices that can double or quadruple the number of lines scanning the TV screen to make the picture sharper.

resolution clarity of the picture on the screen.

Russell Hafferkamp and his dog, Syd, have everything they need to watch TV, including a large-screen television with a built-in line doubler to create a sharper picture.

San Francisco Chronicle/Laura Cerri

Doubler technology will be especially important for the development of Web TV because people who are sitting far across the room won't be able to see the image on the screen without better picture resolution. However, the cost of such a home theater system today is prohibitive for most people.

A 125-inch projection TV with video player, laserdisc player, quadrupler, digital satellite dish and cable access runs about $250,000.[7] The high cost will discourage widespread adoption of this technology soon, but as the price drops, larger screens could become the standard.

Flat Panel Video Display Screens. About the same size as today's TV screens or larger, but only about 4 inches deep, flat panel video display screens hang on the wall like a picture, instead of requiring the large cabinet that houses today's TV and computer screens. Sony introduced its first flat panel video screen in 1998 with a price tag starting at $4,000. Screens like this, once they are affordable, will make all video technologies much more convenient to use.[8]

WHAT'S HAPPENING HERE? *MEDIAMORPHOSIS*

mediamorphosis the intense rate of change that occurs when all media change simultaneously.

This constantly changing media landscape has been called **mediamorphosis**, a word coined by information designer Roger Fidler to describe the way today's media are evolving. Fidler combined the words *media* and *morphosis* (a scientific term used to describe the way an organism or any of its parts undergoes change) to create a new word to describe the simultaneous changes taking place in the media world today.

Digital media forms "do not arise spontaneously and independently from old media," says Fidler. Digital media are related and connected to old media. *Mediamorphosis* "encourages us to examine all forms [of communication media] as members of an interdependent system, and to note the similarities and relationships that exist among past, present and emerging forms."[9]

The digital media that are emerging will be similar to the old media, yet different in ways that will make them distinct from their predecessors, says Fidler. Because of the interdependence of all media, this change will be more intense because changes will happen simultaneously.

ARE OLD MEDIA DYING?

Will the development of digital media mean the death of old media? Some observers have predicted, for example, that the medium of print is dead. "The end of the book is near!" is a headline that has appeared frequently. Yet book sales continue to be healthy and are currently at an all-time high.

The history of the evolution of media shows that the introduction of a new medium does not mean the end of an old medium. The continuing overall growth and expansion of the media industries during the last century support this conclusion.

When television was introduced, for example, radio did not disappear. Instead, radio adapted to its new place in the media mix, delivering music, news and talk. Today, radio exists very comfortably alongside television.

Movies, which also were threatened by the introduction of television, responded by delivering more spectacular and more explicit entertainment than people could see on television, and today movies still play an important role in the business of media.

"When newer forms of communication media emerge, the older forms usually do not die—they continue to evolve and adapt,"[10] says Fidler. In this way, the different media compete for the public's attention and jockey for positions of dominance, but no medium has yet disappeared. Instead, each medium contributes to the development of its successors. Together, all media that now exist will contribute to the media that are yet to be invented.

DIGITAL MEDIA CONVERGENCE

In 1978, Nicholas Negroponte at the Massachusetts Institute of Technology began popularizing a theory called **convergence**. This theory gave a name to the process by which the work of the various media industries was beginning to intersect, and MIT was among the first places to foresee and identify this trend.

convergence the process by which the various media industries intersect.

Nicholas Negroponte, of the Massachusetts Institute of Technology's Media Lab, popularized the concept of convergence.

Copyright ©Louis Fabian Bachrach

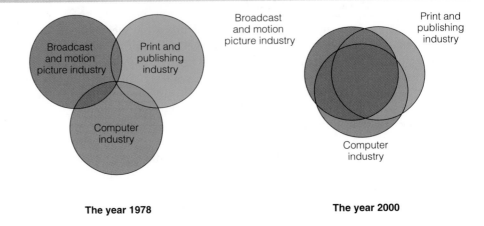

Figure 9.2 How the MIT Media Lab described convergence.

Source: MIT Media Lab.

The media industries not only were combining economically, as media companies began to buy and sell each other, but the technology of the industries also was merging, according to MIT, which meant that eventually the products the media companies produced would begin to resemble each other.

Negroponte also said that the combination of the media industries with the computer industry would create a new type of communication. To identify what was happening, Negroponte created two diagrams (See Figure 9.2) to show the position of the media industries in 1978 and his projected vision for those industries in the year 2000. He listed three segments of the media business: (a) print and publishing; (b) broadcast and motion pictures and (c) the computer industry.

The first diagram displays the alignment of the media industries in 1978, which shows them with a small amount of integrated territory. In the second diagram, which shows Negroponte's predictions for the year 2000, the three segments of the media industries are completely overlapping.[11]

Negroponte's forecast is a very accurate prediction of exactly what happened, and helped establish the framework for today's thinking about future media.

Today's economic and technological convergence in the media industries is the most important reason for the development of digital media. Each of the media industries is equally well-positioned to take advantage of new developments, and each of the media industries will benefit from convergence.

Today, many media companies, because of their size, also have the money available to invest in new technologies. These companies also have a shared interest in seeing their investments succeed. So convergence is likely to continue at a very rapid pace, which means that many digital media products will become available quickly.

Which Digital Media Products Will Succeed?

As digital media products flood the marketplace, some will succeed, and many will not. However, the potential reward if consumers adopt a digital media product is so big that all types of media companies are willing to take the risks associated with developing new products. For consumers, this means a confusing array of product choices bombarding the marketplace as each company tries to develop the one product that a large group of consumers will embrace.

There are parallels between the early history of traditional media and the emerging technologies that are being used to create a new popular product that the public craves that will eventually result in the development of a brand new medium.

Digital Media Lessons From History

In the early 1900s, when movies first were introduced as flickering images on a small screen, the moving images were something consumers hadn't seen before, but many people saw the silent movies as just a passing fad (see Chapter 8).

The inventions that had been introduced by Thomas Edison and his colleagues at the time made the movies technologically possible, but the movies also needed creative minds like director D. W. Griffith and stars like Mary Pickford to create epic stories that people wanted to see.

When new inventions brought sound to the movies, the success of the new medium was unstoppable. This combination of technological development, creative expression and consumer demand was crucial for the movies' enduring prosperity.

The same collision of economics, technology and creativity that drove the early days of the movie industry is behind today's race to develop digital media. Today, media and computer entrepreneurs are hoping to capitalize on fast-moving developments in technology to be the first to deliver a new creative product that large numbers of people want.

DIGITAL MEDIA AND THE WEB

The first sign of the expansion of the Internet to consumer and educational users in the early 1990s was the adoption by businesses and private users of electronic mail, or **e-mail**, technology. With a computer, a modem and a telephone line, just about anyone can learn how to communicate electronically online. It is projected that more than 70 percent of people with computers in the United States will be online at home by the year 2001. (See Impact/ Industry, p. 212.)[12]

"The driving force for achieving large subscriber gains is the incorporation of the Internet by consumers as part of their routine," says Veronis, Suhler & Associates, a media research company. "The Internet has become a tool that allows users to economize on what has become their scarcest resource—time. Virtually all of the leading Internet applications allow users to accomplish tasks more quickly than they can through alternative means."[13]

Just as telephone answering machines changed voice communication by allowing people to send and receive messages on their own time schedule, e-mail allows people to communicate and receive information at their convenience. People who are online at home today are most likely to use the technology to gather news and information or to send and receive e-mail.[14] (See impact/Industry, p. 212)

E-mail at school, work or at home is the way most people first experience communicating in an electronic environment. E-mail is easy to use and convenient, and it is a text-based system, which means that people type in messages on a keyboard, which is a familiar tool.

Familiarity and convenience are very important in the adoption of new technologies because people's fear of something they don't understand, and

e-mail electronic messages delivered online.

INDUSTRY IMPACT

Digital Media and the Web

Access to digital media in the U.S. is skyrocketing, with people going online at home as well as at work.

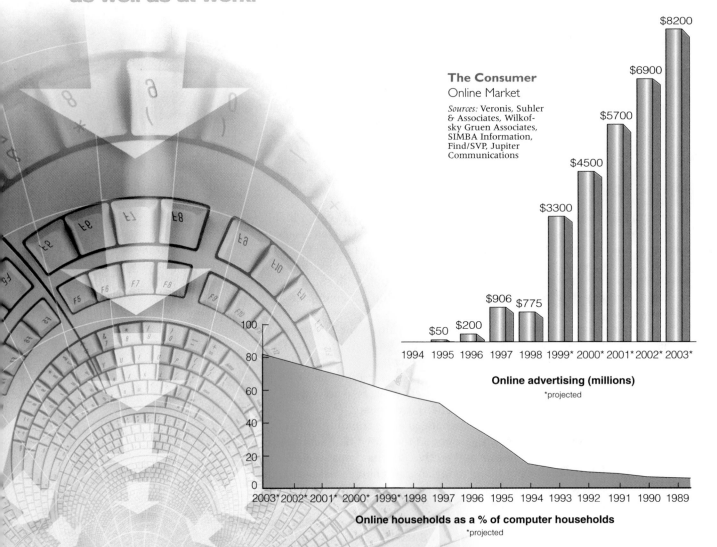

The Consumer Online Market

Sources: Veronis, Suhler & Associates, Wilkofsky Gruen Associates, SIMBA Information, Find/SVP, Jupiter Communications

$8200
$6900
$5700
$4500
$3300
$906
$775
$50
$200

1994 1995 1996 1997 1998 1999* 2000* 2001* 2002* 2003*

Online advertising (millions)
*projected

Online households as a % of computer households
*projected

2003* 2002* 2001* 2000* 1999* 1998 1997 1996 1995 1994 1993 1992 1991 1990 1989

Experts predict that more than 70% of people with computers in the U.S. will be online at home by the year 2001.

Sources: Veronis, Suhler & Associates, Wilkofsky Gruen Associates, Electronic Industries Association U.S. Bureau of the Census, Odyssey Inc. Ventures, Fine/SVP.

Paul Saffo developed the 30-year rule, which says that a new idea takes about 30 years to be adopted within a culture.

Steve Castillo Photos

misunderstandings about how new technologies work, can keep them from changing their current habits.

PREDICTING THE PACE OF CHANGE

Just how quickly consumers will adopt new technology is predictable, according to Paul Saffo, a director of the Institute for the Future in Menlo Park, California. Saffo theorizes that for the past five centuries the pace of change has always been 30 years, or about three decades, from the introduction of a new idea to its complete adoption by the culture.

Saffo called his theory the **30-year rule**, which he has divided into three stages. In the first decade, he says, there is "lots of excitement, lots of puzzlement, not a lot of penetration." In the second decade, "lots of flux, penetration of the product into society is beginning." In the third decade, the reaction to the technology is "'Oh, so what? Just a standard technology and everybody has it.'"[15]

By Saffo's standard, American society is probably entering its second stage of acceptance of online technology because use of the Internet by consumers started growing quickly beginning in 1988, when less than one-half of 1 percent of the U.S. population was online.[16] (See Figure 9.1, p. 204)

Saffo's description of the second decade of change coincides with the fluctuation seen in the media marketplace. People are faced with choices that seem to emerge daily: different combinations of new and existing media technology that are "guaranteed" to create the best digital world. While this technological transformation is underway, the digital media world seems very confusing.

30-year rule A theory about change, developed by Paul Saffo, which says that it takes about 30 years for a new idea to be adopted into the culture.

The most confusing, yet promising, place of all is the newest digital media
development, the World Wide Web.

WWW.COM: UNDERSTANDING THE WORLD WIDE WEB

Exchanging text through e-mail is a simple electronic operation, but several
more developments were necessary for people to be able to share text, graphics,
audio and video online. These developments made the creation of the World
Wide Web possible.

The person most responsible for creating the World Wide Web is Tim Berners-Lee, a British native with an Oxford degree in physics (see Impact/Profile,
p. 217). Working in 1989 in Geneva, Switzerland, at the CERN physics laboratory, Berners-Lee created several new programming languages.

HTML hypertext markup
language.

HTTP hypertext transfer
protocol.

links electronic connections
from one source of information to another.

These new programming languages included **HTML** (**hypertext markup
language**) and **HTTP** (**hypertext transfer protocol**) that allowed people
to create and send text, graphics and video information electronically and also
to set up connections (called **links**) from one source of information to
another. (These developments were very important in the Web's early days,
but today, just a few years later, people can create their own Web pages without knowing HTML and HTTP.)

After he had invented the language and mechanisms that would allow
people to share all kinds of information electronically, Berners-Lee gave this
invention its name—the World Wide Web. "The original goal was working
together with others," says Berners-Lee. "The Web was supposed to be a creative tool, an expressive tool."[17]

browser software that allows
people to search electronically
among many documents to find
what they want online.

Berners-Lee also created the first **browser,** which allows people to search
electronically among many documents to find what they want. The browser
was further defined by Marc Andreessen and his colleagues at the University
of Illinois, and in 1994 they introduced software called Mosaic, which
allowed people to put text and pictures in the same online document. One of

I M P A C T

profile

Tim Berners-Lee: The Man Who Invented the Web

By Robert Wright

You might think that some-one who invented a giant electronic brain for Planet Earth would have a pretty impressive brain of his own. And Tim Berners-Lee, 41, the creator of the World Wide Web, no doubt does. But his brain also has one short-coming, and, by his own account, this neural glitch may have been the key to the Web's inception.

Berners-Lee isn't good at "random connections," he says. "I'm certainly terrible at names and faces." (No kidding. He asked me my name twice during our first two hours of conversation.) Back in 1980 he wrote some software to help keep track of such links—a memory substitute. The rest is history.

This prosthetic extension of his mind took a vast evolutionary leap a decade later, and then grew to encompass the world. It is the reason that today you can be online looking at a photo, then mouse-click on the photographer's name to learn about her, then click on "Nikon" to see the camera she uses—traveling from computers in one end of the world to those in another with no sense of motion.

Copyright 1998–2000 by Seth Resnick

Berners-Lee is the unsung—or at least undersung—hero of the information age. Even by some of the less breathless accounts, the World Wide Web could prove as important as the printing press. That would make Berners-Lee comparable to well, Gutenberg, more or less. Yet so far, most of the wealth and fame emanating from the Web have gone to people other than him.

Marc Andreessen, co-founder of Netscape, drives a Mercedes-Benz and has graced the cover of several major magazines. Berners-Lee has graced the cover of none, and he drives a 13-year-old Volkswagen

Rabbit. He has a smallish, barren office at MIT, where his nonprofit group, the World Wide Web Consortium, helps set technical standards for the Web, guarding its coherence against the potentially deranging forces of the market.

Is Berners-Lee's Volkswagen poisoning his brain with carbon monoxide? He wonders about this by way of apologizing for the diffuseness of his answers. "I'm not good at sound bites," he observes. True, alas. But what he lacks in snappiness he makes up in peppiness.

Spouting acronyms while standing at a blackboard, he approaches the energy level of Robin Williams. He is British (an Oxford physics major), but to watch only his hands as he talks, you'd guess Italian. Five, six years ago, during his "evangelizing" phase, this relentless enthusiasm was what pushed the Web beyond critical mass.

The breathtaking growth of the Web has been "an incredibly good feeling," he says, and is "a lesson for all dreamers...that you can have a dream and it can come true."

Time magazine, May 19, 1997. © 1997 Time Inc. Reprinted by permission.

the successors to Mosaic is Netscape Navigator, currently the most widely used commercial browser.

Another level of help for Web access is the **search engine.** This is a tool used to locate information in a computer database. Some familiar search engines are Lycos, Infoseek, Excite and Yahoo! These devices turn your typed request for information into digital bits that then go and search for what you want and return the information to you.

search engine the tool used to locate information in a computer database.

I M P A C T
on you   *Top Web Search Sites*

There are different ways to search the Web. Search engines use software that crawls the Web and records the text on every page. When you make a query, the search engine goes into the depths of the page to find relevant keywords. A directory is an organized selection of categories, such as Travel and Food. The content within those categories has been hand-picked by humans. When you submit a query, it pulls up relevant sites from the ones in that directory.

TOP WEB SEARCH SITES

There are different ways to search the Web. Search engines use software that crawls the Web and records the text on every page. When you make a query, the search engine goes into the depths of the page to find relevant keywords. A directory is an organized selection of categories, such as Travel and Food. The content within those categories has been hand-picked by humans. When you submit a query, it pulls up relevant sites from the ones in the directory.

	Address	Type	How much of Web it searches	Comments
fast :::: Search	www.alltheweb.com	search engine	25%	Plans to access 100% of the Web over next year.
AltaVista	www.altavista.com	search engine	15.5%	One of the oldest search engines, recently invested in by CMGI.
Ask Jeeves	www.askjeeves.com	search engine	7 million answers	Lets users make queries in form of a question.
eXcite	www.excite.com	portal	5.6%	Plans to add more pages to its search and access about 50% of the Web
Google!	www.google.com	search engine	7.8%	Ranks Web sites based on how often they're linked to from other sites.
GO Network	www.go.com	portal	8%	The Mickey Mouse Corp. soon will own all of go.com.
looksmart	www.looksmart.com	directory	N/A	Has more than 60,000 categories of information.
LYCOS *Your Personal Internet Guide*	www.lycos.com	directory	2.5%	Recently switched from a search engine to a directory model.
Northern Light	www.northernlight.com	search engine	16%	Named for a clipper ship built in Boston in 1853 and known for its technology
YAHOO!	www.yahoo.com	directory	7.4%	Most-visited search site — more than 38.9 million visitors.

To encourage people to use their systems, both Berners-Lee and Andreessen placed their discoveries in the public domain, which meant that anyone with a computer and a modem could download them from the Internet and use them for free. *This culture of free information access, coupled with a creative, chaotic lack of direction, still permeates the Web today.*

The process of putting documents on the Web drew its terminology from print, the original mass medium. Placing something on the Web is called **publishing,** and begins with a **home page,** which is like the front door to the site, the place that welcomes the user and explains how the site works. However, even though Web sites are similar to published documents in the way they are described, what is created on the Web has none of the legal limitations or protections placed on other published documents. (See Chapter 14, p. 335, and Impact/Point of View, "A Wrong Kind of Education", p. 219)

publishing placing items on the Web.

home page the first page of a website that welcomes the user.

WHAT'S ON THE WEB?

Once Berners-Lee had created the tools for access so that all types of text and video images could become available on the Web, it was left to anyone who could use the tools to create whatever they wanted and make it available to anyone who wanted it.

"Nobody ever designed the Web," says Canadian sociologist Craig McKie, who maintains his own website. "There are no rules, no laws. The Web also exists without national boundaries."[18] Any type of information—pictures, voice, graphics and text—can travel virtually instantly to and from anyone with a computer and access to the Internet anywhere in the world.

There are Web sites devoted to every imaginable aspect of human communication. One woman, who learned that a friend had cancer, researched information about cancer treatment on the Web and then established a cancer information site to help others.

One Web site gave a digital image of the new Giants baseball park under construction in San Francisco, with video images sent every five seconds by cameras posted near the building site. The sponsoring group, Whole Earth Networks, fed the images to the Web until the park was completed in the year 2000.

An auto dealer in the Midwest created a Web page to advertise his dealership and uses the site to sell cars, demonstrating potential commercial uses for the Web. Now, he says, at least 10 percent of his buyers are online customers who shop their local dealership, bargain their price online and then drive up to 400 miles from the neighboring state to save money.

Banking has moved online, allowing electronic transactions that can occur anytime, not just when someone can get to an ATM or visit a bank. Several companies have created virtual banks, which are totally online, without any established offices, just online branches.

Early in 1998, the Web exploded with images of a dancing baby created by a software developer and popularized by the television program *Ally McBeal.* The baby drew even more attention when *Ally McBeal* won the Golden Globe Award for Best Television Series and the sequence, showing the main character dancing with the baby on the program, appeared as part of the Golden Globe broadcast.

Universal access, limited only by the available technology, is what gives the Web the feeling and look of what has been called "anarchy"—a world without rules. The Web is a new *medium,* but its growth to become a true *mass medium* for a majority of people seeking information and entertainment is limited only by digital technology and economics.

COMMERCIALIZING THE WEB

When television was introduced to the public in the late 1940s, the assumption from the beginning was that it would be a commercial medium—that is, the programming would be paid for by the advertisers who bought the commercials surrounding the programming. This concept of advertisers underwriting the programs was a natural evolution from radio, where commercials also paid for the programming.

The Web, however, began as a free medium. Many people pay an online service such as America Online to organize and deliver information and entertainment from many sources, including the Web, but the actual information—what's on the Web—is available for free.

Paying for Media on the Web

"Even as Internet use continues its dramatic surge, many if not most Internet ventures are losing money....The standing joke on the Web is that the letters 'ISP' don't really stand for 'Internet Service Provider' but for 'I'm still profitless.'"[19] People are still unwilling to pay for most of the information that's available on the Web.

Slate, the online literary magazine published by Microsoft, planned to start charging subscribers in 1997, but then decided against it. Editor Michael Kinsley said, "It would be better to establish a brand name with wide readership first."[20]

Nathan Myhrvold, who directs technology operations at Microsoft, says that Internet users will not pay for access to one site when "a million free sites are just a click away....There's no incentive until people are too addicted to the Net to turn off their computers, yet are bored with what's available."[21]

Myhrvold says that once people exhaust what's available for free on the Web, they may be willing to pay. The situation is similar, he says, to people who were previously satisfied with network and local television, but who now pay for cable or satellite TV to get access to expanded programming.

I M P A C T

point of view   *A Wrong Kind of Education*

By Esther Dyson
President, Electronic Frontier Foundation

The Net can't solve family problems any more than television can. The only good thing about television is that at least it is relatively harmless and keeps kids off the streets.

By contrast, the Net is both better, because it encourages participation, and worse, because you can get into real trouble on the Net, just as you could wandering outside your home. There still needs to be someone to guide you. And no, you should not necessarily be picking your own friends over the Net. The same freedom that can be liberating—whether the sheer ability to wander, or the chance to overcome limitations of looks, disabilities, geography, income, and other constraints—can be dangerous for children (and for adults, but that's another issue).

That's why there's such strong pressure to regulate content on the Internet. Cyberspace gives kids as much power as adults, but not as much wisdom. Children can roam from home much more eas-

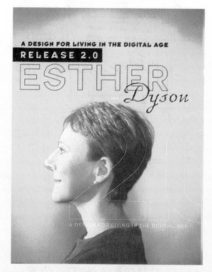

Jacket of *RELEASE 2.0* by Esther Dyson. Used by permission of Broadway Books, a division of Random House, Inc. Photo by Austin MacRae.

ily and cheaply than they could before. They can get to bad places on the Net much more easily than most downtowns, nightclubs, red-light districts, foreign countries, or friends' houses. And in cyberspace, no one knows if you're under 15—not even other 13-year-olds. In our current society, children get exposed all the time to messages meant for adults and not for children (at least according to the cigarette companies).

But on the Internet, they have the opportunity to interact with other people as adults. Even a socially inept child may be able to convince some adults online that he, too, is a grown-up; socially misfit adults, of course, are the least likely to pick up the signals that a person is not an adult—or to take advantage of that fact if they do.

Your friends who are looking for trouble can certainly find it online. Kids can find one another, talk about their parents—or drugs or sex—in a medium inaccessible to many parents and teachers.

Many parents feel uneasy in an environment that their child may understand better than they do. This particular problem will diminish as you and your generation become the parents and teachers of tomorrow, but the ability of children to operate in an adult world will persist.

The good news is that the Net does allow you to experiment more safely than you could in "real life."

Esther Dyson, *RELEASE 2.0*, New York: Broadway Books, 1997, pp. 95–96.

Some explicit Web sites charge for access, and some information sites, such as *The Wall Street Journal*, charge a nominal fee (the Journal claims to have 160,000 online subscribers).

Other sites, such as the sports network ESPN, give away some information and then charge for "premium" services. Online, interactive gamemakers, who offer videogames on the Web, charge by the hour or use a tiered pricing structure—free, basic and premium. "Everybody's fishing right now," says Chris Sherman, director of games for Concentric Networks, "and nobody knows what they're going to catch."[22]

BUYING PRODUCTS ON THE WEB

What makes the Web different from traditional media is its capacity to combine information, entertainment and commerce. People cannot only retrieve information and entertainment from the Web; they can buy things. The Web is interactive, which means that people can send information back and forth. Retailers can use the Web to sell products directly, without setting up a store or spending a lot of money on expensive advertising.

Two of the most successful commercial operations on the Web offer traditional media—*Amazon.com* sells books and *CD Now* (ww.cdnow.com) sells CDs. Amazon.com (See Impact/Profile on p. 28) sells many books at a discount, and features book reviews and author profiles, and it advertises that it can search more than one million titles. At CD Now, you can listen to 30 seconds of a song before buying it.

"The Internet has the potential to be the best sales tool—the best advertising and direct marketing vehicle—ever devised," says *Los Angeles Times* media critic David Shaw. "The Internet can turn any advertiser—any product manufacturer or service provider—into the equivalent of a direct marketer. On the Internet, consumers looking for a particular product or service can shop over the entire country—the entire world—looking at photographs and comparing prices, features and terms, and then buy what they want with a credit card and arrange to have the purchase delivered to their home."[23]

Most Web sites now carry some form of advertising. These appear as banners across the top of the Web site, or run as borders alongside the site's pages. But just like traditional media, advertising can crowd out the original message and turn consumers away. While few commercial online operations have been successful (and many have gone out of business) new Web site entrepreneurs continue to test the market to develop a pricing structure that will pay the bills.

IMPACT

digital

Internet Revolution Misses African Americans, Latinos

Rural Residents, Poor Also Left Behind, Government Survey Shows

By Ramon G. McLeod

Whites and Asians are at least twice as likely as blacks and Latinos to have access to the Internet, a racial "digital divide" that the federal government is beginning to see as a civil rights issue.

In a strongly worded report released [in 1999] by the Commerce Department, people who live in rural areas also were identified as among groups lagging in access to the Internet.

"These findings are meaningful because the Internet itself is meaningful. It is no longer simply a technological marvel. It is having a very significant impact on peoples' lives. The way things are now you can forget higher paying jobs if you don't know how to use it and you can't use it if you don't have access," said Kelly Levy, director of the domestic policy office for the National Telecommunications and Information Administration, a Commerce Department agency.

The report, titled "Falling Through the Net," showed Web use growing in all parts of U.S. society, but growth was far less among blacks, Latinos, the poor and rural groups.

Produced by a survey of 48,000 households, the study found that fully 40 percent had a computer of some kind and

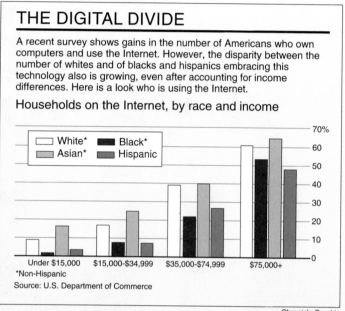

THE DIGITAL DIVIDE

A recent survey shows gains in the number of Americans who own computers and use the Internet. However, the disparity between the number of whites and of blacks and hispanics embracing this technology also is growing, even after accounting for income differences. Here is a look who is using the Internet.

Households on the Internet, by race and income

Legend: White* | Black* | Asian* | Hispanic

(Bar chart with income categories: Under $15,000; $15,000–$34,999; $35,000–$74,999; $75,000+; vertical axis 0 to 70%)

*Non-Hispanic
Source: U.S. Department of Commerce

Chronicle Graphic

that about one-quarter had Internet access at home.

But the details of the survey found great differences by race, income and location.

About 30 percent of white households had home access to the Internet as did about 26 percent of Asian households. On the other hand, only about 12 percent of black households had home access. Similarly, only about 13 percent of Latino households had home access.

The numbers rise when other access points—work, schools, libraries, and the like—are counted, but the division remains very large.

When asked if they had access to the Internet "anywhere," the government survey found that 37 percent of whites and 35 percent of Asians said they had

some kind of access. Among African Americans, only about 19 percent answered that they had access; only 16 percent of Latinos said they could get on the Web.

Money and location matter too, the study showed. About 60 percent of households with income over $75,000 had home Internet access. Rural households were less likely to have access at every income level when compared with their urban counterparts.

"Many Americans are being left behind," said Larry Irving, the Commerce Department assistant secretary for communications and information, at a Washington news conference to release the 108-page report.

"It is now one of America's leading economic and civil rights issues," Irving said.

San Francisco Chronicle, July 9, 1999, A11.

Electronic game players are among the small number of people who are willing to pay for online media. Here, game enthusiasts check out the offerings at Electronic Entertainment Expo, a videogame trade show.

Laura Noel

Tracking Online Buyers

Because the Web is such a targeted medium—the seller can know exactly who the buyer is—the Web holds better potential for monitoring consumers' buying habits than traditional methods of advertising. Ultimately Web advertisers "can achieve the merchandiser's dream—targeting an audience far more precisely than it can with either newspapers or television by advertising a product only on sites that draw people likely to be interested in that product," says David Shaw.

"Moreover, they will be able to get nearly instantaneous electronic feedback on whether their ads are effective: How many people saw the ad? How many 'clicked' on it and went on to a more detailed presentation? How many bought the product right then, online?"[24]

Software already is available that offers "tracking"—information for advertisers. Many sites give advertisers information about how many "hits" the sites receive—how many times people looked at the site. But this is not very reliable information because advertisers have no way to track how much of the ad people read, how much time they spent at the site, or most importantly, if they eventually bought a product that was advertised.

One company has developed "ad robots" that allow a company to, in effect, eavesdrop on chat room conversations while the user is online. If someone mentions online that they are having a problem with their car, for example, the robot would recognize the pattern of words in the discussion and send the person an ad for car repair.[25] But the future of direct consumer measurement on the Web is still uncertain and will become clearer only when the Web itself has further defined its direction.

Rhymes with Orange   Hilary B. Price

Reprinted with special permission of King Features Syndicate.

THE FUTURE OF DIGITAL MEDIA AND THE WEB

The future of digital media is bound only by the needs of consumers and the imaginations of media developers, as diverse as the people who are online today and going online tomorrow. The new media universe could become a purer reflection of the real universe than any medium yet created, with unprecedented potential, like all mass media, to both reflect and direct the culture.

"The Internet is still in its infancy, and its potential is enormous," writes David Shaw. "As technology continues to improve and its audience continues to grow—as users and advertisers alike become more comfortable with it and knowledgeable about it—the Internet could ultimately attract the kind of audience and generate the kind of advertising revenue that would enable it to revolutionize human communication even more dramatically than Johann Gutenberg's first printing press did more than 500 years ago." [26]

IN FOCUS

- The Internet is a combination of thousands of computer networks sending and receiving data from all over the world.

- Because of its global size and the absence of government controls, the Internet is completely different from traditional media.

- Digital media are the fastest growing type of media.

- Some examples of currently emerging digital media technologies are: immersive virtual reality systems, holographic theaters, personal channels, intelligent video agents, digital paper, portable tablets, line doublers and quadruplers for TV screens, and flat panel display screens.

- Information designer Roger Fidler coined the term "mediamorphosis" to describe the simultaneous evolution of several media industries at once.

- Nicholas Negroponte first created the concept of "convergence" in 1978 to describe the process by which the technologies of all the media industries are merging.

- The same collision of economics, technology and creativity that drove the development of traditional media are behind today's race to develop digital media.

- Electronic mail (e-mail) is the way most people first experience communicating in an electronic environment.

- Paul Saffo first defined the 30-year rule governing people's willingness to adopt new ideas.

- Tim Berners-Lee is the person most responsible for creating the World Wide Web.

- The free culture of the Web originated with its founders, who placed their discoveries in the public domain, which meant that anyone could use them for free.

- On the Web, any type of information—pictures, voice, graphics and text—can travel virtually instantly to and from anyone with a computer and access to the Internet anywhere in the world.

- While a few Web sites, such as explicit sites and online gaming sites, charge for their services, most people remain unwilling to pay for what's on the Web.

- What makes the Web different from traditional media is its capacity to combine information, entertainment and commerce.

- Many Web sites now carry some form of advertising.

- Marketers are developing tracking software to monitor consumers' online habits.

- The future of digital media is bound only by needs of consumers and the imaginations of developers, as diverse as the people who are online today and going online tomorrow.

WORKING THE WEB www

- **Electronic Frontier Foundation**
  www.eff.org
- **Electronic Rights Defense Committee**
  www.erights.qc.ca
- **The Industry Standard**
  www.thestandard.com
- **Journal of Electronic Publishing**
  www.press.umich.edu/jep
- **MIT Media Lab Project**
  casr.www.media.mit.edu/groups/casr/papert.html

INFOTRAC COLLEGE EDITION EXERCISES

Using InfoTrac College Edition, a fully searchable online database of articles and abstracts, do the following exercises as directed by your instructor:

1. Look up the three of the following keywords to get more information on the following new media:

   - virtual reality

   - digital paper

   - flat panel video display

- intelligent video agent

- PDAs (personal data assistants)

Print the articles and either:

a. write a brief paper on your findings, or

b. bring the articles to class and be prepared to discuss them.

2. E-mail has become much more common in recent years, but problems have emerged with its use. Use the keywords "e-mail" or "junk e-mail" to gather more information about users' problems with the new technology. Print at least three articles about a specific e-mail problem and either:

a. write a brief paper on your findings, or

b. bring the articles to class and be prepared to discuss them.

3. Read "Impact/Profile: Tim Berners-Lee: The Man Who Invented the Web" in Chapter 9. Using the keywords "Tim Berners-Lee," look up more articles about Berners-Lee. Print at least two of them and either:

a. write a brief paper on your findings, or

b. bring the articles to class and be prepared to discuss them.

4. Read "Impact/Point of View: A Wrong Kind of Education" in Chapter 9. Esther Dyson discusses children using the Internet in the article. Using the keywords "children Internet" on InfoTrac College Edition, find and print at least three articles that discuss the problems with children on the Web. Then write a brief paper citing your InfoTrac sources in which you analyze the problem and offer solutions.

5. Read "Impact/Digital: Internet Revolution Misses African Americans, Latinos" in Chapter 9. Using the keywords "black Internet," "Internet hispanic" or "Internet black," find and print at least three articles about the phenomenon. Then either:

a. write a brief paper on your findings, or

b. bring the articles to class and be prepared to discuss them.

CHAPTER 10

Advertising

got milk?

The advertising industry contends that the ultimate test of any product is the marketplace, and that (*advertising*) may stimulate consumers to try a new product or a new brand, but consumers will not continue to buy an unsatisfying product.

Louis C. Kaufman, author, Essentials of Advertising

What's Ahead

The American Marketing Association defines *advertising* as "any paid form of nonpersonal presentation and promotion of ideas, goods, or services by an identified sponsor." American consumers pay for most of their media (newspapers, magazines, radio and television) by watching, listening to and reading advertisements.

You pay directly for books, movies and recordings, although these media use advertising to sell their products. But the broadcast programs you want to hear and see and the articles you want to read are surrounded by advertisements placed by advertising people who want to sell you products.

PAYING FOR OUR PLEASURES: ADVERTISING AND THE MEDIA

Advertising is not a medium. Advertising carries the messages that come to you from the people who pay for the American media. The price for all types of

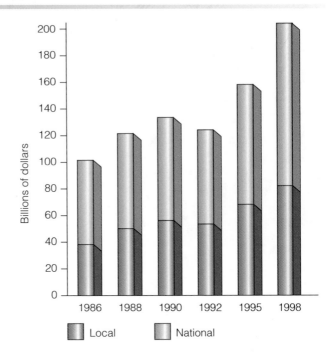

Figure 10.1 How U.S. Advertisers Spend Their Money: Local vs. National. Sixty percent of the money spent for advertising in the United States goes for national ads, and 40 percent goes to local advertising.

Data from McCann-Erickson *Insider's Report,* December 1998.

Total: $201 billion

advertising in America (including billboards and direct mail, as well as print and broadcast advertising) is nearly $200 billion a year (see Figure 10.1).

Americans were not the first consumers. In 1200 B.C., the Phoenicians painted messages on stones near the paths where people often walked. In the sixth century B.C., ships that came into port sent criers around town with signboards to announce their arrival. In the 13th century A.D., the British began requiring trademarks to protect buyers and to identify faulty products. The first printed advertisement was prepared by printer William Caxton in England in 1478 to sell one of his books.

Advertising became part of the American experience even before the settlers arrived. "Never was there a more outrageous or more unscrupulous or more ill-informed advertising campaign than that by which the promoters for the American colonies brought settlers here," writes historian Daniel Boorstin.

> *Brochures published in England in the seventeenth century, some even earlier, were full of hopeful overstatements, half-truths, and downright lies, along with some facts which nowadays surely would be the basis for a restraining order from the Federal Trade Commission. Gold and silver, fountains of youth, plenty of fish, venison without limit, all these were promised, and of course some of them were found. [1]*

Advertising in Newspapers

The nation's first newspaper advertisement appeared in *The Boston News-Letter*'s first issue in 1704 when the newspaper's editor included an ad for his own newspaper. The penny press of the 1800s counted on advertising to underwrite its costs. In 1833, the *New York Sun* candidly stated in its first issue: "The object of this paper is to lay before the public, at a price within the means of everyone, all the news of the day, and at the same time afford an advantageous medium for advertising."[2]

Three years later, the *Philadelphia Public Ledger* reported that "advertising is our revenue, and in a paper involving so many expenses as a penny paper, and especially our own, the only source of revenue."[3] Because they were so dependent on advertisers, newspapers in the 1800s accepted any ads they could get. Eventually they got complaints from customers, especially about the patent medicines that promised cures and often delivered hangovers. (Many of these medicines were mostly alcohol.)

Products like Anti-Corpulene pills claimed they would help someone lose 15 pounds a month. "They cause no sickness, contain no poison and never fail."[4] Dr. T. Felix Couraud's Oriental Cream guaranteed that it would "remove tan, pimples, freckles, moth patches, rash and skin diseases and every blemish on beauty."[5]

The newspaper publishers' response to complaints was to develop an open advertising policy, which allowed the publishers to continue accepting the ads. Then publishers criticized ads on their editorial pages. The *Public Ledger's* policy was that "Our advertising columns are open to the 'public, the whole public, and nothing but the public.' We admit any advertisement of any thing or any opinion, from any persons who will pay the price, excepting what is forbidden by the laws of the land, or what, in the opinion of all, is offensive to decency and morals."[6] But some editors did move their ads, which had been mingled with the copy, to a separate section.

Advertising historian Stephen Fox writes:

> *Advertising was considered an embarrassment…the wastrel relative, the unruly servant kept backstairs and never allowed into the front parlor….A firm risked its credit rating by advertising; banks might take it as a confession of financial weakness.*
>
> *Everyone deplored advertising. Nobody—advertiser, agent, or medium—took responsibility for it. The advertiser only served as an errand boy, passing the advertiser's message along to the publisher: the medium printed it, but surely would not question the right of free speech by making a judgment on the veracity of the advertiser.*[7]

Advertising in Magazines

Until the 1880s, magazines remained wary of advertising. But Cyrus H. K. Curtis, who founded *The Ladies' Home Journal* in 1887, promoted advertising as the way for magazines to succeed. Once when he was asked what made him successful, he answered, "Advertising. That's what made me whatever I am….I use up my days trying to find men who can write an effective advertisement."[8]

When Curtis hired Edward Bok as editor, Bok began a campaign against patent medicine ads and joined with *Collier's* and the American Medical Association to seek government restraints. Congress created the Federal Trade Commission in 1914, and part of its job was to monitor deceptive advertising. The FTC continues today to be the major government watchdog over advertising (see page 339).

Advertising on Radio

WEAF in New York broadcast its first advertising in 1922, selling apartments in New Jersey. B. F. Goodrich, Palmolive and Eveready commercials followed. In September 1928, the Lucky Strike Dance Orchestra premiered on NBC, and Lucky Strike sales went up 47 percent. More cigarette companies moved to radio, and Camel cigarettes sponsored weekly, then daily, programs.

Sir Walter Raleigh cigarettes sponsored the Sir Walter Raleigh Revue. In one hour, the sponsor squeezed in 70 references to the product.

The theme song ("rally round Sir Walter Raleigh") introduced the Raleigh Revue in the Raleigh Theater with the Raleigh Orchestra and the Raleigh Rovers; then would follow the adventures of Sir Walter in Virginia and at Queen Elizabeth's court, with ample mention of his cigarettes and smoking tobacco.[9]

In 1938, for the first time, radio collected more money from advertising than magazines.

Advertising on Television

Television began as an advertising medium. Never questioning how television would be financed, the networks assumed they would attract commercial support. They were right. In 1949, television advertisers totaled $12.3 million. In 1950, the total was $40.8 million. In 1951, advertisers spent $128 million on television.[10]

direct sponsorship a program that carries an advertiser's name in the program title.

In a practice adopted from radio, television programs usually carried **direct sponsorship**. Many shows, such as *Camel News Caravan*, carried the sponsor's name in the title and advertised a product (Camel cigarettes). Advertising agencies became television's programmers. "Given one advertiser and a show title often bearing its name, viewers associated a favorite show with its sponsor and—because of a 'gratitude factor'—would buy the products."[11]

Alfred Hitchcock became legendary for leading into his show's commercials with wry remarks about the sponsor: "Oh dear, I see the actors won't be ready for another sixty seconds. However, thanks to our sponsor's remarkable foresight, we have a message that will fill in here nicely."[12] But Hitchcock's sarcasm was the exception, and most TV programs today welcome advertising support without comment.

HOW ADVERTISEMENTS WORK

The word *advertise* originally meant to take note or to consider. By the 1700s, that meaning had changed. To advertise meant to persuade. "If we consider democracy not just a political system," says Daniel J. Boorstin, "but as a set of institutions which do aim to make everything available to everybody, it would not be an overstatement to describe advertising as the characteristic rhetoric of democracy."[13]

Advertising Shares Common Characteristics

Boorstin says that advertising in America shares three characteristics: repetition, style and ubiquity.

Repetition. When Robert Bonner bought the *New York Ledger* in 1851, he wanted to advertise his newspaper in the competing *New York Herald*, owned by James Gordon Bennett. Bennett limited all of his advertisers to the same size typeface, so Bonner paid for an entire page of the *Herald*, across which he repeated the message "Bring home the *New York Ledger* tonight." This is an early example of the widespread practice of repeating a simple message for effect.

An Advertising Style. At first, advertising adopted a plain, direct style. Advertising pioneer Claude Hopkins, says Boorstin, claimed that "Brilliant writing has no place in advertising. A unique style takes attention from the subject....One should be natural and simple…in fishing for buyers, as in fishing for bass, one should not reveal the hook."[14]

The plain-talk tradition is a foundation of what advertisers call modern advertising. But advertising today often adopts a style of hyperbole, making large claims for products. Boorstin calls this "tall talk."

The tall-talk ad is in the P. T. Barnum tradition of advertising. Barnum was a carnival barker and later impresario who lured customers to his circus acts with fantastic claims. You may recognize this approach in some of the furniture and car ads on television, as an announcer screams at you that you have only a few days left until all the chairs or all of the cars will be gone.

Both plain talk and tall talk combine, Boorstin says, to create advertising's *new myth*:

> *This is the world of the neither true nor false—of the statement that 60 percent of the physicians who expressed a choice said that our brand of aspirin would be more effective in curing a simple headache than any other brand….It is not untrue, and yet, in its connotation it is not exactly true."[15]*

Ubiquity. In America, advertising can be and is everywhere. Advertisers are always looking for new places to catch consumers' attention. Ads appear on shopping carts, on video screens at sports stadiums, atop parking meters.

> *The ubiquity of advertising is, of course, just another effect of our uninhibited efforts to use all the media to get all sorts of information to everybody everywhere. Since the places to be filled are everywhere, the amount of advertising is not determined by the needs of advertising, but by the opportunities for advertising, which become unlimited.[16]*

In some cases this ubiquity works to advertising's disadvantage. Many advertisers shy away from radio and TV because the ads are grouped so closely together. In 1986, in an attempt to attract more advertisers, TV began selling the "split-30" ad, which fits two 15-second ads into a 30-second spot. Even 10-second ads are available. Wherever these shorter commercials are sold, the station runs twice as many ads for different products, crowding the commercial time even more.

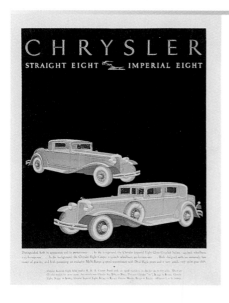

Sixty years after this ad for luxury transportation appeared in the May 1931 issue of *Fortune* magazine (left), this issue of *Fortune* magazine still carried a similar upscale appeal (right), targeting the same audience.

(Left) Courtesy Daimler-Chrysler Corporation (Right) Courtesy Daimler-Chrysler Corporation/Vic Huber Photography

Grabbing Your Attention

To sell the products, advertisers must catch your eye or your ear or your heart (preferably all three). A study by the Harvard Graduate School of Business Administration reported that the average American is exposed to 500 ads a day. With so many ads competing for your attention, the advertiser must first get you to read, to listen, or to watch one ad instead of another. "The immediate goal of advertising [is to] tug at our psychological shirt sleeves and slow us down long enough for a word or two about whatever is being sold." [17]

How Ads Appeal to Consumers

You make your buying decisions based on several sources of information besides advertising: friends, family and your own experience, for example. To influence your choices, the advertising message must appeal to you for some reason as you sift through the ads to make judgments and choose products. Humanities and human sciences professor Jib Fowles in his book *Mass Advertising as Social Forecast* enumerated 15 appeals, which he calls an "inventory of human motives" that advertisers commonly use in their commercials:

1. *Need for sex.* Surprisingly, Fowles found that only 2 percent of the television ads he surveyed used this appeal. It may be too blatant, he concluded, and often detracts from the product.

2. *Need for affiliation.* The largest number of ads use this approach: You are looking for friendship. Advertisers can also use this negatively, to make you worry that you'll lose friends if you don't use a certain product.

3. *Need to nurture.* Every time you see a puppy or a kitten or a child, the appeal is to your maternal or paternal instincts.

4. *Need for guidance.* A father or mother figure can appeal to your desire for someone to care for you, so you won't have to worry. Betty Crocker is a good example.

5. *Need to aggress.* We all have had a desire to get even, and some ads give you this satisfaction.

Reprinted by permission
of Nick Hobart.

"Of course, Brian, this victory wouldn't have been possible without fresh, white overalls."

Which of the 15 advertising appeals listed here can you identify in this current billboard ad?

©Evan Agostini/Gamma Liaision

6. *Need to achieve.* The ability to accomplish something difficult and succeed identifies the product with winning. Sports figures as spokespersons project this image.

7. *Need to dominate.* The power we lack is what we can look for in a commercial: "Master the possibilities."

8. *Need for prominence.* We want to be admired and respected, to have high social status. Tasteful china and classic diamonds offer this potential.

9. *Need for attention.* We want people to notice us; we want to be looked at. Cosmetics are a natural for this approach.

10. *Need for autonomy.* Within a crowded environment, we want to be singled out, to be "a breed apart." This can also be used negatively: You may be too ordinary if you don't use a particular product.

11. *Need to escape.* Flight is very appealing; you can imagine adventures you cannot have. The idea of escape is pleasurable.

12. *Need to feel safe.* To be free from threats, to be secure is the appeal of many insurance and bank ads.

13. *Need for aesthetic sensations.* Beauty attracts us, and classic art or dance makes us feel creative, enhanced.

14. *Need to satisfy curiosity.* Facts support our belief that information is quantifiable, and numbers and diagrams make our choices seem scientific.

15. *Physiological needs.* Fowles defines sex (item no. 1) as a biological need, and so he classifies our need to sleep, eat, and drink in this category. Advertisements for juicy pizza are especially appealing late at night.[18]

FINDING THE AUDIENCE: WHICH DEMOGRAPHIC ARE YOU?

Advertisers target their messages to an audience according to the audience's needs. But an advertiser also seeks to determine the audience's characteristics. This analysis of observable audience characteristics is called **demographics**

Demographics are composed of data about a target audience's sex, age, income level, marital status, geographic location and occupation. These data are observable because they are available to advertising agencies through census data and other sources. Advertising agencies use demographic audience analysis to help advertisers target their messages.

A motorcycle dealer certainly wouldn't want to advertise in a baby magazine, for example; a candy manufacturer probably wouldn't profit from advertising in a diet and exercise magazine. Advertising agencies try to match

demographics data about consumers' characteristics, such as age, sex, income level, marital status, geographic location, and occupation.

IMPACT

on you   *Digital Big Brother*

Tomorrow's Plugged-In World Could Pose a Threat to Consumer Privacy

By Deborah Solomon

I t's 2001 and you're surfing the Net, looking for information on breast cancer to help your mom, who's recently found a lump.

You buy a book, check out some Web sites, even go to a chat room on the subject. A few days later, your new employer has some bad news: Your health coverage has been denied because of a "pre-existing condition"— breast cancer.

The health plan came to that erroneous conclusion after buying information about your habits from a marketing firm, which has been tracking your every move.

If George Orwell thought 1984 was going to be bad, he'd freak at what's coming in the next century.

Soon, what we watch, what we read, even what we keep in our refrigerators, may be accessible to someone other than ourselves.

That's because companies are working on ways to network our homes—linking every appliance together and connecting them all to the Internet. High-tech companies want to connect our TVs with our PCs, our refrigerators with the Internet and our cell phones with our ovens.

But the futuristic ideas gaining steam in Silicon Valley worry privacy advocates, who fear all this

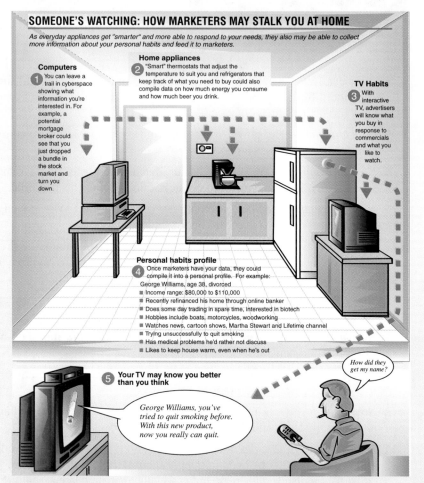

SOMEONE'S WATCHING: HOW MARKETERS MAY STALK YOU AT HOME

As everyday appliances get "smarter" and more able to respond to your needs, they also may be able to collect more information about your personal habits and feed it to marketers.

Computers
1. You can leave a trail in cyberspace showing what information you're interested in. For example, a potential mortgage broker could see that you just dropped a bundle in the stock market and turn you down.

Home appliances
2. "Smart" thermostats that adjust the temperature to suit you and refrigerators that keep track of what you need to buy could also compile data on how much energy you consume and how much beer you drink.

TV Habits
3. With interactive TV, advertisers will know what you buy in response to commercials and what you like to watch.

Personal habits profile
4. Once marketers have your data, they could compile it into a personal profile. For example:
George Williams, age 38, divorced
■ Income range: $80,000 to $110,000
■ Recently refinanced his home through online banker
■ Does some day trading in spare time, interested in biotech
■ Hobbies include boats, motorcycles, woodworking
■ Watches news, cartoon shows, Martha Stewart and Lifetime channel
■ Trying unsuccessfully to quit smoking
■ Has medical problems he'd rather not discuss
■ Likes to keep house warm, even when he's out

5. **Your TV may know you better than you think**

George Williams, you've tried to quit smoking before. With this new product, now you really can quit.

How did they get my name?

connectivity poses major security risks for consumers.

While privacy on the Internet has long been a concern, consumer advocates say the sheer number of devices that will soon be hooked to the Net and the data about consumers that will become available to companies are dangerous.

Most of the concern centers around the loss of control consumers experience once they enter cyberspace. If everything is linked to the Net, privacy advocates say, consumers won't be able to avoid leaving records of their personal information and won't be able to control how companies use that data.

San Francisco Chronicle, July 26, 1999, B-1. Reprinted by permission.

a client's product to a thoroughly defined audience so that each advertising dollar is well spent.

Defining the audience is very important because the goal of advertising is to market a product to people who have the desire for the product and the ability to buy the product. Audience analysis tells an advertiser whether there are enough people who can be targeted for a product to make the advertising worthwhile.

WHAT'S WRONG WITH ADVERTISING?

The study of advertising provokes three main criticisms, according to Louis C. Kaufman, author of *Essentials of Advertising:*

1. *Advertising adds to the cost of products.* Critics of advertising maintain that advertising, like everything that is part of manufacturing a product, is a cost. Ultimately, the consumer pays for the cost of advertising. But the industry argues that advertising helps make more goods and services available to the consumer, and that the resulting competition keeps prices lower.

2. *Advertising causes people to buy products they do not need.* Says media scholar Michael Schudson:

   Most blame advertising for the sale of specific consumer goods, notably luxury goods (designer jeans), frivolous goods (pet rocks), dangerous goods (cigarettes), shoddy goods (some toys for children), expensive goods that do not differ at all from cheap goods (nongeneric over-the-counter drugs), marginally differentiated products that do not differ significantly from one another (laundry soaps), and wasteful goods (various unecological throw-away convenience goods).[19]

   The advertising industry contends that the ultimate test of any product is the marketplace, and that advertising may stimulate consumers to try a new product or a new brand, but consumers will not continue to buy an unsatisfying product.

3. *Advertising reduces competition and thereby fosters monopolies.* Critics point to the rising cost of advertising, especially television, which limits which companies can afford to launch a new product or a new campaign. The industry argues that advertising is still a very expensive way to let people know about new products. "The cost of launching a nationwide advertising campaign may be formidable," writes Louis C. Kaufman, "but the cost of supporting larger, nationwide sales forces for mass-marketed goods would be greater still."[20]

To answer these and other criticisms, the American Association of Advertising Agencies (called the 4As) introduced—what else?—an advertising campaign to explain their point of view. The AAAA ads questioned the assumptions that many people make about advertising (see above). Criticism of advertising also extends to the types of products sold in some ads.

Does advertising work? According to media scholar Michael Schudson:

Apologists are wrong that advertising is simply information that makes the market work more efficiently—but so too are the critics of advertising who believe in its overwhelming power to deceive and to deflect human minds to its ends. Evaluating its impact is more difficult than these simplicities of apology and critique will acknowledge.[21]

A mural advertising Evian bottled water covers a wall of the Hyatt Hotel on Sunset Strip in West Hollywood.

AP/Wide World Photos

WORKING IN ADVERTISING

About 6,000 advertising agencies are in business in the United States, but most of them are small operations, earning less than $1 million a year. Advertising agencies buy time and space for the companies they represent. For this, they are usually paid a commission (commonly 15 percent). Many agencies also produce television and radio commercials and print advertising for their clients.

Depending on the size of the agency, the company may be divided into as many as six departments: marketing research, media selection, creative activity, account management, administration and public relations.

Marketing research examines the product's potential, where it will be sold, and who will buy the product. Agency researchers may survey the market themselves or contract with an outside market research company to evaluate potential buyers.

Media selection suggests the best combination of buys for a client—television, newspapers, magazines, billboards.

Creative activity thinks up the ads. The "creatives" write the copy for TV, radio and print. They design the graphic art and often they produce the commercials. They also verify that the ad has run as many times as it was scheduled to run.

Account management is the liaison between the agency and the client. Account executives handle client complaints and suggestions and also manage the company team assigned to the account.

Administration pays the bills, including all the tabs for the account executives' lunches with clients.

Public relations is an extra service that some agencies offer for companies that don't have a separate public relations office.

All of these departments work together on an ad campaign. An advertising campaign is a planned effort that is coordinated for a specific time period. A campaign could last anywhere from a month to a year, and the objective is a coordinated strategy to sell a product or a service. Typically, the company assigns the account executive a team of people from the different departments to handle the account. The account executive answers to the people who control the agency, usually a board of directors.

The members of the campaign team coordinate all types of advertising—print and broadcast, for example—to make sure they share consistent content. After establishing a budget based on the client's needs, the campaign team creates a slogan, recommends a strategy for the best exposure for the client, approves the design of print and broadcast commercials and then places the ads with the media outlets.

Advertising agencies tend to be clustered in big cities such as New York, Los Angeles, San Francisco and Chicago. In part, this is by tradition. The agencies may be near their clients in the city. They also have access to a larger pool of talent and facilities such as recording studios. But technology may enable greater flexibility.

THE BUSINESS OF ADVERTISING

The advertising business and the media industries are interdependent—that is, what happens in the advertising business directly affects the media industries. The advertising business is very dependent on the nation's economic health. If the national economy is expanding, the advertising business and the media industries prosper. If the nation falls into a recession, advertisers typically reduce their ad budgets, which eventually leads to a decline in advertising revenue for the agencies and also for the media industries where the agencies place their ads. During a recession, advertisers also may change their advertising strategies—choosing radio over television because it is much less expensive, for example.

The advertising industry today, therefore, must be very sensitive to economic trends. The success of an ad agency is best measured by the results an ad campaign brings. The agency must analyze the benefits of different types of advertising and recommend the most efficient combination for their clients.

Commercials on Television

Even though the cost seems exorbitant, sponsors continue to line up to appear on network television. "Advertisers must use television on whatever terms they can get it, for television is the most potent merchandising vehicle ever devised," writes TV producer Bob Shanks in his book *The Cool Fire: How to Make It in Television*. Shanks is talking about national advertisers who buy network time—companies whose products can be advertised to the entire country at once.

Minutes in every network prime-time hour are divided into 10-, 15- and 30-second ads. If an advertiser wants to reach the broad national market, television is an expensive choice because the average price for the TV time for a 30-second commercial is $100,000. The price tag can go as high as $2 million for a widely watched program such as the Super Bowl.

National advertising on programs like *3rd Rock From the Sun* is bought by national advertising agencies, which handle the country's biggest advertisers—Procter & Gamble and McDonald's, for example. These companies usually have

Advertisers must learn to adapt their messages for new audiences as new technology, such as the Internet, create new outlets for advertising.

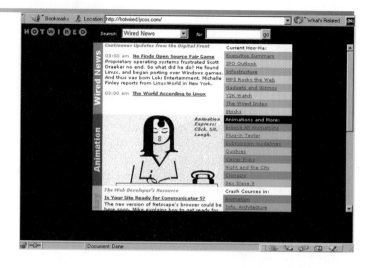

CPM   stands for cost-per-thousand, the cost of an ad per 1,000 people reached. (M is the Roman Numeral for 1,000.)

in-house advertising and public relations departments, but most of the advertising strategy and production of commercials for these companies is handled by the agencies. National agencies buy advertising space based on a careful formula, calculated on a cost-per-thousand **(CPM)** basis—the cost of an ad per 1,000 people reached.

Making a TV commercial for national broadcast is more expensive per minute than making a television program because each company wants its ads to be different from the rest. The price to create a TV commercial can run as much as $1 million a minute. That may be why, as one producer said, "the commercials are the best things on TV."[22]

Network television commercials certainly are the most visible type of advertising, but not everyone needs the reach of network television. The goal of well-placed advertising is to deliver the best results to the client for the lowest cost, and this may mean looking to other media.

Using the Internet, Print and Radio

Different types of media deliver different types of audiences. The Internet offers a large potential audience, but consumers can also quickly click past ads on the Web, so no one is quite sure how effective Web ads are. Network television delivers a large, diverse audience, at a high price. Advertising agencies also buy less expensive time and space in local television, radio, newspapers and magazines to target a specific audience by demographics: age, education, gender and income. (See Figure 10.2.) Language also can be a targeting factor. A radio station with a rock format delivers a different group from an easy-listening station. *The New York Times* delivers a different reader from the *Honolulu Advertiser*. *Sports Illustrated* targets a different group from *The Ladies' Home Journal*.

The competition among different media for advertisers is heavy:

- The American Newspaper Publishers Association commissions a study that reveals that only one in five prime-time adult viewers could remember the last ad they had seen on television.

- Print advertisers claim that remote channel changers zap many TV ads, making TV commercials an unreliable way to deliver an audience.

- *Time* advertises that more airline customers read its magazine than read *Newsweek*.

- AT&T launches a talking website to "express themselves better" to consumers.

- *Newsweek* advertises that it delivers more people for the money than *Time*.

- *Cosmopolitan* says that airline companies should advertise in its magazine because women who travel often don't watch daytime television.

- "Radio is the medium working women don't have to make time for," boasts the Radio Advertising Bureau (RAB). Whereas working women spend 15 percent of their daily media time reading a newspaper, they spend half of their media time with radio, says the RAB.[23]

Advertising agencies gather demographic information provided by Nielsen and Arbitron for broadcast and by the Audit Bureau of Circulations for print; the audience is converted into numbers. Based on these numbers, agencies advise advertisers about ways to reach buyers for their products.

Advertising Locally

Karen's Yogurt Shoppe, a small downtown business, does not need to advertise on *Frasier* or in *The New York Times*. Karen and other local businesses only need to reach their neighbors. Businesses larger than the yogurt shop, such as a car dealer or a furniture store, may buy local television or radio time, but most of the local advertising dollar goes to newspapers.

A local advertising agency can design a campaign, produce the ad, and place the ad just like the national agencies, but on a much smaller scale. Some small companies design and place their own ads directly with the local media.

To attract customers, local media often help companies design their ads. Newspapers, for example, will help a small advertiser prepare an ad using ready-made art. A radio or television station may include the services of an announcer or access to a studio in the price for a series of spot ads. Broadcast stations sometimes trade ads for services offered by the advertiser—dinner for two at the local restaurant in return for two spot ads, for example. Then the station gives the dinners away on one of its programs.

Advertising Sales Representatives. What if you manufacture sunglasses in Dubuque, Iowa, and you hire a local advertising agency to sell your product nationally? The agency tells you that they believe a good market for your product exists on the West Coast. How is the agency going to find out the most efficient way to sell your sunglasses in Los Angeles?

In this situation, many advertising agencies would contact a **rep firm**—a company of advertising sales representatives who sell advertising time and space in their market to companies outside the area. In this case, the agency in Dubuque would first decide who were the most likely customers for your sunglasses. If the agency decided that L.A.-area males age 18–24 are the best potential customers, the agency would budget a certain

rep firm a company of advertising sales representatives who sell advertising time and space in their market to companies outside the area.

Figure 10.2 Where Advertising Dollars Are Spent. Advertising income in the U.S. is evenly divided between print and broadcast. Online advertising has grown to 4% of total spending on advertising.

Source: The Veronis, Suhler & Associates *Communications Industry Forecast* 1999-2003.

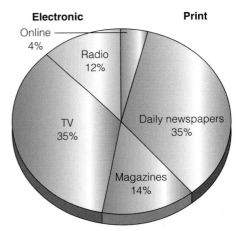

Shares for major media ad spending in the United States, 2000*

*projected

IMPACT
digital

Targeting Gets More Precise; Wall Separating Content from Ads Gets Wobbly

By George Anders

Tony Nethercutt points to a big white swatch of emptiness as his computer pulls up a page on the World Wide Web. Then he coyly tells his audience: "All that space is still available. It can still be yours. But there's a great land rush going on for advertising space on the Internet. Eventually, there will be a bidding war for sites like this."

Across the table, two Clorox Inc. executives listen eagerly to the ad salesman's presentation. They are looking for new ways to promote their Armor All line of car cleansers. Online advertising is new territory for them, but Mr. Nethercutt beckons with a $50,000 opportunity to reach a targeted audience. His proposal: Put their message on the Web pages of Kelley Blue Book Inc., the bible of used car data.

After a moment's pause, Clorox marketing manager Cary Rosenzweig nods his head. "I'm very supportive," he says. "This is the right thing to do…"

Blurring Some Lines

This surge is happening in part because advertisers see new ways cyberspace can fit their strategies. Some global marketers, such as General Motors Corp., are spending more online as they hunt for alternatives to television. Meanwhile, dozens of start-ups want to make a splash in online commerce, and their business plans

Tony Nethercutt

Photo: *Wall Street Journal*

practically force them to buy Internet ads.

Moreover, the online world is accommodating advertisers in ways that print and broadcast media would find impossible. Some of these ways are technological, including an exceptional ability to target specific customers. Others involve a willingness to blur the division between content and advertising, which traditional media regard as almost sacred. If the money is right, many online publishers are willing to strike whatever sort of partnerships an advertiser might want.

"There are so few rules here," says Anil Singh, senior vice president, sales, at Yahoo! Inc., the internet directory company in Santa Clara, Calif. Mr. Singh, who oversees a cyberspace sales force of about 100 people, relishes the way his company can help advertisers meet their goals. "Creativity is crucial," he says.

The Unknowns

Still, whether online advertising can live up to its champions' hopes is unclear. Rates are steep enough that some marketers wonder whether they can get enough response to justify the cost. Most advertisers pay at least as much to reach an Internet audience—typically $10 to $40 per 1,000 viewers—as they would for TV or magazine ads.

And online audiences often greet ads with a yawn, as measured by "click-through rates" of sometimes 1 percent or less. The rates show how often computer users point their mouse at an ad and ask for more information. "A lot of Internet banner ads are like billboards on the side of the highway," says Martha Deevy, a senior vice president at Charles Schwab & Co., a brokerage firm. "People drive right past them and don't bother to look."

Still, the people who sell space on the Internet often have something new and supposedly better than last month's way of advertising. These days, many are promoting "sponsorships," which cost more than simple banner ads at the corner of a Web page but showcase a message much more prominently. Also popular are "rich media" ads with video-like images, including flying golf balls and wiggling fingers, that are meant to engage Web surfers.

The Wall Street Journal, November 30, 1998, p. 1. Reprinted by permission.

amount of money for advertising in the Los Angeles area and then call the ad reps there.

The rep firm, in return, takes a percentage (usually 15 percent) of the advertising dollars they place. Ad reps are, in effect, brokers for the media in their markets.

Each rep firm handles several clients. Some ad reps sell only broadcast advertising and some specialize in print ads, but many rep firms sell all types of media. In this case, each L.A. ad rep would enter the demographics ("demos") for your product into a computer. Based on ratings, readership and the price for the ads, each rep would come up with a CPM (cost per thousand people reached) for your product. The rep then would recommend the most efficient buy—how best to reach the people most likely to want your sunglasses.

Each rep then presents an L.A. advertising plan for your product to the agency in Dubuque. Usually the buy is based on price: The medium with the lowest CPM gets the customer. But a rep who cannot match the lowest CPM might offer incentives for you to choose his or her plan: If you agree to provide 50 pairs of sunglasses, for example, the rep's radio station will give away the glasses as prizes during a local program, each time mentioning the name of your product. So even though the ad time you buy will cost a little more, you will also get promotional announcements every time the station gives away a pair of sunglasses. Other ad reps might offer different packages.

The agency in Dubuque then would decide which package is the most attractive and would present that proposal to you. This entire process can take as little as 24 hours for a simple buy such as the one for your sunglasses account, or as long as several weeks for a complicated campaign for a big advertiser.

REGULATING ADVERTISERS

Government protection for consumers dates back to the beginning of this century when Congress passed the Pure Food and Drug Act in 1906, mainly as a protection against patent medicine ads (see Edward Bok's campaign against patent medicine advertising, Chapter 3). The advertising industry itself has adopted advertising standards, and in some cases the media have established their own codes.

Advertising Liquor

Although you regularly see advertisements on television for beer and wine, the TV networks do not advertise hard liquor. For three decades, the Distilled Spirits Council of the United States, operating under a voluntary Code of Good Practice, did not run television ads. In 1996, some liquor companies decided to challenge the voluntary ban by placing ads on local television.

Seagram's, the first company to challenge the ban, advertised Royal Crown whiskey on a local TV station in Texas. "We believe distilled spirits should have the same access to electronic media, just the same way beer and wine do," said Arthur Shapiro, executive vice president in charge of marketing and strategy for Seagram's in the United States.[24]

The Federal Trade Commission and the Bureau of Alcohol, Tobacco and Firearms regulate the spirits industry, but neither agency has the authority to ban liquor ads on television. Some members of Congress have said they will introduce legislation to ban most alcohol advertising from TV from 7 A.M. to 10 P.M. Even though they could gain a great deal of income from advertising hard liquor, the TV networks maintain that they will not accept the ads.

Although ads for beer and wine regularly appear on TV, companies that produce hard liquor had voluntarily agreed not to use television. But in 1996, some hard liquor companies challenged the ban by placing ads on local TV.

AP/Wide World Photos

Advertising That Deceives the Consumer

Government oversight is the main deterrent against deceptive advertising. This responsibility is shared by several government agencies.

1. *The Federal Trade Commission (FTC)*, established in 1914, can "stop business practices that restrict competition or that deceive or otherwise injure consumers."[25] If the FTC determines that an ad is deceptive, the commission can order the advertiser to stop the campaign. The commission also can require corrective advertising to counteract the deception. In 1993, for example, the FTC launched an investigation of the nation's weight-loss clinics, charging that they were using deceptive advertising.

2. *The Food and Drug Administration (FDA)* oversees claims that appear on food labels or packaging. If the FDA finds that a label is deceptive, the agency can require the advertiser to stop distributing products with that label. Orange juice that is labeled "fresh," for example, cannot be juice that has been frozen first.

3. *The Federal Communications Commission (FCC)* enforces rules that govern the broadcast media. The FCC's jurisdiction over the broadcast industry gives the commission indirect control over broadcast advertising. In the past, the FCC has ruled against demonstrations of products that were misleading and against commercials that the FCC decided were tasteless.

Other government agencies, such as the Environmental Protection Agency and the Consumer Product Safety Agency, also can question the content of advertisements. Advertising agencies have formed the National Advertising Review Board (NARB) to hear complaints against advertisers. This effort at self-regulation parallels those of some media industries, such as the movie industry's ratings code and the recording industry's record labeling for lyrics.

TECHNOLOGY TRANSFORMS THE FUTURE

The future of advertising will parallel changes in the media, in technology, and in demographics. As more U.S. products seek international markets, advertising must be designed to reach those markets. American agencies today collect nearly half of the *world's* revenue from advertising. (See Figure 10.3).

International advertising campaigns are becoming more common for global products, such as Coca-Cola and McDonald's, and this has meant the creation of international advertising. Cable News Network (CNN) announced in 1991 that it would be selling advertising on CNN worldwide, so that any company in any nation with CNN's service could advertise its product to a worldwide audience. Overall, billings outside the United States are commanding an increasing share of U.S. agencies' business (see Figure 10.4).

A second factor in the future of advertising is changing technology. As new media technologies create new outlets, the advertising community must adapt. Advertisers are trying to figure out how to reach consumers on their computer screens. Or a tennis instructional video could include advertising for tennis products. One company is using lasers to create advertising in the evening sky.

A third factor in the future of advertising is shifting demographic patterns. As the ethnicity of the nation evolves, marketing programs must adapt to reach new audiences. Future television ads could include dialogue in both English and

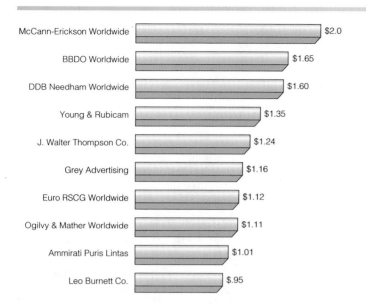

Figure 10.3 The Top 10 U.S. Ad Agencies by Gross Income for 1998 (in billions).

Source: *Ad Age Data Place*, April 19, 1999.

Spanish. Some national ad campaigns already include multilingual versions of the same ad, targeted for different audiences.

The challenges for the advertising business are as great as the challenges for the media industries. The advertising industry will do what it has always done to adapt—follow the audience. The challenge for advertising will be to learn how to efficiently and effectively match the audience to the advertising messages the media deliver.

IN FOCUS

- Advertising carries the messages that come to you from the sponsors who pay for the American media.

- As early as 1200 B.C., the Phoenicians painted messages on stones to advertise. In 600 B.C., ship captains sent criers around to announce that their ships were in port. In the 13th century A.D., the British began requiring trademarks to protect buyers.

- Newspapers were the first medium to use advertising in 1704. Magazines, radio and television followed.

- Daniel Boorstin says that advertising in America shares three characteristics: repetition, an advertising style and ubiquity.

- Advertising can catch your attention, according to Jib Fowles, in 15 ways, including playing on your need to nurture, your need for attention and your need to escape.

- Advertising provokes three main criticisms: advertising adds to the cost of products; advertising causes people to buy products they do not need; advertising reduces competition and thereby fosters monopolies.

- Today's advertising agencies use sophisticated technology to track demographics to help deliver the audience the advertiser wants.

Figure 10.4 Advertising goes global: In 1998, the United States accounted for 49 percent of the world's spending on advertising.

Source: McCann-Erickson *Insider's Report*, December 1998.

**Total worldwide ad spending
1998 ($436 billion)**

■ The advertising business and the media industries are interdependent—what happens in the advertising business directly affects the media industries. The advertising business is very dependent on the nation's economic health.

■ The industry is divided into national and local advertising. Advertising sales representatives broker local accounts to out-of-town advertisers.

■ The media compete with each other for the advertising dollar, and some media are better than others for particular products.

■ In 1996, the distilled spirits industry challenged the industrywide voluntary ban on liquor advertising on TV that has lasted for three decades. Although the TV networks still refuse to carry the ads, the liquor industry is placing the ads on local TV stations. Seagram's was the first company to break the ban, advertising on a local TV station in Texas.

■ Protection for consumers from misleading advertising comes from government regulation (Federal Trade Commission, Food and Drug Administration, and Federal Communications Commission, for example); from advertising industry self-regulatory groups (National Advertising Review Board, for example); and from codes established by the media industries.

■ The future of advertising will parallel the development of international markets, the refinement and expansion of new media technologies (especially the Internet), and changing demographics.

WORKING THE WEB

■ **Advertising Age**
adage.com
■ **Advertising Council**
www.adcouncil.org
■ **American Advertising Federation**
www.aaf.org
■ **Federal Trade Commission**
www.ftc.gov

INFOTRAC COLLEGE EDITION EXERCISES

Using InfoTrac College Edition, a fully searchable online database of articles and abstracts, do the following exercises as directed by your instructor.

1. Read "Impact on You: Digital Big Brother" and "Impact/Digital: Targeting Gets More Precise" in Chapter 10. Using the keywords "Internet Web advertising," look up at least three articles on web advertising and privacy issues. Then, write a brief paper on your findings on one of two topics:

a. how marketers gather information on consumers, or

b. how advertisers are being lured to the Internet.

2. Television and radio ads are some of the most lucrative forms of advertising. Look up the keywords "television ads," "radio advertising," or

"broadcast advertising." Find at least three articles about broadcast ads and either:

a. write a brief paper on you findings, or

b. bring the articles to class and be prepared to discuss them.

3. What effects do advertisements have on children? There have been many studies on this topic. Enter the keywords "advertising children" to research information on how advertisers target children. Print at least three articles and either:

a. write a brief paper on your findings, or

b. bring the articles to class and be prepared to discuss them.

4. How do advertisers attempt to reach minorities and specific ethnic groups? Use the keywords "advertising minorities" or "advertising ethnic" to search for more information. Print at least three articles on the subject. Then bring the articles to class for a small-group discussion. Be prepared to offer your opinion on these techniques.

5. Use the keywords "advertising research" to find at least two articles on the subject of research into advertising. Be specific in your choices about an issue about advertising that interests you. Then, using your InfoTrac College Edition articles as your sources, write a brief paper on this issue of advertising research.

11

Public Relations

What's Ahead

At the end of the day, we all want to go home and say "I had lunch with (*Melanie*) Griffith."

Ruth Cohen, Public Relations Specialist

You may think that the cash rebate program offered by many of today's car manufacturers is a new idea, but in 1914 Henry Ford announced that if he sold 300,000 Model Ts that year, each customer would receive a rebate. When the company reached its goal, Ford returned $50 to each buyer.[1] This was good business. It also was good public relations. Like Henry Ford, public relations people today work to create favorable images—for corporations, public officials, products, schools, hospitals and associations.

Scholars have defined three methods to encourage people to do what you want them to do: power, patronage and persuasion. Power involves ruling by law, but it also can mean ruling by peer pressure—someone does something because his or her friends do. Patronage is a polite term for bribery—paying someone with favors or money to do what you want.

The third method—persuasion—is the approach of public relations. Like advertising, public relations is not a mass medium. Public relations is a media support industry. In the classic definition, public relations involves creating an understanding for, or goodwill toward, a company, a person or a product.

HOW PUBLIC RELATIONS GREW

One of the first political leaders to realize the importance of public relations was Augustus Caesar, who commissioned statues of himself in the first century to be erected throughout the Roman Empire to enhance his image.[2] Many political leaders have ordered heroic images of themselves printed on coins and stamps.

Today's public relations approach can be traced to the beginning of the 20th century. Journalists were an important reason for the eventual emergence of the public relations profession.

THE PRESS AND PUBLIC RELATIONS

Before 1900, business had felt that it could work alongside the press, or even ignore it. Many stories that appeared in the press promoted companies that bought advertising. Then the Industrial Revolution arrived, and some industrialists exploited workers and collected enormous profits. Ida Tarbell and Lincoln Steffens began to make business people uncomfortable, writing stories for magazines like *McClure's* about the not-so-admirable characteristics of some companies (see Chapter 3).

> *No longer could the railroads butter up the press by giving free passes to reporters. No longer would the public buy whitewashed statements like that of coal industrialist George F. Baer, who in 1902 told labor to put their trust in "the Christian men whom God in His infinite wisdom has given control of the property interests of the country."* [3]

President Theodore Roosevelt fed public sentiment against the abuses of industry when he started his antitrust campaigns.

> *With the growth of mass-circulation newspapers, Roosevelt's canny ability to dominate the front pages demonstrated a new-found power for those with causes to promote. He had a keen sense of news and knew how to stage a story so that it would get maximum attention. His skill forced those he fought to develop similar means. He fully exploited the news media as a new and powerful tool of presidential leadership, and he remade the laws and the presidency in the process.* [4]

CORPORATE AND INSTITUTIONAL PUBLIC RELATIONS

The first publicity firm was called The Publicity Bureau and opened in Boston in 1900 to head off the growing public criticism of the railroad companies. The best-known early practitioner of public relations was Ivy Lee, who began his PR career by opening an office in New York with George F. Parker. Lee and Parker represented coal magnate George F. Baer when coal workers went on strike. A former newspaper reporter, Lee issued a "Declaration of Principles" that he mailed to city editors. This declaration became a manifesto for early public relations companies to follow.

Reacting to criticism that The Publicity Bureau had worked secretly to promote the railroads, Lee wrote:

> *This [the firm of Lee & Parker] is not a secret press bureau. All our work is done in the open. We aim to supply news….In brief, our plan is, frankly and openly, on behalf of business concerns and public institutions, to supply to the press and public of the United States prompt and accurate information concerning subjects which it is of value and interest to the public to know about.[5]*

Lee and Parker dissolved their firm in 1908 when Lee went to work as a publicity agent for the Pennsylvania Railroad. Eventually John D. Rockefeller hired Lee to counteract the negative publicity that began with Tarbell's investigation of Standard Oil. (Lee worked for the Rockefellers until he died in 1934.)

The idea of in-house corporate public relations grew as Chicago Edison Company and American Telephone & Telegraph began promotional programs. The University of Pennsylvania and the University of Wisconsin opened publicity bureaus in 1904, and the Washington, D.C., YMCA hired a full-time publicist to oversee fund-raising in 1905—the first time a publicist was hired for this job.[6]

GOVERNMENT PUBLIC RELATIONS

During World War I, the government set up the Committee on Public Information, organized by former newspaper reporter George Creel, blurring the line between propaganda and publicity. Creel recruited journalists, editors, artists and teachers to raise money for Liberty Bonds and to promote the nation's participation in the war. One of the people who worked for Creel was Edward L. Bernays. Both Bernays and Ivy Lee have been called the father of public relations.

In 1923, Bernays wrote the first book on public relations, *Crystallizing Public Opinion*, and taught the first course on the subject. Bernays was interested

In what was the largest public relations drive of its time, the Office of War Information promoted the role of the United States in World War II.

The Library of Congress

Doris Fleischman, a public relations pioneer, began her career in the 1920s. Her husband, Edward L. Bernays, pictured below, wrote the first book on public relations, *Crystallizing Public Opinion.*

Top and Bottom: Bettmann/CORBIS

in mass psychology—how to influence the opinions of large groups of people. Procter & Gamble, General Motors and the American Tobacco Company were among his clients. "Public relations," Bernays wrote in 1955, "is the attempt, by information, persuasion, and adjustment, to engineer public support for an activity, cause, movement, or institution."[7] In 1985, Bernays further defined public relations as "giving a client ethical advice, based on research of the public, that will win the social goals upon which the client depends for his livelihood."[8]

To sell the New Deal in the 1930s, Franklin D. Roosevelt used every tactic he knew. Comfortable with the press and the public alike, and advised by PR expert Louis McHenry Howe, FDR

> *projected an image of self-confidence and happiness—just what the American public wanted to believe in. He talked to them on the radio. He smiled for the cameras. He was mentioned in popular songs. He even allowed himself to be one of the main characters in a Rodgers and Hart musical comedy (played by George M. Cohan, America's favorite Yankee Doodle Dandy).[9]*

To gain support for the nation's entry into World War II, the federal government mounted the largest public relations drive in its history, which centered around the Office of War Information, led by former newscaster Elmer Davis. Public relations boomed with the postwar economy, and more women began to enter the field.

WOMEN IN PUBLIC RELATIONS

Doris E. Fleischman was among the first women in public relations when she joined her husband, Edward L. Bernays, in his PR firm. Fleischman was an equal partner with Bernays in their public relations business. An early advocate of public relations as a profession for women, Fleischman wrote in 1931 that "one finds women working side by side with men in forming the traditions and rules that will govern the profession of the future."[10]

Two other women who were public relations pioneers were Leone Baxter and Anne Williams Wheaton. Baxter formed Baxter and Whitaker in San Francisco with her husband, Clem Whitaker—the first public relations agency to specialize in political campaigns. In 1957, President Dwight Eisenhower appointed Anne Williams Wheaton as his associate press secretary.[11]

DEVELOPMENT OF ETHICS CODES

In the 1930s, the requirements for someone to work in public relations were loose, and many people who said they worked in public relations were press agents who were not above tricks to get attention for their clients. Henry Rogers, co-founder of what was then the world's largest entertainment PR firm, Rogers & Cowan (based in Beverly Hills), admitted that in 1939 he created a "best-dressed" contest to promote little-known actress Rita Hayworth.

There had been no contest, but Rogers dubbed Hayworth the winner of this fictional event. *Look* magazine gave Hayworth a ten-page spread. "Press agents, and that's what we were, would dream up all sorts of phony stories," he said. "Journalists knew they were phony but printed them because they looked good in print."[12]

During the 1950s, the question of ethics in public relations arose publicly when Byoir and Associates, hired by a railroad company to counteract the expansion of trucking, was charged with creating "front" organizations to speak out against the trucking industry. In court, Byoir's agency argued that they were exercising free speech. In 1961 the U.S. Supreme Court upheld Byoir's right to represent a client even if the presentation was dishonest, but this left the ethical issue of honesty unresolved.

The Public Relations Society of America (PRSA) established its first code of ethics in 1954 and expanded that code in 1959 with a Declaration of Principles.[13] That ethics code still exists today to guide the business of public relations. (Excerpts from the PRSA code are in Chapter 15.) PR professionals continue to argue among themselves about the differences between the profession's beginnings as press agentry (which often meant fabricating stories) and the concept of ethically representing a client's business, as Edward L. Bernays described.

Public relations grew throughout the 1960s and 1970s with the encouragement of television, the federal government and corporate America. In 1961, for example, the federal government had 1,164 people working as writer-editors and public affairs specialists. Today, the total number of people working in federal government public information jobs is nearly 4,000,[14] making the federal government the nation's largest single employer of public information people. (Public information is the name given to the job of government public relations.)

HOW PUBLIC RELATIONS WORKS

Public relations is an industry of specialties. The most familiar public relations areas are financial public relations, product public relations and crisis public relations, but there are many other specialty areas.

Financial Public Relations

People in financial public relations provide information primarily to business reporters. "Business editors like a PR staff that can provide access to top management," wrote James K. Gentry in the *Washington Journalism Review*, "that knows its company well or can find needed information quickly, that demonstrates ethics and honesty and that knows and accepts the difference between news and fluff."

Gentry then listed comments gathered from editors about what makes a bad PR operation:

- "Companies that think they can hide the truth from the public or believe it's none of the public's business."

- "I despise it when a PR person intercepts our calls to a news source but then isn't capable of answering our questions."

- "When they hire an outside PR firm to handle the job."

- "The 'no-comment' attitude. When they have little or no interest in going beyond the press release."

- "People who either get in the way of your doing your job, complain too much or are no help at all."[15]

Product Public Relations

Product PR uses public relations techniques to sell products and services. Many companies have learned that seeking publicity for a product often is less expensive than advertising the product. Public relations "is booming partly because of price," reports *The Wall Street Journal*. A PR budget of $500,000 is considered huge, whereas an ad budget that size is considered tiny.

At its best, PR can work better than advertising. Coleco Industries Inc. kicked off its Cabbage Patch Kids in 1983 with press parties thrown in children's museums, to which editors and their children were invited—and at which all received dolls to "adopt." "Reporters who adopted dolls felt a part of the process," a Coleco spokeswoman says. They had "a personal interest in…continuing to publicize it."[16]

The initial publicity for the Cabbage Patch dolls snowballed, as Cartier's used the dolls to display jewelry in its windows and First Lady Nancy Reagan gave dolls to two Korean children who were in the United States for surgery. Richard Weiner, who handled the publicity, charged Coleco $500,000. (See Impact on You, How Public Relations Sells You Products, p. 253).

On a smaller budget, the Wieden & Kennedy agency in Seattle contracted Bigger Than Life, Inc., which makes large inflatables to manufacture a 2 1/2-story pair of tennis shoes. The company attached the shoes to the Westin Copley Place hotel during the Boston Marathon and to the Westin Hotel in downtown Cincinnati during the March of Dimes walk-a-thon.

Pictures of the shoes appeared in *The New York Times*, the *Cincinnati Enquirer* and in newspapers as far away as Japan. Wieden & Kennedy estimated that buying the same advertising would have cost $7 million.

Crisis Public Relations

This aspect of public relations goes back as far as Edward Bernays responding to the charges against Standard Oil. The term *crisis public relations* has been used to describe the situation facing Johnson & Johnson after its product Tylenol was identified as the carrier of a poison that killed seven people in and near Chicago in 1982.

Johnson & Johnson and Burson-Marsteller, the company's PR agency, were credited with exceptional professionalism in handling the crisis. The Public Relations Society of America honored the companies for their performance. This is an example of responsible public relations in a crisis—when PR must counteract overwhelming negative information.

"The poisonings called for immediate action to protect the consumer," explained Johnson & Johnson's Lawrence G. Foster, who was vice president of public relations at the time, "and there wasn't the slightest hesitation about being completely open with the news media. For the same reasons, Johnson & Johnson decided to recall two batches of the product, and later to withdraw it nationally. During the crisis phase of the Tylenol tragedy, virtually every public relations decision was based on sound, socially responsible business principles, which is when public relations is most effective."[17]

Johnson & Johnson sampled public opinion about its activities with nightly telephone surveys. Pulling the product from the shelves cost $100 million, but as soon as Tylenol was out of the stores, the company was viewed as acting responsibly. The challenge then was to rebuild the product's 37 percent share of the market.

The 2,500-member Johnson & Johnson sales force visited retailers and people in the medical community to rebuild confidence in Tylenol. Then Burson-Marsteller organized a televised 30-city satellite press conference for 600 journalists to give local media an equal chance at a nationwide story, which ensured broad coverage.

After relaunch of the product, Tylenol immediately regained a 24 percent share of the market and later regained its position as the nation's top-selling

I M P A C T

on you

How Public Relations Sells You Products

Tickle Me Elmo and Sing & Snore Ernie benefit from public relations

By Bruce Horovitz

Sometimes, the best way to sell to a kid is to target Mom and Dad. Just ask Tyco, maker of Tickle Me Elmo and Sing & Snore Ernie. Tyco employed very different marketing strategies for Ernie and Elmo. But both relied heavily upon one thing: public relations. The purpose each time was to get the good word out to the parents, and it worked. Ernie [was] the top-selling toy of 1997, just as Elmo was in 1996.

For Ernie, Tyco appealed indirectly to parents by coaxing retailers and trade publications to hype the toy. For Elmo, Tyco appealed directly to parents by pulling in talk show host Rosie O'Donnell as an avid fan.

The Elmo rage began shortly after Tyco's PR firm, Freeman Public Relations of Clifton, N.J., sent 200 Elmo dolls to producers of the Rosie O'Donnell Show, as well as to O'Donnell's then one-year-old son.

O'Donnell, one of daytime TV's most popular and influential talk show hosts, distributed the dolls to her audience in October 1996. But that was just the beginning. O'Donnell requested 200 more dolls for charity. Then, she asked for 200 more for a December show.

Meanwhile, former *Today Show* host Bryant Gumbel was sent an Elmo doll. He played with it on

Francis Hogan/Electronic Publishing Services Inc.

the air. And producers of the *Live with Regis & Kathie Lee* talk show featured Elmo on a November 1996 show. "It was wonderful publicity," says Neil Friedman, president of the Tyco Preschool division of Mattel. Sing & Snore Ernie didn't get the Rosie O'Donnell seal of approval. But it got lots of positive PR.

In February 1997, Ernie was one of the most visible products at Toy Fair, the industry's top marketing event.

In June, more than 100 members of the media, and their families, were invited to the Sesame Place amusement park in Pennsylvania. They got previews and samples of Ernie.

In October, *Family Fun* magazine named Ernie "Toy of the Year." Shortly after that, a survey of retailers in *Playthings* magazine, a trade publication, named Ernie and Elmo "co-toys" of the year.

"At that point, we knew we had a big hit," says Friedman. In fact, he says, Tyco sold 20 percent more Ernies (in 1997) than Elmos (in 1996). And the key has been getting the word out to parents.

"It's very difficult to market to kids under four years old," says Friedman. "For us, marketing to moms is a better way to go."

Bruce Horovitz, "Marketing to Kids Means Playing for Keeps," *USA Today,* December 18, 1997, p. 3B. Copyright 1997, *USA TODAY*. Reprinted with permission.

Odwalla, Inc., CEO Stephen Williamson drinks a bottle of spring water during a news conference at the company's headquarters.

AP/Wide World Photos

brand.[18] The Tylenol case is often used as an example of very effective crisis public relations.

In October 1996, Odwalla Inc. was faced with a similar crisis when *E. coli* bacteria was traced to unpasteurized apple juice that had been sold by the natural juice company. The bacteria eventually was held responsible for the death of a 16-month-old girl in Colorado and more than 50 cases of severe illness.

Odwalla, the leading manufacturer of unpasteurized juices, had made its reputation on natural, unfiltered products. But as soon as the bacteria was detected, Odwalla announced an immediate recall of 13 products in the seven western states and British Columbia. Then the company worked with the Food and Drug Administration to scour the Odwalla processing facilities, which were found to be free of the bacteria. The company continued the investigation, including the processors who supplied fruit for the juice.

At the same time, Odwalla Chief Executive Officer Stephen Williamson said that the company was exploring all methods of processing the juice to kill the bacteria. Eventually the company announced that it would use a method of flash pasteurization, which the company said would keep more flavor than traditional pasteurization while maintaining better taste.

One month after the outbreak, Odwalla took out full-page ads in several newspapers, an "open letter" to its customers, thanking them for their support and offering sympathy for people diagnosed with *E. coli*-related illnesses after drinking Odwalla juices. "I think Odwalla is making all the right moves," said Pam Smith, a retail stock analyst. Smith's advice for any company facing such a crisis was "Be brutally honest, no matter what the results. And show your customers that you care about their safety."[19]

The Odwalla episode and the Tylenol crisis indicate how important specialization in crisis public relations can be within the public relations business.

THE BUSINESS OF PUBLIC RELATIONS

The estimated number of people in the country involved in public relations is 161,000,[20] and more than 4,000 firms in the United States offer PR-related services. The largest public relations firms employ more than 1,000 people. Several major corporations have 100 to 400 public relations specialists, but most public relations firms have fewer than four employees.[21]

Public relations people often deal with advertising agencies as part of their job, and because PR and advertising are so interrelated, several large public relations firms have joined several large advertising agencies. For example, J. Walter Thompson (advertising) bought Hill & Knowlton (public relations), and then in 1987 J. Walter Thompson Group was bought by a London firm, WPP Group PLC. Combined agencies can offer both public relations and advertising services to their clients, and the trend toward advertising/public relations combinations continues today.[22]

The difference between public relations and advertising at the nation's largest agencies can be difficult to discern. Advertising is an aspect of marketing that aims to sell products. People in advertising usually *aren't* involved in a company's policymaking. They implement the company's policies after company executives decide how to sell a product or a corporate image or an idea.

Public relations people, in comparison, usually *are* involved in policy. A PR person often contributes to decisions made about how a company will deal with the public, the press and its own employees.

Types of Clients

Public relations people work for several types of clients, including governments, nonprofit organizations, industry and business.

Government. As noted previously, the federal government is the nation's largest employer of public information people. State and local governments also hire people to handle PR. Related to government are PR people who work for political candidates and for lobbying organizations. Media consultants also are involved in political PR. These people counsel candidates and officeholders about how they should present themselves to the public through the media.

Education. Universities, colleges and school districts often hire public relations people to promote these educational institutions and to handle press attention from the consequences of decisions that educators make.

Nonprofit Organizations. This includes hospitals, churches, museums and charities. Hospital PR is growing especially fast as different health care agencies compete with each other for customers.

Industry. AT&T's early use of public relations strategies was one type of industry PR. Many industries are government-regulated, so this often means that the industry PR person works with government agencies on government-related issues that affect the industry, such as utility rate increases or energy conservation programs.

Business. This is the best-known area of public relations. Large companies keep an in-house staff of public relations people, and these companies also often hire outside PR firms to help on special projects. Product publicity is one of the fastest-growing aspects of business-related public relations.

Within many large businesses are people who handle corporate PR, sometimes called financial PR. They prepare annual reports and gather financial data on the company for use by the press. They also may be assigned directly

In Washington. D.C., with the Washington Monument in the background, participants in the ninth annual National Race for the Cure run and walk past the Museum of American History. The race, which raises funds for breast cancer research, education and treatment programs, is an example of a nonprofit event that uses public relations techniques.

AP/Wide World Photos

to the executives of a corporation to help establish policy about the corporation's public image. Many companies sponsor charity events to increase their visibility in the community.

In an example of corporate public relations, General Telephone Company of California (GTE) lent technical assistance, equipment, charitable contributions, volunteers, graphics, printing and media assistance to the World Games for the Deaf. The "Tell-A-Bike Relay" consisted of two teams of eight experienced cyclists apiece, riding from Santa Barbara to Santa Monica. Instead of passing batons, each team passed a message. One team was a deaf team, the other a hearing team made up of GTE employee volunteers. The hearing team spoke the message; the deaf team signed it. As a result, the California Public-Private Partnership Commission recognized GTE and the World Games for the Deaf with its award in the public initiatives category.

Athletic Teams and Entertainment Organizations. A professional sports team needs someone to travel with them and handle the press requests that inevitably come at each stop. Sports information people also are responsible for the coaches', the owner's and the team's relationship with the fans. College and university sports departments often hire public relations people to handle inquiries from the public and from the press.

In 1939, Henry Rogers learned how to use press agentry to gather publicity for Rita Hayworth. Today, entertainment public relations agencies promote movies and also handle TV personalities and well-known athletes who appear on the lecture circuit.

International. As the nation's consumer market broadens, more attention is being given to developing business in other countries. This means more opportunities in international PR. Hill & Knowlton and Burson-Marsteller, for example, are the two biggest U.S. public relations firms now operating in Japan.[23]

What Do Public Relations People Do?

Responsibilities of PR people include the following: (For some insight on how public relations people make use of modern technology, see Impact/Digital, "The Internet and the Web.")

Writing. News releases, newsletters, correspondence, reports, speeches, booklet texts, radio and TV copy, film scripts, trade paper and magazine articles, institutional advertisements, product information and technical materials.

Editing. Special publications, employee newsletters, shareholder reports and other communications for employees and for the public.

Media Relations and Placement. Contacting news media, magazines, Sunday supplements, freelance writers and trade publications with the intent of getting them to publish or broadcast news and features about or originated by the organization. Responding to media requests for information or spokespersons.

Special Events. Arranging and managing press conferences, convention exhibits, open houses, anniversary celebrations, fund-raising events, special observances, contests and award programs.

Speaking. Appearing before groups and arranging platforms for others before appropriate audiences by managing a speaker's bureau.

Production. Creating art, photography and layout for brochures, booklets, reports, institutional advertisements and periodicals; recording and editing audio- and videotapes; preparing audiovisual presentations.

Research. Gathering data to help an organization plan programs; monitoring the effectiveness of public relations programs. This is a fast-growing area of public relations that includes focus groups to test message concepts; research to target specific audiences; surveys of a company's reputation to use for improving the company's image; employee and public attitude surveys; and shareholder surveys to improve relations with investors.

Programming and Counseling. Establishing a program for effective public relations within the company.

Training. Working with executives and other people within the organization to prepare them to deal with the media.

Management. Overseeing the costs of running the public relations program; paying the bills.[24]

PUBLIC RELATIONS AND THE MEDIA

Public relations work often means finding ways to attract the attention of the press. Says Seymour Topping, managing editor of *The New York Times*,

> PR people do influence the news, but really more in a functional manner rather than in terms of giving new editorial direction. We get hundreds of press releases every day in each of our departments. We screen them very carefully for legitimate news, and very often there are legitimate news stories. Quite a lot of our business stories originate from press releases. It's impossible for us to cover all of these organizations ourselves.[25]

IMPACT

digital

Negative PR Spreads Quickly on the Web

The Two-Way Public Relations Highway

G.A. Andy Marken

" I didn't hear the one that hit me," a friend of Hawkeye's said just before he died in one episode of *M*A*S*H*.

The same is true of all the shots people are firing at your company and your products on the Internet and Web. Unless you're maintaining constant vigilance you'll never know—until it's too late.

Most marketing and public relations people love the Internet and Web.

Outbound Traffic

The technologies give them a chance to bombard editors, analysts, user groups and even individual users in a whole new way.

They're intrigued with the possibility of using new Push technology to make certain their

news and information are delivered to as many of their audiences as possible. They are in love with spam techniques that allow them to shotgun a single message to millions of people around the globe with a click of the mouse.

The technologies also allow many PR people to be what they've secretly wanted to be all along—editors and publishers. It's easy to be a publisher. My dentist has a Web site. My carwash has a Web site. My son has two Web sites. The Web is so popular that there are more than 500,000 Web sites already posted and industry analysts estimate that 50 new sites are added every day.

Broadcast Complaints

Just as it's easy for us to develop, control and send messages, so can dissatisfied customers and our competition.

In the pre-Internet days we used to say that a satisfied customer will tell one or two prospects but a dissatisfied customer will tell 10 or more. With the Internet and Web those same dissatisfied customers can tell millions of people...and they're doing it every day around the globe.

Don't take our word for it. Get on the Web. Go to your favorite search engine and look for Anti-Disney, Anti-McDonald's, Anti-Ford, Anti-Gun Regulation, Anti-Microsoft, Anti-AT&T, Anti-BofA, Anti-Judaism (or any race, religion or orientation), Anti-(company name) and Anti-(product name).

You'll find a range of sites from highly polished to amateurish Web pages waging a war of words against individual companies, products, services and concepts.

---

publicity uncontrolled use of media by a public relations firm to create events and present information to capture press and public attention.

People in public relations provide **publicity**, which creates events and presents information so the press and the public will pay attention. Publicity and advertising differ: An *advertising* message *is paid for; publicity is free.* Advertising is a *controlled* use of media, because the message and where it will appear are governed by the person or company that places the ad. Publicity is considered an *uncontrolled* use of the media, because the public relations person provides information to the press but has no control over how the information will appear—the press writes the story. "We know how the media work," says David Resnicow of the PR firm Ruder Finn & Rotman, "and we make judgments on that, providing access to events as it becomes necessary." [26]

It is precisely because people in the media and people in PR know how each other work that they argue about the role of public relations in the news. The *Columbia Journalism Review* studied the relationship between corporate public relations and *The Wall Street Journal* by examining the stories in the *Journal* on a specific day and comparing the stories to press releases issued by PR people.

Specific companies were mentioned in 111 articles. Nearly half of the news stories in the *Journal* that day, *CJR* reported in its analysis, were based solely

Multiple Platforms

As if the individual Web sites weren't bad enough, there are thousands of online forums, mailing lists, chat rooms, discussion groups and Usenet groups gathering on the Internet every day. When these virtual groups gather, people exchange positive and negative information, rumors, misinformation and even disinformation about companies, products and even individuals

It's a tedious task but any organization that isn't monitoring Internet traffic and Web activity could find itself in serious trouble because of the slanted, malicious and downright libelous information. In short, they could suddenly have a public relations nightmare on their hands.

Shots Read Round the World

Disney's policy of providing domestic partners support regardless of the sexual orientation of the couples produced all types of fanatic messages on the Internet. Religious groups and "correct thinking people" quickly fanned their indignation to the other media.

McDonald's spent an estimated $16 million over a seven-year period before it won a libel suit in the U.K. For all of its legal expense McDonald's was awarded $94,000. But the company can't put a price on the lost customers and tarnished reputation caused by the negative Web sites and the rumors that flew around the world about the company and its activities.

Suddenly the Internet and Web don't look like the friendly skies for corporate marketing and public relations.

Ignorance is No Excuse

Unfortunately the vast majority of PR people spend very little time understanding the depth and breadth of the Internet and the communities it serves. They view the internet as an open communications pipeline where they can send out their news to target audiences, research competitors' Web sites and occasionally spend time in their firm's or product's user forum.

Companies and agencies spend hundreds and thousands of dollars on audio, video and print clipping services to analyze how their messages are being picked up, interpreted and used by the conventional media. They spend little or no time or effort finding out what people are saying in real-time in cyberspace about them.

Just as with *M*A*S*H*'s Hawkeye's friend, what you don't hear can hurt you...and it could be fatal.

Source: *Public Relation Quarterly*, Spring 1998, 43(1), p. 31(3). Reprinted by permission.

on press releases. In 32 of the stories that were based on press releases, reporters paraphrased the releases almost verbatim; in the 21 remaining cases, only a small amount of additional reporting had been done.

The *Journal's* executive director, Frederick Taylor, responded to *CJR's* analysis by saying, "Ninety percent of daily coverage is started by a company making an announcement for the record. We're relaying this information to our readers."[27]

In a specific example of what is called press release journalism, *New York Times* reporter Douglas C. McGill published a story in the *Times* about the discovery of the original model that Michelangelo used to create his famous statue of David. McGill attributed the story to Professor Frederick Hartt, who had made the discovery.

Hartt had signed a contract with Abbeville Press to write a book about the Michelangelo discovery, and the book's photographer was David Finn, the chief executive officer of the public relations agency Ruder Finn & Rotman. Two public relations people from Ruder Finn & Rotman had called McGill at the *Times* and offered him the story.

IMPACT
point of view   *PR Blunders List Highlights Big Gaffes*

By Burton St. John

The top 10 PR foul-ups of 1997 were recently released by Fineman Associates, a San Francisco public relations agency. With few exceptions, the list reveals a dangerous combination—companies making what *The Wall Street Journal*'s Yumiko Oho called "klutzy moves" while under media scrutiny. In fact, all the blunders on the list were widely reported from such sources as Reuters, the Associated Press, the Newhouse News Service and Bloomberg Business News.

With only a hint of irony, Fineman's list leads with Proctor & Gamble's use of its own list— a ranking of the "least kissable" celebrities, as reflected in a poll of 1,000 men and women. P&G's poll was designed to get its mouthwash, Scope, publicity. It did.

Rosie O'Donnell, who made the list, belittled the product on her daytime talk show, saying, "If you're a dope, you use Scope," and handing out bottles of Listerine to her studio audience. Her tirades were also extensively reported in such publications as *TV Guide, Brandweek* and *Reputation Management*.

When *The Wall Street Journal* asked P&G's Bill Dobson about the promotion's future, he said, "We probably won't do the least-kissable portion of it, just

Mitchell Gerber/CORBIS

because it has the potential to offend whoever's on that list."

The American Medical Association also places prominently on the list, because of its ill-fated attempt to place its seal of approval on Sunbeam products. Through a series of poor or mis-

communications with Sunbeam, a five-year endorsement deal was announced to widespread media coverage—without the final approval of the AMA's top leadership.

The AMA subsequently refuted the unprecedented

agreement, but the story eventually led to the resignations of AMA's vice president and general counsel. The AMA is now facing a $20 million lawsuit from Sunbeam (which, in itself, is drawing some criticism—the *St. Petersburg Times* call the suit "a dumb move").

American Airlines is the dominant airline at Dallas/Ft. Worth International, and a major player throughout Texas. Consequently, the airline has been receiving considerable attention and criticism from the media concerning its position against the expansion of Dallas' Love Field—and the competition such expansion could bring from Southwest Airlines. In fact, one wouldn't be surprised if American Airlines decided to take a low profile in the face of such scrutiny.

So it appears quite remarkable that the airline decided to promote its first Austin-Miami flight with a Fidel Castro look-alike greeting passengers at the gate. Also remarkable—the telling of Cuban jokes over the flight's intercom.

In addition, the airline printed a pilot's manual that, Fineman said, "characterized Latin Americans as drunk and unruly passengers, likely to call in a bomb threat rather than miss a plane." Although the FAA obviously didn't see the "pilot's manual,"

Reuters did; Hence American Airlines' spot on the blunder list. Others who made the list:

- Sloan-Kettering, which sent out surveys to black women that featured questions about voodoo, white racism and stereotypical diet ("do you ever eat chitterlings?"). The company told *The Wall Street Journal* that it was merely trying to find out why black women apparently didn't trust the "medical establishment."

- The Babe Ruth League in Boca Raton, Fla., which insisted that 12-year-old Melissa Raglin wear a jockstrap and cup, or else be removed as catcher. The league told the Associated Press that the rule was for Raglin's protection.

- Philip Morris—more specifically its president, James Morgan, who said cigarettes have minimal addictive effect. "If they are behaviorally addictive or habit forming, they are much more like caffeine," said Morgan, "or, in my case, Gummy Bears....I don't like it when I don't eat my Gummy Bears, but I'm certainly not addicted to them."

- Eat Me Now Foods, and its president Steve Corri. The company made Crave, test tubes filled with white sugar. When

parents objected that the product resembled a drug, Corri fought back saying "[they're] just constipated hypocrites....It is their problem not mine." When this *San Jose Mercury News* story went national, Corri pulled Crave off the shelves.

- Converse, which signed Dennis Rodman to shill its footwear. The *Boston Globe* reported the deal just days after Rodman attacked a court-side reporter by kicking him in the groin.

- Corning, Inc., which, with a "no comment," snubbed a local reporter's inquiry about possible declines in the fiber optics business. "The resulting story in the *Corning Leader* concluded that Corning was in 'a state of emergency,'" said Fineman. The story went national and Corning's stock plummeted overnight.

- Nike, which, in the face of extensive strikes in its Southeast Asian facilities, maintained that its workers there are "better off than most and that abuses are isolated." The story received national attention through the Newhouse News Service and prompted Garry Trudeau to excoriate Nike repeatedly in the syndicated strip *Doonesbury*.

Source: *St. Louis Journalism Review*, February 1998, 28(203), p. 12(1).

McGill added considerable research to the story, but when the connection was discovered, McGill told *Manhattan inc.* magazine that he felt uncomfortable. "I wasn't especially happy that the story was handed to me by a public relations agent. But once I heard about it, I thought it was an important story for *Times* readers no matter who it came from. The whole thing made me uneasy. It showed a high degree of sophistication from Ruder Finn." [28]

PUBLIC RELATIONS PROFESSIONALISM

Clever ways to attract attention are trademarks of today's successful public relations professional. According to Jeff and Marie Blyskal, who interviewed hundreds of PR people for their book *PR: How the Public Relations Industry Writes the News*:

> *At the highest level of the profession, PR people are low-key, candid, creative, knowledgeable, warm, witty, charming, friendly, personable, self-confident. The best ones communicate as well as or better than some of the best journalists today; they are true communications technicians. We have found few hollow shells of human beings, bereft of moral conviction and marching in step with whatever "orders" their clients or employers bark out. Many were genuinely excited about their profession; some were swell-headed; only a few harkened back to their journalism days to assure us they were really "okay."*
>
> *Then, too, we saw no cabals or international PR conspiracies to control the public's mind—though quietly controlling minds is, in fact, what PR people attempt to do on a case-by-case basis. PR people have chosen their profession, and most seem reasonably satisfied with being effective advocates for their clients....Some will even admit that what they do is manipulation, but manipulation with a noble, higher goal in mind: defending or advancing the cause of their client. There are two sides to every story, goes the argument. They are, in a sense, the equivalent of attorneys in the court of public opinion.[29]*

TECHNOLOGY CHANGES THE FUTURE

Like the future of advertising, the future of public relations is tied closely to the future of the media industries. The basic structure of the business will not change, but public relations practitioners will find themselves facing the same challenges as people in the advertising business.

Growing international markets will mean that, in the future, many U.S. public relations firms will expand overseas. Global communications will mean that public relations agencies will work internationally on some projects, and that the agencies will have to adjust to the cultural differences that global exposure brings.

New technologies, especially the Internet, mean new ways to deliver public relations messages. Eventually, satellite technology will streamline all print, audio and video, giving PR agencies the same access to distributing information to news organizations that the news organizations now possess themselves.

As in the advertising industry, shifting demographic patterns mean growing potential markets for public relations services.

IN FOCUS

■ Modern public relations emerged at the beginning of the 20th century as a way for business to respond to the muckrakers and to Theodore Roosevelt's antitrust campaign.

■ The first publicity firm in the country, called The Publicity Bureau, opened in Boston in 1900.

■ The best-known early practitioner of public relations was Ivy Lee, who wrote a "Declaration of Principles" to respond to the secret publicity activities of The Publicity Bureau.

■ The Chicago Edison Company and American Telephone & Telegraph were the first companies to begin in-house promotional programs.

■ The Committee on Public Information, headed by George Creel, promoted the war effort during World War I. The Office of War Information, headed by newscaster Elmer Davis, promoted the country's efforts during World War II.

■ Edward L. Bernays wrote the first book on public relations, *Crystallizing Public Opinion*. Both Bernays and Ivy Lee have been called the father of public relations.

■ Franklin Roosevelt, assisted by public relations expert Louis McHenry Howe, successfully used public relations to promote the New Deal.

■ Among the pioneering women who joined the public relations business were Doris E. Fleischman, Leone Baxter, and Anne Williams Wheaton. Doris Fleischman and Edward Bernays were equal partners in the Bernays public relations firm. Doris Fleischman was an early advocate of public relations as a career for women.

■ The Public Relations Society established the profession's first code of ethics in 1954.

■ Public relations expanded quickly in the 1960s and 1970s to accommodate television, the federal government and corporate America.

■ Today 161,000 people work in public relations nationwide. More than 4,000 firms offer PR-related services.

■ Public relations people work in government, education, industry, business, nonprofit agencies, athletic teams, entertainment companies and international business.

■ Public relations people use persuasion and publicity to attract attention for their clients.

■ The main difference between advertising and public relations is that advertising messages are controlled and public relations messages are uncontrolled.

■ The trademark of today's public relations is a sophisticated approach to news. People who work in public relations have been called "attorneys in the court of public opinion."

■ Public relations agencies face the same challenges as advertising agencies: expanding worldwide markets, the development of new technologies and changing demographic patterns.

WORKING THE WEB www

- **Directory of Public Relations Agencies and Resources on the Web**
  www.webcom.com/impulse/prlist.html
- **Online Public Relations**
  www.connectingonline.com/anchors/online_public_relations.html
- **Public Relations Society of America**
  www.prsa.org
- **Small Business Resources Index for Public Relations Resources**
  www.inc.com/idx_t_cc.html

INFOTRAC COLLEGE EDITION EXERCISES

Using the InfoTrac College Edition's fully searchable online database of articles and abstracts, do the following exercises as directed by your instructor.

1. Using InfoTrac College Edition, type in the keywords "Edward L. Bernays" and learn more about this early public relations pioneer. Then print the articles and either:

   a. write a brief paper on your findings, or

   b. bring the articles to class for a small-group discussion.

2. Learn more about specific examples of crisis public relations by typing in the keywords "public relations case studies," "crisis public relations" or "Odwalla." Pick a specific case and find at least two articles about that case. Print the articles and either:

   a. write a brief paper on your findings, or

   b. bring the articles to class for a small-group discussion.

3. Think of a major U.S. corporation—"Disney public relations" or "Microsoft public relations," for example—and, using InfoTrac College Edition, find at least three articles about that corporation's public image or strategies. Print the articles and either:

   a. write a brief paper on your findings, or

   b. bring the articles to class for a small-group discussion.

4. Read "Impact/Digital: Negative PR Spreads Quickly on the Web," in Chapter 11. Use the keywords "public relations Internet" and search for other examples of the way the Internet is revolutionizing public relations. Print the articles and either:

   a. write a brief paper on your findings, or

   b. bring the articles to class for a small-group discussion.

5. The moral and ethical aspects of public relations are often debated. Use the keywords "public relations moral and ethical aspects" to find at least three articles on the subject. Print the articles and either:

   a. write a brief paper on your findings, or

   b. bring the articles to class for a small-group discussion.

12

Mass MEDIA and Social Issues

What's Ahead

N o medium is excessively *dangerous* if its users understand what its dangers are.

Neil Postman, author, Amusing Ourselves to Death

How do the media affect what we do? In 1994, when O. J. Simpson was arrested and charged with murder, calls to domestic violence hotlines in Los Angeles jumped 80 percent.[1] On November 7, 1991, within minutes after basketball star Earvin "Magic" Johnson announced on TV that he had tested positive for the HIV virus, callers flooded the San Francisco AIDS Foundation hotline at more than 15 times the normal rate.[2]

These two examples of media effects are anecdotal evidence—pieces of a very complex picture. Today, scholars understand that the media have different effects on different types of people with differing results. Generalizations about the media's effects are easy to make but difficult to prove. "We do not fully understand at present what the media system is doing to individual behavior, much less to American culture," according to William L. Rivers and Wilbur Schramm. "The media cannot simply be seen as stenciling images on a blank mind. That is too superficial a view of the communication process."[3]

ASSESSING THE IMPACT: EARLY MEDIA STUDIES

The concept that the media have different effects on different types of people is relatively new. Early media observers felt that an absolute one-to-one relationship existed between what people read, heard and saw and what people did with that information. They also believed that the effects were the same for everyone.

The magic bullet theory, sometimes called the hypodermic needle theory, alleged that ideas from the media were in direct causal relation to behavior. The theory held that the media could inject ideas into someone the way liquids are injected through a needle. This early distrust of the media still pervades many people's thinking today, although the theory has been disproved.

Media research, like other social science research, is based on a continuum of thought, with each new study advancing slightly the knowledge from the studies that have come before. This is what has happened to the magic bullet theory. Eventually, the beliefs that audiences absorbed media messages uncritically and that all audiences reacted the same to each message were proven untrue. Research disclosed that analyzing media effects is a very complex task.

Some media research existed before television use became widespread in the mid-1950s, but TV prompted scholars to take an even closer look at media's effects. Two scholars made particularly provocative assertions about how the media influence people's lives. David M. Potter and Marshall McLuhan arrived at just the right moment—when the public and the scholarly community were anxiously trying to analyze media's effects on society.

In his book *People of Plenty*, published in 1954, Potter first articulated an important idea: that American society is a consumer society driven primarily by advertising. Potter, a historian, asserted that American advertising is rooted in American abundance.

> *Advertising is not badly needed in an economy of scarcity, because total demand is usually equal to or in excess of total supply, and every producer can normally sell as much as he produces....It is when potential supply outstrips demand—that is, when abundance prevails—that advertising begins to fulfill a really essential economic function.*

Potter then warned about the dangers of advertising. "Advertising has in its dynamics no motivation to seek the improvement of the individual or to impart qualities of social usefulness....It has no social goals and no social responsibility for what it does with its influence."[4] Potter's perspective was important in shaping the critical view of modern advertising. *People of Plenty* is still in print today.

In the 1960s, Canadian Marshall McLuhan piqued the public's interest with his phrase "The medium is the message," which he later parodied in the title of his book *The Medium Is the Massage*. One of his conclusions was that the widespread use of television was a landmark in the history of the world, "retribalizing" society and creating a "global village" of people who use media to communicate.

McLuhan suggested that electronic media messages are inherently different from print messages—to watch information on TV is different from reading the same information in a newspaper. McLuhan never offered systematic proof for his ideas, and some people criticized him as a charlatan, but his concepts still are debated widely.

Scholars who analyze the media today look for patterns in media effects, predictable results and statistical evidence to document how the media affect us. Precisely because the media are ubiquitous, studies of their effects on American society are far from conclusive. In this chapter you will learn about some of the major studies that have examined the media's effects and some of the recent assertions about the role that the media play in our lives.

Media research today includes media effects research and media content analysis. Effects research tries to analyze how people use the information they receive from the media—whether political advertising changes people's voting behavior, for example. (See the discussion of *The People's Choice*, page 274.) Content analysis examines what is presented by the media—how many children's programs portray violent behavior, for example. (See the discussion of George Gerbner, page 271.) Sometimes these two types of analysis (effects research and content studies) are combined in an attempt to evaluate what effect certain content has on an audience.

The Payne Fund Studies

The prestigious Payne Fund sponsored the first major study of media, conducted in 1929. It contained 12 separate reports on media effects. One of these studies concentrated on the effects of movies on children. In his interviews, researcher Herbert Blumer simply asked teenagers what they remembered about the movies they had seen as children.

Using this unsystematic approach, he reported that the teenagers had been greatly influenced by the movies because they *said* they had been greatly influenced. Blumer's conclusion and other conclusions of the Payne Fund studies about the media's direct one-to-one effect on people were accepted without question, mainly because these were the first major studies of media effects, and the results were widely reported. This became known as the **magic bullet theory**, the belief that media messages directly and measurably affect people's behavior.

magic bullet theory the assertion that media messages directly and measurably affect people's behavior.

The Payne Fund studies also contributed ammunition for the Motion Picture Producers and Distributors Association Production Code, adopted in 1930, which regulated movie content (see Chapter 8).

"Five thousand hours, and his vital signs are still strong."

The Cantril Study

The Martians who landed in New Jersey on the Mercury Theater "War of the Worlds" broadcast of October 30, 1939 (see Chapter 5) sparked the next major study of media effects, conducted by Hadley Cantril at Princeton University. The results of the Cantril study contradicted the findings of the Payne Fund studies and disputed the magic bullet theory.

The Cantril researchers wanted to find out why certain people believed the Mercury Theater broadcast and others did not. After interviewing 135 people, Cantril concluded that high critical thinking ability was the key. Better-educated people were much more likely to decide that the broadcast was a fake. This might seem to be a self-evident finding today, but the importance of the Cantril study is that it differentiated among listeners: People with different personality characteristics interpreted the broadcast differently.

The Lasswell Model

In 1948, Harold D. Lasswell designed a model to describe the process of communication that is still used today. Lasswell said that this process can be analyzed by answering five questions:

> Who?
> says what?
> on which channel?
> to whom?
> with what effect?

In other words, Lasswell said that the process of communication can be analyzed by determining who the sender is and what the sender says. Next, you must identify which channel—meaning the method—of communication the sender used. Then you must examine the audience and define the effect on that audience. Because Lasswell described the communication process so succinctly, most of the communications research that followed has attempted to answer his five questions.

TELEVISION AND CHILDREN'S BEHAVIOR

The 1950s were a time of adjustment because of the addition of the new medium of television, which was seen first as a novelty and then as a necessity. Since 1960, four of the major studies of the effects of television have focused on children.

Television in the Lives of Our Children

Published in 1961 by Wilbur Schramm, Jack Lyle and Edwin Parker, *Television in the Lives of Our Children* was the first major study of the effects of television on children. Researchers interviewed 6,000 children and 1,500 parents, as well as teachers and school officials.

Schramm and his associates reported that children were exposed to television more than to any other mass medium. On average, 5-year-old children watched television 2 hours every weekday. TV viewing time reached 3 hours by the time these children were 8 years old. In a finding that often was subsequently cited, Schramm said that from the ages of 3 to 16, children spent more time in front of the television set than they spent in school.

Children used television for fantasy, diversion and instruction, Schramm said. Children who had troubled relationships with their parents and children who were classified as aggressive were more likely to turn to television for fantasy, but Schramm could find no serious problems related to television viewing. Schramm also found, in support of Cantril, that different children showed different effects.

Television and Social Behavior

Television and Social Behavior, a six-volume study of the effects of television, was funded by $1 million appropriated by Congress in 1969 after the violent decade of the 1960s. The U.S. Department of Health, Education, and Welfare, which sponsored the study, appointed a distinguished panel of social scientists to undertake the research.

The study's major findings, published in 1971, concerned the effects of television violence on children. A content analysis of one week of prime-time programming, conducted by George Gerbner of the University of Pennsylvania, reported that eight out of ten prime-time shows contained violence. The conclusions of *Television and Social Behavior* failed to make a direct connection between TV programming and violent behavior, however. The report said that there was a "tentative" indication that television viewing caused aggressive behavior. According to the study, this connection between TV violence and aggressive behavior affected only *some* children who were already classified as aggressive children and *only* in some environments.

Even though the report avoided a direct statement about violent behavior in children as a result of television viewing, the U.S. Surgeon General called for immediate action against violence on television. The television industry dismissed the results as inconclusive.

The Early Window

Several studies since 1971 have suggested that television violence causes aggression among children. In their 1988 book *The Early Window: Effects of Television on Children and Youth*, psychologists Robert M. Liebert and Joyce Sprafkin urged caution in drawing broad conclusions about the subject:

> *Studies using various methods have supported the proposition that TV violence can induce aggressive and/or antisocial behavior in children. Whether the effect will hold only for the most susceptible individuals (e.g., boys from disadvantaged homes) or whether it will hold for a wider range of youngsters obviously depends in part upon the measure being used....The occurrence of serious violent or criminal acts results from several forces at once. Researchers have said that TV violence is a cause of aggressiveness, not that it is the cause of aggressiveness. There is no one, single cause of any social behavior.* [5]

Television Advertising to Children

The effects of advertising on adults have been analyzed widely, but in 1979 the advertising of children's products became an object of serious government attention with the release of the 340-page report *Television Advertising to Children* by the Federal Trade Commission.

The report, based on a two-year study, was designed to document the dangers of advertising sugar-based products to children, but embedded in the report was some provocative information about children's advertising. Children are an especially vulnerable audience, said the FTC. The report concluded:

- The average child sees 20,000 commercials a year, or about 3 hours of TV advertising a week.

IMPACT

on you   *Do Movies Cause Teenagers to Smoke?*

By Richard Klein

Photodisc

Toward the end of the hit film comedy *My Best Friend's Wedding*, Julia Roberts is hunched on the floor of a hotel hallway, her back propped against the door. The man she wants to marry is in the room getting news of her betrayals. We see her extract—from her bra, it appears—a pack of Marlboros. Hesitantly, shakily she lights a cigarette. The viewer is supposed to see the cigarette and her nervous smoking as a visible counterpart to the panicky feelings of imminent loss that are sweeping over her….

Smoking, once again, is hot in the entertainment media. Half the movies released between 1990 and 1995 featured a major character who chose to light up on screen, a significant increase compared with 29 percent in the 1970s, according to a recent study at the University of California, San Francisco. And the trend appears to be accelerating….

In the last four and a half years, American teenagers have been the object of the most sustained and systematic anti-smoking campaign ever mounted, directed at them from their earliest age by every adult institution of authority, particularly by the Clinton White House. Yet teenage smoking during the same period has increased alarmingly. The President himself announced a 30 percent increase in smoking among 10th graders and 40 percent among 9th graders. Children are smoking more and starting earlier.

Who can doubt that they are being influenced by the new aura of cool that surrounds smoking in the media? When television isn't preaching the evils of tobacco, it's putting cigarettes in the hands of unlikable characters, the ones we love to hate. On the silver screen, the sexiest, most bewitching stars make smoking look glamorous again. Somewhere along the way, all that preaching has backfired….

But it's an old story. We always love a bad girl, and the bad girl smokes….Our leaders often assume that teenagers read naïvely and will imitate what they are told is good for them and avoid what is disapproved. But one consequence of such assumptions is the present forms of censorship, which, however well meaning, may reinforce the behavior they seek to banish.

Young people need information, not preaching, about the harm that smoking does to their development, to their bodies and to their futures. Confronted instead with censorship, they become skilled in and devoted to reading between the lines. In the end, the censor always incites aggressive curiosity about the very thing it aims to keep from view.

The censorship effect has clearly been at work in America in recent years, especially where teenagers, inherently curious and skeptical of authority, are concerned.

The abyss between what can be said and shown about smoking and the fact that more than 25 million adults continue legally to smoke, despite the warnings, constitutes an enigma that gets the attention of every adolescent. They don't fail to notice either that there's a lot of secret smoking going down.

Richard Klein, "After the Preaching, the Lure of the Taboo," *The New York Times*, August 24, 1997, 2-1, 31. Copyright © 1997 by The New York Times Co. Reprinted by permission.

- Many children regard advertising as just another form of programming and do not distinguish between programs and ads.

- Televised advertising for any product to children who do not understand the intent of the commercial is unfair and deceptive.

The report called for a ban on advertising to very young children, a ban on sugared products in advertising directed to children under age 12, and a requirement for counter-ads with dental and nutritional information to balance any ads for sugared products.[6]

This report and subsequent research about children's advertising suggest that younger children pay more attention to television advertising than older children. But by sixth grade, children adopt what has been called a "global distrust" of advertising.[7]

TELEVISION AND VIOLENCE

Television and Behavior: Ten Years of Scientific Progress and Implications for the Eighties, published in 1982 by the National Institute of Mental Health, compiled information from 2,500 individual studies of television. According to the National Institute of Mental Health, three findings of these 2,500 studies, taken together, were that:

1. A direct correlation exists between televised violence and aggressive behavior, yet there is no way to predict who will be affected and why.

2. Heavy television viewers are more fearful, less trusting and more apprehensive than light viewers.

3. Children who watch what the report called "pro social" programs (programs that are socially constructive, such as *Sesame Street*) are more likely to act responsibly.

Most of the latest studies of the media's role have continued to reinforce the concept that different people in different environments react to the media differently.

In 1994, cable operators and network broadcasters agreed to use an independent monitor to review programming for violent content. The agreement came after Congress held hearings on the subject in 1993 and threatened to introduce regulations to curb violence if the industry didn't police itself. The agreement also called for the development of violence ratings for TV programming and endorsed a "V" chip—*V for violence*—technology that would be built into a television set to allow parents to block programs rated as violent.

The monitoring will be "qualitative" rather than "quantitative," the agreement said. This means that the programs will be examined for content, not just for incidents of violence, a system that is very controversial. The Telecommunications Act of 1996 established a ratings code for content (see Chapter 14).

This agreement continues a tradition of media self-regulation. That is, the audio and video media industries have responded—often reluctantly—to congressional pressure by offering to monitor themselves rather than invite the government to intrude on the content of their programs.

THE MEDIA AND NATIONAL POLITICS

The media have transformed politics in ways that could never have been imagined when President Franklin D. Roosevelt introduced what were called

Fireside Chats in 1933. Roosevelt was the first president to use the media effectively to stimulate public support. The newest technology of FDR's era—radio—gave him immediate access to a national audience. (See Chapter 5.) Roosevelt's media skill became an essential element in promoting his economic programs. Today, politics and the media seem irreversibly dependent on each other, one of the legacies of Roosevelt's presidency.

The Fireside Chats

In March 1933, just after he was inaugurated, FDR looked for a way to avoid a financial panic after he announced that he was closing the nation's banks. For a week the country cooled off while Congress scrambled for a solution. On the Sunday night eight days after his inauguration, Roosevelt used radio to calm the nation's anxiety before the banks began to reopen on Monday. FDR went down to the basement of the White House to give his first Fireside Chat.

There was a fireplace in the basement, but no fire was burning. The president could not find his script, so he borrowed a mimeographed copy from a reporter. In his first address to the nation as president, FDR gave a banking lesson to his audience of 60 million people: "I want to talk for a few minutes with the people of the United States about banking....First of all, let me state the simple fact that when you deposit money in a bank, the bank does not put the money into a safe deposit vault. It invests your money in many different forms." When he finished, he turned to people in the room and asked, "Was I all right?"[8] America had its first media president, an elected leader talking directly to the people through the media.

Roosevelt's chats are cited as a legendary example of media politics, yet he gave only eight of them in his first term of office. His reputation for press access also was enhanced by his other meetings with the press: In 13 years in office he held more than 900 press conferences.

The People's Choice

The first major study of the influence of media on politics was *The People's Choice*, undertaken precisely because FDR seemed to be such a good media politician. This comprehensive examination of voter behavior in the 1940 presidential election was quite systematic.

Researchers Paul Lazarsfeld, Bernard Berelson and Hazel Gaudet followed 3,000 people in rural Erie County, Ohio, from May to November 1940 to determine what influenced the way these people voted for president. The researchers tracked how people's minds changed over the six-month period and then attempted to determine why. (It is important to remember that this study was undertaken before television. Radio became the prevailing medium for political advertising in 1932, when the two parties spent more money for radio time than for any other item.[9])

What effect, the researchers wanted to know, did the media have on people's choosing one candidate over another? The results were provocative. Lazarsfeld and his colleagues found that only 8 percent of the voters in the study were actually *converted*. The majority of voters (53 percent) were *reinforced* in their beliefs by the media, and 14 percent were *activated* to vote. Mixed effects or no effects were shown by the remaining 25 percent of the people.

Lazarsfeld said that opinion leaders, who got their information from the media, shared this information with their friends. The study concluded

Reprinted by permission of *Milwaukee Sentinel*.

that instead of changing people's beliefs, the media primarily activate people to vote and reinforce already-held opinions. *The People's Choice* also revealed that:

- Family and friends had more effect on people's decisions than the media did.
- The media had different effects on different people, reinforcing Cantril's findings.
- A major source of information about candidates was through other people.

This finding that opinion leaders often provide and shape information for the general population was a bonus—the researchers hadn't set out specifically to learn this. This transmission of information and ideas from mass media to opinion leaders to friends and acquaintances is called the **two-step flow** of communication.

two-step flow the transmission of information and ideas from mass media to opinion leaders and friends.

The Unseeing Eye

In 1976, a second study of the media and presidential elections, called *The Unseeing Eye: The Myth of Television Power in National Elections*, revealed findings that paralleled those of *The People's Choice*. With a grant from the National Science Foundation, Thomas E. Patterson and Robert D. McClure supervised interviews with 2,707 people from early September to just before Election Day in the November 1972 race between George McGovern and Richard Nixon. The study did not discuss political media events, but it did analyze television campaign news and political advertising. (The role of journalists and news reporting is discussed in Chapter 13.)

The researchers concluded that, although 16 percent of the people they interviewed were influenced by political advertising, only 7 percent were manipulated by political ads. The researchers defined people who were influenced as those who decided to vote for a candidate based mostly on what they knew and only slightly on what the ads told them. The 7 percent of the people in the survey who were manipulated, according to Patterson and McClure, were people who cited political advertising as a major factor in their choices. Patterson and McClure concluded that political advertising on TV has little effect on most people.

> *By projecting their political biases…people see in candidates' commercials pretty much what they want to see. Ads sponsored by the candidate who shares their politics get a good response. They like what he has to say. And they like him. Ads sponsored by the opposing candidate are viewed negatively. They object to what he says. And they object to him.*[10]

It is important to remember, however, that in some elections a difference of a few percentage points can decide the outcome. This is why political advertising continues to play such an important campaign role, in an effort to reach the percentage of the population that remains vulnerable.

Election Campaigns on Television

So far, no convincing systematic evidence has been presented to show that the media change the voting behavior of large groups of people. Yet, since John F. Kennedy debated Richard Nixon during the 1960 presidential campaign, a deeply felt view has persisted among many people that the media—television in particular—have changed elections and electoral politics.

Kennedy's debate with Nixon in 1960 was the first televised debate of presidential candidates in American history. Kennedy's performance in the debates often is credited for his narrow victory in the election. In his book *Presidents and the Press*, media scholar Joseph C. Spear wrote:

> *As the panel began asking questions, Nixon tended to go on the defensive, answering Kennedy point by point and ignoring his huge audience beyond the camera. Kennedy, by contrast, appeared rested, calm, informed, cocksure. Whatever the question, he aimed his answer at the millions of Americans viewing the program in their living rooms.*

John F. Kennedy's debate with Richard Nixon in 1960 was the first televised debate of presidential candidates. Kennedy's performance in the debates often is credited for his narrow victory in the election.

UPI-Bettmann/CORBIS

It was an unmitigated disaster for Nixon. In the second, third, and fourth debates, he managed to recover somewhat from his initial poor performance, but it was too late. Surveys showed that an overwhelming percentage of the television audience had judged Kennedy the victor.[11]

One legacy of Kennedy's television victory is that today, national political campaigns depend almost entirely on TV to promote presidential candidates. Television is a very efficient way to reach large numbers of people quickly, but campaigning for television also distances the candidates from direct public contact. Television advertising also is very expensive, and the cost of national campaigns in the past 20 years has skyrocketed (see Table 12.1). According to University of Southern California political scientist Herbert Alexander, gubernatorial and senatorial candidates devote 40 to 60 percent of their campaign budgets to advertising.

Alexander is quick to point out that not all of this money goes to television. In congressional elections, according to Alexander, "fewer than half the candidates use TV. Many of them are in districts like Los Angeles, where the media markets are much larger than the political jurisdictions."[12] Television advertising in such markets delivers a bigger audience than candidates need, so they use direct mail or print advertising. But a candidate running for Congress in Des Moines, Iowa, might use television because the entire district would be included in the local station's coverage, says Alexander.

In presidential politics, the cost of radio and television advertising is rising quickly. During the 1984 presidential general election, Republican media expenditures were $23.9 million; the Democrats spent $21.5 million. In 1996, President Clinton and Republican challenger Bob Dole each spent $40 million for media advertising. The amount of money that each presidential candidate spends for media has doubled in the last 12 years.[13]

Congressional candidates in 1992 spent an estimated $678 million, which was one-third more than in 1986. California Republican challenger Michael Huffington spent a record $29 million in 1994 in an unsuccessful attempt to beat incumbent Democrat Dianne Feinstein in a race for the U.S. Senate.[14]

Historian James David Barber describes the public's role in politics:

Particularly since television has brought national politics within arm's length of nearly every American, the great majority probably have at least some experience of the quadrennial passing parade. But millions vote their old memories and habits and interests, interpreting new perceptions that strike their senses to coincide with their prejudices and impulses.

At the other end of the participation spectrum are those compulsive readers of The New York Times *who delve into every twitch and turn of the contest. Floating in between are large numbers of Americans who pick up on the election's major events and personalities, following with mild but open interest the dominant developments. Insofar as the campaign makes a difference, it is this great central chunk of* The People *who swing the choice. They respond to what they see and hear. They are interested but not obsessed. They edit out the minor blips of change and wait for the campaign to gather force around a critical concern. They reach their conclusions on the basis of a widely shared common experience. It is through that middling throng of the population that the pulse of politics beats most powerfully, synchronizing to its insistent rhythm the varied vibrations of discrete events.[15]*

TABLE 12.1

The Rising Cost of Running for President				
Costs of the U.S. Presidential/Vice Presidential general election campaigns, 1984–1996 (millions of dollars)				
	1984		**1988**	
	Reagan	**Mondale**	**Bush**	**Dukakis**
Media cost	$23.9	$21.5	$31.5	$23.5
Total campaign cost	$47.3	$45.0	$54.4	$54.4
Percentage of cost for media	50.5%	47.8%	58.0%	43.0%

*Reported amounts as of November 25, 1996.

Sources: Herbert F. Alexander and Brian A Haggerty, *Financing the 1984 Election*, Lexington, Mass.: D. C. Heath, 1987; Herbert Alexander and Monica Bauer, *Financing the 1988 Election*, Boulder, Colo.: Westview Press, 1991; Federal Elections Commission and Herbert E. Alexander, Citizens' Research Foundation, University of Southern California.

The rising cost of running for public office can exclude people without the means to raise huge sums of money. If "The People who swing the choice," described by Barber, cannot easily participate in the political process, eventually they may choose not to participate at all, eroding the number of people who run for office, vote in elections and work in political campaigns.

Today, the media are essential to American politics, changing the behavior of politicians as well as the electorate, raising important questions about governance and the conduct of elections. (For further insight on the rising cost of election campaigns on TV, see Table 12.1.)

MASS MEDIA REFLECTS CULTURAL VALUES

Because media research is a continuing process, new ideas will emerge in the next decade from today's ideas and studies. Several provocative recent studies have extended past boundaries of media research.

Silencing Opposing Viewpoints

Elisabeth Noelle-Neumann has asserted that because journalists in all media tend to concentrate on the same major news stories, the audience is assailed on many sides by similar information. Together, the media present the consensus; journalists reflect the prevailing climate of opinion. As this consensus spreads, people with divergent views, says Noelle-Neumann, may be less likely to voice disagreement with the prevailing point of view. Thus, because of a **"spiral of silence,"** the media gain more influence because opponents of the consensus tend to remain silent. The implication for future research will be to ask whether the media neutralize dissent and create a pattern of social and cultural conformity.

spiral of silence the belief that people with divergent views may be reluctant to challenge the consensus of opinion offered by the media.

	1992			**1996**	
	Bush	**Clinton**	**Perot**	**Dole/Kemp***	**Clinton/Gore***
Media cost	$42.6	$32.2	$39.5	$40.0	$40.0
Total campaign cost	$100.5	$115.3	$69.6	$130.6	$156.0
Percentage of cost for media	42.0%	28.0%	56.0%	30.6%	25.6%

Losing a Sense of Place

In his book *No Sense of Place*, published in 1985, Joshua Meyrowitz provided new insight into television's possible effects on society. In the past, says Meyrowitz,

> *parents did not know what their children knew, and children did not know what their parents knew they knew. Similarly, a person of one sex could never be certain of what a member of the other sex knew....Television undermines such behavioral distinctions because it encompasses children and adults, men and women, and all other social groups in a single informational sphere or environment. Not only does it provide similar information to everyone but, even more significant, it provides it publicly and often simultaneously.* [16]

This sharing of information, says Meyrowitz, means that subjects that rarely were discussed between men and women, for instance, and between children and adults, have become part of the public dialogue.

A second result of television viewing is the blurred distinction between childhood and adulthood, says Meyrowitz. When print dominated the society as a medium, children's access to adult information was limited. The only way to learn about "adult" concepts was to read about them, so typically a child was not exposed to adult ideas or problems, and taboo topics remained hidden from children.

In a video world, however, any topic that can be portrayed in pictures on television challenges the boundaries that print places around information. This, says Meyrowitz, causes an early loss of the naïveté of childhood.

> *Television removes barriers that once divided people of different ages and reading abilities into different social situations. The widespread use of television is equivalent to a broad social decision to allow young children to be present at wars and funerals, courtships and seductions, criminal plots and cocktail parties....Television*

thrusts children into a complex adult world, and it provides the impetus for children to ask the meanings of actions and words they would not yet have heard or read about without television.[17]

Meyrowitz concedes that movies offered similar information to children before television, but he says that the pervasiveness of television today makes its effects more widespread. Television is blurring social distinctions—between children and adults, and between men and women. Complicating the current study of media effects is the increase in the variety and number of available media sources.

Linking TV to School Performance

Many studies about children and television, such as the National Institute of Mental Health report, have concentrated on the effects of the portrayals of violence. But in 1981, a California study suggested a link between television viewing and poor school performance.

The California Assessment Program (CAP), which tests academic achievement, included a new question on the achievement test: "On a typical weekday, about how many hours do you watch TV?" The students were given a choice ranging from zero to six or more hours.

An analysis of the answers to that question from more than 10,000 sixth graders was matched with the children's scores on the achievement test. The results suggested a consistent relationship between viewing time and achievement. Students who said they watched a lot of television scored lower in reading, writing and mathematics than students who didn't watch any television. The average scores for students who said they viewed six or more hours of television a day were six to eight points lower than for those children who said they watched less than a half-hour of television a day.

Because the study didn't include information about the IQ score or income levels of these students, the results cannot be considered conclusive. The study simply may show that children who watch a lot of television aren't studying. But the results are particularly interesting because of the number of children who were included in the survey.[18]

Further research could examine whether children are poor students *because* they watch a lot of television or whether children who watch a lot of television are poor students for other reasons.

Stereotyping Women

Journalists often use shorthand labels to characterize ethnic and other groups. In his 1922 book *Public Opinion*, political journalist Walter Lippmann first identified the tendency of journalists to generalize about other people based on fixed ideas.

When we speak of the mind of a group of people, of the French mind, the militarist mind, the bolshevik mind, we are liable to serious confusion unless we agree to separate the instinctive equipment from the stereotypes, the patterns, the formulae which play so decisive a part in building up the mental world to which the native character is adapted and responds....Failure to make this distinction accounts for oceans of loose talk about collective minds, national souls, and race psychology.[19]

I M P A C T

point of view

Magazine Ads Should Portray People of Color More Accurately

By Lawrence Bowen and Jill Schmid

For most of its life as a nation, America has been referred to as the world's "melting pot." The emphasis has been on the "melt"—not what was in the pot. *E Pluribus Unum* was to be both motto and model, with acculturation and assimilation the keys to nation building. Institutional imperatives called for an "integrated" society where people of color could work together and live in harmony.

Mass media, in general, and advertising, in particular, were seen as important windows on the melting pot, where progress, or the lack thereof, would be readily apparent. Television brought the window into America's living room, and a number of window gazers were quick to point out that the view was suburban, predominantly young, white, and middle class....

In the past decade, we've seen the "melting pot" metaphor challenged by multiculturalists calling for separate but equal approaches of life, liberty, and the pursuit of happiness. It's likely that something like "peaceful coexistence" or "different strokes for different folks" may eventuate, but meanwhile, many are caught between the pot and those who would stir it. Not the least among them are those marketers and their adver-

Ms. Foundation for Women. Photo by Pam Francis.

tising agencies who must serve up appealing images that are politically correct and racially sensitive, images that motive us to buy....

Overall, it is encouraging to note greater use of African Americans in mainstream magazine advertising. Simple inclusion is a necessary first step, but it does not equal integration or fair representation. Asians and Latinos are still woefully under-represented. Moreover, there are few advertisements in which minorities appear alone and, when they do appear, they are outnumbered by whites. Minorities continue to be used as "tokens" or as questionable links to some product attribute....

It's easy for an advertiser to simply add minority models to diffuse criticism; and, if one were to simply count the number of times minorities appear in advertisements, the increase could be viewed as progress. However, it is not that simple, and this analysis is very direct in pointing out that the actual number of times minorities are included in advertisements in an equal fashion to white models or as independent, potential consumers is really quite small.

Only a concerted effort from all sectors of the community can correct that condition by beginning to portray all minority groups, not just blacks, in a variety of different occupations and social settings. Industry will need to assume a lead role. And like most change, enlightened self-interest will light the path.

If companies are truly trying to reach minority markets, they must do a better job of not just including minorities in their mainstream advertising, but also showing the minorities in various occupations, in meaningful roles, and in a variety of settings. Minorities read mainstream magazines and buy mainstream products. It's time they receive mainstream treatment.

Excerpted from: Lawrence Bowen and Jill Schmid, "Minority Presence and Portrayal in Mainstream Magazine Advertising: An Update." *Journalism and Mass Communication Quarterly,* Spring 1997, 134–146.

The image of women portrayed by the media has been a subject of a significant contemporary study by many media researchers. Observers of the stereotyping of women point to past and current media portrayals showing very few women in professional roles and the lack of women shown as strong, major characters. The media's overall portrayal of women in mass culture is slowly improving, but in her book *Loving with a Vengeance: Mass-Produced Fantasies for Women*, Tania Modleski says that the portrayal in popular fiction of women in submissive roles began in 1740 with the British novel *Pamela*, which was then published in America by Benjamin Franklin in 1744.

Modleski analyzed the historical content of gothic novels, Harlequin Romances and soap operas. Her study reveals:

> *In Harlequin Romances, the need of women to find meaning and pleasure in activities that are not wholly male-centered such as work or artistic creation is generally scoffed at.*
>
> *Soap operas also undercut, though in subtler fashion, the idea that a woman might obtain satisfaction from these activities [work or artistic creation]….Indeed, patriarchal myths and institutions are…wholeheartedly embraced, although the anxieties and tensions they give rise to may be said to provoke the need for the texts in the first place.[20]*

The implication in Modleski's research is that women who read romance novels will believe they should act like the women in the novels they read. A stereotype that has existed since 1740 is unlikely to change quickly.

MULTICULTURALISM AND THE MASS MEDIA

For the year 2000, the U.S. census allows Americans to use more than one racial category to describe themselves, and the categories have been changed to reflect America's changing face. In the past, people were forced to choose one category from among the following: Black; White; Asian or Pacific Islander; American Indian or Alaskan Native; or "Other—specify in writing." In the last census (1990), about 10 million people checked "Other"—nearly all of Latino descent.

The new range of choices for the year 2000 census is: White; Black or African American; Asian; Hawaiian Native or Pacific Islander; American Indian or Alaska Native; and Hispanic or Latino. People who identify with more than one group also will be able to check more than one description, such as African American and Asian, for example. All government forms will be required to use the new categories by the year 2003.

The cast of Fox television's *Damon*, launched in 1998, reflected an attempt by the network to present a diverse set of characters.

© Fox Broadcasting Company

This new method will allow people to identify themselves to the government and shows the evolving social landscape of the U.S. population. Yet the American media have been very slow to acknowledge America's changing population patterns. In fact, critics charge that the media have responded reluctantly to reflect accurately America's growing multicultural mix.

During the last century, selected media outlets, such as African-American and Latino newspapers and magazines, have been able to cater to specific audiences. But the mainstream media, especially daily newspapers and the TV networks, have traditionally represented the interests of the mainstream culture. Scores of media studies have documented stereotypical representation, and a lack of representation, of people of color in all areas of the culture.

Media scholar Carolyn Martindale, for example, in a content analysis of *The New York Times* from 1934 to 1994, found that most nonwhite groups were visible "only in glimpses." According to Martindale, "The mainstream press in the U.S. has presented minorities as outside, rather than a part of, American Society."[21]

After examining 374 episodes of 96 prime-time series on ABC, CBS, NBC, Fox, WB and UPN, the Center for Media and Public Affairs for the National Council of La Raza concluded that only 2 percent of prime-time characters during the 1994–1995 season were Latinos, and most of the roles played by those characters were minor. The study, "Don't Blink: Hispanics in Television Entertainment," also revealed that, although Latino characters were portrayed more positively than they had been in the past, they were most likely to be shown as poor or working class.[22]

Based on a comprehensive analysis of the nation's newspapers, a 56-page *News Watch* report issued at a convention of the nation's African American,

Asian, Latino and Native American journalists concluded that "The mainstream media's coverage of people of color is riddled with old stereotypes, offensive terminology, biased reporting and a myopic interpretation of American society."[23]

To counteract stereotyping, the Center for Integration and Improvement of Journalism at San Francisco State University (which sponsored the study) offered the following Tips for Journalists:

- Apply consistent guidelines when identifying people of race. Are the terms considered offensive? Ask individual sources how they wish to be identified.

- Only refer to peoples' ethnic or racial background when it is relevant.

- When deciding whether to mention someone's race, ask yourself: Is ethnic/racial identification needed? Is it important to the context of the story?

- Consult a supervisor if you are unsure of the offensiveness or relevance of a racial or ethnic term.

- Use sensitivity when describing rites and cultural events. Avoid inappropriate comparisons. For example, Kwanza is not "African-American Christmas."

- Be specific when using ethnic or racial identification of individuals. Referring to someone as Filipino American is preferred to calling that person Asian. The latter term is better applied to a group.

The issue of accurate reflection by the media of a complex society invites analysis as traditional media outlets struggle to reflect the evolving face of an America that is growing more diverse every day.

ALTERNATIVE LIFESTYLES AND THE MASS MEDIA

An understanding of the media portrayals of Americans' diverse lifestyles received extra attention in 1997, when the television program *Ellen* portrayed two women exchanging a romantic kiss. Although promoted as the nation's first female television kiss, the first romantic lesbian relationship actually had been shown on *L.A. Law* in 1991. (See Impact/Point-of-View, "From Here to Immodesty: Milestones in the Toppling of TV's Taboos," pages 316–317.)

The subject of alternative lifestyles has remained primarily a subject for the nation's lesbian and gay newspapers and magazines, although in 1996, *The New Yorker* ran a controversial cover that portrayed two men kissing on a Manhattan sidewalk.

Bringing the issue to mainstream TV, as the *Ellen* program did, presents a dilemma for the TV networks because, when notified beforehand about the content of the program, some local TV stations refused to show the episode. The reluctance of television to portray alternative lifestyles is as much a reflection of the networks trying to protect their economic interests as it is a reflection of the nation's social values.

In 1993, newspapers faced a similar dilemma when cartoonist Lynn Johnston, who draws the very popular syndicated strip *For Better or Worse*, decided to reveal that Lawrence, one of the teenagers in the comic strip, is gay. Most newspapers published the strip, but 19 newspapers cancelled their contracts for the comic, which is carried by Universal Press Syndicate of

The alternative lifestyle portrayed by the ABC program *Ellen* prompted this protest outside the network's offices.

Kansas City. One newspaper editor who refused to carry the strip explained that "We are a conservative newspaper in a conservative town." Another editor said that he "felt the sequence condoned homosexuality 'almost to the point of advocacy.'" [24]

Responding to criticism that, by revealing Lawrence's sexual preference, she was advocating homosexuality, Johnston said, "You know, that's like advocating left-handedness. Gayness is simply something that exists. My strip is a reality strip, real situations, real crises, real people." One newspaper executive at a paper that carried the strip wrote, "It seems to me that what we're talking about here isn't the rightness or wrongness of homosexuality. It is about tolerence." [25]

UNDERSTANDING MASS MEDIA AND SOCIAL ISSUES

Scholars once thought that the effects of media were easy to measure, as a direct relationship between media messages and media effects. Contemporary scholars now know that the relationship between mass media and social issues is complex.

Communications scholar Neil Postman poses some questions to ask about mass media and social issues:

- *"What are the main psychic effects of each [media] form?"*

- *"What is the main relation between information and reason?"*

- *"What redefinitions of important cultural meanings do new sources, speeds, contexts, and forms of information require?"*

- *"How do different forms of information persuade?"*
- *"Is a newspaper's 'public' different from television's 'public'?"*
- *"How do different information forms dictate the type of content that is expressed?"*[26]

These questions should be discussed, says Postman, because "no medium is excessively dangerous if its users understand what its dangers are....This is an instance in which the asking of the questions is sufficient. To ask is to break the spell." [27]

IN FOCUS

- Media scholars look for patterns in the effects of media, rather than anecdotal evidence.

- David Potter, in *People of Plenty*, described the United States as a consumer society driven by advertising.

- Canadian scholar Marshall McLuhan introduced the term *global village* to describe the way the media bring people together through shared experience.

- The magic bullet theory, developed in the 1929 Payne Fund studies, asserted that media content had a direct causal relationship to behavior.

- Hadley Cantril challenged the magic bullet theory. Cantril found that better-educated people listening to "War of the Worlds" were more likely to detect that the broadcast was fiction. Today, scholars believe that the media have different effects on different people.

- In 1948, political scientist Harold D. Lasswell described the process of communication as: who? says what? on which channel? to whom? with what effect?

- In 1961, Wilbur Schramm and his associates revealed that children used TV for fantasy, diversion and instruction. Aggressive children were more likely to turn to TV for fantasy, said Schramm, but he could find no serious problems related to TV viewing.

- The 1971 report to Congress, *Television and Social Behavior*, made a faint causal connection between TV violence and children's violent behavior, but the report said that only some children were affected, and these children already had been classified as aggressive.

- Several subsequent studies have suggested that TV violence causes aggression among children. Researchers caution, however, that TV violence is not *the* cause of aggressiveness, but only *a* cause of aggressiveness.

- The Federal Trade Commission report, *Television Advertising to Children*, said that children see 20,000 commercials a year and that younger children are much more likely to pay attention to TV advertising than older ones.

- The summary study by the National Institute of Mental Health in 1982 asserted that a direct connection exists between televised violence and aggressive behavior, but there is no way to predict who will be affected and why.

- Media politics began in 1933 with President Franklin Roosevelt's Fireside Chats. John F. Kennedy broadened the tradition when he and Richard Nixon appeared in the nation's first televised debate of presidential candidates in 1960.

- The first major study of politics and the media, *The People's Choice*, concluded that only 8 percent of the voters in the study were actually converted by media coverage of the 1940 campaign.

- The 1976 study *The Unseeing Eye* revealed that only 7 percent of the people in the study were manipulated by TV ads. The researchers concluded that political advertising has little effect on most people.

- The rising cost of national political campaigns is directly connected to the expense of television advertising. Television is a very efficient way to reach large numbers of people quickly, but campaigning for television also distances the candidates from direct public contact.

- Elisabeth Noelle-Newmann has asserted that, because of what she calls a "spiral of silence" supporting the consensus point of view, the media have more influence because opponents of the consensus tend to remain silent.

- Joshua Meyrowitz says that television viewing blurs the distinction between childhood and adulthood.

- A study by the California Assessment Program of children's TV viewing habits seems to support the idea that children who watch a lot of TV do not perform as well in schoolwork as children who watch less television.

- Walter Lippmann first identified the tendency of journalists to generalize about groups of people and create stereotypes.

- Scholar Tania Modleski says that the media's inaccurate portrayals of women is not new but began in 1740 with publication of *Pamela*, the first novel.

- The year 2000 census categories for racial designations reflect the multicultural nature of the U.S. population, yet the mass media have been slow to acknowledge America's changing population patterns.

- The mainstream media, especially daily newspapers and the TV networks, have traditionally represented the interests of the mainstream culture.

- A study of *The New York Times* from 1934 to 1994 found that most non-white groups were visible "only in glimpses."

- A study by the National Council of La Raza concluded that only 2 percent of prime-time characters during the 1994–1995 TV season were Latinos, and most of the roles played by those characters were minor.

- The Center for Integration and Improvement of Journalism has offered *Tips for Journalists* as guidelines to help reporters cover multicultural issues with sensitivity.

- The lesbian character on the 1997 TV program *Ellen* and the homosexual character Lawrence in the cartoon strip *For Better or Worse* focused attention on media portrayals of alternative lifestyles.

WORKING THE WEB www

■ **American Society of Newspaper Editors Minority Employment Report**
www.asne.org/kiosk/diversity/97minsrv.htm

■ **Association for Asian Studies**
www.easc.indiana.edu/~aas

■ **Diversity in Electronic Media**
www.mediaaccess.org/program/diversity/index.html

■ **Hispanic Magazine Online**
www.hisp.com

■ **Hotline (politics)**
www.cloakroom.com

■ **Political Junkie**
www.politicaljunkie.com

INFOTRAC COLLEGE EDITION EXERCISES

Using the InfoTrac College Edition's fully searchable online database of articles and abstracts, do the following exercises as directed by your instructor.

1. Marshall McLuhan was one of the first social scientists to study the effects of mass communication on people. Using the keywords "Marshall McLuhan," look for more information on McLuhan's theories. Print at least two articles that you find and either:

   a. write a brief paper on your findings, or

   b. bring the articles to class for a small-group discussion.

2. Using the keywords "Mercury Theater" find an article about the famous "War of the Worlds" broadcast of 1938. Learn more about the effects of Orson Welles' famous radio play on the public. Print at least one article and bring it to class for discussion.

3. Look up the subject heading "children television" on InfoTrac and choose three articles on the effects of television on children. Print them and either:

   a. write a brief paper on your findings, or

   b. bring the articles to class for a small-group discussion.

4. Read "Impact/Point of View: Magazine Ads Should Portray People of Color More Accurately" in Chapter 12 and then, using the keywords "advertising ethics" look up at least two articles about the controversy. Print the articles and either:

   a. write a brief paper on your findings, or

   b. bring the articles to class for a small-group discussion.

5. Using the keywords "television violence," look up at least three articles on the subject. Choose a specific aspect of television violence (say, television violence on TV dramas or cop shows) and print at least two articles on that subject. Print the articles and either:

   a. write a brief paper on your findings, or

   b. bring the articles to class for a small-group discussion.

13

Media Ownership and Press Performance

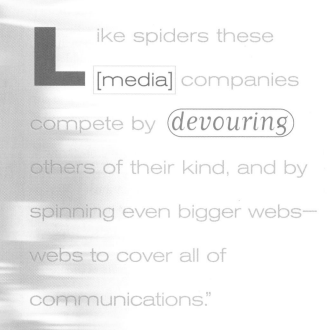

"Like spiders these [media] companies compete by *devouring* others of their kind, and by spinning even bigger webs— webs to cover all of communications."

Ken Auletta, The New Yorker

In 1822, James Madison observed about the media's role in a democracy that "a popular government, without popular information, or the means of acquiring it, is but a prologue to a farce or a tragedy; or perhaps both."[1]

One hundred years later, political columnist Walter Lippmann wrote, "The press is no substitute for institutions. It is like the beam of a searchlight that moves restlessly about, bringing one episode and then another out of darkness into vision."[2]

Because the media are this country's main source of information, it is important to examine who owns the media and how well journalists, working within that system of ownership, fulfill their responsibility of reporting on events. How well does today's system of media ownership in the United States allow the media to bring the important and necessary "popular information" to the people, as envisioned by Madison? How well do journalists shine that searchlight to bring "one episode and then another out of darkness into vision," as Lippmann described? That is what this chapter is about.

OWNERSHIP: WHO CONTROLS THE MESSAGES?

In some media industries, ownership is controlled by more companies today than in the 1950s. There are six major movie studios today, for example, compared to the Big Five of the 1940s; the number of companies that own broadcast stations has increased since the 1940s, and so has the number of magazine publishers. The number of companies that publish newspapers and the number of companies that produce records, however, have declined.

Overall, American media ownership has been contracting rather than expanding since its heyday in the 1960s. The emergence of some new media, such as cable, is inviting more people into the media business, but the trend is for fewer companies to own more media businesses and for fewer companies to own more aspects of the media business. Here is some media ownership information compiled from previous chapters, with some new facts added. (See Impact/Point of View, "Who's Left Out at the Media Ball," p. 293.)

- The top ten newspaper chains own one-fifth of the nation's dailies; group owners (companies that own more than one newspaper) hold four out of five newspapers published in America every day.

- Twenty corporations control more than 50 percent of annual magazine revenue.

- One broadcast company can own more than 500 radio stations.

- More than half of the nation's TV stations are network affiliates.

- Almost all of America's movies are distributed by one of the six large studios.

- The majority of recording company profits are collected from six major labels.

- America's top six book publishing companies account for 40 percent of total annual publishing revenue.

- In 1999, America Online merged with Time Warner, the largest media merger in the nation's history.[3]

Media Concentration

Media concentration involves four trends:

1. *Concentration of ownership* within one industry, such as print and broadcast chain ownership and broadcast network affiliation.

2. *Cross-media ownerships*—companies that own more than one type of medium.

3. *Conglomerate ownership*—companies that own media properties and that are involved in businesses other than the media business.

4. *Vertical integration*—companies that control several aspects of a single media industry, such as production and distribution. (See Chapter 1 for more information about these categories.)

More than 40 years ago, *New Yorker* press critic A. J. Liebling warned about the danger of one-newspaper towns:

> *As the number of cities in the United States with only a single newspaper ownership increases, news becomes increasingly nonessential to the newspaper. In the mind of the average publisher, it is a costly and uneconomic frill, like the free lunch that*

IMPACT

point of view *Who's Left Out at the Media Ball?*

By John Lippman and Bruce Orwall

And then there was NBC. The TV network, owned by General Electric Co., is now the only major broadcast operation not owned or affiliated with a Hollywood movie studio, following Viacom Inc.'s planned acquisition of CBS Corp.

Conventional wisdom—on Wall Street as well as in Hollywood—now has it that NBC needs to find a dance partner, in this age of media conglomeration and vertical integration.

But who? Each of the other networks has now paired off with one of the big producers of movies and TV programming: Walt Disney Co. owns ABC, News Corp. owns Fox, Time Warner Inc.'s Warner Bros. Studio operates the fledgling WB network, and Viacom's Paramount Pictures units owns 50 percent of UPN.

Notably left out of the action are Sony Corp., Seagram Co., and a host of smaller players that include Barry Diller's USA Networks Inc. Nobody wants to be a wallflower, and NBC would be a great catch, one that would secure a broadcast distribution system for shows, as well as enhanced opportunities for cross-media advertising. USA Networks already held some talks with NBC last year.

But integrating a network can be a lot harder than simply acquiring one, as Disney is finding with ABC. And those looking for NBC to pair off quickly with a studio could find the wait a bit longer than expected. For starters, a recent Federal Communications Commission decision now allows broadcasters to own more than one station in the same market. That has opened up a vast world of potential deals involving TV station groups that are widely expected to occur before NBC aligns with any studio.

The Wall Street Journal, September 8, 1999, B-1. Reprinted by permission.

The Big Four

A quartet of entertainment giants have operations that bestride both movies and television.

	MOVIE STUDIO	TV STATIONS	TV NETWORK	CABLE PROGRAMMING
Time Warner	✓		✓	✓
News Corp.	✓	✓	✓	✓
Walt Disney	✓	✓	✓	✓
Viacom/CBS	✓	✓	✓	✓

The Wallflowers

Pressure could be mounting on companies with gaps in their entertainment holdings.

	MOVIE STUDIO	TV STATIONS	TV NETWORK	CABLE PROGRAMMING
NBC		✓	✓	✓
Seagrams	✓	✓ [1]		✓ [1]
Sony	✓	✓ [2]		
USA Networks	✓	✓	✓ [3]	✓

[1] Through stake in USA networks
[2] Minority stake
[3] Plans announced but rollout delayed

Daniel Pelavin.

Martin Kozlowski.

AOL's Steve Case (left) hugs Time Warner's Gerald Levin to celebrate the $162 billion merger of the two companies in 1999.

Reuters Newmedia Inc/CORBIS

saloons used to furnish to induce customers to buy beer....With the years, the quantity of news in newspapers is bound to diminish from its present low. The proprietor, as Chairman of the Board, will increasingly often say that he would like to spend 75 cents now and then on news coverage but that he must be fair to his shareholders.[4]

Today, about 2 percent of American cities have competing newspapers. Liebling's fears could apply to all forms of ownership concentration. The issue of concentration centers on one question, what former newspaper editor Norman E. Isaacs calls "the internal war between public purpose and making money" and what the book publishing industry calls the war between "culture and commerce."

"For an author, the increased concentration means decreased access to the market and fewer outlets for publication," write economists Michael J. Robinson and Ray Olszewski, summarizing statements made by the Authors Guild about concentration in the publishing industry. "Its impact on the marketplace for ideas...is to introduce the risk of corporate pressure being placed on editors and on the production process, pressure that would not be a problem with the existence of independent companies. Mergers and acquisitions reduce the number of diverse and antagonistic sources."[5]

In the advertising business, some executives are even more candid. "It's big for big's sake," one advertising executive told *The Wall Street Journal*. "Advertising is really a personal service," said a second ad executive, "and the bigger it gets, the more impersonal it becomes."[6]

Competition and Convergence

Today's media companies are profit-centered. They are also driven by *convergence* (the melding of the communications, computer and electronics industries described in Chapter 1) to seek business alliances that will help them compete in the next century. Media companies are owned by people who want to make money. As in all industries, there are people who want to make money quickly and people who take the long-term view about profits, but certainly none of them wants to lose money.

Traditionally, making money has been a goal supported by the vast majority of Americans. But the way these companies make money is the debate. Does the legacy of First Amendment protection for news-gathering organizations mean that they have a special responsibility to provide the information people need in a democracy? Should entertainment-producing companies provide a diversity of cultural outlets for creativity? Will the adoption of corporate values benefit or harm the mass media industries?

WHY MEDIA PROPERTIES ARE SELLING

Turnover in ownership is highest in the newspaper and broadcast industries. Several factors have affected the market for these properties.

1. Newspaper and broadcast properties are attractive investments. Many report profits of 10 percent a year, which is about double the profit for a U.S. manufacturing company.

2. Newspapers and broadcast stations are scarce commodities. Because the number of newspapers has been declining and the number of broadcast stations is government regulated, only so many properties are available. As with all limited commodities, this makes them attractive.

3. Many newspapers, especially, have gone through a cycle of family ownership. If the heirs to the founders of the business are not interested in joining the company, the only way for them to collect their inheritance is to sell the newspaper.

4. Newspapers and broadcast stations are easier to buy than to create. Because these businesses require huge investments in equipment, they are expensive to start up.

5. In broadcasting, the major factor that encouraged ownership changes in the 1980s was deregulation. This allowed people who had never been in the broadcast business before to enter the industry, using bank loans to pay for most of their investment. But deregulation had other effects, too. In the 1990s, the introduction of new technologies changed the economics of the industry.

Some new owners of media companies approach broadcast properties as they would any other business—hoping to invest the minimum amount necessary. They hope to hold onto the property until the market is favorable and then sell at a huge profit. Since Congress removed restrictions in 1996 on how many radio stations one company can own, for example, more than 2,200 stations have changed hands.[7]

ADVANTAGES OF CONCENTRATION

Supporters of concentrated ownership say that a large company can offer advantages that a small company could never afford—training for the employees, higher wages and better working conditions. John C. Quinn, executive vice president for news for Gannett, says:

A publisher's instinct for good or evil is not determined by the number of newspapers he owns. A group can attract top professional talent, offering training under a variety of editors, advancement through a variety of opportunities....It can invest in research and development and nuts-and-bolts experience necessary to translate the theories of new technology into the practical production of better newspapers.

Concentrated ownership can provide great resources; only independent, local judgment can use the resources to produce a responsible and responsive local newspaper. That measure cannot be inflated by competition nor can it be diluted by monopoly. [8]

William A. Henry III of *Time* magazine, who won a Pulitzer Prize at the *Boston Globe*, pointed out that several of the newspapers that are considered the nation's best—*The New York Times*, the *Los Angeles Times*, and the *Washington Post*—are chain newspapers, although he acknowledged that these three are still dominated by family owners who hold the majority of stock.

The same arguments that are made against chain ownership can be made against independent ownership, he said.

Most independent owners run papers in ways that comfort them, their friends and their general social class.

A great many reporters have gotten into trouble over the years by going after buddies or business associates of the owners. And a great many more have compromised themselves by writing puffy, uncritical pieces about cultural institutions, department stores, restaurants or socialites favored by the owner or his spouse.[9]

DISADVANTAGES OF CONCENTRATION

The major arguments of those who support concentration are that a corporation can offer financial support to a small newspaper or broadcast station and that responsible, autonomous local management is the key to successful group ownership. Yet several studies have proved that chain newspapers are more likely to support the favored candidates in elections, and that in presidential elections, 85 percent or more of the papers in a chain endorse the same candidate.[10]

This is an example of the consequences of corporate control that forms the major argument against group ownership—that concentration limits the diversity of opinion and the quality of culture available to the public and reduces what scholars call **message pluralism**.

message pluralism
a broad and diverse representation of opinion and culture by the media.

In an article in *The New Republic* entitled "Invasion of the Gannettoids," former newspaper reporter Philip Weiss described what he says happens when corporate culture takes over American journalism:

The problem with Gannett isn't simply its formula or its chairman, but the company's corporate culture. The product is the company—cheerful, superficial, self-promoting, suspicious of ideas, conformist, and implicitly authoritarian. But the Gannett story is more, too. For as many as 6 million daily readers, most of them in one-newspaper towns, Gannett serves as chief interpreter and informer about society—and does so unsustained by ideals of independence or thoroughness.[11]

The loss of message pluralism in television angers critics the most, since broadcasting still is licensed to serve the public "interest, convenience, and necessity." Broadcasters argue that this requirement is out of date because it was adopted when broadcast outlets were scarce. Today, broadcasters say many channels of information are available to the public.

But Ben H. Bagdikian, Dean Emeritus, Graduate School of Journalism at University of California, Berkeley, describes how the loss of message pluralism can affect every aspect of communication:

It has always been assumed that a newspaper article might be expanded to a magazine article which could become the basis for a hardcover book, which, in turn, could be a paperback, and then, perhaps a TV series and finally, a movie. At each step of change an author and other enterprises could compete for entry into this array of channels for reaching the public mind and pocketbook. But today several media giants own these arrays, not only closing off entry points for competition in different media, but influencing the choice of entry at the start.[12]

PRESS PERFORMANCE: HOW WELL DO JOURNALISTS DO THEIR JOBS?

Because the First Amendment to the U.S. Constitution prescribes freedom of the press, it is important to examine how well the press uses that freedom to report on events. To understand how well the press performs, you must first understand who journalists are and how they work. Then you can examine how the public feels about the way members of the press do their job.

The latest study of just who journalists are comes from *The American Journalist in the 1990s*, by David H. Weaver and G. Cleveland Wilhoit, published in 1996. Weaver and Wilhoit surveyed 1,400 American journalists about their jobs. According to Weaver and Wilhoit, today's "typical" journalist "is a white Protestant male who has a bachelor's degree from a public college, is married, 36 years old, earns about $31,000 a year, has worked in journalism about 12 years, does not belong to a journalism association, and works for a medium-sized (42 journalists), group-owned daily newspaper."[13]

Weaver and Wilhoit cautioned, however, that this typical portrait is misleading because there are:

substantial numbers of women, non-Whites, non-Protestant, single, young and old, and relatively rich and poor journalists working in this country for a wide variety of small and large news media, both group and singly owned.

Many of these journalists differ from this profile of the typical journalist. For example, Black and Asian journalists are more likely to be women than men, not to be married, to have higher incomes ($37,000–$42,000) than the typical journalist, to have worked in journalism 10 or 11 years, to be members of at least one journalism association, and to work for larger (100–150 journalists) daily newspapers.

Hispanic journalists are more likely to be Catholic than Protestant, and to be more similar to Blacks and Asians than to the "typical" U.S. journalist on other characteristics. Native American journalists are more likely to be of some other religion besides Protestant or Catholic, to make much less than the other groups (median income of $22,000) and to work for very small newspapers or television stations (3 or 4 journalists).

Following are some other important findings of the study:

1. Employment growth stalls. The substantial growth in the number of journalists working for the media that characterized the 1970s has stalled. The growth rate from 1982 to 1992 was 9 percent. Between 1971 and 1982, the growth rate was 60 percent.

Figure 13.1

"Typical" Journalist Information
Gender - Male
Education - Public College
Marital Status - Married
Average age - 36 years
Journalistic experience - 12 years
Average income - $31,000
"Typical" employer - Medium-sized daily newspaper

Getting the story and getting the story faster and better than the competition are major factors influencing journalistic values.

AP/Wide World Photos

2. **Minorities make some gains.** News organizations have made some progress in attracting minorities, despite the lack of growth in journalism jobs. The current minority news workforce of 8 percent is up from 4 percent in 1982–83....Recent *hires are 12 percent minorities.*

3. **Mixed gains for women.** In spite of more women being hired in the 1980s, they remain at the same workforce percentage as a decade ago: 34 percent. The problem may be one of retention, as well as poor job growth. Salary equity with men has improved.

4. **Abandoning ship.** A serious retention problem in journalism may be just over the horizon. More than 20 percent of those surveyed said they plan to leave the field within five years. That's twice the figure in 1982–*83.*

   This is tied to a significant decline in job satisfaction, with complaints about pay and the need for a different challenge leading the list of major reasons for plans to leave journalism.

5. **Little shift in journalistic values.** *Overall differences in ideas about journalistic roles and reporting practices are not great....Two journalistic responsibilities seen as extremely important by a majority: getting information to the public quickly and investigating government claims.*

6. **Some shift in political values.** More journalists now see themselves as Democrats (44.1% Democrats; 16.3% Republican; 34.4% Independent) than they did in 1982–83, with Democratic Party allegiance strongest among women and minorities. However, journalists tend to regard their news organizations as more politically middle-of-the-road than themselves.[14]

It has not been shown in any comprehensive survey of news gathering that people with liberal or conservative values insert their personal ideology directly into their reporting and that the audience unquestioningly accepts one point of view. The belief in a causal relationship between the media and the audience's behavior is known as the **magic bullet theory.** This belief was disproved long ago (see Chapter 12).

But the assumption that journalists' personal beliefs directly influence their professional performance is common. Although the reporting by some journalists and columnists certainly can be cited to support this idea, the majority of journalists, says media scholar Herbert J. Gans, view themselves as detached observers of events:

> *Journalists, like everyone else, have values, [and] the two that matter most in the newsroom are getting the story and getting it better and faster than their prime competitors—both among their colleagues and at rival news media. Personal political beliefs are left at home, not only because journalists are trained to be objective and detached, but also because their credibility and their paychecks depend on their remaining detached....*
>
> *The beliefs that actually make it into the news are professional values that are intrinsic to national journalism and that journalists learn on the job. However, the professional values that particularly antagonize conservatives (and liberals when they are in power) are neither liberal nor conservative but* reformist, *reflecting journalism's long adherence to good-government Progressivism.*[15]

Some press critics, in fact, argue that journalists most often present establishment viewpoints and are unlikely to challenge prevailing political and social values.[16] In addition, the pressure to come up with instant analyses of news events may lead to conformity in reporting.

In mid-May 1989, for example, thousands of people gathered in Tiananmen Square to demonstrate against the Chinese government. Angered by the demonstrations, the government sent troops to clear the Square, and hundreds of people were killed and injured, most of them students. In his analysis of the way the press reported on the violence, press critic David Shaw argued that journalists misread and misreported events as a pro-democracy uprising that could not be stopped. Shaw called this "consensus journalism"—the tendency among many journalists covering the same event to report similar conclusions about the event, rather than to report conflicting interpretations.

JOURNALISTS' NEWS VALUES

News organizations often are criticized for presenting a consistently slanted view of the news. But as Weaver and Wilhoit observed, news values often are shaped by the way news organizations are structured and the routines they follow. The press in America, it is generally agreed, doesn't tell you what to think but does tell you what and whom to think *about*. This is called **agenda-setting**.

There are two types of agenda-setting: the flow of information from one news organization to another and the agenda of information that flows from news organizations to their audiences.

In the first type of agenda-setting, the stories that appear in the nation's widely circulated print media provide ideas to the other media. The print media, for example, often identify specific stories as important by giving them attention, so that widely circulated print media can set the news agenda on some national issues.

To analyze the second type of agenda-setting—the picture of the world that journalists give to their audiences—is to examine the social and cultural values that journalists present to the public. The most significant recent study of news values was offered by Herbert J. Gans in his book *Deciding What's News*.

Gans identified eight enduring values that emerged in his study of different types of news stories over a long period of time: **ethnocentrism** (the attitude that some cultural and social values are superior), altruistic democracy, responsible capitalism, small-town pastoralism, individualism, moderatism, order and leadership. These values, said Gans, often help define what is considered news. American news conveys the ideas of:

Ethnocentrism. America is a nation to be valued above all others. "While the news contains many stories that are critical of domestic conditions, they are almost always treated as deviant cases, with the implication that American ideas, at least, remain viable," says Gans.

ethnocentrism
the attitude that some cultural and social values are superior.

"No comment."

Altruistic democracy. Politics should be based on public service and the public interest. The news media expect all public officials to be scrupulously honest, efficient and public-spirited.

Responsible capitalism. Open competition will create increased prosperity for everyone. Business people should not seek unreasonable profits, and they should not exploit workers or customers.

Small-town pastoralism. Small agricultural or market towns are favored over other settlements. Suburbs are usually overlooked as a place where news happens. Big cities are viewed as places with "urban" problems.

Individualism. A heroic individual is someone who struggles against difficulties and powerful forces. Self-made people are admired.

Moderatism. Moderation is valued, excesses and extremism are not.

Order. Importance is placed on political order. "The values in the news derive largely from reformers and reform movements, which are themselves elites. Still, the news is not simply a compliant support of elites, or the establishment, or the ruling class; rather, it views nation and society through its own set of values and with its own conception of the good social order."

Leadership. Attention is focused on leaders. The president is seen as the nation's primary leader and protector of the national order.[17]

These values exist throughout American society and, indeed, come from historical assumptions based in our culture. As Gans suggests, this news ideology both supports and reflects elements of the social order.

BLURRING DISTINCTIONS: NEWS, REALITY SHOWS AND ADVERTISING

Today's TV reality shows, such as *Cops*, *Real Stories of the Highway Patrol*, and *America's Most Wanted* are blurring the distinction between what is news and what is recreated drama. These shows portray events and use interviews with crime victims and reenactments of events in a documentary style that imitates news stories. These reality shows, or docudramas, can make it difficult for an audience to distinguish true news footage when they see it.

"Infomercials"—programs that pretend to give viewers information but that are really advertisements for the sponsors' products—also are making it harder to discern what is reporting and what is advertising. The line between news and entertainment on television becomes even more tricky when advertisers produce programs that look like news but are really advertisements.

The effect of this merging of entertainment and news, as well as the entertaining graphics and the lighthearted presentation style of most local TV newscasts, are making it more difficult for viewers to separate fact from fiction, reality from reenactment and news from advertising. The result could be a decline in the audience's trust in television news to deliver accurate information.

THE PUBLIC'S PERCEPTION OF THE PRESS

Two astute observers of the press who have been critical of its performance are James Reston and Norman Corwin. "The truth is that most American newspaper people are really more interested in dramatic spot news, the splashy story, than in anything else," said *The New York Times* columnist James Reston. "They want to be in on the big blowout, no matter how silly, and would rather write about what happened than whether it made any sense."[18]

IMPACT

on you

Public Sees Papers as Biased, Sensationalist, Study Shows

By Susan Sward

The public believes that U.S. newspapers seek out sensational stories, show too much bias and make too many errors, according to a report released yesterday by the American Society of Newspaper Editors.

Readers believe that sensational stories are pursued "because they're exciting and they sell papers," according to a three-year project studying the public's attitudes about media credibility. People don't believe these stories deserve the attention and play they get."

The report's findings were gleaned from three sources—a national telephone survey of 3,000 people, 16 focus groups, and a 12-page questionnaire given to about 1,700 journalists working at U.S. newspapers with a circulation of 5,000 or more.

Among the findings:

- Seventy-eight percent of U.S. adults believe there is bias in the news media. The same number believe that powerful people can get stories into the paper or keep them out. They also believe that these powerful people can influence a newspaper to "spike or spin" a story.

- Eighty-seven percent say they would rather see a newspaper hold a story until the facts can be double-checked than rush it into print.

- While almost half of the public conclude that errors occur during the rush to meet deadlines, 27 percent blame sloppiness and laziness for the mistakes.

- Half of the public believe there are individuals or groups that get a "special break" and 45 percent think some people "don't get a fair shake" and instead get unfavorable treatment in the media. African Americans, Latinos, the poor, conservatives, religious organizations and people on welfare were often cited as objects of such unfavorable treatment.

- Television is viewed as having two clear strengths: immediacy (93 percent believe it is the first to break the news) and expediency (60 percent believe television provides a better overview of the most important news).

- Seventy-four percent also think television puts more emphasis on the personalities of newsmakers than on issues.

Matthew Wilson, executive editor of the *San Francisco Chronicle*, said, "These findings should be taken very seriously by reporters and editors. Clearly, the industry needs to do a better job not only in its coverage but also in explaining news decisions and the reporting process to readers."

Other news executives around the country had mixed reactions to the report.

Tom Rawlins, senior editor of the *St. Petersburg Times* in Florida, said he blames some of the dis-

Broadcast producer and writer Norman Corwin said about local television news people:

> *The average local newscast, almost everywhere in the country, is a kind of succotash served in dollops and seasoned by bantering between anchorpersons, sportspersons, weatherpersons and person-persons. And these people had better be good-looking, sparkling or cute—weathermen with party charm, anchorladies with good teeth and smart coiffures, sportscasters with macho charisma. It doesn't matter if they have a news background or not* [19]

Reston and Corwin are members of the media who are critical of their own profession. The public's perception of how well members of the press perform

connect between public and newspapers on the growth of newspaper chains.

Noting that his paper has the benefit of being owned by the nonprofit Pointer Institute, he said the paper's former editor, Nelson Pointer, always emphasized: "I make money so I can put out newspapers. I don't put out newspapers to make money."

Rawlins said it is hard for chain newspapers to have enough reporters and editors to be in touch with their communities and to build public confidence in their publications when "you are being squeezed for more profits...to meet some corporate headquarter's expectations."

A thorough survey of journalists reveals areas of agreement with the public's assessment. Journalists agree with public opinion on the importance of accuracy—that it's more important to get a story right than to get it first. Most everyone—both journalists and the consumers of journalism—wants newspapers to

present context and explanation, in addition to the facts.

The Findings In Brief

- The public and the press agree that there are too many factual errors and spelling or grammar mistakes in newspapers. Both put the major blame on deadline pressures.

- The public perceives that newspapers don't consistently demonstrate respect for, and knowledge of, their readers and communities. Journalists are much less critical of themselves.

- The public suspects that the points of view and biases of journalists influence what stories are covered. While some journalists agree that particular people or groups sometimes get overly favorable (or unfavorable) coverage, they are less likely to perceive a problem of bias in newspapers.

- The public believes that newspapers over-cover sensational stories because they're exciting and they sell papers. They don't believe these stories deserve the attention and play they get. While most journalists dispute the charge, others argue they're just providing what readers want.

- The public feels that newsroom values and practices are sometimes in conflict with their own priorities for their newspapers. The journalists' responses suggest that they're correct in this view.

- Members of the public who have had actual experience with the news process are the most critical of media credibility. The same is true of journalists who have been the subjects of the news stories.

American Society of Newspaper Editors, from "Gaining Our Credibility: Perspectives of the People and the Press." Used by permission.

their responsibility is equally important; only recently have the media begun to survey the public for their opinions about the news media.

Since 1986 Times Mirror has sponsored several ongoing studies of the public's feelings about the press conducted by the Gallup organization. For these surveys, Gallup has personally interviewed 1,000–3,021 people nationwide and then doubled back to ask the same respondents additional questions to clarify earlier findings. Among the findings of these surveys, which Times Mirror calls *The People & the Press*, are:

- By a ratio of 4 to 1, the people who were surveyed said that the major news organizations—*The Wall Street Journal, CBS News, ABC News, NBC News, Newsweek* and *Time*—are believable.

- 79 percent of the people surveyed said that news organizations "care about how good a job they do"; 72 percent said the press is "highly professional."

- In 1989, a majority (54 percent) said reporters get the facts straight; 44 percent said that the press often was inaccurate. The inaccuracy rating has increased 10 percent since 1985 (see Figure 13.2).

- In 1989, more than two-thirds of the people (68 percent) said that journalists tend to favor one side, compared to 53 percent who felt the press were biased in 1985 (see Figure 13.2).

- The press is "pretty independent," according to 33 percent of the people, but 62 percent said the press is "often influenced by the powerful," including the federal government, big business, advertisers and special-interest groups.

- 77 percent of the people interviewed in 1989 said that the press invades people's privacy. This was the most widely held criticism among the people surveyed.

- The people who have negative opinions about the press are those who consume the most news and are among the most vocal and powerful segments of American society.[20]

These surveys are the most comprehensive of their kind undertaken. They show that members of the public seem to support the press as an institution, but with specific misgivings about the way journalists do their job. It is also important to note that the people who pay the most attention to the news are the most critical about how the press performs.

Furthermore, the public is not a cheering section roused to its feet to defend the First Amendment. In fact, only one in three people surveyed by Gallup was able to cite the First Amendment as the source of press freedoms in America.

Figure 13.2   The Public Rates the Press

Accuracy of News Organizations

Question: In general, do you think news organizations get the facts straight, or do you think that their stories and reports are often inaccurate?

Fairness of News Organizations

Question: In presenting the news dealing with political and social issues, do you think that news organizations deal fairly with all sides, or do they tend to favor one side?

Data from *The People & the Press*, 1989.

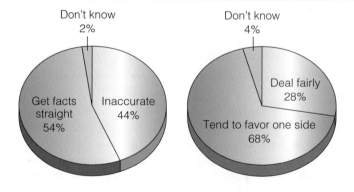

After the first survey appeared, Times Mirror received nearly 8,000 letters from people commenting on the results. One person wrote: "No question: No free press, no democracy. They go together like pie and ice cream." But a second person wrote, "Does a free press strengthen democracy? Absolutely, but it must be a *responsible press*. It must be *honest*. It must have *integrity*. And it must be willing to admit its mistakes *as loudly* as it claims its triumphs."[21]

UNDERSTANDING MEDIA OWNERSHIP AND PRESS PERFORMANCE

The media system described by Walter Lippmann and James Madison at the beginning of this chapter delivers a diversity of messages and opinions to an alert and informed public that uses this information to make intelligent decisions.

Media ownership that becomes concentrated in a few corporations could limit the society's access to "popular information, or the means of acquiring it," that Madison foresaw as an essential part of democratic government. A press that does not fulfill its public duty, as "the beam of a searchlight" that Lippmann described, risks losing the freedom that the First Amendment prescribes.

To maintain the public's trust, the owners of media companies and members of the press must be willing to undergo constant scrutiny about whether they are meeting their responsibilities. A critical view of ownership issues and press performance issues is important because American media was founded in the belief that the press will perform conscientiously, and that the public will have access to a variety of ideas and opinions through diverse media outlets.

IN FOCUS

- Ownership issues center around: (1) concentration; (2) cross-media ownership; (3) conglomerate ownership; (4) vertical integration.

- Media properties are selling rapidly because they are attractive investments; they are scarce commodities; they are easier to buy than to launch; many newspapers have gone through a cycle of family ownership and broadcast deregulation has lifted many restrictions.

- The major arguments of people who support concentration are that a corporation can offer financial support and that responsible local management is the key to successful group ownership.

- The major argument against group ownership is that concentration limits the diversity of opinion and the quality of culture available to the public-the loss of message pluralism.

- *The American Journalist* study (published in 1996) indicates that today's "typical" journalist is a 36-year-old Protestant white male with a bachelor's degree, is married and has children, does not belong to a journalism association, and earns about $31,000 a year.

- Consensus journalism is the tendency of journalists covering the same event to report similar conclusions about the event, rather than to report conflicting interpretations.

- The press in America doesn't tell you what to think. It *does* tell you what and whom to think *about*. This is called agenda-setting.

- There are two types of agenda-setting: the flow of information from one news organization to another (the broadcast media, for example, often develop stories that first appeared in the print media) and the flow of information from news organizations to their audiences.

- Herbert J. Gans, in his book *Deciding What's News*, identified eight enduring news values: ethnocentrism, altruistic democracy, responsible capitalism, small-town pastoralism, individualism, moderatism, order and leadership.

- *The People & the Press* survey sponsored by the *Los Angeles Times* found that most people believe that news organizations care about how well they do their jobs; more than two-thirds of the people surveyed said journalists tend to favor one side; 62 percent felt that the press is influenced by special interests; 77 percent of the people felt that the press invades people's privacy. People who consume the most news also are most critical of the press' performance.

- The merging of entertainment and news is making it more difficult for TV viewers to separate fact from fiction, reality from re-enactment and news from advertising.

WORKING THE WEB www

- **Corporate Watch**
  www.corpwatch.org/
- **Cross Media Ownership Rules Campaign**
  www.alliance.aust.com/CMOC
- **FAIR-Fairness and Accuracy in Reporting**
  www.fair.org/
- **Investigative Journalism on the Internet**
  www.vir.com/~sher/julian.htm
- **Public Journalism Bibliography**
  poynter.org/research/biblio/bib_pj.htm

INFOTRAC COLLEGE EDITION EXERCISES

Using the InfoTrac College Edition's fully searchable online database of articles and abstracts, do the following exercises as directed by your instructor.

1. Read "Impact/Point of View: Who's Left Out at the Media Ball?" in Chapter 13. Then, using InfoTrac College Edition and the keywords "media merger" (or one particular merger—"Time Warner AOL," for example), find at least two articles about media mergers. Print the articles and either:

   a. write a brief paper on you findings, or

   b. bring the articles to class for a small-group discussion.

2. Gannett is the world's largest newspaper chain. Using the keyword "Gannett" or the name of a particular Gannett paper listed in Chapter 13, look

up at least two articles on one of the newspapers or an issue within the chain. Print the articles about two different newspapers and either:

a. write a brief paper on your findings, or

b. bring the articles to class for a small-group discussion.

3. Using the keywords "media criticism," find at least two articles that are critical of some aspect of press performance. Print the articles and either:

a. write a brief paper on your findings, or

b. bring the articles to class for a small-group discussion.

4. Television reality shows have big audiences but blur the distinction between news, reality and advertising. Using the keywords "television reality shows" and/or "infomercials," look up at least two articles on the subject. Then print the articles and either:

a. write a brief paper on your findings, or

b. bring the articles to class for a small-group discussion.

5. Using the keywords "Freedom Forum" or "Newseum," look up information about the Freedom Forum or the Newseum, the world's first news museum. Print at least two of the articles and bring them to class for discussion about what these organizations do to promote a better understanding of media.

LAW and regulation

W e presume that governmental (regulation) of the content of speech is more likely to interfere with the free exchange of ideas than to encourage it.

*U.S. Supreme Court Justice John Paul Stevens, striking
down the Communications Decency Act*

What's Ahead

Freedom of the Press

Government Attempts to Restrict Press Freedom

Prior Restraint

Censorship

Libel Law

Privacy Law

Fair Trial and Right of Access

Regulating Broadcast

*Understanding the Telecommunications Act
   of 1996*

Understanding the Communications Decency Act

*Advertising and Public Relations Law
   and Regulation*

According to the precedent-setting *New York Times* v. *Sullivan* case, which helped define press freedom, the media's role is to encourage "uninhibited, robust and wide open debate." Arguments among the public, the government, and the media about the best way for the media to maintain this public trusteeship form the core of challenges and rebuttals to legal and regulatory limits on the media. Writes *New York Times* columnist Tom Wicker, "Even though absolute press freedom may sometimes have to accommodate itself to other high constitutional values, the repeal or modification of the First Amendment seems unlikely....If the true freedom of the press is to decide for itself what to publish and when to publish it, the true responsibility of the press must be to assert and defend that freedom."[1]

The media are businesses operating to make a profit, but these businesses enjoy a special trust under the U.S. Constitution. The legal and regulatory issues faced by the media are attempts by the government to balance this special trust with (1) the interests of individuals and (2) the interests of government.

FREEDOM OF THE PRESS

All legal interpretations of the press's responsibilities attempt to determine exactly what the framers of the U.S. Constitution meant when they included the First Amendment in the Bill of Rights in 1791. The First Amendment established the concept that the press should operate freely:

> *Congress shall make no law respecting an establishment of religion, or prohibiting the free exercise thereof; or* abridging the freedom of speech, or of the press; *or the right of the people peaceably to assemble, and to petition the Government for a redress of grievances.*

In his book *Emergence of a Free Press,* Leonard W. Levy explained:

> *By freedom of the press the Framers meant a right to engage in rasping, corrosive, and offensive discussions on all topics of public interest....The press had become the tribune of the people by sitting in judgment on the conduct of public officials. A free press meant the press as the Fourth Estate, [as]...an informal or extraconstitutional fourth branch that functioned as part of the intricate system of checks and balances that exposed public mismanagement and kept power fragmented, manageable, and accountable.*[2]

A discussion of the restrictions and laws governing the press today can be divided into six categories: (1) federal government restrictions, (2) prior restraint, (3) censorship, (4) libel, (5) privacy and (6) the right of access.

GOVERNMENT ATTEMPTS TO RESTRICT PRESS FREEDOM

At least four times in U.S. history before 1964, the federal government felt threatened enough by press freedom to attempt to restrict that freedom. These four notable attempts to restrict the way the media operate were: the Alien and Sedition Laws of 1798, the Espionage Act of 1918, the Smith Act of 1940 and the Cold War congressional investigations of suspected Communists in the late 1940s and early 1950s. All four of these challenges were attempts by the government to control free speech.

The Alien and Sedition Laws of 1798

Under the provisions of the Alien and Sedition Laws of 1798, 15 people were indicted, 11 people were tried and ten were found guilty. The Alien and Sedition Laws, as discussed in Chapter 2, set a fine of up to $2,000 and a sentence of up to two years in jail for anyone who was found guilty of speaking, writing or publishing "false, scandalous and malicious writing or writings" against the government, Congress or the president. The laws expired in 1801, and when he became president that year, Thomas Jefferson pardoned everyone who had been found guilty under the laws.[3]

The Espionage Act of 1918

Although Henry Raymond challenged censorship of Civil War reporting (see Chapter 2), journalists and the general population during that war accepted government control of information. But during World War I, Congress passed the Espionage Act of 1918. Not all Americans supported U.S. entry into the war, and to stop criticism, the Espionage Act made it a crime to say or write anything that could be viewed as helping the enemy. Under the act, 877 people were convicted. Many, but not all, of them were pardoned when the war ended.[4]

The most notable person cited under the Espionage Act of 1918 was Socialist party presidential candidate Eugene V. Debs, who was sentenced to two concurrent ten-year terms for giving a public speech against the war. At his trial Debs said, "I have been accused of obstructing the war. I admit it. Gentlemen, I abhor war. I would oppose the war if I stood alone."[5] Debs was released from prison by a presidential order in 1921.

The Smith Act of 1940

During World War II, Congress passed the Smith Act of 1940, which placed some restrictions on free speech. Only a few people were cited under it, but the press was required to submit stories for government censorship. President Roosevelt created an Office of Censorship, which worked out a voluntary "Code of Wartime Practices" with the press. It spelled out what information the press would not report about the war, such as troop and ship movements. The military retained power to censor all overseas war reporting.[6] The Office of Censorship also issued guidelines for news broadcasts and commentaries, called the *Code of Wartime Practices for American Broadcasters* (see Impact/Point of View page 314). The government exercised special influence over broadcasters because it licensed broadcast outlets.

HUAC and the Permanent Subcommittee on Investigations

The fourth major move challenging the First Amendment protection of free speech came in the late 1940s and early 1950s, culminating with the actions of the House Un-American Activities Committee (HUAC) against the Hollywood Ten (see Chapter 8) and the Army-McCarthy hearings before the Permanent Subcommitee on Investigations presided over by Senator Joseph R. McCarthy.

These congressional committees set a tone of aggressive Communist-hunting. When television broadcasts of McCarthy's investigation of Communist influence in the army and other reports eventually exposed his excesses, McCarthy's colleagues censured him by a vote of 67 to 22. But while the hearings were being held, they established a restrictive atmosphere that challenged free expression.

Senator Joseph McCarthy explains his theory of communism during the Army-McCarthy hearings. Army counsel Joseph N. Welch, who was defending people who had been declared subversive by McCarthy, is seated at the table.

Bettmann/CORBIS

PRIOR RESTRAINT

prior restraint the power of government to stop information from being published or broadcast.

Prior restraint means censoring information before the information appears or is published. The framers of the Constitution clearly opposed prior restraint by law. However, in 1931 the U.S. Supreme Court established the circumstances under which prior restraint could be justified.

Near v. *Minnesota*

J. M. Near published the weekly *Saturday Press*, which printed the names of people who were violating the nation's Prohibition laws. Minnesota authorities obtained a court order forbidding publication of *Saturday Press*, but the U.S. Supreme Court overturned the state's action. In *Near* v. *Minnesota* in 1931, the Court condemned prior restraint but acknowledged that the government could limit information about troop movements during war and could control obscenity. The Court also said that "the security of community life may be protected against incitements to acts of violence and the overthrow of orderly government."[7]

Saturday Press had not violated any of these prohibitions, so the court order was lifted. But future attempts to stop publication were based on the *Near* v. *Minnesota* decision, making it a landmark case.

In two important cases since *Near* (the Pentagon Papers and the *Progressive* case), courts were asked to bar publication of information to protect national security. In two other situations (military offensive in Grenada and the Persian Gulf), the federal government took action to prevent journalists from reporting on the government's activities.

The Pentagon Papers

In June 1971, *The New York Times* published the first installment of what has become known as the Pentagon Papers, excerpts from what was properly titled *History of U.S. Decision-Making Process on Vietnam Policy*. The Pentagon Papers detailed decisions that were made about the Vietnam War during the Kennedy and Johnson administrations. The documents were labeled top secret, but they were given to the *Times* by one of the report's authors, Daniel Ellsberg, an aide to the National Security Council. Ellsberg said he believed that the papers had been improperly classified and that the public should have the information.

After the first three installments were published in the *Times*, Justice Department attorneys received a restraining order against the *Times*, which stopped publication for two weeks while the *Times* appealed the case. While the case was being decided, the *Washington Post* began publishing the papers, and the *Post* was stopped, but only until the *Times* case was decided by the U.S. Supreme Court.

In *The New York Times Co.* v. *United States*, the Court found that the government had failed to prove that prior restraint was necessary. The *Times* and the *Post* then printed the papers, but publication had been delayed for two weeks. It was the first time in the nation's history that the federal government had stopped a newspaper from publishing. Legal fees cost the *Post* and the *Times* more than $270,000.[8]

The *Progressive* Case

The next instance of prior restraint happened in 1979 when editors of *The Progressive* magazine announced that they planned to publish an article by Howard Morland about how to make a hydrogen bomb. The author said that

Daniel Ellsberg, author of the Pentagon Papers, and his wife, Barbara, after a court hearing in Los Angeles. Ellsberg gave the papers to *The New York Times*.

J. P. Laffont/CORBIS Sygma

the article was based on information from public documents and from interviews with government employees. The Department of Justice brought suit in
Wisconsin, where the magazine was published, and received a restraining
order to stop the information from being printed (*United States* v. *The Progressive*). *The Progressive* did not publish the article as planned.

Before the case could reach the Supreme Court, a Wisconsin newspaper
published a letter from a man named Charles Hansen that contained much of
the same information as the Morland article. Hansen sent eight copies of the
letter to other newspapers, and the *Chicago Tribune* published it, saying that
none of the information was proprietary.[9] Six months after the original
restraining order, *The Progressive* published the article.

Restricting the Press at Grenada

In an incident that never reached the courts but that was a type of prior
restraint, the Reagan administration in 1983 kept reporters away from the
island of Grenada, where the administration had launched a military offensive. This caused a press blackout beginning at 11 P.M. on October 24, 1983.

The administration didn't officially bar the press from covering the invasion, but the Pentagon refused to transport the press and then turned back
press yachts and airplanes that attempted to enter the war zone. About a
dozen print journalists and photographers were able to get in, but no television crews were allowed.

More than 400 journalists from 170 news organizations around the world
who couldn't get to Grenada were left on Barbados, waiting for the news to
get to them. Charles Lachman of the *New York Post* flew to Barbados, then to
St. Vincent. Then he and some other reporters paid $6,000 to charter a boat
to Grenada. It was five days after the invasion when they arrived and discovered that one of the casualties of the military's action had been a hospital.[10]

News Blackouts and Press Pools

The Gulf War posed the toughest battleground yet for the rights of reporters
versus the rights of the military to restrict access.

On Saturday, February 23, 1991, about three weeks into the Gulf War, the
Defense Department announced the first total news blackout in U.S. military
history. For 24 hours, defense leaders were told to issue no statements about
the actions of U.S. troops. Military officials said that instantaneous transmission of information from the battlefield meant that live TV pictures could be
picked up by Iraq. Press organizations protested the ban, but the military
argued that modern communications technology necessitated the blackout.

Pentagon rules for war coverage, reached in cooperation with journalists,
imposed stricter limits on reporting in the Persian Gulf than in any other U.S.
war. Reporters had to travel in small "pools," escorted by public affairs officers. Every story produced by the pool was subject to military censorship.
This system, called **pool reporting**, had been created in response to
reporters' complaints about news blackouts during the Grenada incident. An
unprecedented number of journalists—1,300 in Saudi Arabia alone—posed a
challenge for military press officers.

pool reporting an arrangement that places reporters in
small, supervised groups to
cover an event.

In a commentary protesting the restrictions, *The New Yorker* magazine said,
"The rules, it is clear, enable the Pentagon to promote coverage of subjects
and events that it wishes publicized and to prevent reporting that might cast
it, or the war, in a bad light."[11] Yet, in a *Los Angeles Times* poll of nearly 2,000
people two weeks after the fighting started, 79 percent approved of the Pentagon's restrictions and 57 percent favored even further limits.[12] When the war

IMPACT

point of view

Excerpts from the 1943 Code of Wartime Practices for American Broadcasters

During World War II, the Office of War Information tried to control what was broadcast from the United States. Following are some of the rules that radio broadcasters were expected to follow.

News Broadcasts and Commentaries

It is requested that news in any of the following classifications be kept off the air unless made available for broadcast by appropriate authority or specifically cleared by the Office of Censorship.

(a) Weather—Weather forecasts other than those officially released by the Weather Bureau.

(b) Armed forces—Types and movements of United States Army, Navy, and Marine Corps units, within or without continental United States.

Programs

(a) Request programs—No telephoned or telegraphed requests for musical selections should be accepted. No requests for musical selections made by word-of-mouth at the origin of broadcast, whether studio or remote, should be honored.

(b) Quiz programs—Any program which permits the public accessibility to an open microphone is dangerous and should be carefully

supervised. Because of the nature of quiz programs, in which the public is not only permitted access to the microphone but encouraged to speak into it, the danger of usurpation by the enemy is enhanced.

(c) Forums and interviews—During forums in which the general public is permitted extemporaneous comment, panel discussions in which more than two persons participate, and interviews by authorized employees of the broadcasting company, broadcasters should devise methods guaranteeing against the release of any information which might aid the enemy....

(d) Special-events reporting (ad lib)—Reporters and commentators should guard against use of descriptive material which might be employed by the enemy in plotting an area for attack....

Foreign Language Broadcasts

(a) Personnel—The Office of Censorship, by direction of the president, is charged with the responsibility of removing from the air all those engaged in foreign language broadcasting who, in the judgment of appointed authorities in the Office of Censorship, endan-

ger the war effort of the United Nations by their connections, direct or indirect, with the medium.

(b) Scripts—Station managements are requested to require all persons who broadcast in a foreign language to submit to the management in advance of broadcast complete scriptsor transcriptions of such material.

(c) Censors and monitors—In order that these functions can be performed in a manner consistent with the demands of security, station managers are reminded that their staffs should include capable linguists as censors and monitors whose duty it will be to review all scripts in advance of broadcast and check them during broadcast against deviation....

Broadcasters should ask themselves, "Is this information of value to the enemy?" If the answer is "Yes," they should not use it. If doubtful, they should measure the material against the Code....

The Office of Censorship
Byron Price, Director
December 1, 1943.

U.S. Government Office of Censorship, *Code of Wartime Practices for American Broadcasters.* Washington, D.C.: Government Printing Office, 1943, pp. 1–8.

ended, many members of the U.S. press in the Middle East complained bitterly about their lack of access, but the military and the public seemed satisfied with the new rules for wartime coverage.

By contrast, when the United States offered humanitarian aid to Somalia in 1992, the military offered the press unprecedented access, hoping to create a favorable impression of the military.

When should the government be able to prevent information from reaching the public? When should the press have access? The Supreme Court has not yet specifically answered this question, and the press and publishers remain vulnerable to military restrictions.

CENSORSHIP

Different media industries historically have reacted differently to threats of **censorship**, the practice of suppressing material that is considered morally, politically, or otherwise objectionable. Most threats of censorship concern matters of morality, especially obscenity.

In America, censorship is almost always an issue after the fact. Once the material is printed or displayed, it can be judged obscene and therefore censored. The motion picture and recording industries have accepted some form of self-regulation to avoid government intervention. The electronic media are governed by laws in the federal criminal code against broadcast obscenity, and the federal Cable Act of 1984 bars obscenity on cable TV.

Print media have been the most vigorous defenders of the right to publish. The print media, of course, were the earliest media to be threatened with censorship, beginning with the philosopher Plato, who suggested in 387 B.C. that Homer's *Odyssey* be expurgated for immature readers.

censorship The practice of suppressing material that is considered morally, politically, or otherwise objectionable.

Local Efforts

More than 2,000 years after Homer's *Odyssey* was threatened with censorship, Boston officials banned the sale of the April 1926 issue of H. L. Mencken's magazine *The American Mercury*. The local Watch and Ward Society had denounced a fictional story in the magazine as "salacious." The title character of the story, "Hatrack," was a prostitute whose clientele included members of various religious congregations who visited her after church.

In Boston, surrounded by his supporters, Mencken sold a copy of the magazine at a prearranged time to a member of the Watch and Ward. The chief of the Boston Vice Squad arrested Mencken and marched him to jail, where he spent the night before going to court the next morning.

"Mencken passed an uneasy night," says Mencken's biographer Carl Bode, "knowing that he could be found guilty and perhaps even be imprisoned....Returning to court he listened to Judge Parmenter's brief analysis of the merits of the case and then to his decision: 'I find that no offense has been committed and therefore dismiss the complaint.'" Mencken spent $20,000 defending the *Mercury* but, according to Bode, "the net gain for both the *Mercury* and Mencken was great. The *Mercury* became the salient American magazine and Mencken the international symbol of freedom of speech."[13]

Mencken was defending his magazine against local censorship. Until 1957, censorship in America remained a local issue because the U.S. Supreme Court

IMPACT

on you

By Sheila Muto

Questions about what can be seen on television shows and what should be cut continue to preoccupy producers and the public. But this much is certain: new series will contain scenes that were unthinkable and dialogue that was unmentionable in the early days of television….

"There's no such thing as broadcast standards" today, says Steven Bochco, co-creator of *NYPD Blue* and *Hill Street Blues*. He adds: "It's really what you can get away with. Then it becomes a new standard."

It is illuminating to see how much prime-time standards have loosened since the 1950s, when the word "damn" shocked viewers, and the 1960s, when network executives refused to air an episode of *Dr. Kildare* because it involved rape.

From Here to Immodesty: Milestones in the Toppling of TV's Taboos

1939 NBC begins the first regular network broadcasts.

1950 Arthur Godfrey becomes one of the first people to swear on national TV when he utters the words "damn" and "hell" during a live CBS program.

1950 The first bare breasts appear—unintentionally—when talk-show host Faye Emerson accidentally falls out of her plunging neckline. (The 1977 miniseries *Roots* is the first to intentionally show bare breasts.)

1951 TV's first pregnant character in prime time is a woman in the Barbour clan on *One Man's Family*, a long-running radio program that made its way to TV in 1949.

1952 Ozzie and Harriet Nelson are the first TV couple shown sleeping in the same bed. "There was no controversy because they were so darn wholesome," says Alex McNeil, author of Total Television, an encyclopedia of network and cable shows.

1952 Lucille Ball's pregnancy is featured in seven episodes of *I Love Lucy*—without the word "pregnant" uttered once.

1961 Actress Yvette Mimieux wears a scanty bikini and bares her navel in a *Dr. Kildare* episode titled "Tyger, Tyger." No other navels are shown for the next decade: *I Dream of Jeannie* is launched in 1965 and runs for five years without showing Barbara Eden's, which is hidden under waist-high harem pants; Cher ends the taboo on the *Sonny and Cher Comedy Hour* in the 1970s.

had not considered a censorship case. Today, censorship still is primarily a local issue, but two landmark Supreme Court cases—*Roth* v. *United States* and *Miller* v. *California*—established the major criteria for local censorship.

Roth v. United States. Two cases were involved in this 1957 decision. Samuel Roth was found guilty in New York of sending obscenity through the mail, and David S. Alberts was found guilty of selling obscene books in Beverly Hills. The case carries Roth's name because his name appeared first.

The Supreme Court upheld the guilty verdict and established several precedents:

- Obscenity is not protected by the First Amendment.

- Obscenity is defined as material "utterly without redeeming social importance."

1962 In an episode of *The Defenders*, a doctor speaks out in favor of abortion, which at the time is illegal in all 50 states. Some stations refuse to air the episode, and the show's regular sponsor pulls out. More than 10 years later, *Maude* experiences a similar backlash when its two-part abortion episode airs.

1968 *Star Trek* features the first interracial kiss. In an episode titled "Plato's Stepchildren," a man who has the power to control the actions of others forces Capt. James Kirk, played by William Shatner, and Lt. Uhura, played by Nichelle Nichols, to kiss.

1970 ABC's *The Odd Couple* features the first lead characters who are divorced. Ironically, *The Mary Tyler Moore Show*, which premiered on CBS five days earlier, was originally to have been about a divorced woman. However, CBS told the show's creators that a divorcee was too controversial to be the main character of a weekly comedy, so Mary Richards was rewritten as a woman who recently ended a long engagement.

1971 During its first season, *All in the Family* brings one of the first homosexual characters to prime time. In the episode "Judging Books by Covers," Archie Bunker scorns his son-in-law's effeminate friend, unaware that one of his own tough beer-drinking buddies is gay.

1973 In an episode of *All in the Family*, titled "Gloria, the Victim," Gloria is almost raped and suffers through the aftermath of reporting the crime.

1980 A man is beheaded in the miniseries *Shogun*.

1983 *The Bay City Blues*, a short-lived series from Steven Bochco revolving around the professional and personal lives of a minor-league baseball team, shows a locker room full of naked men.

1991 The first scene of one woman kissing another airs when a bisexual attorney on *L.A. Law* played by Amanda Donohoe kisses a straight attorney played by Michele Greene.

1992 NBC's *Seinfeld* features an episode on masturbation called "The Contest." Although nine of 10 advertisers pull out of the episode, they are quickly replaced.

Wall Street Journal, September 15, 1995, B-1. Reprinted by permission of *Wall Street Journal,* (c) 1995 Dow Jones & Co., Inc. All rights reserved worldwide.

- Sex and obscenity are not synonymous. Obscene material is material that appeals to "prurient [obsessively sexual] interest."
- A test of obscenity is "whether to the average person, applying contemporary community standards, the dominant theme of the material taken as a whole appeals to prurient interest."[14] (This last description of obscenity has become known as the **Roth test**.)

> **Roth test** a standard court test for obscenity, named for one of the defendants in an obscenity case.

Miller v. California. In the late 1960s, a California court found Marvin Miller guilty of sending obscene unsolicited advertising material through the mail. The case reached the U.S. Supreme Court in 1973. The decision described just which materials a state could censor and set a three-part test for obscenity.

According to the Supreme Court, states could censor material that met this three-part local test for obscenity. The local court should determine:

1. Whether "the average person, applying contemporary community standards," would find that the work, taken as a whole, appeals to the prurient interest.

2. Whether the work depicts or describes, in a patently offensive way, sexual conduct specifically defined by the applicable state law.

3. Whether the work, taken as a whole, lacks serious *Literary, Artistic, Political* or *Scientific* value—often called the **LAPS test**. [15]

LAPS test a yardstick for local obscenity judgments, which evaluates an artistic work's Literary, Artistic, Political or Scientific value.

The combination of the Roth and Miller cases established a standard for obscenity, leaving the decision on specific cases to local courts. The result is that there are widely differing standards in different parts of the country because local juries decide what is offensive in their communities. Books that are available to readers in some states are unavailable in other states.

School Boards as Censors. Many censorship cases begin at school and other local government boards, where parents' groups protest books, magazines and films that are available to students. For example:

- A school board in New York removed 11 books from school libraries, including the novels *Slaughterhouse-Five* by Kurt Vonnegut and *Black Boy* by Richard Wright, plus a work of popular anthropology, *The Naked Ape* by Desmond Morris.

- A school district in California required students to have parental permission to read *Ms.* magazine in the school library.

- A school board in Minnesota banned four books, including *Are You There, God? It's Me, Margaret* by Judy Blume, a writer well known for her young adult books.

- The state of Alabama ordered 45 textbooks pulled from the shelves after a federal judge said the books promoted "secular humanism."[16]

One-third of all censorship incidents involve attempts to censor library books and school curricula.[17] These types of cases usually are reversed on appeal, but while the specific issues are being decided, the books, magazines, and films are unavailable. Moreover, censorship efforts are increasing.

National Efforts to Control Speech

The Meese Commission on Pornography. Censorship activities were encouraged from the federal level by the issuance in July 1986 of the Final Report of the Attorney General's Commission on Pornography, called the Meese Commission (named for Attorney General Edwin Meese). The 1986 report reversed the conclusion of the 1970 Commission on Obscenity and Pornography, which had found that no convincing evidence existed to show that pornography causes harm.

The 1986 commission concluded that pornography does cause harm, and that even when sexually explicit material doesn't actually portray violence, it may be harmful to society and the family. The 1986 commission urged Congress to require convicted pornographers to give up the profits from producing and distributing offensive material, but the commission's arguments were not convincing, and no substantial legislation resulted.

The Hazelwood Case. In 1988, the U.S. Supreme Court for the first time gave public school officials considerable freedom to limit what appears in student publications. The case, *Hazelwood* v. *Kuhlmeier*, became known as the Hazelwood Case because the issues originated at Hazelwood High School in Hazelwood, Missouri.

The high school paper, funded mostly from the school budget, was published as part of a journalism class. The principal at Hazelwood regularly reviewed the school paper before it was published, but in this case he deleted two articles that the staff had written.

One of the deleted articles covered the issue of student pregnancy and included interviews with three students who had become pregnant while attending school, using pseudonyms instead of the students' names. The principal said he felt that the anonymity of the students was not sufficiently protected, and that the girls' discussion of their use or nonuse of birth control was inappropriate for a school publication. By a vote of 5 to 3, the U.S. Supreme Court agreed.

"Even though the legal rights of children have gained broader recognition in recent years, it remains that children are not adults and that they have no explicit or implied right to behave with the full freedom granted to adults," wrote Jonathan Yardley, a *Washington Post* columnist. "Freedom entails the responsibility to exercise it with mature judgment, and this neither young children nor adolescents possess."

The same newspaper, however, carried an editorial that opposed the decision. "Even teenagers," the *Post* editorial said, "should be allowed to publish criticism, raise uncomfortable questions and spur debate on subjects such as pregnancy, AIDS and drug abuse that are too often a very real aspect of high school culture today."

The decision is significant because it may change the way local officials monitor school publications. At Hazelwood, however, the principal's action drew the attention of the *St. Louis Post-Dispatch*, which published the censored articles, bringing them a much wider audience than the students at Hazelwood High.

LIBEL LAW

"Americans have increasingly begun to seek the refuge and vindication of litigation," writes legal scholar Rodney A. Smolla in his book *Suing the Press*. "Words published by the media no longer roll over us without penetrating; instead, they sink in through the skin and work inner damage, and a consensus appears to be emerging that this psychic damage is serious and must be paid for."[18]

Four cases show how prominent the media are as targets of litigation:

- In 1983, actress Carol Burnett sued the *National Enquirer* for $10 million for implying in an article that she was drinking too much and acting rude in a Washington, D.C., restaurant.

- In late 1984, General William C. Westmoreland filed a $120 million suit against CBS, charging that he was defamed in a 1982 CBS documentary, *The Uncounted Enemy: A Vietnam Deception*.

- At the same time, former Israeli Defense Minister Ariel Sharon sought $50 million in a libel suit against *Time* magazine, claiming that *Time* wrongly characterized his role in a 1982 massacre of Palestinian refugees.

IMPACT *digital*

High Court Strikes Down Internet Smut Law

By Edward Felsenthal and Jared Sandberg

The Supreme Court has called off the traffic cops on the information superhighway.

The court struck down a federal law designed to keep smut off the Internet, making it much harder for Congress and states to keep Internet users from saying and doing whatever they want.

The 7-2 decision, which praised the vast democratic potential of cyberspace, concluded that it is entitled to the fullest possible free-speech protection. But the ruling could allow for some narrow, carefully designed regulations to protect Internet users from copyright violations, invasions of privacy and consumer fraud.

"The interest in encouraging freedom of expression in a democratic society outweighs any theoretical but unproven benefit of censorship," Justice John Paul Stevens wrote for the majority.

Industry executives and free-speech advocates were elated. "The Supreme Court has written the First Amendment for the 21st century," said Jerry Berman, exec-

Steve Greenberg, *Editor & Publisher.*

• In 1989 entertainer Wayne Newton was awarded $6 million in damages after he sued NBC-TV for a story that linked him to organized-crime figures. NBC appealed the case, and eventually the award was overturned, but legal costs were in the millions.

libel a false statement that damages a person's character or reputation by exposing that person to public ridicule or contempt.

These four cases involve the law of **libel**, which is only one recognized restraint on press freedom in the United States. (A libelous statement is one that unjustifiably exposes someone to ridicule or contempt.) All of these cases indicate the media's legal vulnerability.

How can the country accommodate both the First Amendment concept of a free press and the right of the nation's citizens to keep their reputations from being unnecessarily damaged?

The Sullivan Case Establishes a Landmark

Modern interpretation of the free speech protections of the First Amendment began in 1964 with the landmark *New York Times* v. *Sullivan* case. With

utive director of the Center for Democracy and Technology. Attorney Bruce Ennis, who represented the 50-odd groups challenging the law, called the ruling "the legal birth certificate of the Internet."

The ruling strikes down the so-called Communications Decency Act, a provision of the 1996 Telecommunications Act that made it a crime to transmit "indecent" material to minors, punishable by two years in prison and a $250,000 fine. Although the law didn't explicitly hold online services responsible for material transmitted by users, many feared they could be found in violation if indecent material turned up on a site they promoted.

Internet access providers had worried that the law would require them to continually sift through the online content and communications of their sub-scribers in order to avoid lawsuits. Though the industry has responded with a variety of software tools that prevent kids from accessing racy fare, such tools aren't foolproof.

Had the act been upheld, "it's likely that a large business like ours would be targeted and pulled under," said Theodore Claypoole, corporate counsel at commercial online service CompuServe Corp.

Executives have also fretted about having to abide by conflicting Internet regulations around the world. But George Vradenburg, senior vice president and general counsel at America Online Inc., said the decision may also make other countries think hard before regulating on-line content. "It's an important precedent to the rest of the world that the U.S. is going to allow the Internet to grow without content restrictions," he said.

Excerpts From the Ruling

- *Through the use of chat rooms, any person with a phone line can become a town crier with a voice that resonates farther than it could from any soapbox. Through the use of Web pages, mail exploders, and newsgroups, the same individual can become a pamphleteer.*

- *We presume that governmental regulation of the content of speech is more likely to interfere with the free exchange of ideas than to encourage it.*

- *Moreover, the Internet is not as 'invasive' as radio or television... Users seldom encounter content 'by accident.'*

—Justice John Paul Stevens striking down the Communications Decency Act

Wall Street Journal, June 27, 1997 p. B-1. Reprinted by permission of *Wall Street Journal,* (c)1997 Dow Jones &Co., Inc. All Rights Reserved Worldwide.

this case, the U.S. Supreme Court began a process that continues today to define how the press should operate in a free society. Many of today's arguments about the free press's role in a libel case derive from this decision.

The Sullivan case began in early 1960 in Alabama, where civil rights leader Dr. Martin Luther King Jr. was arrested for perjury on his income tax form (a charge of which he was eventually acquitted). The Committee to Defend Martin Luther King bought a full-page ad in the March 29, 1960, *The New York Times*, which included statements about harassment of King by public officials and the police. The ad included a plea for money to support civil rights causes. Several notable people were listed in the ad as supporters, including singer Harry Belafonte, actor Sidney Poitier and former First Lady Eleanor Roosevelt.

L. B. Sullivan, who supervised the police and fire departments as commissioner of public affairs in Montgomery, Alabama, demanded a retraction from the *Times*, even though he had not been named in the ad. The *Times* refused, and Sullivan sued the *Times* for libel in Montgomery County, where 35 copies of the March 29, 1960, *Times* had been distributed for sale.[19]

The trial in Montgomery County lasted three days, beginning on November 1, 1960. The jury found the *Times* guilty and awarded Sullivan $500,000. Eventually the case reached the U.S. Supreme Court. In deciding the suit the Court said that although the *Times* might have been negligent because it did not spot some misstatements of fact that appeared in the ad, the *Times* did not deliberately lie—it did not act with what the court called *actual malice*. To prove libel, a *public official* must show that the defendant published information with *knowledge of its falsity* or out of *reckless disregard* for whether it was true or false, the court concluded.[20] The Sullivan decision thus became the standard for subsequent libel suits: Public officials in a libel case must prove actual malice.

Redefining the Sullivan Decision

Three important cases further defined the Sullivan decision.

Gertz* v. *Robert Welch. A 1974 decision in *Gertz* v. *Robert Welch* established the concept that the expression of opinions is a necessary part of public debate, and so opinions—an editorial or a restaurant review, for example—cannot be considered libelous. The Gertz case also expanded the definition of public *official* to public *figure*. Today, people involved in libel suits are classified as *public figures* or *private figures*.

The criterion that distinguishes public and private figures is very important. People who are defined as private citizens by a court must show only that the libelous information was false and that the journalist or news organization acted negligently in presenting the information. *Public figures must show* not only that the libelous information was false but that the information was published with *actual malice*—that the journalist or the news organization knew that the information was untrue or that the journalist or news organization deliberately overlooked facts that would have proved that the published information was untrue.

Herbert* v. *Lando. A 1979 decision in *Herbert* v. *Lando* established the concept that because a public figure suing for libel must prove actual malice, the public figure can use the discovery process (the process by which potential witnesses are questioned under oath before the trial to help define the issues to be resolved at the trial) to determine a reporter's state of mind in preparing the story. Because of this decision, today reporters are sometimes asked in a libel suit to identify their sources and to give up notes and tapes of the interviews they conducted to write their stories.

Masson* v. *New Yorker Magazine. In 1991, the U.S. Supreme Court reinstated a $10 million libel suit brought against *The New Yorker* magazine by psychoanalyst Jeffrey M. Masson. Masson charged that author Janet Malcolm libeled him in two articles in *The New Yorker* and in a book when she deliberately misquoted him. Malcolm contended that the quotations she used were tape recorded or were written in her notes.

Malcolm wrote, for example, that Mr. Masson said, "I was like an intellectual gigolo." However, this exact phrase was not in the tape-recorded transcript of her interview. Masson contended that he never used the phrase.

Issues in the case include whether quoted material must be verbatim and whether a journalist can change grammar and syntax. When the case was heard again in 1994, the court found that Malcolm had changed Masson's words but that the changes did not libel Masson. The Masson case is the most important recent example of a continuing interest in defining the limits of libel.

Charges and Defenses for Libel

To prove libel under today's law, someone must show that:

1. The statement was communicated to a third party.
2. People who read or saw the statement would be able to identify the person, even if that person was not actually named.
3. The statement injured someone's reputation or income or caused mental anguish.
4. The journalist or the print or broadcast organization is at fault.

Members of the press and press organizations that are faced with a libel suit can use three defenses: truth, privilege and fair comment.

Truth. The first and best defense against libel, of course, is that the information is true. True information, although sometimes damaging, cannot be considered libelous. Publishing true information, however, can still be an invasion of privacy, as explained later in this chapter. Furthermore, truth is a successful defense only if truth is proved to the satisfaction of a judge or jury.

Privilege. The press is free to report what is discussed during legislative and court proceedings, even though the information presented in the proceedings by witnesses and others may be untrue or damaging. This is called **qualified privilege**.

qualified privilege the freedom of the press to report what is discussed during legislative and court proceedings.

Fair Comment. The courts also have carefully protected the press's freedom to present opinions. Because opinions cannot be proved true or false, the press is free to comment on public issues and to laud a play or pan a movie, for example.

Today's Libel Laws and the Media

The four cases listed at the beginning of the Libel Law section (on pages 319–320) all involved public figures. The jury in the Carol Burnett case originally awarded her $1.6 million, but the amount was reduced to $150,000 on appeal. The Westmoreland case was settled before it went to the jury. CBS issued a statement acknowledging that Westmoreland had acted faithfully in performing his duties, but the combined legal costs for both parties were more than $18 million.[21]

In the Sharon case, the jury found that *Time* had defamed Sharon and reported false information but that the magazine did not act with actual malice, so no judgment was levied against *Time*. Sharon's legal costs were $1 million. The jury awarded Wayne Newton $19.2 million in 1986, but in 1990, the court threw out the award altogether, ruling that there was not enough evidence to prove actual malice.

In several of these cases, members of the press were faulted for their reporting methods, even when the news organizations were not found guilty.

Jenny Jones said the $25 million libel verdict "shocked" her.

AP/Wide World Photos

Although *Time* magazine was exonerated in the Sharon case, for example, the jury issued a statement that said that "certain *Time* employees, particularly correspondent David Halevy, acted negligently and carelessly in reporting and verifying the information which ultimately found its way into the published paragraph of interest in this case."[22] These cases show that the press must always be diligent.

Most successful libel judgments eventually are reversed or reduced when they are appealed. According to a study of all libel suits brought in the United States from 1974 through 1984, only about 10 percent of the cases were won. Although 20 judgments of $1 million or more were awarded between 1980 and 1984, none of these was upheld on appeal. However, in 1999 a Michigan jury returned a $25 million civil judgment against *The Jenny Jones Show* (see Impact/Point of View, "It's Time Shock-Talk TV Took Some Responsibility," pp. 326–327).[23]

The major cost of a libel suit for the media is not the actual settlement but the defense lawyers' fees. Large media organizations carry libel insurance, but a small newspaper, magazine, book publisher or broadcast station may not be able to afford the insurance or the legal fees. The average libel case today costs about $150,000 in legal fees alone.[24] These costs sometimes cause the press to be self-censoring.

"Since the Supreme Court ruled in favor of *The New York Times* in *The New York Times* v. *Sullivan* in 1964, no country in the world has offered more legal protection for those wishing to speak out frankly and fearlessly," writes eminent libel lawyer Floyd Abrams. "Yet today, American libel law manages to achieve the worst of two worlds: It does little to protect reputation. It does much to deter speech."[25]

From 1995 to 1996, the dollar amounts awarded in libel cases against journalists have increased significantly, according to the Libel Defense Resource Center. The average libel award in 1996 amounted to $2.4 million, and included a $2.3 million award against a small newspaper, the *Ottumwa Courier* in Iowa, although the Iowa case was reversed on appeal. The $2.3 million amount is more than double the $1 million median libel award in 1995, and more than 10 times the two-year median of $175,000 in 1992 and 1993. "This year [1996] has been very disturbing," said Sandra Baron, executive director of the Libel Resource Center. "It reflects profound concerns by these juries."[26]

A Proposal for Libel Law Reform

Lawyer Floyd Abrams has proposed three major reforms in American libel law:

1. Publishers and broadcasters should be encouraged to print corrections quickly. When the media do offer timely corrections, no suit would be allowed.

2. Damages should be limited to amounts actually lost by those who sue. Abrams suggests that the actual amount of lost wages should be awarded, and that the limit on emotional injury be $100,000.

3. The court should be able to require that the losing side pay the legal fees for the winning side.[27]

"The libel explosion does chill the courage of the press," says legal scholar Rodney A. Smolla, "and in that chill all of us suffer, for it threatens to make the press slavishly safe, pouring out a centrist, spiceless paste of consensus thought. All of us lose if we permit the trivialization of free speech."[28]

PRIVACY LAW

The public seems to feel that invasion of privacy is one of the media's worst faults. As noted in Chapter 13, three out of four people interviewed in the Times Mirror survey said that news organizations invade people's privacy. However, libel suits are much more common in the United States than suits about invasion of privacy. Because there is no Supreme Court decision covering privacy like *The New York Times* v. *Sullivan* covers libel, each of the states has its own privacy protections for citizens and its own restrictions on how reporters can get the news and what can be published.

Privacy is an ethical issue as well as a legal one. (See Chapter 15 for a discussion of the ethics of privacy.) Generally, the law says that the media can be guilty of invasion of privacy in four ways:

1. By intruding on a person's physical or mental solitude.
2. By publishing or disclosing embarrassing personal facts.
3. By giving someone publicity that places the person in a false light.
4. By using someone's name or likeness for commercial benefit.

If they are successful, people who initiate privacy cases can be awarded monetary damages to compensate them for the wrongdoing. However, most privacy cases do not succeed.

Physical or Mental Solitude

The courts in most states have recognized that a person has a right not to be pursued by the news media unnecessarily. A reporter can photograph or question someone on a public street or at a public event, but a person's home and office are private. For this reason, many photographers request that someone who is photographed in a private situation sign a release form, designating how the photograph can be used.

One particularly notable case establishing this right of privacy is *Galella* v. *Onassis*. Jacqueline Onassis, widow of former President John F. Kennedy, charged that Ron Galella, a freelance photographer, was pursuing her unnecessarily. He had used a telephoto lens to photograph her on private property and he had pursued her children at private schools. Galella was ordered to stay 25 feet away from her and 30 feet away from her children.

Embarrassing Personal Facts

The personal facts the media use to report a story should be newsworthy, according to the courts. If a public official is caught traveling with her boyfriend on taxpayers' money while her husband stays at home, information about the boyfriend is essential to the story. If the public official is reported to have contracted AIDS from her contact with the boyfriend, the information

IMPACT

point of view

It's Time Shock-Talk TV Took Some Responsibility

$25 Million 'Jenny Jones' Verdict Should Help

By John Carman

The *Jenny Jones* verdict threatens to introduce a disturbing new element into TV's shock-talk jungle—responsibility.

Naturally, the industry is aghast.

If yesterday's verdict somehow stands up on appeal, it could spoil the long and lavish party for Jones, Jerry Springer, Ricki Lake and their ilk.

A Michigan jury decided the producers of the syndicated TV show were negligent, to the tune of $25 million, in the case of a *Jenny Jones* guest who murdered a gay man who had revealed he had a crush on him.

Jonathan Schmitz is serving a 25- to 50-year prison term for shooting Scott Amedure three days after the show's "secret admirer" segment was taped in 1995. Because of the murder, the show never aired.

Amedure's family brought a wrongful-death suit against Telepictures, which produces

Jenny Jones, and Warner Bros. Television, which syndicates it. Both are units of the entertainment giant Time Warner.

Ruling that the defendants negligently caused Amedure's death, the jury awarded his family $5 million for his pain and suffering, $10 million for their loss of his companionship, $10 million for the loss of his future earnings, and $6,500 for funeral expenses.

Jones issued a statement calling the verdict "outrageous"—she ought to know outrageous when she sees it—and Telepictures President Jim Paratore said the jury had been "misled and distracted" by the Amedure's attorney, Geoffrey Fieger, and his "inflammatory rhetoric."

Paratore said the verdict will be appealed.

(*Jenny Jones* airs locally on KRON, Channel 4. The station is owned by the Chronicle Publishing Co.)

There were perfunctory gasps elsewhere in the broadcasting business, too, and professed fears that the verdict will clamp a chill-

ing effect on television's burgeoning realm of reality programs.

Good. This is a corner of TV that needs not only a good chill, but maybe a chest cold, a full bout of pneumonia and a funeral dirge.

Shows that stage outlandish surprises and spontaneous confrontations ought to take responsibility for the consequences. Amedure's death was a consequence.

But in the circus world of TV today, responsibility is a stuffy and antiquated notion. *Jenny Jones* and shows like it coax participants onto the air, exploit them, and then cast them to the wolves.

Granted, it's a stretch to compare the *Jenny Jones* case with the tragic massacre in Littleton, Colo., last month. But there is something worth pondering. While it's a desultory exercise to pin the blame for Littleton on everyone's favorite scapegoat, the media, it may be true that the media are part of an array of contributing factors.

That certainly includes the anything-goes ambience of the worst daytime talk shows, where hooting, jeering, name-calling, psychological

probably is not relevant to the story and could be covered under this provision of privacy law.

In reality, however, public officials enjoy very little legal protection from reporting about their private lives. Information available from public records, such as court proceedings, is not considered private. If the public official's husband testifies in court about his wife's disease, this information could be reported.

Attorney Ven Johnson (center) hugged Frank Amedure Sr. and Patricia Graves, parents of Scott Amedure, who was slain by a fellow talk-show guest.

AP/Wide World Photos

ambushes, freely vented rage and fistfights are commonplace.

There's a subtler connection. Jeanne Albronda Heaton, an Ohio University psychologist and co-author of *Tuning In Trouble*, a 1995 book about the unsavory talk shows, points out that these shows promote the idea, appealing but infantile, that one's problems are always someone else's fault.

In Littleton, Eric Harris and Dylan Klebold apparently lashed out in murderous anger at peers they blamed for their problems.

After yesterday's *Jenny Jones* verdict, some media observers expressed concern that journalism as well as entertainment could be affected. Is a critic, for example, now responsible for the effects of a bad review?

But there is a distinction. Journalists describe and evaluate the action, but they don't set the stage. *Jenny Jones* and similar shows do, deliberately setting up what Heaton calls "a kind of parade of pathology with nobody minding the shop and nobody responsible for the outcome." Heaton wrote that before Amedure was shot.

Yesterday, Heaton said that in talking with talk-show producers and harried, youthful assistant producers when she was researching her book, she was astonished to find that "the idea of ethics was laughable. To them the only thing that matters is ratings."

Since Amedure was killed, money has continued to speak louder than murder. Even the Jones show, which never acknowledged a whit of responsibility, has continued to stage sexual ambushes and surprises.

The verdict reintroduces the idea that TV shows generate consequences other than enriching producers, stars and TV stations. It's time, the jurors were saying, to stop passing the buck.

San Francisco Chronicle, May 8, 1999, A-1. Reprinted by permission.

False Light

A writer who portrays someone in a fictional version of actual events should be especially conscious of **false light** litigation. People who believe that what a writer or photographer *implies* about them is incorrect (even if the portrayal is flattering) can bring a false-light suit.

The best-known false-light suit is the first, *Time Inc.* v. *Hill*. In 1955, *Life* magazine published a story about a Broadway play, *The Desperate Hours*, that

false light the charge that what was implied in a story about someone was incorrect.

portrayed a hostage-taking. The author of the play said he based it on several real-life incidents. One of these involved the Hill family, a husband and wife and their five children who had been taken hostage in their Philadelphia home by three escaped convicts. The Hills told police that the convicts had treated them courteously, but the Hills were frightened by the events and eventually moved to Connecticut.

When *Life* decided to do the story about the play, the cast went to the Hills' old home, where *Life* photographed the actors in scenes from the play—one son being roughed up by the convicts and a daughter biting a convict's hand. None of these incidents had happened to the Hills, but *Life* published the photographs along with a review of the play.

The Hills sued Time Inc., which owned *Life* magazine, for false-light invasion of privacy and won $75,000, which eventually was reduced to $30,000. When the case went to the U.S. Supreme Court, the Court refused to uphold the decision, saying that the Hills must prove actual malice.[29] The Hills dropped the case, but *the establishment of actual malice* as a requirement in false-light cases *was important.*

In 1974, in *Cantrell* v. *Forest City Publishing Co.,* the U.S. Supreme Court held that a reporter for the Cleveland *Plain Dealer* had wrongly portrayed the widow of an Ohio man who was killed when a bridge collapsed. The story talked about the woman as if the reporter had interviewed her, although he had only interviewed her children. She was awarded $60,000 in her false-light suit, and the Supreme Court upheld the verdict. "Eight justices held that a properly instructed jury had come to the correct conclusion in finding actual malice," writes legal scholar Ralph L. Holsinger. "There was enough evidence within the story to prove that the reporter's word portrait of Mrs. Cantrell was false. The story indicated that he had seen her and perhaps had talked with her. He had done neither."[30]

Only a few false-light cases have been successful, but the lesson for the press is that truthful portrayal of people and events avoids the problem altogether.

Right of Publicity

This facet of privacy law is especially important in the advertising and public relations industries. A portable toilet seems a strange fixture to use to establish a point of law, but a case brought by former *Tonight Show* host Johnny Carson demonstrates how the right of publicity protects someone's name from being used to make money without that person's permission.

In *Carson* v. *Here's Johnny Portable Toilets,* Carson charged in 1983 that a Michigan manufacturer of portable toilets misappropriated Carson's name to sell the toilets. The manufacturer named his new line "Here's Johnny Portable Toilets," and advertised them with the phrase "The World's Foremost Commodian." Carson said he did not want to be associated with the product and that he would be. Since he began hosting *The Tonight Show* in 1957, he said, he had been introduced by the phrase "Here's Johnny." The court agreed that "Here's Johnny" violated Carson's right of publicity.

This right can cover a person's picture on a poster or name in an advertisement. In some cases, this right is covered even after the person dies, so that the members of the immediate family of a well-known entertainer, for example, are the only people who can authorize the use of the entertainer's name or likeness.

FAIR TRIAL AND RIGHT OF ACCESS

The answers to two other questions that bear on press freedoms and individual rights remain discretionary for the courts: When does media coverage influence a jury so much that a defendant's right to a fair trial is jeopardized? How much access should the media be granted during a trial?

Fair Trial

The best-known decision affecting prejudicial press coverage of criminal cases is *Sheppard* v. *Maxwell*. In 1954, Dr. Samuel Sheppard of Cleveland was sentenced to life imprisonment for murdering his wife. His conviction followed reams of newspaper stories, many of which proclaimed his guilt before the jury had decided the case. The jurors, who went home each evening, were told by the judge not to read newspapers or pay attention to broadcast reports, but no one monitored what the jurors did.

Twelve years later, lawyer F. Lee Bailey took Sheppard's trial to the U.S. Supreme Court, where the conviction was overturned on the premise that Sheppard had been a victim of a biased jury. In writing the decision, Justice Tom C. Clark prescribed several remedies. He said that the reporters should have been limited to certain areas in the courtroom, that the news media should not have been allowed to interview the witnesses and that the court should have forbidden statements outside of the courtroom.

Courtroom Access

The outcome of the Sheppard case led to many courtroom experiments with restrictions on the press. The most widespread practices were restraining (gag) orders and closed proceedings. With a gag order, the judge limited what the press could report. Closed proceedings excluded the press from the courtroom. But since 1980, several court cases have overturned most of these limitations so that today the press is rarely excluded from courtroom proceedings, and the exclusion lasts only as long as it takes the news organization to appeal to a higher court for access.

Cameras in the courtroom is a sticky issue between judges, who want to avoid the disruption that cameras present, and broadcast newspeople, who want to photograph what is going on. In selected cases, however, cameras have been allowed to record complete trials. In 1994, for example, Court TV broadcast the entire trial of O. J. Simpson. Cameras in the courtroom is a state-by-state decision. Some states allow cameras during civil but not criminal trials. Other states ban them altogether. The courts and the press are not yet completely comfortable partners.

REGULATING BROADCAST

All of the American media are expected to abide by the country's laws. Regulation of the media comes from government agencies that oversee aspects of the media business. The print industry is not regulated specifically by any government agency. The largest single area of regulation comes from the Federal Communications Commission, which oversees broadcasting. Other regulating agencies, such as the Federal Trade Commission, scrutinize specific areas that relate to the media, such as advertising.

The concept behind broadcast regulation since 1927 has been that the airwaves belong to the public and that broadcasters are trustees operating in the public interest. The history of U.S. broadcast regulation can be traced to government's early attempt to organize the airwaves. (For information on the Radio Act of 1912 and the Radio Act of 1927, see Chapter 5.) The Federal Communications Commission, based in Washington, D.C., now has five commissioners who are appointed by the president and are approved by the Senate. Each commissioner serves a five-year term and the chairperson is appointed by the president.

Today FCC regulation touches almost every aspect of station operations. Most importantly, U.S. broadcast stations must be licensed by the FCC to operate. Because the print media are unregulated by any government agency, the government exercises more direct control over the broadcast media than over the print media.

Like the print media, broadcasters must follow court rulings on issues such as libel, obscenity and the right of privacy. But broadcast stations also must follow the regulations that the FCC establishes.

The Telecommunications Act of 1996 Transforms the Marketplace

On February 8, 1996, President Clinton signed the Telecommunications Act of 1996, the most far-reaching reform in the way the U.S. government regulates mass media in more than 60 years. The Telecommunications Act will affect all aspects of the media industries, especially broadcast, cable, telephone and computer networks.

The Telecommunications Act of 1996 promises to transform the nation's media industries. The last time the government intervened in a similar way to affect the development of the media business was in 1934, when Congress created the Federal Communications Commission (FCC) to regulate broadcasting in the "public interest, convenience and necessity."

The Telecommunications Act is merely an extension of the philosophy of deregulation—that free competition, with less government regulation, even-

Courtesy of Don Wright, *The Palm Beach Post.*

tually will improve consumers' choices and encourage investment in new technologies. The theory is that free competition will lower costs for consumers and give them access to more types of media.

Critics, however, say that the Act will help large media companies get bigger because only the large companies can afford to spend the money necessary to upgrade their equipment and delivery systems in order to take advantage of new markets. This philosophy of open competition, as established in the Telecommunications Act of 1996, will govern the media industries in the next century.

Goal: To Sell You "The Bundle"

"It's War!" declared *The Wall Street Journal* on September 16, 1996. The battlefield was telecommunications and the goal was **"The Bundle."** This term is being used in telecommunications to describe the combination of services that the media industries will be able to offer you in the future. Following passage of the 1996 Telecommunications Act, large companies began positioning themselves to deliver the combination of telecommunications services that they think consumers will want.

"The Bundle" the combination of telecommunications services that the media industries will be able to offer consumers in the future.

"Thanks to a combination of deregulation and new technologies, war has broken out in the communications market," says the *Journal.* "Everybody has joined the fray—long-distance telephone giants, the regional [local telephone] Bell companies and the cable-TV operators, the satellite outfits, the fledgling digital wireless phone firms and the Internet service providers. Even your old-fashioned power company.

"And they all want the same thing: to invade one another's markets and sell you one another's products and services.

"In short, they want to sell you the Bundle."[31]

Your long-distance telephone company, such as AT&T, MCI or Sprint, would like to become your local telephone company, as well as the provider of your online access services.

This same long-distance company also would like to provide your TV programs, replacing the local cable system, adding these charges to your monthly telephone bill. Local telephone companies, the Regional Bell Operating Companies (**RBOCs**), sometimes called Baby Bells, want their slice of revenue, too, so in some areas of the country they are moving into the cable business. Some cable companies have announced plans to offer telephone service.

RBOCs Regional Bell Operating Companies, or "Baby Bells."

"The act so completely dismantles the existing regulatory structure that the telecommunications industry begins to look like a free-for-all," said Howard Anderson, founder and manager of Yankee Group, a Boston-based consulting firm. "Everyone is already trying to build multimedia networks to deliver everything from telephone and mobile services to Internet access and video-on-demand."[32]

Targeting the "Power User"

This "bundling" of services would mean that you would pay one monthly bill for several types of media services to a single company, which, of course, would dramatically increase that company's portion of media revenue. "The goal for these companies is two-fold," says Richard Siber, a wireless analyst for Andersen Consulting in Boston. "One is locking in a customer for life and providing one-stop shopping. And the other is revenue maximization, getting you to use their products more and more."[33] *Business Week* magazine called this intense competition for customers a "Telescramble."

IMPACT

on you

By Thomas E. Weber

Privacy Concerns: Can Online Public Data Be Too Public?

Does the Internet know too much? Privacy advocates think so. And, increasingly, average users are inclined to agree. No wonder: Web sites have gotten downright nosy, openly demanding answers to personal questions and secretly tracking users' movements online. It is easy to get the impression that, in the age of the Internet, no secret is safe.

But it isn't that simple. Americans routinely relinquish all sorts of personal data—and they were doing so long before they ever heard of the Internet. Consumers who have applied for a credit card, earned a frequent-flier mile or signed up for a supermarket discount club have given marketers the means to look over their shoulders. And a tradition of public access to government records means that highly personal details—from divorce filings to bankruptcy judgments—have long been open to inspection by all....

The Federal Trade Commission grilled marketers and technologists about online privacy to determine whether the government needs to institute new safeguards or whether businesses can be trusted to regulate themselves.

Either way, consumers will ultimately have to decide where to draw the privacy line. Will Web surfers continue to swap personal details for "free" access to online information? Or will they shun businesses they deem too intrusive? And while they're at it, will the Internet debate galvanize

them to begin clamoring for more privacy off-line, fighting back against junk-mailers and telemarketers? Here…are some key issues to consider.

No Secrets?

Privacy and Internet Growth
Fears about privacy top other concerns among those who haven't yet moved onto the Internet. Pecentage of nonusers who would be more likely to begin using the Internet if:

Privacy would be protected — 52%
Cost was reduced — 44%
Users had more control over marketing messages — 38%
Use became less complicated — 37%

Perception and Reality
Despite widespread concerns about online privacy, few users say they have actually been victimized by an invasion of privacy – especially compared with incidents off-line.

Personally experienced invasion of privacy on the Internet — 5%
Experienced invasion of privacy on an online service — 7%
Experienced invasion of privacy off-line — 26%

Unease Over E-Mail
Electronic mail causes more concern about privacy than other widely used forms of communication. Percentage of those very or somewhat concerned about the confidentiality of:

☐ Users   ☐ Nonusers

E-mail — 59% / 81%
Telephone — 48% / 61%
Fax — 51% / 59%
U.S. mail — 30% / 44%

Filling In the Blanks
Faced with nosy Web sites asking personal questions, most users have at some point declined to answer. Most of those users said they understood and agreed with the site's privacy policy.

Declined to give information — 79%
Provided information requested by a site — 61%
Responded with false information — 8%

Source: Louis Harris & Associates Inc.

The primary target is the so-called "power-user," someone who uses a lot of media at home or in business. While the average consumer spends about $100 a month on media services, an upscale customer averages $300 a month, or $3,000 to $3,500 a year. Income for the local telephone companies alone totals $90 billion a year; the long-distance market annually collects $73 billion.[34] The Telecommunications Act of 1996 has created this battlefield for consumers' attention because the financial incentives are so huge. The economic future of every media company in the country will, in some way, be affected by this battle. That is why it is so important to understand this single piece of legislation, which is expected to have such a dramatic effect on consumers and on the future of the nation's media industries.

UNDERSTANDING THE TELECOMMUNICATIONS ACT OF 1996

The major provisions of the Telecommunications Act affect telecommunications, broadcast and cable. The Communications Decency Act, which is part of the Telecommunications Act, regulates access to cable and television programming and monitors the content of computer networks, including the Internet.

Universal Service

The Telecommunications Act of 1996 establishes, for the first time in federal legislation, a goal of universal service—meaning that everyone in the United States should have access to affordable telecommunications services. "In a time when we increasingly use information as a commodity, telecommunications are becoming increasingly important for the delivery of that commodity,"[35] according to the Benton Foundation, a public interest group. The intent of the Act is to make telecommunications available to everyone.

What should be in the "universal service" package, of course, will be defined by the FCC. Does "universal service" mean only a telephone, or should "universal service" include access to a modem to connect a computer to the Internet? The FCC must decide what exactly constitutes "universal service" and whether access to a computer and a modem will be part of that service, in an effort to use telecommunications to improve the economies of rural areas and central cities, as well as the rest of the nation.

Deregulation of "Free Media"

The Telecommunications Act continues a policy of deregulation of commercial radio and television ownership that began in the 1980s. Radio and over-the-air broadcast television are viewed as "free media." Unlike cable stations, which require extra equipment and charge consumers for their services, over-the-air broadcasting is available to anyone with a radio or television—and 98 percent of U.S. households have a TV set. Over-the-air broadcasting therefore has the largest potential audience.

Relaxed Ownership and Licensing Rules

Before the Act passed, broadcast companies were allowed to own only 12 television stations. The Act eliminates television station limits altogether and instead uses a station's potential audience to measure ownership limits. The Act allows one company to own television stations that reach up to 35 percent of the nation's homes. Existing television networks (such as NBC and ABC) can begin new networks, although they are not allowed to buy an existing network. NBC could not buy ABC, for example, but NBC could begin a second network of its own, such as NBC2.

Before the Act passed, radio broadcasters were allowed to own 20 AM or 20 FM radio stations nationwide. The Telecommunications Act removes the limit on the number of radio stations a company can own and, in each market, the number of stations that one owner can hold depends on the size of the market. In a large market with 45 or more commercial radio stations, for example, a broadcaster may own eight stations; in a market with 14 stations, a broadcaster may own up to five stations.

The Act also allows cross-ownership. This means that companies can own television and radio stations in the same broadcast market. Companies also can own broadcast and cable outlets in the same market.

In 1999, the FCC further relaxed TV station ownership rules by allowing one broadcast company to own two TV stations in the same market. A company could buy a second station in the same market, says the FCC, as long as eight other stations with different owners are still operating in the market after the deal.

Each broadcast station in the country, television and radio, is licensed by the FCC. In the past, renewal has been a complicated process. Television stations were required to renew their licenses every five years and radio every seven. The Telecommunications Act extends the renewal period for both radio and television to every eight years.

Local Phone Competition

Cable companies have services available to 90 percent of all homes in the Unites States, but only about 60 percent of American homes have cable. About 94 percent of all homes have a telephone. This means that, in the future, cable and telephone companies will be competing to deliver telecommunications services to home customers.

To encourage competition for delivery of video services, the Telecommunications Act allows the local telephone companies to get into the video delivery business. The Act repeals the FCC's "telco-cable cross-ownership" restrictions (**"telco"** is an abbreviation for "telephone company"). Local telephone companies will be able to deliver video services either by an agreement with a cable operator or by creating their own delivery system. In turn, the cable companies are allowed to enter the business offered in the past by local telephone companies.

telco an abbreviation for "telephone company."

Large cable companies also want to deliver new types of telephone services. Cable operator TCI, for example, is developing a service with long-distance carrier Sprint to carry messages to and from wireless pocket phones.[36]

To add to competition in the local telephone business, the Act also allows long-distance carriers to offer local telephone service to compete with the Regional Bell (local telephone) companies. Within two months of the Act's passage, the long-distance carrier AT&T had filed to be allowed to offer local telephone service in all 50 states.[37]

"If we get this right," said former FCC Chairman Reed Hundt, "you'll be buying communications services like shoes. Different styles, different vendors."[38] Until all the rules are in place, however, the choices promise to be confusing for consumers and frustrating for people in the media industries who are trying to position themselves for a new future that hasn't yet been defined.

Unregulated Cable Rates

The rates that cable companies can charge have been regulated since 1992. In an attempt to control spiraling cable charges to consumers, Congress passed the 1992 Cable Act to regulate rates. The cable companies, facing competition from the local telephone companies, argued that Congress should remove rate regulation to allow the cable companies to compete and to help raise cable income.

The Telecommunications Act removed most rate regulation for all cable companies. All that remains is regulation to monitor the "basic tier" of cable service, often called "basic cable."

UNDERSTANDING THE COMMUNICATIONS DECENCY ACT (CDA)

Along with the major provisions of the Telecommunications Act to increase competition, Congress also added three provisions to control content. These provisions in the legislation, called the Communications Decency Act, attempt to define and control the users' access to specific types of programs and content.

Program Blocking

The Telecommunications Act required cable owners to take steps within 30 days after the bill was signed to ensure that cable shows "primarily dedicated to sexually oriented programming or other programming that is indecent" did not accidentally become available to people who did not subscribe to the programs. This meant that every cable operator would have to provide a free "lock box" to every cable subscriber's home to block programs, whether or not the customer requested it.

On March 9, 1996, the day the program blocking provision of the Act was scheduled to go into effect, Playboy Enterprises successfully won a temporary restraining order, which prevented the application of the law. "Attorneys for Chicago-based Playboy argued that the provision violated constitutional protections of free speech and equal protection. Justice Department attorneys argued that the government has the right and duty to regulate the distribution of indecent material if it can be viewed or heard by children."[39]

Indecent Material on the Internet

The Communications Decency Act made it a felony to send indecent material over computer networks. The Act also "prohibited using a telecommunications device to:

- Make or initiate any communication that is obscene, lewd, lascivious, filthy or indecent with intent to annoy, abuse, threaten or harass another person.

- Make or make available obscene communication.

- Make or make available an indecent communication to minors.

- Transmit obscene material—including material concerning abortion—or for any indecent or immoral use."[40]

The Act relied on a very broad definition of the term "indecent," and courts have generally ruled that such speech is protected under the First

Amendment. Under the Act's provisions, violators could be charged with a felony and fined up to $250,000.

More than 50 opponents of the Act's indecency provision, including the American Library Association and the American Civil Liberties Union, went to court in Philadelphia to challenge the law. On June 12, a three-judge Philadelphia panel unanimously declared that the Internet indecency provision was unconstitutional, and the judges blocked enforcement of the law. The judges issued a restraining order, which meant that the Internet indecency provisions could not be enforced and violations could not even be investigated.

The federal government had argued that the Internet should be regulated like radio and television, but the judges said that material on the Internet deserved the same protection as printed material. In presenting the court's opinion, Judge Stewart R. Dalzell made very strong arguments defending access to the Internet. "Just as the strength of the Internet is chaos," he wrote, "so the strength of our liberty depends upon the chaos and cacophony of the unfettered speech the First Amendment protects."[41]

In 1997, the U.S. Supreme Court struck down the Communications Decency Act (see Impact/Digital, "High Court Strikes Down Internet Smut Law," pp. 320–321), making it much harder for Congress to limit Internet access in the future. What is interesting is that the courts are defining an electronic delivery system—the Internet—as if it were a print medium.

This is important because Congress and the President, through the FCC, have historically regulated the broadcast industries, but none of the regulations that apply to the broadcast media also applies to print. The content of the print media, by law and by practice, has historically remained unregulated because of the First Amendment's protection of free expression.

Violent Programming: TV Ratings and the V-Chip

A third provision of the CDA affects television programming. Under pressure from Congress, television executives agreed to devise a voluntary ratings system for television programs by January 1997. The *Broadcasting and Cable* magazine called the imposition of the ratings system a "stunning defeat" for the television industry, which had long resisted all content regulation.[42]

Jack Valenti, President of the Motion Picture Association of America (MPAA), led the ratings task force (Valenti also helped establish the current system of movie ratings). In January 1997, the task force announced the new ratings system, which *applies to all programming except sports, news magazines and news shows.*

The new ratings divide programming into six categories:

TVY—Appropriate for all children but specifically designed for a very young audience, including children ages two to six. Programs not expected to frighten younger children.

TV7—Designed for children age seven and above. More appropriate for children who are able to distinguish between make-believe and reality. May include mild physical or comedy violence.

TVG—Most parents would find these programs suitable for all ages. Little or no violence, no strong language and little or no sexual dialogue or situations.

TVPG—May contain some material that some parents would find unsuitable for younger children. Programs' themes may call for parental guidance. May contain infrequent coarse language, limited violence, some suggestive dialogue and situations.

TV14—May contain some material that many parents would find unsuitable for children younger than 14. These programs may contain sophisticated themes, sexual content, strong language and more intense violence.

TVMA—Specifically designed to be viewed by adults and therefore may be unsuitable for children younger than 17. May contain mature themes, profane language, graphic violence and explicit sexual content.

Unlike movies, which are rated by an independent board, the TV shows will be rated by producers, networks, cable channels, syndicators and other people who originate the programs.[43] These ratings evaluate violence and sexual content, and the results are displayed on the screen at the beginning of each program and coded into each TV program. The codes will be read by a "V-chip." This microchip device is required in all new television sets. The V-chip allows parents to program the TV set to eliminate shows the parents find objectionable.

Six months after this rating system was adopted, in response to some public criticism that the first system did not address violence and sexual content, the majority of TV executives agreed to an additional ratings system that is more descriptive about program content. Using this system, a program will receive a general rating (TVY, TV7, TVG, TVPG, TV14 and TVMA) and a specific rating for violent or sexual content. The program and violent content labels are:

V	Violence
S	Sexual content
L	Vulgar language
D	Suggestive dialogue
FV	Fantasy violence on children's shows

A program could receive TV14, plus an L, for example, or a TV7, and an FV. All of the broadcast networks agreed to use specific program content ratings, except NBC, which said it would offer its own advisory labels for violence and sexual content, similar to the "viewer discretion" warnings that the networks traditionally had used.

ADVERTISING AND PUBLIC RELATIONS LAW AND REGULATION

Advertising and public relations are governed by legal constraints and by regulation.

Legal Decisions Govern Advertisers

The New York Times v. *Sullivan* was a crucial case for advertisers as well as for journalists. Since that decision, two other important court cases have defined the advertising and public relations businesses—the Central Hudson case for advertising (which is defined as "commercial speech" under the law) and the Texas Gulf Sulphur case for public relations.

Central Hudson Case. In 1980, in *Central Hudson Gas & Electric Corp.* v. *Public Service Commission*, the U.S. Supreme Court issued the most definitive opinion yet on commercial speech. During the energy crisis atmosphere of the 1970s, the New York Public Utilities Commission had banned all advertising by public utilities that promoted the use of electricity. Central Hudson Gas & Electric wanted the ban lifted, so the company sued the commission. The commission said the ban promoted energy conservation; the Supreme Court disagreed, and the decision in the case formed the basis for commercial speech protection today. "If the commercial speech does not mislead, and it concerns lawful activity," explains legal scholar Ralph Holsinger, "the government's power to regulate it is limited....The state cannot impose regulations that only indirectly advance its interests. Nor can it regulate commercial speech that poses no danger to a state interest."[44]

The decision prescribed standards that commercial speech must meet to be protected by the First Amendment. The main provisions of the standards are that (1) the advertisement must be for a lawful product and (2) the advertisement must not be misleading. This has become known as the *Hudson test*.

To be protected, then, an advertisement must promote a legal product and must not lie. This would seem to have settled the issue, but controversy continues. Should alcohol advertising be banned? What about advertisements for condoms or birth control pills? Courts in different states have disagreed on these questions, and no Supreme Court decision on these specific issues exists, leaving many complex questions undecided. The Hudson test remains the primary criteria for determining what is protected commercial speech.

The Texas Gulf Sulphur Case. The most important civil suit involving the issue of public relations occurred in the 1960s in *Securities and Exchange Commission* v. *Texas Gulf Sulphur Company*. The Texas Gulf Sulphur (TGS) Company discovered ore deposits in Canada in late 1963 but did not announce the discovery publicly. TGS quietly purchased hundreds of acres surrounding the ore deposits. Although TGS officers began to accumulate more shares of the stock, the company issued a press release that said that the rumors about a discovery were "unreliable."

When TGS announced that it had made a "major strike," the company was taken to court by the Securities and Exchange Commission. The U.S. court of appeals ruled that TGS officers had violated the disclosure laws of the Securities and Exchange Commission. The court also ruled that TGS had issued "a false and misleading press release." Company officers and their friends were punished for withholding the information.

The case proved conclusively that a company's failure to make known material information (information likely to be considered important by reasonable investors in determining whether to buy, sell, or hold securities) may be in violation of the antifraud provision of the Securities and Exchange Acts. The TGS case remains today as a landmark in the history of public relations law.[45]

The decision in the Texas Gulf Sulphur case means that public relations people can be held legally responsible for information that is not disclosed about their companies. This case says that public relations people at publicly held corporations (businesses with stockholders) are responsible not only to their companies, but also to the public.

The Government Regulates Advertisers

The main regulatory agency for advertising and public relations issues is the Federal Trade Commission (FTC), although other agencies such as the Securities and Exchange Commission and the Food and Drug Administration sometimes intervene to question advertising practices.

In 1914, the Federal Trade Commission assumed the power to oversee deceptive interstate advertising practices under the Federal Trade Commission Act. Today, the FTC's policy covering deceptive advertising says: "The Commission will find an act or practice deceptive if there is a misrepresentation, omission or other practice that misleads the consumer acting reasonably in the circumstances, to the consumer's detriment."[46] The FTC can fine an advertiser who doesn't comply with an FTC order.

The Federal Trade Commission's five members serve seven-year terms. They are appointed by the president and confirmed by the Senate, and no more than three of the members can be from one political party. The commission acts when it receives a complaint that the staff feels is worth investigating. The staff can request a *letter of compliance* from the advertiser, with the advertiser promising to change the alleged deception without admitting guilt.

Next, the advertiser can argue the case before an administrative law judge, who can write a consent agreement to outline what the advertiser must do to comply with the law. A cease-and-desist order can be issued against the advertiser, although this is rare.

Finally, because the FTC's members are presidential appointees, the commission's actions often reflect the political climate under which they operate. In the 1970s, the FTC became a very active consumer advocacy agency. This was challenged in the 1980s, when presidential policy favored easing regulations on business practices.

Under President Clinton in the 1990s, the FTC moved aggressively to cite companies for wrongdoing. For example, in 1997, the FTC conducted hearings to determine whether the government should impose safeguards on information access on the Internet to protect consumers' privacy. (See Impact/On You, "Privacy Concerns, Can Online Public Data Be Too Public?" p. 332.)

In summary, legal and regulatory issues governing advertising and public relations, then, are stitched with the same conflicting values that govern all aspects of media law and regulation. The courts, the FCC, the FTC and other government agencies that monitor the media industries are the major arbiters of ongoing constitutional clashes that attempt to balance the business needs of the media industries, the constitutional guarantee of freedom of speech and the government's role as a public interest representative.

IN FOCUS

- Until 1964, the First Amendment faced four notable government challenges: the Alien and Sedition Laws of 1798, the Espionage Act of 1918, the Smith Act of 1940 and the Cold War congressional investigations of suspected Communists in the late 1940s and early 1950s.

- Prior restraint has rarely been invoked by American courts. The two most recent cases involved the publication of the Pentagon Papers by *The New York Times* and the publication of directions to build a hydrogen bomb in *The Progressive* magazine. In both cases, the information eventually was printed, but the intervention of the government delayed publication.

- Attempts by the Reagan administration to limit reporters' access to Grenada during the U.S. invasion in October 1983 were a subtle form of prior restraint.

- Pentagon rules for 1991 war coverage, reached in cooperation with journalists, imposed stricter restrictions on reporting in the Gulf War than in any other U.S. war. In contrast, when the U.S. government delivered humanitarian aid to Somalia in 1992, the military encouraged press coverage.

- *Roth* v. *United States* established the Roth test for obscenity: "whether to the average person, applying contemporary community standards, the dominant theme of the material taken as a whole appeals to prurient interest."

- *Miller* v. *California* established a three-part local test for obscenity: whether "the average person, applying contemporary community standards," would find that the work, taken as a whole, appeals to the prurient interest; whether the work depicts or describes, in a patently offensive way, sexual conduct specifically defined by the applicable state law; and whether the work, taken as a whole, lacks serious literary, artistic, political or scientific value—often called the LAPS test.

- The 1986 Final Report of the Attorney General's Commission on Pornography totally contradicted the findings of a similar study done in 1970. The 1986 report called for a nationwide crackdown on obscenity, linking sex crimes and other antisocial behavior to hard-core pornography. The commission's arguments were not convincing, and no substantial legislation resulted.

- In the 1988 Hazelwood case, the U.S. Supreme Court gave public school officials considerable freedom to limit what appears in student publications.

- In 1964, *The New York Times* v. *Sullivan* case set a precedent, establishing that to be successful in a libel suit, a public official must prove actual malice.

- *Gertz* v. *Robert Welch* established the concept that the expression of opinions is a necessary part of public debate. Because of the *Herbert* v. *Lando* decision, today reporters can be asked in a libel suit to identify their sources and to surrender their notes. The *Masson* v. *New Yorker Magazine* case addressed the journalist's responsibility for direct quotations.

■ To prove libel, a person must show that the statement was communicated to a third party; that people who read or saw the statement would be able to identify the person, even if that person was not actually named; that the statement injured the person's reputation or income or caused mental anguish; and that the journalist or the print or broadcast organization is at fault.

■ The press can use three defenses against a libel suit: truth, privilege and fair comment.

■ Invasion-of-privacy lawsuits are much less common than libel suits. There is no U.S. Supreme Court decision governing invasion of privacy, so each state has its own interpretation of this issue.

■ Generally, the media can be guilty of invading someone's privacy by intruding on a person's physical or mental solitude, publishing or disclosing embarrassing personal facts, giving someone publicity that places the person in a false light or using someone's name or likeness for commercial benefit.

■ *Sheppard* v. *Maxwell* established the legal precedent for limiting press access to courtrooms and juries.

■ Unlike print, the broadcast media are regulated by a federal agency, the Federal Communications Commission.

■ The Telecommunications Act of 1996 is the most far-reaching reform in the way the U.S. government regulates mass media in more than 60 years. Following passage of the Telecommunications Act, large companies began positioning themselves to deliver the combination of telecommunications services that they think consumers will want.

■ The major provisions of the Telecommunications Act of 1996 affect telecommunications, broadcast and cable.

■ The Communications Decency Act, which is part of the Telecommunications Act, regulates access to cable and TV programming and monitors the content of computer networks, including the Internet.

■ In 1997, the U.S. Supreme Court blocked the Internet indecency provisions of the Communications Decency Act.

■ The Communications Decency Act also established a system of ratings for TV programming.

■ The FCC under President Clinton moved to a policy of deregulation of station ownership and re-regulation of broadcast programming.

• The Hudson test for advertising means that, to be protected by the First Amendment, an advertisement must promote a legal product and must not lie.

• The Texas Gulf Sulphur case established the concept that a publicly held company is responsible for any information it withholds from the public.

• The main government agency regulating advertising is the Federal Trade Commission. This agency adopted aggressive policies of protecting consumers' rights in the 1990s.

WORKING THE WEB www

- **Communications Decency Act**

  http://www.findlaw.com/casecode/supreme.html

- **Copyright Principles Proposed by the National Humanities Alliance**

  http://www.ninch.cni.org/ISSUES/COPYRIGHT/PRINCIPLES/NHA_Compact/html

- **Copyright on the Net**

  http://www.benedict.com/home/htm

- **Fair Use on the Net**

  http://www.fairuse.stanford.edu

- **Reporters Committee for Freedom of the Press**

  http://www.rcpf.org.rcfp

INFOTRAC COLLEGE EDITION EXERCISES

Using the InfoTrac College Edition's fully searchable online database of articles and abstracts, do the following exercises as directed by your instructor.

1. Read "Impact/Point of View: Excerpts From the 1943 Code of Wartime Practices for American Broadcasters" in Chapter 14. Then, using Info-Trac, look up one of the following sets of keywords:

   - war reporting

   - wartime censorship

   - war correspondents

   Find at least three articles on the subject of reporters covering wars, print them and either:

   a. write a brief paper on your findings, or

   b. bring the articles to class for a small-group discussion.

2. Read "Impact on You: From Here to Immodesty: Milestones in the Toppling of TV's Taboos" in Chapter 14. Using InfoTrac College Edition, enter keywords "television censorship" and/or "sex in television" and find at least three other articles on the subject of censorship. Print them and either:

   a. write a brief paper on your findings, or

   b. bring the articles to class for a small-group discussion.

3. Sen. Joseph McCarthy and the Pentagon Papers represent two unique chapters in media history about censorship. Using InfoTrac College Edition, look up articles on "Joseph McCarthy," "HUAC" or "Army-McCarthy" and gather more information about McCarthy's Senate hearings to identify Communists. Or, using the keywords "Pentagon Papers," gather information about that chapter of journalism history. Print at least three articles about either subject and bring them to class for a small-group discussion.

4. Read "Impact/Digital: High Court Strikes Down Internet Smut Law" in Chapter 14. Then, using InfoTrac College Edition, look up the keywords "Internet censorship" and/or "privacy law" and find at least three articles on the subject. Print the articles and bring them to class for a small-group discussion.

5. Read Impact/Point of View: It's Time Shock-Talk TV Took Some Responsibility" in Chapter 14. Using the keywords "libel law," "newspaper libel" or "libel and slander," look up at least three articles on libel. Print them and either:

a. write a brief paper on your findings, or

b. bring the articles to class for a small-group discussion.

15

ETHICS

What's Ahead

Recognize that gathering and (reporting) information may cause harm or discomfort. Pursuit of the news is not a license for arrogance.

Society of Professional Journalists Code of Ethics

"**M**ost of us would rather publish a story than not," explained journalist Anthony Brandt in an *Esquire* magazine article about ethics.

We're in the business of reporting, after all; most of us believe the public should know what's going on, has a right to know, has, indeed, a responsibility to know, and that this right, this responsibility, transcends the right to privacy, excuses our own pushiness, our arrogance, and therefore ought to protect us from lawsuits even when we are wrong.

But most reporters also know there are times when publishing can harm or ruin people's lives. Members of the press sometimes print gossip as truth, disregard the impact they have on people's lives, and are ready to believe the worst about people because the worst sells....We in the media have much to answer for.[1]

ORIGIN OF ETHICAL CONCEPTS IN JOURNALISM

Discussions about how journalists answer for what they do center on *ethics*. The word derives from the Greek word *ethos*, meaning the guiding spirit or traditions that govern a culture. Part of America's culture is the unique First Amendment protection, so any discussion of ethics and the American media acknowledges the cultural belief that the First Amendment privilege carries with it special obligations. Among these obligations are professional ethics.

Journalists are no more likely to exploit their positions than people in other professions, but when journalists make the wrong ethical choices, the consequences can be very damaging. "It may well be that if journalism loses touch with ethical values, it will then cease to be of use to society, and cease to have any real reason for being," writes media ethics scholar John Hulteng. "But that, for the sake of all of us, must never be allowed to happen."[2]

Journalists sometimes make poor ethical judgments because they work quickly and their actions can be haphazard; because the lust to be first with a story can override the desire to be right; because they sometimes don't know enough to question the truthfulness of what they're told; because they can win attention and professional success quickly by ignoring ethical standards; and because journalists sometimes are insensitive to the consequences of their stories for the people they cover. Consider these actual situations:

1. *Creating composite characters.* A journalist for a prestigious magazine admitted that he sometimes embroidered the events he wrote about or created composite characters in his articles without telling his readers. Was the journalist presenting fiction as fact, or was he simply using journalistic license?

2. *Insider friendships.* A nationally syndicated political columnist coached a presidential candidate before a televised debate and then praised the candidate's performance on a nationwide TV program. Did the columnist get too close to a news source, or did he simply help a friend?

3. *Reporting personal information.* A reporter verified that a well-known public figure was dying of AIDS, although the news figure would not admit his illness. Did the reporter infringe on the person's privacy, or did the readers deserve to know about the extent of this growing health hazard?

4. *Staging sensational events.* A television news magazine program showed a Chevrolet truck exploding when struck near the gas tank. But the explosion was staged, and the collision did not cause the explosion. Did the network exploit a story for its shock value, or will the public understand this type of tragedy better by viewing the staged demonstration?

DEFINING ETHICAL DILEMMAS

Ethical dilemmas faced by the media can be described using four categories: truthfulness, fairness, privacy and responsibility. Falsehood is the issue for the journalist who embroidered characters in example 1. Bias is the question for the columnist who coached the presidential candidate in example 2. Invasion of privacy is the debate facing the reporter who published the AIDS information in example 3. The television network that staged the explosion in example 4 could be criticized for acting irresponsibly.

Some ethical debates are easier to resolve than others. These four incidents and several other examples are described here to demonstrate how vulnerable the media can be to ethical lapses.

TRUTHFULNESS

Truthfulness in reporting means more than accuracy and telling the truth to get a story. Truthfulness also means not misrepresenting the people or the situations in the story to readers or viewers. Another aspect of truthfulness is the responsibility of government officials to not use the media for their own ends.

Misrepresentation

The journalist described in example 1 was *The New Yorker* magazine writer Alistair Reid, who acknowledged in 1984 that in more than 20 years as a writer for *The New Yorker*, he had modified facts five separate times. In a "Letter from Barcelona," Reid had described some Spaniards sitting in "a small, flyblown bar," jeering at a televised speech by Spanish chief of state Francisco Franco. In fact, Reid said that he watched the speech at the home of a one-time bartender and that two of the main characters were composites. This was particularly surprising because *The New Yorker* prides itself on its fact-checking department. Reid said that he created the fictional environment and characters to protect his sources from retribution by the government.

A more celebrated case of a journalist embroidering the facts is Janet Cooke, who was a reporter for the *Washington Post* in 1980 when she wrote "Jimmy's World," a story about an 8-year-old heroin addict. After she was awarded the Pulitzer Prize for the story in April 1981, reporters began to check up on her background, and the *Post* learned that she had lied on her résumé. The editors then questioned her for several hours about the story. She was allowed to resign.

"'Jimmy's World' was in essence a fabrication," she wrote in her resignation letter. "I never encountered or interviewed an 8-year-old heroin addict. The September 19, 1980, article in the *Washington Post* was a serious misrepresentation which I deeply regret. I apologize to my newspaper, my profession, the Pulitzer board and all seekers of truth."[3]

A month later, columnist Michael Daly of the New York *Daily News* resigned, admitting that he had invented a British soldier in a story about Ireland. He said he had recreated the adventures of "Christopher Spell" from a description given to him by another soldier, who had witnessed the events. "The question of reconstruction and using a pseudonym—I've done it a lot," said Daly. "No one has ever said anything."[4]

Misrepresenting people by creating composite characters, as in these three cases, causes readers to question the facts in all stories: Which are actual people and which are composites? Is the story fiction or fact?

Disinformation

In October 1986, the press learned that in August 1986 the Reagan administration had launched a **disinformation** campaign to scare Libyan leader

disinformation the planting by government sources of inaccurate information.

Moammar Qadhafi. Selected U.S. government sources had planted stories with reporters that U.S. forces were preparing to strike Libya. The first report of the bogus preparations appeared in the August 25, 1986, *Wall Street Journal.*

On the basis of this story and a statement by White House spokesman Larry Speakes that the article was "authoritative," other newspapers, including the *Washington Post,* carried the story. This brings up the ethical question of the government's responsibility not to use the press for its own ends. State Department spokesman and former television reporter Bernard Kalb resigned when he learned about the disinformation campaign, saying "Faith in the word of America is the pulsebeat of our democracy."

In 1988, the Drug Enforcement Administration (DEA) admitted it had used police nationwide to stage phony drug seizures and attract press attention to help DEA agents gain the confidence of drug kingpins. Law enforcement officials defended the practice as a way to outsmart criminals; the press responded that scams like these raise ethical questions similar to the planted Qadhafi story. How is the public to differentiate between true stories and those that are planted by the government?

FAIRNESS

Fairness implies impartiality—that the journalist has nothing personal to gain from a report, that there are no hidden benefits to the reporter or to the source from the story being presented. Criticism of the press for unfairness results from debates over close ties that sometimes develop between reporters and the people they write about—called *insider friendships;* reporters who accept personal or financial benefits from sources, sponsors, or advertisers—called *conflicts of interest;* and reporters who pay their sources for stories—called *checkbook journalism.*

Insider Friendships

The columnist in example 2 was ABC News commentator George Will; the candidate was Ronald Reagan. In 1980, Will coached Reagan before he faced President Jimmy Carter for a televised debate. On the ABC program *Nightline,* after the debate, Will compared Reagan's performance to that of a "thoroughbred." In 1983, when Will's actions were reported, Will admitted that he would not do the same thing again.

In 1987, *The Wall Street Journal* reported that in December 1986, ABC's Barbara Walters had carried a private message from arms merchant Manucher Ghorbanifar to President Reagan after she conducted an exclusive interview with Ghorbanifar for an ABC story. Ghorbanifar was a central figure in the arrangements during 1985 and 1986 between the White House and the Iranian government to send arms to Iran in exchange for American hostages. Walters did not report on ABC that she had delivered a message to the president.

"After the interviews, Mr. Ghorbanifar asked to speak with Ms. Walters again and asked that she send his views to the president," stated network spokesman Tom Goodman. "Believing that her information could be of assistance to the remaining hostages (held in Lebanon), and before informing her management, Ms. Walters did that and also gave her information to the appropriate editors" at the network.[5]

The New York Times reporter Judith Miller, who covered the Middle East for three years, criticized Walters for becoming a participant in a story she covered. "We're in the business of publishing what we know....We don't deliver messages," said Miller.[6]

IMPACT

point of view

The Diana Effect: Will Anything Change?

By Richard Lambert

Princess Diana used, and was used by, the international media. Her looks, charm, and obvious sympathy were powerful weapons in her efforts to build an identity, first as a future queen and, later, as a royal outcast. But she was unable to control the instrument which was the main source of her power.

The public hunger for more could be satisfied only by ever bolder and more intrusive reporting. So it was that on the day after her death, the British tabloid newspapers—which were everywhere being cursed as being directly responsible for the tragedy—saw their sales surge as the public rushed for details.

Of course, no citizen—public or private—should be subject to the brutal persecution by hordes of reporters that has become commonplace in most parts of the world.

Where the press is unable to control its own behavior—as in the UK—then legal rights of privacy should be devised, provided always that freedom of information is also a legal right. That such freedom is not available in the UK, which also has arbitrary and unpredictable libel laws, is one explanation for the shortcomings to be found in large sections of the British press.

We all have to answer very serious questions about the way we responded to Princess Diana's death. It's clear that the news brought a genuine surge of emotion and distress to millions of people around the world. What was startling, and even sinister, was the way that the media fed off that response and helped to create a mood which seemed almost cult-like in its intensity. Dissent became impossible: as the hysteria mounted, as Diana appeared to be moving along the path to beatification, choosing *not* to grieve was presented as an act of betrayal.

This was not a tabloid-driven phenomenon. Television broadcasters everywhere reinforced the public mood with the same soft images, the same reverential tones, the same unwillingness to question whether we were indeed mourning the passing of a great public servant, as opposed to a tragic and vulnerable figure. The serious press followed suit.

Writing in the London *Times*, the admirable John Lloyd observed: "it had been one of the received wisdoms of anti-communism that whenever one met the People capitalized, one knew something undemocratic to be afoot. A People's princess is not a People's democracy, to be sure; but in recasting the people as the People we move into dangerous territory."

As Diana's army surged and roamed the streets of London, supported and encouraged by the world's media, there was a sense of danger in the air: a glimpse of something illiberal and unsettling.

Reprinted from *Columbia Journalism Review,* November/December 1997. ©1997 by *Columbia Journalism Review.*

Part of the job of being a reporter is learning to be friendly with many different types of people. In both the Walters and Will examples, the reporters became part of the stories they were supposed to be covering. How can the public trust a reporter who becomes more than an outside observer of events and instead takes part in the story? Insider friendships can remove a reporter's necessary detachment.

Conflicts of Interest

Reporters with conflicts of interest are divided between at least two loyalties, and the ethical question is: How will the stories the reporters write and the integrity of the organizations for which they work be affected?

In 1984, *The Wall Street Journal* fired stock tip columnist R. Foster Winans for allegedly leaking stories in advance to a group of friends who paid Winans for his help and then used the information to make profitable stock market investments. An investigation by the Securities and Exchange Commission had prompted the *Journal* to question Winans.

In 1985, Winans was found guilty of 59 counts of fraud and conspiracy. "What made the conduct here a fraud was that Winans knew he was not supposed to leak the timing or contents of his articles or trade on that knowledge," wrote Judge Charles E. Stewart in his decision on the case. "Here, the fraudulent taking and misuse of confidential information stolen from *The Wall Street Journal* placed immediately in jeopardy probably its most valuable asset—its reputation for fairness and integrity."[7] Winans was sentenced to 18 months in jail, $5,000 in fines, five years' probation, and 400 hours of community service.

A different type of conflict of interest happens when reporters accept free meals and passes to entertainment events (freebies) and free trips (junkets). In a 1986 survey of 34 newspapers, nearly half said they accepted free tickets to athletic events, and nearly two-thirds accepted free tickets to artistic events.[8]

In 1986, Walt Disney World invited journalists from all over the world to attend its 15th anniversary celebration in Orlando, Florida, and more than 10,000 journalists and their guests accepted the invitation. Most of the press guests let Disney pay for the hotel, transportation, and meals. *Variety* called the event "one of the biggest junkets in showbiz history," at an estimated cost to Disney, the airlines, hotels, and tourism agencies of $8 million. In an editorial about the junket, *The New York Times* said: "Accepting junkets and boondoggles does not necessarily mean that a reporter is being bought—but it inescapably creates the appearance of being bought."[9]

Checkbook Journalism

In 1994, U.S. Olympic skater Tonya Harding reportedly received $600,000 for appearing on *Inside Edition* after she was charged with participating in an attack on her opponent, Nancy Kerrigan.[10]

When Pulitzer Prize–winning journalist Teresa Carpenter decided to write a book about a Tufts University Medical School professor who murdered a Boston prostitute, she says other writers were offering money to all of the main people involved in the case. According to Carpenter, even the owner of a local massage parlor, who was a minor figure in the case, left a message on Carpenter's phone machine that said, "Without compensation there will be no information."[11]

After New York's "Son of Sam" serial killer David Berkowitz signed a lucrative film and book deal, the state passed a law to prohibit criminals from prof-

Public figures such as Monica Lewinsky often try to use their celebrity status to earn money.

AP/Wide World Photos

iting from such contracts. But on December 10, 1991, the U.S. Supreme Court overturned the law as an infringement on free speech.

Besides the ethical questions about whether journalists and criminals should profit from crime, there are other hazards in any kind of checkbook journalism. One danger is that a paid interviewee will sensationalize the information to bring a higher price, so the interviewee's veracity cannot always be trusted.

A second hazard is that such interviews often become the exclusive property of the highest bidder, shutting out smaller news organizations and independent journalists from the information. In 1999, Las Vegas radio station KVBC-FM offered Monica Lewinsky $5 million for an exclusive interview. She never took the offer. She subsequently was interviewed by ABC's Barbara Walters, but ABC did not pay for the interview.

A third possibility is that the person, who is paid by the news organization to comment, could possibly carry a hidden agenda, such as in an incident involving ABC News and former U.S. Secretary of State Henry Kissinger. In 1989, ABC News paid Kissinger to appear on ABC to analyze how the United States should respond to the events in Tiananmen Square. The student demonstrations in China threatened U.S. business ties there. Neither ABC nor Kissinger revealed during Kissinger's commentary that Kissinger's company had extensive investments in China at the time.

Can an influential person who is being paid for his analysis comment dispassionately about events when those events could affect his business? What responsibility did ABC have to tell its audience about Kissinger's ties to China?

PRIVACY

Reporting on AIDS and on rape are the most visible examples of a complex ethical dilemma: How does the press balance the goal of truthfulness and fact-finding with the need for personal privacy? Is the private grief that such a report may cause worth the public good that can result from publishing the information?

Reporting on AIDS

Because many people who contract AIDS are homosexual, announcing that a person's illness is AIDS can reflect on the person's private sexual behavior. One argument in favor of the press reporting the nature of the illness in these cases is that covering up the information means that the public won't understand the widespread extent of the public health problem that AIDS represents.

"Covering up the truth, by doctors or journalists, stigmatizes other sufferers—the less widely the disease is acknowledged, the less easily they can be accepted. And it shields communities and industries from understanding the full, devastating effect of AIDS," argued *Newsweek* in a story called "AIDS and the Right to Know."[12] The counterargument is that a person's illness and death is strictly a private matter and that publishing the information will harm the person's reputation.

The case of the public figure with AIDS in example 3 describes two situations that occurred in the early years of the AIDS crisis. In 1986, New York lawyer Roy Cohn died of AIDS without acknowledging before his death that he suffered from the disease. Entertainer Liberace also withheld information about his illness before he died in 1987.

Roy Cohn became a public figure in the 1950s during the McCarthy hearings (see Chapter 8), as counsel for the Senate committee investigating Communist activity in the 1950s. As a lawyer in the 1980s, he defended many organized crime figures, and he lived a high-profile existence in New York City. A week before Cohn died, columnists Jack Anderson and Dale Van Atta published a story saying that Cohn was being treated with azidothymidine (AZT), used exclusively for AIDS patients.

Journalist William Safire criticized Anderson and Van Atta in *The New York Times*, saying "Doctors with some sense of ethics and journalists with some regard for a core of human privacy are shamed by [this] investigative excess."[13] After Cohn's death, *Harper's* magazine published copies of the hospital records on which Van Atta had based his column.

Liberace's illness was first revealed in the *Las Vegas Sun* about two weeks before he died. *Sun* publisher Brian Greenspun appeared on ABC's *Nightline* to defend publishing the information before the entertainer's death. Because only the *Sun* had access to the documentation, other members of the media who wrote about Liberace's illness attributed the information to the *Sun*. After Liberace died, the Riverside County coroner confirmed that Liberace suffered from a disease caused by AIDS.

A third example of a story about someone dying of AIDS represents one journalist's answer to the debate. *Honolulu Star-Bulletin* managing editor Bill Cox announced in a column published September 1, 1986, that he was going on disability leave because he had AIDS. "As a journalist," he wrote, "I have spent my career trying to shed light in dark corners. AIDS is surely one of our darkest corners. It can use some light."[14]

Reporting on Rape

Privacy is an important issue in reporting on rape cases. Common newsroom practice forbids the naming of rape victims in stories. In 1989, editor Geneva Overholser of *The Des Moines Register* startled the press community when she wrote an editorial arguing that newspapers contribute to the public's misunderstanding of the crime by withholding not only the woman's name, but an explicit description of what happened.

In 1990, the *Register* published a five-part series about the rape of Nancy Ziegenmeyer, with Ziegenmeyer's full cooperation. Ziegenmeyer had contacted the *Register* after Overholser's column appeared, volunteering to tell her story. The Ziegenmeyer series has provoked wide-ranging debate among editors about this aspect of privacy.

Is there more benefit to society by printing the victim's name, with the victim's permission, than by withholding it? Should the press explicitly describe sexual crimes, or is that merely sensationalism, preying on the public's salacious curiosity?

The Cohn, Liberace and Ziegenmeyer cases demonstrate how complex privacy issues in today's society have become. When is it in the public interest to divulge personal information about individuals? Who should decide?

RESPONSIBILITY

The events that journalists choose to report and the way they use the information they gather reflect on the profession's sense of public responsibility. Most reporters realize that they often change the character of an event by covering that event. The mere presence of the media magnifies the importance of what happens.

The media can be exploited by people in trouble or by people who covet the notoriety that media coverage brings. The media can exploit an event for its shock value to try to attract an audience. The following two specific examples demonstrate how differently individual media organizations and individual members of the media interpret their responsibility to the public.

A Staged Accident Demonstration

In 1992, *Dateline NBC* broadcast a story questioning the safety of General Motors trucks. To demonstrate the alleged problems with the trucks, NBC hired a company to stage an accident. In the newsfootage of the accident used in the broadcast, the truck's gas tank appeared to explode on impact. General Motors threatened to sue NBC, saying the footage had been edited to give the appearance of an explosion, that the company hired by NBC to stage the crash used spark igniters to cause the fire, and that the staff of *Dateline NBC* knowingly aired footage that was an inaccurate portrayal of a staged event. This is example 4.

After a month-long NBC-commissioned investigation, NBC president Robert Wright admitted that NBC News employees made "'seriously flawed judgments' and violated numerous (news) division guidelines in putting together a much-criticized story." The president of NBC News, who originally denied the GM charges, was forced to resign, as were three staff members directly involved with the story. The reporter on the story, who said she had argued against using the footage, was reassigned.[15]

The NBC incident demonstrates the important responsibility that reporters share for the information they present to the public. The credibility of any news organization rests on the truthfulness of the information the reporters present, and slanting the information, or portraying inaccurate information, even in just one story, ultimately can cause readers and viewers to doubt the believability of all stories presented by that organization.

A Live TV Raid

In 1993, three Cable News Network reporters accompanied Fish and Wildlife agents in Jordan, Montana, on an investigation of a ranch owned by Paul Berger, 72. Dressed in street clothes, like the Fish and Wildlife agents, the reporters spent 10 hours searching the ranch, along with the agents. The agents targeted Berger because they said they had reason to believe he was

IMPACT digital

Internet Gossip Columnist Drudge Defends His Online Ethics

By Karen Kaplan

Matt Drudge screwed up his face and squirmed in his chair. The attacks were coming from both sides. To his right, Marty Kaplan, associate dean at USC's Annenberg School of Communications, was calling him a bottom feeder in the "information ecosystem" that is the news business. To his left, *Slate* Editor Michael Kinsley was taking easy shots at the man he once called—with some admiration, actually—an "unreliable source of information."

Drudge, arguably the Internet's premier news and gossip columnist, had heard such insults before. No less a media authority than *Columbia Journalism Review* Publisher Joan Konner had dismissed him as "your next-door neighbor gossiping over the electronic fence."

So Drudge struck back. He said that Konner hadn't talked to him or even read his electronic dispatch, known as the *Drudge Report,* before passing judgment.

"So," retorted Kinsley, "you were crushed that she doesn't have higher standards than you do?"

From an apartment in Hollywood, Drudge dishes dirt on politics and the entertainment industry. He rejects the label "journalist" in favor of "reporter," and once boasted of being 80% accurate.

At Annenberg, he tried to make the case that his brand of news reporting is the wave of the future. In his view, every hack with access to the World Wide Web is a poten-

AP/Wide World Photos

tial journalist. The established media are critical of him, he said, because they are threatened by the Internet's ability to undermine their control.

The argument wasn't entirely convincing, and neither were Drudge's attempts at looking wounded by the scorn it elicited.

Drudge: "I'm not welcome at any party in this town."

Kinsley: "You're having your 15 minutes of fame right now, and you're enjoying it."

Drudge: "You said it was over last summer."

Kinsley: "I was wrong. I was less than 80% accurate."

Despite the laughs, it's not all fun and games for Drudge anymore. He faces a $30-million libel suit from Sidney Blumenthal, a Clinton aide who, Drudge wrote, "has a spousal abuse past that has been effectively covered up."

The allegation was retracted almost immediately, but not before Drudge became a media establishment symbol for all that's wrong with the freewheeling Internet. The episode prompted a story in *The New York Times*…and a profile of Drudge in…*Vanity Fair.*

The irony, of course, is that by breaking the conventions of the media elite, Drudge has earned the high profile that gains him admission to their world. But that doesn't mean Drudge is prepared to accept them into his.

"They just don't know what to do with" the *Drudge Report,* he said. "But they're going to have to start accepting it."

Karen Kaplan, "Online Gossip Columnist Drudge Debates Establishment Media," *Los Angeles Times,* November 17, 1997, p. D-3. Reprinted by permission.

poisoning eagles who were preying on his sheep. During the aerial and ground search, agents wore recording devices that documented the raid for CNN.

"This was a case where government agents became reporters and reporters became government agents," asserted Berger's attorney, Henry Rossbacher. Eventually a jury found that Mr. Berger was not guilty of poisoning eagles, mainly because the search of the ranch did not turn up any poisoned eagles, although Berger was found guilty of lacing two sheep carcasses with poison, a misdemeanor. CNN aired the video of the raid in a 12-minute program called "Ring of Death," which portrayed the search as a complete success for the agents. Mr. Berger then sued CNN, claiming that the network violated his Fourth Amendment rights against unreasonable search and seizure. CNN admitted no wrongdoing. "Investigative journalism is an important part of today's television market and entitled to all the safeguards of the First Amendment," the network said.[16]

This case "raises ethical issues for the press, particularly at a time when new shows profiling law enforcement are proliferating, and reporters are increasingly eager to ride along on the execution of search warrants," reported *The Wall Street Journal.* "While a reporter's presence could work to a suspect's benefit—by keeping investigators from becoming abusive or bearing witness to a police failure to find incriminating evidence—critics worry that it more often than not inspires uncivil police theatrics. The allure of access often tempts the media into deals that give the authorities substantial power to shape both the content and timing of stories."[17]

Are members of the media, as CNN contends, merely conduits for information? Or do they have a responsibility to protect the interests of the people they cover—in this case, the innocent as well as the guilty? And how did CNN's presence during the ranch raids change the event from a private to a public arrest? Does CNN have any responsibility for the person involved to report who actually faced charges, of which he was eventually found innocent? How are the ethics of live TV coverage different from the ethics for print coverage of the same event?

Bizarro by Dan Piraro is reprinted by permission of Chronicle Features, San Francisco, CA.

PHILOSOPHICAL PRINCIPLES OF JOURNALISTIC ETHICS

Scholars can prescribe only guidelines for moral decisions because each situation presents its own special dilemmas. First it is important to understand the basic principles that underlie these philosophical discussions.

In their book *Media Ethics*, Clifford G. Christians, Kim B. Rotzoll and Mark Fackler identify five major philosophical principles underlying today's ethical decisions: Aristotle's golden mean, Kant's categorical imperative, Mill's principle of utility, Rawls' veil of ignorance and the Judeo-Christian view of persons as ends in themselves.

- *Aristotle's golden mean.* "Moral virtue is appropriate location between two extremes." This is a philosophy of moderation and compromise, often called the *golden mean.* The journalistic concept of fairness reflects this idea.

- *Kant's categorical imperative.* "Act on that maxim which you will to become a universal law." Eighteenth-century philosopher Immanuel Kant developed this idea, an extension of Aristotle's golden mean. Kant's test— that you make decisions based on principles that you want to be universally applied—is called the *categorical imperative.* This means you would act by asking yourself the question, "What if everyone acted this way?"

- *Mill's principle of utility.* "Seek the greatest happiness for the greatest number." In the 19th century, John Stuart Mill taught that the best decision is one with the biggest overall benefit for the most human beings.

- *Rawls' veil of ignorance.* "Justice emerges when negotiating without social differentiations." John Rawls' 20th-century theory supports an egalitarian society that asks everyone to work from a sense of liberty and basic respect for everyone, regardless of social position.

- *Judeo-Christian view of persons as ends in themselves.* "Love your neighbor as yourself." Under this longstanding ethic of religious heritage, people should care for one another—friends as well as enemies—equally and without favor. Trust in people and they will trust in you.[18]

In American society, none of these five philosophies operates independently. Ethical choices in many journalistic situations are not exquisitely simple. What is predictable about journalistic ethics is their unpredictability. Therefore, journalists generally adopt a philosophy of "situational" ethics: Because each circumstance is different, individual journalists must decide what is best in each situation.

Should the press adopt Rawls's idea of social equality and cover each person equally, or should public officials receive more scrutiny than others because they maintain a public trust? Is it a loving act in the Judeo-Christian tradition to allow bereaved parents the private sorrow of their child's death by drowning, or is the journalist contributing to society's greater good by warning others about the dangers of leaving a child unattended? Questions like these leave the press in a continually bubbling cauldron of ethical quandaries.

HOW THE MEDIA DEFINE ETHICS

Ethical dilemmas might seem easier to solve with a rule book nearby, and several professional media organizations have tried to codify ethical judgments to ensure the outcomes in difficult situations. Codes of ethics can be very general ("Truth is our ultimate goal"—Society of Professional Journalists); some are very specific ("We will no longer accept any complimentary tickets, dinners, junkets, gifts or favors of any kind"—*The San Bernardino* [California] *Sun*); and some are very personal ("I will try to tell people what they ought to know and avoid telling them what they want to hear, except when the two coincide, which isn't often"—CBS commentator Andy Rooney).[19]

Some ethical decisions carry legal consequences—for example, when a journalist reports embarrassing facts and invades someone's privacy (see Chapter 14). First Amendment protections shield the media from government enforcement of specific codes of conduct, except when ethical mistakes also are judged by the courts to be legal mistakes.

In most cases, however, a reporter or a news organization that makes an ethical mistake will not face a lawsuit. The consequences of bad ethical judgments usually involve damage to the newsmakers who are involved and to the individual journalist, damage to the reputation of the news organization where the journalist works and damage to the profession in general.

PROFESSIONAL ETHICS CODES

Professional codes of ethics set a leadership tone for a profession, an organization or an individual. Several groups have attempted to write rules governing how the media should operate. Television stations that belonged to the National Association of Broadcasters, for example, once subscribed to a code of conduct developed by the National Association of Broadcasters. This code covered news reporting and entertainment programming.

One provision of the NAB code said "Violence, physical or psychological, may only be projected in responsibly handled contexts, not used exploitatively. Programs involving violence should present the consequences of it to its victims and perpetrators." Members displayed the NAB Seal of Approval before broadcasts to exhibit their compliance with the code.

In 1976, a decision by a U.S. federal judge in Los Angeles abolished the broadcast codes, claiming that the provisions violated the First Amendment. Today, codes of ethics for both print and broadcast are voluntary, with no absolute penalties for people who violate the rules. These codes are meant as guidelines. Many media organizations, such as CBS News, maintain their own detailed standards and hire people to oversee ethical conduct. Other organizations use guidelines from professional groups as a basis to develop their own philosophies. Advertising and public relations organizations also have issued ethical codes.

Three widely used codes of ethics are the guidelines adopted by the Society of Professional Journalists, the Radio-Television News Directors Association and the Public Relations Society of America.

The Society of Professional Journalists Code of Ethics. This code lists specific canons for journalists. Following are the code's major points:

> ***Seek Truth and Report It.*** Test the accuracy of information from all sources and exercise care to avoid inadvertent error. Deliberate distortion is never permissible.

> • Identify sources whenever feasible. The public is entitled to as much information as possible on sources' reliability.

> • Make certain that headlines, news teases and promotional material, photos, video, audio, graphics, sound bites and quotations do not misrepresent. They should not oversimplify or highlight incidents out of context.

- Never distort the content of news photos or video. Image enhancement for technical clarity is always permissible. Label montages and photo illustrations.

- Avoid misleading reenactments or staged news events.

- Never plagiarize.

- Avoid stereotyping by race, gender, age, religion, ethnicity, geography, sexual orientation, disability, physical appearance or social status.

- Distinguish between advocacy and news reporting. Analysis and commentary should be labeled and not misrepresent fact or context.

- Distinguish news from advertising and shun hybrids that blur the lines between the two.

- Recognize a special obligation to ensure that the public's business is conducted in the open and that government records are open to inspection.

Minimize Harm. Show compassion for those who may be affected adversely by news coverage. Use special sensitivity when dealing with children and inexperienced sources or subjects.

- Be sensitive when seeking or using interviews or photographs of those affected by tragedy or grief.

- Recognize that gathering and reporting information may cause harm or discomfort. Pursuit of the news is not a license for arrogance.

- Show good taste. Avoid pandering to lurid curiosity.

- Balance a criminal suspect's fair trial rights with the public's right to be informed.

Act Independently. Avoid conflicts of interest, real or perceived.

- Remain free of associations and activities that may compromise integrity or damage credibility.

- Refuse gifts, favors, fees, free travel and special treatment, and shun secondary employment, political involvement, public office and service in community organizations if they compromise journalistic integrity.

Be Accountable. Clarify and explain news coverage and invite dialogue with the public over journalistic conduct.

- Encourage the public to voice grievances against the news media.

- Admit mistakes and correct them promptly.

- Expose unethical practices of journalists and the news media.

- Abide by the same high standards to which they hold others.[20]

Radio-Television News Directors Association Code of Broadcast News Ethics. The RTNDA offers a seven-point program for broadcasters:

1. *Strive to present the source or nature of broadcast news material in a way that is balanced, accurate and fair.*

   A. *They will evaluate information solely on its merits as news, rejecting sensationalism or misleading emphasis in any form.*

   B. *They will guard against using audio or video material in a way that deceives the audience.*

C. *They will not mislead the public by presenting as spontaneous news any material which is staged or rehearsed.*

D. *They will identify people by race, creed, nationality or prior status only when it is relevant.*

E. *They will clearly label opinion and commentary.*

F. *They will promptly acknowledge and correct errors.*

2. *Strive to conduct themselves in a manner that protects them from conflicts of interest, real or perceived. They will decline gifts or favors which would influence or appear to influence their judgments.*

3. *Respect the dignity, privacy and well-being of people with whom they deal.*

4. *Recognize the need to protect confidential sources. They will promise confidentiality only with the intention of keeping that promise.*

5. *Respect everyone's right to a fair trial.*

6. *Broadcast the private transmissions of other broadcasters only with permission.*

7. *Actively encourage observance of this Code by all journalists, whether members of the Radio-Television News Directors Association or not.*[21]

The Public Relations Society of America Standards. The Code of Professional Standards, first adopted in 1950 by the Public Relations Society of America, has been revised several times since then. Here are some excerpts:

- A member shall deal fairly with clients or employers, past, present, or potential, with fellow practitioners, and with the general public.

- A member shall adhere to truth and accuracy and to generally accepted standards of good taste.

- A member shall not intentionally communicate false or misleading information, and is obligated to use care to avoid communication of false or misleading information.

- A member shall be prepared to identify publicly the name of the client or employer on whose behalf any public communication is made.

- A member shall not guarantee the achievement of specified results beyond the member's direct control.[22]

THE MEDIA'S RESPONSE TO CRITICISM

Prescriptive codes of ethics are helpful in describing what journalists should do, and informal guidelines can supplement professional codes (see Impact/Point of View, "The Ethicist: I'm Not a Prude, but..."). Moreover, most journalists use good judgment. But what happens when they don't? People with serious complaints against broadcasters sometimes appeal to the Federal Communications Commission (see Broadcast Regulation, Chapter 14), but what about complaints that must be handled more quickly? The press has offered three solutions: press councils, readers' representatives and correction boxes.

News Councils

News councils originated in Great Britain. They are composed of people who formerly worked or currently work in the news business, as well as some laypeople. The council reviews complaints from the public, and when the members determine that a mistake has been made, the council reports its findings to the offending news organization.

In 1973, the Twentieth-Century Fund established a National News Council in the United States, which eventually was funded through contributions from various news organizations. The council was composed of 18 members from the press and the public. The council was disbanded in 1984, largely because some major news organizations stopped giving money to support the idea, but also because several news managers opposed the council, arguing that the profession should police itself.

Today, only two news councils exist in the United States, the Minnesota News Council and the Honolulu Community Media Council. The Minnesota council is the oldest. Since 1970, the council's 24 members, half of them journalists and half of them public members such as lawyers and teachers, have reviewed complaints about the state's media. Half of the complaints have been ruled in favor of the journalists.

The council has no enforcement power, only the power of public scrutiny.[23] Media ethics scholar John Hulteng writes:

> It would seem that—as with the [ethical] codes—the great impact of the press councils is likely to be on the responsible editors, publishers and broadcasters who for the most part were already attempting to behave ethically… An additional value of the councils may be the mutual understanding that grows out of the exchange across the council table between the members of the public and the managers of the media. These values should not be dismissed as insignificant, of course. But neither should too much be expected of them.[24]

Readers' Representatives

The *readers' representative* (also called an ombudsperson) is a go-between at a newspaper who responds to complaints from the public and regularly publishes answers to criticism in the newspaper. About two dozen newspapers throughout the country, including the *Washington Post, The Kansas City Star* and the Louisville *Courier-Journal*, have tried the idea, but most newspapers still funnel complaints directly to the editor.

Correction Boxes

The *correction box* is a device that often is handled by a readers' representative but that also has been adopted by many papers without a readers' representative. The box is published in the same place, usually a prominent one, in the newspaper every day. As a permanent feature of the newspaper, the correction box leads readers to notice when the newspaper retracts or modifies a statement. It is used to counter criticism that corrections sometimes receive less attention from readers than the original stories.

THE IMPORTANCE OF PROFESSIONAL ETHICS

Readers' representatives and correction boxes help newspapers handle criticism and to avert possible legal problems that some stories foster. But these solutions address only a small percentage of issues. In newsrooms every day, reporters face the same ethical decisions that all people face in their daily

I M P A C T

point of view

By Randy Cohen

*I am the father of two early-adoles-
cent boys, who are both active Web
surfers. I'm not a prude, but I
think exposure to the more extreme
sexual images available online is not
a good thing at their ages. I could
retain a secret list of the Web sites they
visit. But is that ethical? Is it equivalent to putting a hidden TV camera in
their room (which I would consider a
violation of their privacy), or is it an
acceptable way for a parent to keep
informed and be able to initiate discussion of this tricky topic?*
—William S. Kessler, Seattle

The Ethicist: I'm Not a Prude, but…

Illustration by Christoph Niemann

Your concern for your sons'
well-being necessitates neither
that you cast them adrift in a
sea of disturbing pornography
nor that you abandon your
respect for their privacy and fill
your house with hidden cameras, tiny microphones and
cagey men in dark glasses who
would make everyone uneasy at
the dinner table.

There's nothing wrong with
being involved with what your
kids see online; it is deception
that is unsettling. Just as you
probably wouldn't sneak a look at
their diaries to learn what they're
writing, you shouldn't surrepti-
tiously tap their computer to find
out what they're reading. If you
intend to retain a list of the sites
they visit, tell them. That way,
you can discuss those sites with
them, just as you might discuss a
book that you saw them reading
around the house.

But especially at this age, your
boys may find any parental
scrutiny—even of the most
innocuous activities—embarrassing. The problem is balancing
their right to free inquiry with
your duty to shield them from
truly disturbing images. And here
the solution is not a technical fix
but the more difficult task of
teaching your kids a system of
values. Part of that system
reserves certain activities—drinking, driving, perusing pornography—for adults.

In any case, just as the boys can
hide an ugly and upsetting magazine under the bed, they can
browse online pornography with
a friend's computer. But by creating a situation at home in which
conversation is encouraged and
privacy is respected, you have a
better chance of helping them
deal with the rough stuff.

The New York Times Magazine, July 25,
1999, p. 18. Reprinted by permission of
the author.

lives—whether to be honest, how to be fair, how to be sensitive and
how to be responsible.

The difference is that, unlike personal ethical dilemmas that other
people can debate privately, reporters and editors publish and broadcast the results of their ethical judgments and those judgments become

public knowledge—in newspapers, magazines, books and on radio and television. So potentially, the media's ethical decisions can broadly affect society.

A profession that accepts ethical behavior as a standard helps guarantee a future for that profession. The major commodity that the press in America has to offer is information, and when the presentation of that information is weakened by untruth, bias, intrusiveness or irresponsibility, the press gains few advocates and acquires more enemies. Writes John Hulteng:

> *The primary objective of the press and those who work with it is to bring readers, listeners, and viewers as honest, accurate, and complete an account of the day's events as possible....The need to be informed is so great that the Constitution provides the press with a First Amendment standing that is unique among business enterprises. But as with most grants of power, there is an accompanying responsibility, not constitutionally mandated but nonetheless well understood: that the power of the press must be used responsibly and compassionately.[25]*

IN FOCUS

- The word *ethics* derives from the Greek word *ethos*, which means the guiding spirit or traditions that govern a culture.

- Journalists' ethical dilemmas can be discussed using four categories: truthfulness, fairness, privacy and responsibility.

- Truthfulness means more than telling the truth to get a story. Truthfulness also means not misrepresenting the people or the situations in the story to readers or viewers.

- Truthfulness also means that government agencies should not knowingly provide disinformation to the press.

- Fairness implies impartiality. Criticism of the press for unfairness results from insider friendships, conflicts of interest and checkbook journalism.

- Two important invasion-of-privacy issues are the publication of names of AIDS victims and the publication of the names of rape victims.

- Responsibility means that reporters and editors must be careful about the way they use the information they gather.

- Staged events, such as the GM truck explosion, and live events, such as the ranch raids broadcast by CNN, offer especially perilous ethical situations.

- Five philosophical principles underlying the practical application of ethical decisions are: Aristotle's golden mean, Immanuel Kant's categorical imperative, John Stuart Mill's principle of utility, John Rawls's veil of ignorance and the Judeo-Christian view of persons as ends in themselves.

- Several media professions have adopted ethical codes to guide their conduct. Three of these codes are the guidelines adopted by the Society of Professional Journalists, the Radio-Television News Directors Association and the Public Relations Society of America.

- The U.S. press's three responses to press criticism have been to create news councils, to employ readers' representatives and to publish correction boxes. The National Press Council, created in 1973, was disbanded in 1984.

- Today only two news councils still exist in the United States—the Minnesota News Council and the Honolulu Community Media Council.

WORKING THE WEB www

- **Drudge Report**
  www.drudgereport.com
- **The New Media Monitor**
  www.gpnet.it/dallomo
- **Radio-Television News Directors Ethics Codes**
  www.missouri.edu/~jourvs
- **Smoking Gun (public documents about celebrities and public figures)**
  www.smokinggun.com

INFOTRAC COLLEGE EDITION EXERCISES

Using the InfoTrac College Edition's fully searchable online database of articles and abstracts, do the following exercises as directed by your instructor.

1. Read "Impact/Point of View: The Diana Effect: Will Anything Change?" in Chapter 15. Then, using InfoTrac College Edition, enter keywords "Princess Diana media" to find what's been written in the wake of her death about media coverage. Print at least three articles and either:

   a. write a brief paper on your findings, or

   b. bring the articles to class for a small-group discussion.

2. Search for articles on InfoTrac College Edition using the keywords "media ethics," "TV news ethics" or "journalism ethics." Cite a specific case in which a journalist's (or news organization's) ethics were questioned or condemned. Bring the article to class for discussion. Consider which of the five major philosophical principles underlying ethical decisions listed in Chapter 15 applies to your case.

3. Consider one of the people criticized in the past 20 years for their questionable ethical practices. Using InfoTrac College Edition, you might look up "Janet Cooke" (the *Washington Post* reporter fired for making up a character in a story) or "Stephen Glass," (the *New Republic* reporter caught inventing sources and plagiarizing). Print at least three articles about the person you're researching, and either:

   a. write a brief paper on your findings, or

   b. bring the articles to class and be prepared to do a brief talk about your subject.

4. Read "Impact/Digital: Internet Gossip Columnist Drudge Defends His Online Ethics" in Chapter 15. Then use keywords "Matt Drudge" or "Drudge Report" to find more information on Matt Drudge. Print at least two articles and bring them to class for discussion.

5. Using keywords "media ombudsmen" or "ombudsmen," search for more information on the role of readers' representatives in news organizations. What other kinds of professions have ombudspersons? Print at least two articles, and either:

   a. write a brief paper on your findings, or

   b. bring the articles to class and be prepared to discuss them.

16

A GLOBAL Media marketplace

A

s the (*universe*) behind the screen expands, it will be the people in front who shape the soul of the new machine.

The Economist, "Wired Planet," February 1994

What's Ahead

Students of the media often assume that media in most countries throughout the world operate like the U.S. media. But media industries in different countries are as varied as the countries they serve. Can you identify the countries in the following media situations?

1. Citizens of this country woke up one morning to find that, overnight, their leader had shut down several independent newspapers and broadcast stations. Heavily armed police raided the media outlets and shut them down.

2. In this country, a weekly TV game show features people eating overly spicy foods. The champion is dubbed Super Spiciness King.

3. In this country, a program called *Youth TV* broadcasts racy rock videos, professional wrestling from Madison Square Garden and Oliver Stone's epic *J.F.K.* The station is run by the son of the government's leader.

4. This country's TV License Police can knock on the door of someone's house, fine the person $150 and threaten him or her with jail if the person doesn't pay the annual TV license fee.

DIFFERING STANDARDS OF PRACTICE

The armed police raid in example 1 took place in Nigeria in 1993, when the country's ruler, General Ibrahim Babangida, raided newspapers and magazines owned by his primary rival, millionaire business tycoon Moshood Abiola. One year later, the Nigerian government closed newspapers that were critical of the military government.

The TV game show with the spicy cast (example 2) is very popular in Japan, where *TV Champion* is one of several shows in which contestants vie for modest prizes and national attention by showing *gaman*, or endurance.

The manager of the station where *Youth TV* appears (example 3) is Uday Hussein, Saddam Hussein's son. His station, Channel 2, began broadcasting the new format in 1993. Iraq's Culture Minister Hamid Youssel Hammadi told the *Los Angeles Times,* "We don't want our youth to be more or less split from what is going on outside."

The British are responsible for paying a yearly TV license fee (example 4). The fee is due at the post office each year, so the collectors who find people who haven't paid the fee are actually members of the post office. The government collects more than $2 billion a year from the fees, which allows the British Broadcasting Corporation (BBC) to operate two TV stations without advertising.[1]

These examples help demonstrate the complexity of defining today's international media marketplace, which clearly is a marketplace in rapid transition. This chapter examines four aspects of the global media: (1) the media and government, (2) world media systems, (3) news and information flow and (4) global media markets.

Television owners in Britain pay an annual license fee that supports the British Broadcasting Corporation (BBC). (The BBC news room is shown here).

Courtesy BBC News

POLITICAL THEORIES AND THE MEDIA

No institution as sizable and influential as the mass media can escape involvement with government and politics. The media are not only channels for the transmission of political information and debate, but also significant players with a direct stake in government's regulatory and economic policies, as well as government's attitude toward free speech and dissent. Remember that *the way a country's political system is organized affects the way the media within that country operate.* Media systems can be divided broadly into those systems that allow dissent and those that do not.

To categorize the political organization of media systems, scholars often begin with the 1956 book *Four Theories of the Press,* by Fred S. Siebert, Theodore Peterson and Wilbur Schramm. These four theories, which were originally used to describe the political systems under which media operated in different countries, were: (1) the Soviet theory, (2) the authoritarian theory, (3) the libertarian theory, and (4) the social responsibility theory. A fifth description, the more modern *developmental theory,* updates the original categories.

The Soviet Theory. Historically in the Soviet Union (which dissolved in 1991 into several independent nations and states), the government owned and operated the mass media. All media employees were government employees, expected to serve the government's interests.

Top media executives also served as leaders in the Communist party. Even when the press controls loosened in the 1980s, the mass media were part of the government's policy. Government control came *before* the media published or broadcast; people who controlled the media could exercise *prior restraint.* They could review copy and look at programs before they appeared.

This description of the Soviet press system was conceived before the events of the 1990s challenged the basic assumptions of Soviet government. Many Eastern bloc countries, such as Romania, Slovakia, and the Czech Republic which once operated under Soviet influence, based their media systems on the communist model. Today, the media systems in these countries are in transition.

The Authoritarian Theory. Media that operate under the authoritarian theory can be either publicly or privately owned. This concept of the press developed in Europe after Gutenberg. Until the 1850s, presses in Europe were privately owned, and the aristocracy (which governed the countries) wanted some sort of control over what was printed about them. The aristocracy had the financial and political power necessary to make the rules about what would be printed.

Their first idea was to license everyone who owned a press so that the license could be revoked if someone published something unfavorable about the government. The first colonial newspapers in America, for example, were licensed by the British crown. Licensing wasn't very successful in the United States, however, because many people who owned presses didn't apply for licenses.

The next authoritarian attempt to control the press was to review material after it was published. A printer who was discovered publishing material that strongly challenged the government could be heavily fined or even put to death.

Today, many governments still maintain this type of rigid control over the media. Most monarchies, for example, operate in an authoritarian tradition, which tolerates very little dissent. Media systems that serve at the government's pleasure and with the government's approval are common.

*"And, finally, after a day of record trading on Wall Street,
the entire world was owned by Mickey Mouse."*

The Libertarian Theory. The concept of a libertarian press evolved from
the idea that people who are given all of the information on an issue will be
able to discern what is true and what is false and will make good choices. This
is an idea embraced by the writers of the U.S. Constitution and by other
democratic governments.

This theory assumes, of course, that the media's main goal is to convey the
truth and that the media will not cave in to outside pressures, such as from
advertisers or corporate owners. This theory also assumes that people with
opposing viewpoints will be heard—that the media will present all points of
view, in what is commonly called the free marketplace of ideas.

The First Amendment to the U.S. Constitution concisely advocates the idea
of freedom of the press. Theoretically, America today operates under the libertarian theory, although this ideal has been challenged often by changes in
the media industries since the Constitution was adopted.

The Social Responsibility Theory. This theory accepts the concept of a libertarian press but prescribes what the media should do. Someone who
believes in the social responsibility theory believes that members of the press
will do their jobs well only if periodically reminded about their duties.

This theory grew out of the 1947 Hutchins Commission Report on the Free
and Responsible Press. The commission listed five goals for the press, including
the need for truthful and complete reporting of all sides of an issue. The commission concluded that the American press's privileged position in the Constitution means that the press must always work to be responsible to society.[2]

If the media fail to meet their responsibilities to society, the social responsibility theory holds that the government should encourage the media to comply. In this way the libertarian and the social responsibility theories differ. The
libertarian theory assumes the media will work well without government
interference; the social responsibility theory advocates government oversight
for media that don't act in society's best interest.

The Developmental Theory. A fifth description for media systems that can
be added to describe today's media has been called the developmental or
Third World theory. Under this system, named for the developing nations

where it is most often found, the media *can* be privately owned, but usually are owned by the government. The media are used to promote the country's social and economic goals, and to direct a sense of national purpose. For example, a developmental media system might be used to promote birth control or to encourage children to attend school. The media become an outlet for some types of government propaganda, then, but in the name of economic and social progress for the country.

Although the theory that best describes the American media is the libertarian theory, throughout their history the American media have struggled with both authoritarian and social responsibility debates: Should the press be free to print secret government documents, for example? What responsibility do the networks have to provide worthwhile programming to their audiences? The media, the government, and the public continually modify and adjust their interpretations of just how the media should operate.

WORLD MEDIA SYSTEMS

It has been nearly five decades since scholars began using the four theories of the press to define the world's media systems. With today's transitional period in global history, even the recent addition of the developmental theory still leaves many media systems beyond convenient categorization.

Media systems vary throughout the world. The print media form the basis for press development in North America, Australia, Western Europe and Eastern Europe, where two-thirds of the world's newspapers are published.[3] Many developing countries matured after broadcast media were introduced in the 1920s, and newsprint in these countries often is scarce or government controlled, making radio their dominant communications medium. Radio receivers are inexpensive, and many people can share one radio.

Television, which relies on expensive equipment, is widely used in prosperous nations and in developing countries' urban areas. Yet most countries still have only one television service, usually run by the government.[4] In most developing countries all broadcasting—television and radio—is owned and controlled by the government.

What follows is a description of today's media systems by region: Western Europe and Canada, Eastern Europe, the Middle East and North Africa, Africa, Asia and the Pacific and Latin America and the Caribbean.

WESTERN EUROPE AND CANADA

Western European and Canadian media prosper under guarantees of freedom of expression similar to the First Amendment, but each nation has modified the idea to reflect differing values. For example, in Great Britain the media are prohibited from commenting on a trial until the trial is finished. France and Greece, unlike the United States, give more libel protection to public figures than to private citizens.

Scandinavian journalists enjoy the widest press freedoms of all of Western Europe, including almost unlimited access to public documents. Of the Western nations, Canada is the most recent country to issue an official decree supporting the philosophy of press freedom. In 1982, Canada adopted the Canadian Charter of Rights and Freedoms. Before 1982, Canada did not have its own constitution, and instead operated under the 1867 British North America Act, sharing the British free press philosophy.[5]

Print Media

Johannes Gutenberg's invention of movable type rooted the print media in Western Europe. Today, Western European and Canadian media companies produce many fine newspapers. *The Globe and Mail* of Toronto, *The Times* of London, *Frankfurter Allgemeine* of Germany, *Le Monde* of France and Milan's *Corriere della Sera* enjoy healthy circulations. Whereas Canadian journalists seem to have adopted the U.S. value of fairness as a journalistic ethic, Western European newspapers tend to be much more partisan than the U.S. or Canadian press, and newspapers (and journalists) are expected to reflect strong points of view.

Audio and Video Media

As in the United States, the print media in Western Europe are losing audiences to broadcast and cable. (See Figure 16.1.) Government originally controlled most of Western Europe's broadcast stations. A board of 12 governors, appointed by the queen, supervises the British Broadcasting Corporation (BBC), for example. To finance the government-run broadcast media, countries tax the sale of radios and TVs or charge users an annual fee. Broadcasting in Western Europe is slowly evolving to private ownership and commercial sponsorship.

Western Europeans watch less than half as much television as people in the United States—an average of three hours a day per household in Europe, compared to seven hours a day per household in the United States. One reason for

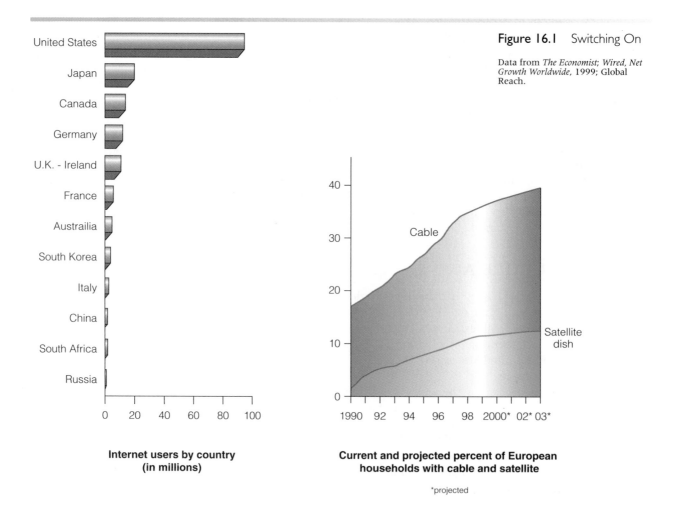

Figure 16.1   Switching On

Data from *The Economist; Wired, Net Growth Worldwide*, 1999; Global Reach.

Internet users by country (in millions)

Current and projected percent of European households with cable and satellite

*projected

the difference in viewing time may be that most Western European TV stations don't go on the air until late afternoon. In the majority of countries, commercials are shown back-to-back at the beginning or the end of a program.[6]

Europe gets much of its programming from the United States. Of the 125,000 hours of TV broadcast in Western Europe each year, only 20,000 hours are produced in Europe. Most of the programming comes from the United States, with a few shows imported from Australia and Japan.[7] U.S. imports are attractive because programs such as *L.A. Law*, which is very popular in Western Europe, are cheaper to buy than to produce.

The European Union (EU) constitutes a single, unified European market. The policy adopted by the EU is "Television Without Frontiers," which promotes an open marketplace for television programs among countries in the EU and between EU countries and the United States.

Some members of the EU (especially France) have proposed quotas to limit imported TV programs, charging that the U.S. imports are an example of "cultural imperialism." Countries that favor quotas fear that the importation of U.S. programs imposes a concentration of U.S. values on their viewers. The United States opposes such quotas, of course, because Western European commercial broadcasting offers a seemingly insatiable market for recycled U.S. programs.

EASTERN EUROPE

The democratization of Eastern Europe is transforming the media in these countries at an unprecedented pace. Some examples:

- In the six months after the Berlin Wall opened in 1990, circulation of East Germany's national newspapers *Neues Deutschland* and *Junge Welt* dropped 55 percent as the East German population, hungry for news from the West, embraced the flashy West German mass circulation daily *Bild*.[8]

- In Poland, Eastern Europe's first private television station, Echo, went on the air in February 1990, with a total cash investment of $15,000. The station broadcast programs from the windowless janitor's room of a student dormitory.[9]

- One week after the 1991 failed coup in the Soviet Union, President Mikhail Gorbachev fired the directors of the Soviet news agency, TASS, who had supported the coup.[10] Then, on December 25, 1991, Gorbachev resigned. Within 24 hours, President Boris N. Yeltsin of Russia announced that the government would maintain control of the nation's broadcast media. TASS moved away from government control and was renamed RITA (Russian Information Telegraph Agency).

Everette E. Dennis, executive director of the Gannett Center for Media Studies, and Jon Vanden Heuvel described the Eastern European challenges in a report issued after a Gannett-sponsored 1990 fact-finding trip:

Mass communication in the several countries of the region was reinventing itself. While grassroots newspapers and magazines struggled for survival, new press laws were being debated and enacted; elements of a market economy were coming into view; the media system itself and its role in the state and society were being redefined, as was the very nature of journalism and the job description of the journalist, who was no longer a propagandist for the state.[11]

Eastern Europe in transition is defining a new balance between the desire for free expression and the indigenous remnants of a government-controlled system.

IMPACT digital

Foie Gras and Chips, Anyone? Internet Shopping Is (Sort of) Catching On in Europe

By John Tagliabue

Milan, Italy—Maria Paola Sassella is often amused by her customers, who are experimenting with what for Europeans is still unfamiliar practice: shopping on the World Wide Web.

For the last year, her company, Vino Please, has been selling wines online (www.vinoplease.it). Customers click on Chianti and Brunello wines to have them delivered anywhere in Italy, and to Germany and Japan—or indeed any country where such sales are permitted. (The United States is not among them.)

"Some examine my products on the Internet, then fax the order in," Ms. Sassella said, with a mix of bemusement and desperation. Many do not pay with a credit card, but pay later by making a bank transfer. Moreover,

Cristiano Cora sends a case of wine on its merry way to an online client of Vino Please.

James Hill for *The New York Times*

she added, with a sigh of resignation, almost all her customers are men, who so far dominate Europe's corner of cyberspace.

While Americans have embraced online shopping, Europeans are just now warming to electronic commerce. From designing her Internet site and persuading diffident wine growers to supply products, Ms. Sassella has received an education in how difficult it is to convince Europeans, who have plenty of small shops and age-old shopping habits, that they should shop on the Web.

Online shopping accounted for just $1.2 billion of Europe's $1.9 trillion in retail sales last year, compared with $8 billion in online sales and $2.6 trillion in total sales in the United States, according to Forrester Research, a market research firm based in Cambridge, Mass.

Yet Ms. Sassella, who is based in Milan, and other European online entrepreneurs, have reasons to be optimistic. Internet use is rising in Europe as its cost falls, thanks in large part to the deregulation of telecommunications. Governments, troubled by Europe's lag behind North America, are pushing for more Internet use in schools, and at work and home. And the introduction of the euro in 11 European countries is giving electronic commerce an additional boost because a single currency makes billing and price comparisons easier.

As a result, online stores are spreading like brush fire. More than 400 operate in Italy, com-

pared with 13 just two years ago. In Germany, more than 1,200 online stores now sell books, and book sales per capita rival those in the United States.

"We always start late," Ms. Sassella said, "but then it takes off."

The New York Times, March 27, 1999, B-1. Reprinted by permission.

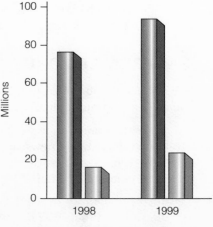

Total internet users

United States ▮   Europe ▮

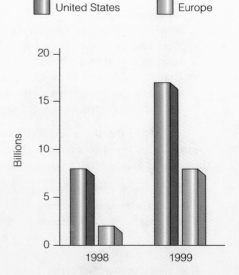

Total online purchases

The New York Times.

In many of these countries, the media played a central role in upsetting the established power structure. Often one of the first targets of the revolutionary movements was the nation's broadcast facilities. For example, in Romania in 1989, opposition leaders of the National Salvation Committee and sympathetic employees barricaded themselves in a Bucharest TV station, rallying the audience to action. "Romania was governed from a hectic studio littered with empty bottles, cracked coffee mugs and half-eaten sandwiches, and run by people who had not slept in days," the Associated Press reported.[12]

Audio and Video Media

Television in the Eastern bloc countries developed under Communist direction because the Communist governments were in power before TV use was widespread. Radio broadcasting also was tightly controlled, although foreign broadcasts directed across Eastern European borders, such as *Voice of America* and *Radio Free Europe,* usually evaded jamming attempts by Radio Moscow.

Print Media

Print media were controlled strictly under communism, with high-ranking party officials forming the core of media management. Because paper supplies were limited, newspapers rarely exceeded 12 pages. *Pravda,* the Soviet Union's oldest newspaper, was founded in 1912 by revolutionary leader Vladimir Lenin, who said that a newspaper should be a "collective propagandist," a "collective agitator" and a "collective organizer."[13] The Eastern European nations developed their press policies following the Soviet model.

In the late 1980s, President Mikhail Gorbachev relaxed media controls as part of his policy of *glasnost.* In 1988, the first paid commercials (for Pepsi-Cola, Sony and Visa credit cards) appeared on Soviet TV, and in 1989, the Soviet daily newspaper *Izvestia* published its first Western ads (including ads for perfume and wines from the French firm Pechiney and for Dresdner, a German bank).

In 1990, the Supreme Soviet outlawed media censorship and gave every citizen the right to publish a newspaper.[14] Within five months, more than 100 newspapers began publication. Then, showing how quickly government positions can change, in early 1991 Gorbachev asked the Supreme Soviet to suspend these press freedoms, but they refused.[15] Less than a year later, the Soviet Union had been replaced by the Commonwealth of Independent States, and Gorbachev's successor, President Boris Yeltsin, continued to relax government control of the press. In 1996, facing bankruptcy, *Pravda* ceased publication.

As the Eastern European governments change and realign themselves, the adjustments facing Eastern European media are unprecedented. According to Dennis and Vanden Heuvel:

> *Once the revolution came, among the first acts of new government was to take (they would say liberate) electronic media and open up the print press. Permitting free and eventually independent media was a vital beginning for democracy in several countries and a clear break with the past. The freeing up of the media system, speedily in some countries and incrementally in others, was the lifting of an ideological veil without saying just what would replace it.[16]*

MIDDLE EAST AND NORTH AFRICA

Press history in the Middle East and North Africa begins with the newspaper *Al-Iraq,* first published in 1817, although the first daily newspaper didn't begin until 1873. With one exception, development of the press throughout this region follows the same pattern as in most developing countries: More newspapers and magazines are published in regions with high literacy rates than in regions with low literacy rates. The exception is Egypt, where less than half the people are literate. Yet Cairo is the Arab world's publishing center.[17] *Al Ahram* and *Al Akhbar* are Egypt's leading dailies.

Print Media

The Middle Eastern press is controlled tightly by government restrictions, through ownership and licensing, and it is not uncommon for opposition newspapers to disappear and for journalists to be jailed or to leave the country following political upheaval.

> *Following the revolution in Iran, all opposition and some moderate newspapers were closed, and according to the National Union of Iranian Journalists (now an illegal organization), more than 75 percent of all journalists left the country, were jailed, or no longer work in journalism.*[18]

The Palestinian press, for example, was subject to censorship by the Israeli government, and all Palestinian newspapers and magazines once required permission from the Israeli government to be published.[19]

Audio and Video Media

The foreign-language press is especially strong in the Middle East because of the large number of immigrants in the area, and foreign radio is very popular. Radio and television are controlled almost completely by the governments within each country, and television stations in smaller countries (Sudan and Yemen, for example) broadcast only a few hours beginning in mid-afternoon.

In the larger Arab states (Jordan, Lebanon, Saudi Arabia and Egypt) TV stations typically broadcast from early morning until midnight. Radio signals beamed from Europe have become one of the region's alternative, affordable sources of news.

> *Because of tight censorship, newspapers and television stations in the Arab world frequently reflect the biases or outright propaganda of their governments. But radio broadcasts from outside the region travel easily across borders and long distances, and many Arabs regard those stations as the most reliable sources of unbiased news.* [20]

The BBC (based in London) and Radio Monte Carlo Middle East (based in Paris) are the main across-the-border program sources.

Also, because of careful government control of television programming, another alternative medium has emerged—the VCR.

> *Saudi Arabia and some of the Gulf countries have the highest VCR penetration levels in the world, in spite of the high cost of the equipment. And since only Egypt, Turkey, Lebanon, and Israel [of the Gulf countries] have copyright laws, pirated films from Europe, the United States, India, and Egypt circulate widely in most countries.... The widespread availability of content that cannot be viewed on television or at the cinema (Saudi Arabia even forbids the construction of cinemas) has reduced the popularity of broadcast programming.*[21]

In the Middle East, as in other developing regions, the government-owned media are perceived as instruments of each country's social and political programs. The rapid spread of technological developments such as the VCR, however, demonstrates new challenges to the insulated Middle Eastern media cocoon.

IMPACT

profile   *Journalists Downplay Personal Courage*

An acid attack that may yet cost Anna Zarkova her sight in one eye does not deter her from reporting crime and corruption for *Trud Daily* in Bulgaria. "I'm just one of many (journalists) who are taking risks," she says. "Change is needed in the system and I'm contributing to that change."

Zarkova, whose reporting has brought threats upon her and her family, was at a bus stop in May when an attacker splashed sulfuric acid on her, badly burning her face. She was one of three women to receive the International Women's Media Foundation Courage in Journalism Award Oct. 19. Like Zarkova, co-recipients Blanca Rosales of *La República* in Lima, Peru, and Elizabeth Neuffer of *The Boston Globe* downplayed their personal courage and spoke instead of doing the right thing.

"I'm not brave," said Neuffer, European bureau chief for the *Globe*, who has reported from Kuwait, Bosnia, Rwanda and Kosovo. "I just got angry [at what I saw] and felt like I couldn't live with myself unless I spoke out."

Rosales has targeted corruption in Peru. In turn, she has been called a threat to national security, and at one point was abducted, held at gunpoint and taunted for several hours before being released. "I have no great courage," she said. "It has more to do with the anger—that makes us capable of facing the challenges."

In a panel discussion moderated by ABC News' Carol Simpson, the three shared the stage with Bonnie Angelo of *Time*, a Lifetime Achievement Award recipient, and Chris Anyanwu, editor of *The Sunday Magazine*, in Lagos, Nigeria.

Anyanwu was a 1995 Courage in Journalism Award winner, but in June of that year was charged with treason for opposing a crackdown on the media by Nigeria's dictator. She was sentenced to life in prison but was freed…after the death of dictator Sani Abachi.

The Freedom Forum and Newseum News, November 1998, p. 10.

Chris Anyannu

Scott Maclay/Photo Editor/The Freedom Forum

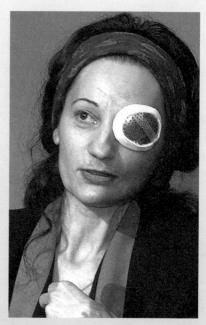

Anna Zarkova

AFRICA

Most of the new nations of Africa were born after 1960, a remarkable year in U.S. media history that witnessed the Kennedy-Nixon debates and the maturing of U.S. television as a news medium. African history is a record of colonialism, primarily by the British, French, Dutch and Portuguese, and the early print media were created to serve the colonists, not the native population.

Print Media

The first English-language newspaper in sub-Saharan Africa, the *Capetown Gazette and African Advertiser*, appeared in 1800; a year later, the first black newspaper, the *Royal Gazette and Sierra Leone Advertiser*, appeared in Sierra Leone.

French settlement in Africa is reflected in the pages of *Fraternité-Matin*, the only major daily in French Africa. A Portuguese settler founded *Noticias*, published in Mozambique. In Kenya, three tabloid newspapers enjoy wide circulations with relative independence: the English-language *Daily Nation* and *The Standard* and the Swahili daily *Taifa Leo*.

Media scholar L. John Martin describes the African media landscape:

> *Africans have never had an information press. Theirs has always been an opinion press. Advocacy journalism comes naturally to them. To the extent that they feel a need for hard news, that need is satisfied by the minimal coverage of the mass media, especially of radio. Soft news—human interest news or what [media scholar Wilbur] Schramm has called immediate-reward news—is equally well transmitted through the folk media, such as the "bush telegraph" or drum; the "grapevine," or word-of-mouth and gossip; town criers and drummers; traditional dances, plays, and song.[22]*

Martin points out that African culture is very diverse, with an estimated 800 to 2,000 language dialects, making it impossible to create a mass circulation newspaper that can appeal to a wide readership. The widest circulating publication is a magazine called *Drum*, published in South Africa but also distributed in West Africa and East Africa.

Today, most newspapers in South Africa, for example, are owned and edited by whites, who publish newspapers in English and in Afrikaans, a language that evolved from South Africa's 17th-century Dutch settlers. South Africa's first Afrikaans newspaper, *Di Patriot*, began in 1875.

In Africa, radio is a much more widely used medium than television, but new technology may change that balance. Here, villagers watch a solar-powered TV in Niger.

John Chaisson/Gamma Liaison

South Africa's highest circulation newspaper is the *Star*, which belongs to the Argus Group, South Africa's largest newspaper publisher. The Argus Group also publishes the *Sowetan*, a handsome newspaper based in Johannesburg, with color graphics, an appealing design and a healthy circulation of about 120,000. Many of the Argus Group's editors spent time in jail for speaking out against apartheid. As South Africa's largest newspaper publisher, the Argus Group owns a total of nine major papers, six of them dailies, in several African states.

From 1985 to 1990, the South African government demonstrated its distaste for dissident speech when it instituted strict limits on domestic and international news coverage in the region. Because of violent demonstrations supporting the opposition African National Congress, President P. W. Botha declared a state of emergency in the country in 1985. In 1988, the government suspended the *New Nation* and four other alternative publications.[23] The suspensions and regulations that prevented journalists from covering unrest show the power of government to limit reporting on dissent.

Audio and Video Media

Radio is a much more important medium in Africa than print or television. One reason for radio's dominance over print is that literacy rates are lower in Africa than in many other regions of the world. Radio is also very accessible and the cheapest way for people to follow the news.

Some governments charge license fees for radio sets, which are supposed to be registered, but many go unregistered. Most stations accept advertising, but the majority of funding for radio comes from government subsidies.[24]

Less than 2 percent of the African public owns a TV set. Television in the region is concentrated in the urban areas, and TV broadcasts last only a few hours each evening. Says L. John Martin, "TV remains a medium of wealthy countries."[25]

ASIA AND THE PACIFIC

The development of media in this region centers primarily in four countries: Japan, with its prosperous mix of public and private ownership; Australia, where media barons contributed their entrepreneurial fervor; India, which has seen phenomenal media growth; and the People's Republic of China, with its sustained government-controlled media monopoly.

Japan

Japan boasts more newspaper readers than any other nation in the world. Japan's three national daily newspapers are based in Tokyo—*Asahi Shimbun, Yomiuri Shimbun* and *Mainichi Shimbun*. These three papers, each of them more than 100 years old, account for almost half of the nation's newspaper circulation.

Broadcast media in Japan developed as a public corporation called the Japanese Broadcasting Corporation (NHK). During World War II, NHK became a propaganda arm of the government, but after the Japanese surrender, the United States established the direction for Japanese broadcasting. Japan created a licensing board similar to the Federal Communications Commission, but an operating board similar to that of Great Britain's BBC. Japan also decided to allow private broadcast ownership.

As a result of this, Japan today has a mixed system of privately owned and publicly held broadcast media. NHK continues to prosper and, according to broadcast scholar Sydney W. Head:

NHK enjoys more autonomy than any other major public broadcasting corporation. In a rather literal sense, the general public "owns" it by virtue of paying receiver fees. The government cannot veto any program or demand that any program be aired. It leaves the NHK free to set the level of license fees and to do its own fee collecting (which may be why it rates as the richest of the world's fee-supported broadcasting organizations). [26]

Private ownership is an important element in the Japanese media, and many broadcasting operations are owned by newspaper publishers. NHK owns many more radio properties than private broadcasters; NHK shares television ownership about equally with private investors.[27] However, Japan has very few cable systems, which will hinder access to global communications networks.

Australia

In Australia, acquisitions by media magnates such as Rupert Murdoch skyrocketed in the 1980s. The Murdoch empire controls an astounding 60 percent of Australia's newspaper circulation, which includes the *Daily Telegraph Mirror* in Sydney and *The Herald-Sun* in Melbourne.

Murdoch, although somewhat burdened with debt because of his acquisitions binge in the 1980s, emerged in the 1990s as Australia's uncontested print media baron after the other major Australian media family, the Fairfaxes, fell into bankruptcy in December 1990.

Broadcasting in Australia is dominated by Australian Broadcasting Corporation (ABC), modeled after the BBC. Three nationwide commercial networks operate in the country, but all three were suffering financial difficulty in the early 1990s, a legacy "of the heydays of the 1980s, when aspiring buyers, backed by eager bank lenders, paid heady prices for broadcast and print assets," reported *Wall Street Journal*.[28]

India

Entrepreneurship is an important element in the print media of India, which gained independence from Britain in 1947. Forty years following indepen-

Figure 16.2 Internet in China, 1997–2003   By 2003, China is projected to have nearly 34 million Internet users.

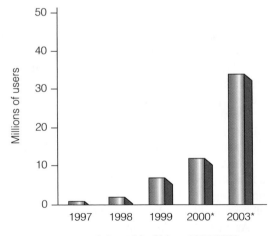

Internet in China, 1997-2003

*projected

dence, in 1987, Indian print media had multiplied 1,000 times—from 200 publications in 1947 to nearly 25,000 publications in 1987.[29]

Broadcasting in India follows its British colonial beginnings, with radio operating under the name All India Radio (AIR) and TV as Doordarshan ("distance view"). Doordarshan uses satellite service to reach remote locations, bringing network TV to four out of five people. As in most developing countries, the network regularly broadcasts programs aimed at improving public life and about subjects such as family planning, health and hygiene.

People's Republic of China

Social responsibility is a very important element of media development in the People's Republic of China, where a media monopoly gives government the power to influence change. At the center of Chinese media are the two party information sources, the newspaper *People's Daily* and Xinhua, the Chinese news agency. These two sources set the tone for the print media throughout China, where self-censorship maintains the government's direction.

A street vendor openly sells pirated movies on the street in Beijing. Pirated U.S. movies sell for about $2 each.

AP/Wide World Photos/Chien-min Chung

Broadcasting in China, as in India, offers important potential for social change in a vast land of rural villages. China's three-tier system for radio includes a central national station; 100 regional, provincial and municipal networks; and grassroots stations that send local announcements and bulletins by wire to loudspeakers in outdoor markets and other public gathering places.[30]

A television set is a prized possession in China, where the Chinese have bought some U.S. programs and accepted some U.S. commercials, but generally produce the programming themselves. The 1989 demonstrations in Tiananmen Square cooled official enthusiasm for relationships with the West, and Chinese media today sometimes use information and entertainment programming from the West to show the dangers of Western influence, proving the power and the reach of a government media monopoly.

In the new market economy in China, there are ten times as many newspapers and magazines today as there were in 1978. The number of newspapers has jumped from 186 in 1978 to 2,200 today. The number of magazines increased from 930 to 8,100. With the increased competition for readers, some of the print media are beginning to look like Western tabloids, running some sensationalist stories.

This sensationalism has angered Party officials, who are trying to maintain control on what is published. In 1996, the president of the popular newspaper *Beijing Youth Daily* was disciplined after the paper ran a story about a poisoning case involving a state-run business. "The leadership of the news media must be tightly held in the hands of those who are loyal to Marxism, the party and the people," said President Jiang Zemin.[31]

LATIN AMERICA AND THE CARIBBEAN

In Latin America, where hectic political change is the norm, media have been as volatile as the region. Media are part of the same power structure that controls politics, business and industry; family dynasties often characterize Latin American media ownership.

Romulo O'Farrill Jr., chairman of the board of Televisa in Mexico, owns more than 150 TV stations and eight newspapers. Mario Vásquez Raña owns more than 50 Mexican newspapers. His name became familiar in the United States in 1986 when he bought a controlling interest in United Press International, but he sold his interest a year later.

Print Media

In Santiago, Chile, the Edwards family has owned *El Mercurio* since 1880; now the *El Mercurio* newspapers total at least 14. *O Estado de São Paulo* in Brazil, owned by the Mesquita family, has represented editorial independence in the region for more than 50 years and often is mentioned as one of the country's best newspapers. Argentina's *La Prensa* refuses government subsidies and has survived great conflicts with people like former dictator Juan Peron, who shut down the newspaper from 1951 to 1955.[32]

Home delivery for newspapers and magazines is uncommon in Latin America; the centers of print media merchandising are street-corner kiosks, where vendors offer a variety of publications. *Manchete*, published in Brazil, is one of the most widely circulated national magazines, similar in size and content to *Life* magazine.[33]

Audio and Video Media

Broadcasting operates in a mix of government and private control, with government often owning a few key stations and regulating stations that are privately owned. But the pattern is varied.

Cuba's broadcast media are controlled totally by the government, for example. In Costa Rica and Ecuador, almost all of the broadcast media are privately owned. In Brazil, private owners hold most of the radio stations and television networks, including TV Globo Network, which claims to be the world's fourth largest network (after the United States' three TV networks).[34]

As in many other developing regions, Latin American media often are targets for political and terrorist threats, and a journalist's life can be very hazardous.

> *Threats to journalists come not only from governments but from terrorist groups, drug lords, and quasi-government hit squads as well. Numerous news organizations have been bombed, ransacked, and destroyed by opponents. Dozens of Latin American journalists have been murdered for their beliefs or for writing articles that contain those beliefs.* [35]

Journalists face danger in this region because the media represent potential opposition to the political power of a country's leadership. Perhaps more than in any other part of the world, the Latin American media are woven into the fiber of the region's revolutionary history.

NEWS AND INFORMATION FLOW

Countries in Latin America and in many other developing nations have criticized what they believe is a Western bias to the flow of information throughout the world. These countries charge that this practice imposes cultural imperialism, centered in Western ideology.

In fact, most of the major international news services are based in the West. The Associated Press, United Press International, Reuters (Great Britain), Agence France-Presse (France), Deutsche Presse-Agentur (Germany) and Agencia Efe (Spain) supply news to the print and broadcast media. Visnews, based in Great Britain, the U.S.-based Cable News Network (CNN) and World International Network (WIN) offer international video services. Sky TV in Europe and Star TV in Asia deliver programs by satellite.

Despite Western dominance of global news organizations, many regions of the world support information services within their own countries and even within their regions. Middle East News Agency (MENA), based in Egypt, serves all of the countries of the Middle East, while News Agency of Nigeria (NAN) limits services to Nigeria, for example.

Within the past 40 years, news services outside the Western orbit have been created—Russian Information Telegraph Agency (RITA); Asian-Pacific News Network in Japan; Caribbean News Agency (CANA); Pan-African News Agency (PANA); Non-Aligned News Agency (NANA), linking the non-aligned nations with the national news agencies, based in Yugoslavia; and Inter Press Service (IPS), based in Rome as an "information bridge" between Europe and Latin America.[36] In 1991, Japan Broadcasting Corporation announced, and then canceled, plans for a worldwide news network, citing the projected start-up cost of more than $1 billion.

New World Information and Communications Order

Even with the creation of these added sources of information, Western news services dominate. Critics of the present system of news and information flow have labeled this issue the New World Information and Communications Order (NWICO), saying that the current system is **ethnocentric**, or promoting the superiority of one ethnic group (in this case, the Western world) over another.

ethnocentric promoting the superiority of one ethnic group over another.

> *Developing world media and newly independent governments have been highly critical of this situation, arguing that coverage from the major services contains ethnocentric occidental values that affect its content and presentation. Coverage from these media most often include political, economic, Judeo-Christian religious, and other social values that are not universal.... In addition, developing world media and governments have argued that Western ethnocentrism creates an unequal flow of information by providing a large stream of information about events in the developed world but only a very small flow from the developing world.[37]*

UNESCO's 1978 Declaration

The United Nations organization UNESCO adopted a declaration in 1978 supporting the principles of self-reliant communications and self-determination for countries as they establish their own communications policies. Critics of the statement, especially journalists, felt that some aspects of the declaration supported government control of the flow of information out of a country, because some news services are official government mouthpieces.

Digital technology has blurred the territorial boundaries between countries. Here, in a remote region of Northern Kenya, a Samburu warrior makes a cellular telephone call.

Sally Weiner Grotta/The Stock Market

The MacBride Report

Four years later, UNESCO, which had appointed a 16-member commission headed by Irish statesman Sean MacBride, received their recommendations at the general conference of UNESCO in Belgrade, Yugoslavia. These recommendations became known as the MacBride Report. The report listed 82 ways to help achieve the New World Information and Communications Order, but after the report was issued neither critics of the current status of communications nor those who opposed the report's recommendations were satisfied:

> *The West objected to the report's skepticism about a free market in communication, including its opposition to advertising, for example; many NWICO supporters objected to its downplaying of government controls (for example, its advocacy of self-imposed rather than government codes of ethics for journalists).*[38]

The Belgrade conference passed a general resolution supporting NWICO, but in 1983, citing opposition to some of the principles outlined in the MacBride Report, the Reagan administration withdrew its $50 million in financial support for UNESCO, seriously crippling the organization because the United States had been its largest contributor.

UNESCO has since turned to other issues. The NWICO still remains a theoretical idea that scholars of global media continue to debate because of its implications for the international media community.

GLOBAL MEDIA MARKETS

Today's media markets are increasingly global. U.S. media companies are looking for markets overseas at the same time that overseas media companies are purchasing pieces of media industries in the United States and other countries. MTV, for example, is available 24 hours a day in St. Petersburg, Russia. Here are some more examples:

- ABC and British Broadcasting Corporation (BBC) have formed a news-gathering partnership to share television and radio news coverage worldwide. This service will compete with CNN to deliver news by satellite.[39]

- Rupert Murdoch expanded his Hong Kong-based satellite TV network, British Sky Network, into India. Murdoch said he planned to offer more than just TV coverage in India. "Our plan is not just to beam signals into India but also to take part in Indian films, make television programs, and broadcast them."[40]

- Jun Murai, who has been called the father of Japan's Internet, created a nonprofit network to connect all of Japan's universities to the Internet, without government approval. Ultimately, he says, he "wants to connect all the computers in this world."[41]

- U.S./British advertising and public relations partnerships are on the rise. The British firm Shandwick is the largest agency in the United Kingdom and the second largest agency in the U.S. More than half of Shandwick's business comes from the U.S.[42]

All of these companies are positioning themselves to manage the emerging global media marketplace. This media marketplace includes news and information services, programming, films and recordings, as well as products and the advertising to sell those products.

Fueling the move to global marketing is the decision by the European countries to eliminate all trade barriers among countries. A further sign of the times is the shrinking proportion of worldwide advertising expenditures accounted for by the United States, which has long been the world's advertising colossus. In recent years, advertising spending by companies outside the United States has overtaken the amount spent by companies in the United States.

CHASING INTERNATIONAL CONSUMERS

International communication on the Internet (see Chapter 1) is just the beginning of an easy, affordable and accessible transfer of information and entertainment back and forth between other countries and the United States. Media companies in the United States also are looking longingly at the large populations in other countries that are just beginning to acquire the tools of communication, making millions of people instantly available for all types of products.

The number of TV sets in the world has jumped to more than 1 billion—a 50 percent jump in the past five years. "TV sets are more common in Japanese homes than flush toilets. Virtually every Mexican household has a TV, but only half have phones. Thai consumers will buy a TV before an electric fan or even a refrigerator....Vans roam Bogotá streets with miniature satellite dishes on the roof and a megaphone blaring promises of hookups for $150. In New Delhi, 'dish wallahs' nail satellite receivers to crowded apartment buildings."[43]

OPENING NEW PATHWAYS FOR IDEAS

Along with the transfer of information in the new global communications future, however, comes the transfer of ideas.

> *Historically, the empowered elite have always sought to suppress the wider distribution of ideas, wealth, rights and, most of all, knowledge.*
>
> *This is as true today as it was 536 years ago, when the German printer Gutenberg invented movable type to print the Bible. For two centuries afterward, government tightly controlled what people could read through the widespread use of "prior restraint"....*
>
> *Just as censorship of the printed word could not continue with the emergence of democracy in 17th-Century Britain and 18th-Century America, so today suppression of the electronic media is thwarted by technology and rapidly growing economies around the world.*[44]

Governments that are accustomed to controlling the information that crosses their borders face unprecedented access within their borders to global information sources. According to media theorist Ithiel de Sola Pool:

> *International communications is often considered a mixed blessing by rulers. Usually they want technical progress. They want computers. They want satellites. They want efficient telephones. They want television. But at the same time they do not want the ideas that come with them.*[45]

IMPACT

digital

Japan's Newest Heartthrobs Are Sexy, Talented and Virtual

By Andrew Pollack

Tokyo—Shiori Fujisaki is a 17-year-old high school junior with long reddish hair and dreamy eyes who is about to release her first record. Shingo Hagiwara is a 21-year-old college sophomore who idolizes her. He goes to nearly every event at which she appears and has bought calendars, posters, watches and mugs with her picture on them.

"Shiori does everything perfectly," he sighed.

Perfect she might be, but Shiori Fujisaki is not real. She is a character in a video game called Tokimeki Memorial, the goal of

which is to get Shiori or one of her friends to date you and fall in love.

Shingo Hagiwara, on the other hand, is quite real. He is one of a growing legion of young Japanese men who have given their hearts to a virtual girl.

So called "love simulation" games, normally sold on CD-ROMS, have become one of the hottest categories in Japan's home video game industry.

The girls in such games are animated characters that have only a limited ability to converse. Players cannot type in whatever they want to say; rather, they use the video game controller merely to pick a topic of conversation or a

multiple-choice reply. In most games, the text of the conversation is also printed on the bottom of the screen....

Some players become so absorbed in their pursuit that the girls become real to them. Some young men send love letters and birthday cards to their favorite characters.

"Everybody has one character for whom he could sacrifice his life," said Mr. Hagiwara, the college student....

Many governments that control the media, especially broadcast media, are expected to continue to control the messages as long as they can supervise access to newsprint and satellites. But this is becoming increasingly difficult.

In 1994, the Chinese government passed regulations to ban satellite dishes and prohibit people from watching foreign broadcasts. Factories that own dishes were required to broadcast only approved programs. But many Chinese simply refused to abide by the edict.[46]

Videos can travel in a suitcase across borders, and video signals can travel unseen to pirated satellite dishes, assembled without government knowledge. The airwaves are truly "borderless." Reports the *Los Angeles Times*,

"Asked once what had caused the stunning collapse of communism in Eastern Europe, Polish leader Lech Wałęsa pointed to a nearby TV set, 'It all came from there.'"[47]

As more and more national media boundaries open up throughout the world, news, information and entertainment will be able to move instantly from each home country to become part of the global media dialogue. In the 1990s, the media industries are entering a media marketplace without boundaries, a global marketplace that is truly "transnational."

> *Optimists declare that the world is headed unstoppably for an electronic Renaissance. How arrogant; how naive. The essence of a technology of freedom is that it endows its users with the freedom to fail. But pessimists are equally wrong to think that failure is inevitable. Nothing is inevitable about this technology except its advance.... As the universe behind the screen expands, it will be the people in front who shape the soul of the new machine.*[48]

IN FOCUS

- The four theories of the press (the Soviet theory, the authoritarian theory, the libertarian theory and the social responsibility theory), plus the developmental theory, still leave many press systems beyond categorization.

- The print media form the basis for press development in North America, Australia, Western Europe and Eastern Europe.

- Radio is often the dominant medium in developing countries; television is in widespread use in prosperous nations and in urban areas of developing countries. Yet most countries still have only one TV service, usually run by the government.

- Today Western European and Canadian media prosper under guarantees of freedom of expression similar to the First Amendment, although each nation has modified the idea to reflect differing values.

- Scandinavian journalists enjoy the widest press freedoms of all of Western Europe, including almost unlimited access to public documents; Canada is the most recent country to issue an official decree supporting press freedom.

- Western European newspapers tend to be much more partisan than either U.S. or Canadian newspapers.

- Western Europeans watch less than half as much TV as people in the United States; most TV stations in Europe don't go on the air until late afternoon.

- Most of Western European programming comes from the United States. U.S. programs are attractive to European broadcasters because buying U.S. programs is cheaper than producing their own.

- Some members of the European Community have proposed quotas on the importation of U.S. programs.

- Eastern Europe, which is in transition, is defining a new balance between the desire for free expression and the remnants of government control.

- In many Eastern European countries, the media played a central role in upsetting the established power structure.

- Television in the Eastern bloc countries developed under Communist direction because the Communist governments were in power before TV use was widespread; radio broadcasting also was tightly controlled.

- The Eastern European nations developed their press policies following the Soviet model.

- In the Middle East and North Africa, more newspapers and magazines are published in regions with high literacy rates than in regions with low literacy rates; the one exception is Cairo, Egypt, which is the Arab world's publishing center.

- The Middle Eastern press is tightly controlled by government restrictions, through ownership and licensing.

- Radio Monte Carlo and the BBC offer alternative radio programming across Middle Eastern borders. VCRs also are very popular.

- In the Middle East, as in other developing regions, the media are perceived as instruments of each country's social and political programs.

- African culture is very diverse, making it impossible to create a mass circulation newspaper that can appeal to a wide readership.

- Suspension of five publications in South Africa during the state of emergency during 1985–1990 demonstrates the power of government to limit reporting on dissent.

- In Africa, radio is a much more important medium than print because it is an inexpensive way for people to follow the news.

- The three major Japanese national dailies account for almost half of the nation's newspaper circulation.

- Japan today has a mixed system of privately owned and publicly held broadcast media.

- Entrepreneurs, including Rupert Murdoch, control large segments of Australia's media; broadcasting in Australia is dominated by the Australian Broadcasting Corporation (ABC).

- Since India's independence in 1947, the number of publications has increased 1,000 times; broadcasting in India follows its British colonial beginnings.

- Chinese media operate under a government monopoly, supported by a belief in the media's social responsibility.

- Media in Latin America are part of the power structure, and media often are owned by family dynasties.

- Journalists in Latin America face danger because the media represent a challenge to political power.

- The New World Information and Communications Order (NWICO), supported by UNESCO, advocated parity for the media in all countries.

- U.S. media companies are looking for markets overseas at the same time that overseas media companies are purchasing pieces of media industries in the United States and other countries.

- Along with the transfer of information in the new global communications future comes the transfer of ideas. Governments that are accustomed to controlling the information that crosses their borders face unprecedented access within their borders to global information sources.

WORKING THE WEB www

- **BBC News**
  news.bbc.co.uk/default/htm
- **Canadian Broadcasting Corporation (CBC) Newsworld**
  www.newsworld.cbc.ca
- **The Electronic Telegraph**
  www.telegraph.co.uk
- **The Exile (from Moscow)**
  www.exile.ru/index/htm
- **Jerusalem Post**
  www.jpost.co.il
- **Mediapolis**
  mediapolis.es
- **World Net Daily**
  www.WorldNetDaily.com

INFOTRAC COLLEGE EDITION EXERCISES

Using the InfoTrac College Edition's fully searchable online database of articles and abstracts, do the following exercises as directed by your instructor.

1. Choose another country and, using InfoTrac College Edition, look up articles about its media. You might consider:
   - "British media"
   - "Russia media"
   - "Mexico media"
   - "China media"
   - "India media"
   - "Africa media"

   Read and print at least three articles about the media in that country. Then either:

   a. write a brief paper on your findings, or

   b. bring the articles to class and be prepared to do a brief talk about your subject.

2. Enter the keywords "global media" or "world media" and read at least three articles about the impact of the global media revolution. Be specific, and narrow your search to a specific part of this issue. Then either:

   a. write a brief paper on your findings, or

   b. bring the articles to class and be prepared to discuss them.

3. Read "Impact/Digital: Foie Gras and Chips, Anyone?" in Chapter 16 about the impact of shopping online. Then, using keywords "Internet

shopping" or "online shopping," find at least three articles about people around the world shopping online. Print the articles and either:

a. write a brief paper on your findings, or

b. bring the articles to class and be prepared to discuss them.

4. Read "Impact/Digital: Japan's Newest Hearthrobs are Sexy, Talented and Virtual" in Chapter 16. Enter keywords "Japanese online" or "Japanese video" to learn more about the virtual worlds of Japanese technology. Print at least two articles and either:

a. write a brief paper on your findings, or

b. bring the articles to class and be prepared to discuss them.

5. Read "Impact/Point of View: Journalists Downplay Personal Courage" in Chapter 16. Using keywords such as "journalists at risk," and "journalists dangers," research at least two articles on the issue. Cite specific examples of dangers that have befallen journalists in other countries and either:

a. write a brief paper on your findings, or

b. bring the articles to class and be prepared to discuss them.

Student Resource Guide

GLOSSARY OF MEDIA TERMS

MEDIA RESEARCH DIRECTORY

Glossary of Media Terms

accreditation certification by the government of members of the press to cover wartime action or other official government business.

affiliates broadcast stations that use broadcast network programming but that are owned by companies other than the broadcast networks.

agenda-setting the principle that members of the press do not tell people what to think but do tell people what and whom to think about.

alternative press newspapers that become outlets for the voices of social protest; also called the dissident press.

analog in mass communications, a type of technology used in broadcasting, whereby video or audio information is sent as continuous signals through the air on specific airwave frequencies.

ancillary rights the revenue opportunity for a movie beyond its theater audience, including television and videocassette sales.

Baby Bells see *RBOCs*.

blanket licensing agreement an arrangement whereby radio stations become authorized to use recorded music for broadcast by paying a fee.

blind booking the practice of renting films to exhibitors without showing the films to the exhibitors first.

block booking the practice of scheduling a large number of movies for a theater, combining a few good movies with many second-rate features.

browser software that allows people to search electronically among many documents to find what they want online.

Bundle the combination of services that the media industries will be able to offer consumers in the future.

CDA Communications Decency Act.

censorship the practice of suppressing material that is considered morally, politically or otherwise objectionable.

channel in mass communication, the medium that delivers the message.

concentration of ownership the trend among the media industries to cluster together in groups.

consumer magazines all magazines sold by subscription or at newsstands, supermarkets and bookstores.

content the multimedia term for information sources and programs that can be digitized for the new communications network.

convergence the blurring of lines between the publishing industry, the communications industry, consumer electronics and computers because of advances in technology.

cooperative news gathering a practice first used by the New York Associated Press, whereby member newspapers share the expenses of acquiring news and returning any profits to the members.

CPM in advertising, cost-per-thousand, which is the cost of an ad per 1,000 people reached. (M is the Roman numeral for 1,000.)

cross-ownership used to describe a company that owns television and radio stations in the same broadcast market.

data compression a process that uses software and hardware to squeeze information into a tiny electronic package.

demand programming request radio that is controlled completely by the listener.

demographics the analysis of data used by advertising agencies to target an audience by sex, age, income level, marital status, geographic location and occupation.

deregulation the process of ending government monitoring of an industry.

digital a way to store and transmit data by reducing it to electronic signals—digits—and then reassembling them for an exact reproduction.

digital audio broadcast (DAB) a technology that uses computer codes to send music and information, which eliminates the static of current broadcast signals and provides more program choices.

digital audiotape (DAT) a new type of audiotape that uses computer codes to produce recordings.

digital film the electronic manipulation of film images.

digital media all emerging communications media that combine text, graphics, sound and video, using computer technology.

digital service line (DSL) provides Internet access that is up to 50 times faster than a dial-up modem.

direct sponsorship radio and television programming in which the advertiser sponsored an entire show, which often bore the name of the product or company in the title.

disinformation the planting by government sources of inaccurate information.

dissident press see *alternative press.*

drive-time audience people who listen to the radio in their cars 6-9 A.M. and 4-7 P.M.

duopoly the control by one company owning two AM or two FM radio stations in the same market area. Duopoly ownership was sanctioned by a 1992 FCC ruling.

e-mail electronic messages delivered on-line.

ethnocentric characterized by the attitude that one culture is superior to others.

ethnocentrism the attitude that some cultural and social values are superior to others.

false light the charge that what a writer implied in a story about someone was incorrect.

FCC Federal Communications Commission. This five-member commission is responsible for administering the provisions of the Telecommunications Act of 1996.

feedback in mass communication, a response sent back to the sender (source) from the receiver.

freelancers in magazine or newspaper publishing, writers who are not on the staff and are paid separately for each article published.

free media used to describe over-the-air broadcast media.

high-definition television (HDTV) a type of television that provides a picture with a clearer resolution than on normal television sets.

home page the first page of a web site that welcomes the user.

HTML hypertext markup language, a computer programming language developed by Tim Berners-Lee that allows people to send text and pictures on the Web.

HTTP hypertext transfer protocol, a computer programming language developed by Tim Berners-Lee that allows people to create links on the Web from one source of information to another.

information disadvantaged used to describe people who do not have access to a telephone, a computer and a modem.

interactive a two-way viewer-controlled electronic process that allows the consumer to select among a variety of services.

Internet a web of interconnected computer networks that sprang from a U.S. government effort to connect government and academic locations. It currently links about 15 million people.

LAPS test the local standard for obscenity established in *Miller* v. *California*: whether a work, taken as a whole, lacks serious *Literary, Artistic, Political* or *Scientific* value.

libel a false statement that damages a person's character or reputation by exposing that person to public ridicule or contempt.

line doublers/line quadruplers devices that can double and quadruple the number of lines scanning the TV screen to make the picture sharper.

links electronic connections from one source of information to another.

magic bullet theory a belief that ideas from the media create a direct causal relationship to behavior.

mass communication communication from one person or group of persons through a transmitting device (a medium) to a large audience or market.

mass media industries used in *Media/Impact* to describe the seven types of media businesses: newspapers, magazines, radio, television, movies, recordings and books.

media plural for *medium.*

mediamorphosis a term coined by information designer Roger Fidler to describe the intense rate of change that occurs when all media change simultaneously.

medium in mass communication, the transmitting device by which a message is carried.

message pluralism a broad and diverse representation of opinion and culture by the media.

MPAA Motion Picture Association of America.

muckrakers turn-of-the-century magazine journalists who wrote articles to expose big business and corrupt government.

multimedia the blending of different types of media—audio, video and data—into a single product or service.

narrowcasting in broadcasting, identifying a specific audience segment and specifically programming for that segment.

navigator a software program that allows someone to browse easily through program services.

NCTA National Cable Television Association.

network a collection of radio or television stations that offers programs, usually simultaneously, throughout the country, during designated program times.

news services originally called wire services, agencies formed to provide information to print and broadcast news operations from locations throughout the world.

NTIA National Telecommunications and Information Administration.

O & O's broadcast stations that are *O*wned and *O*perated by a broadcast network.

pass-along readership an audience of readers who share a magazine with its original owner.

payola a contraction of the words *pay* and *Victrola* (an early record player), used to describe the payment of a fee to a disc jockey in exchange for playing a recording on the air.

penny paper first popularized by Benjamin Day of the *New York Sun* in 1833, a newspaper produced by dropping the price of each copy to a penny and supporting the production cost through advertising.

photojournalism the use of photographs and text to tell a better story than either could tell alone.

pool reporting an arrangement that places reporters in small, supervised groups to cover an event. This device often limits journalists' access to cover an event.

prime time in broadcasting, the hours between 7 P.M. and 11 P.M., when more people watch television than during any other period.

prior restraint the power of government to stop information from being published or broadcast.

program blocking the use of a "lock-box" to block out cable channels.

publicity uncontrolled use of media by a public relations firm to create events and present information to capture press and public attention.

publishing used to denote items placed on the Web.

qualified privilege the freedom of the press to report what is discussed during legislative and covert proceedings.

rating the percentage of audience for a program, based on the total number of households with receivers.

RBOCs Regional Bell Operating Companies that deliver local telephone services; sometimes called Baby Bells.

rep firm a company of advertising sales representatives who sell advertising time and space in their market to advertisers outside their geographic area.

resolution clarity of the picture on the screen.

Roth test the local standard used to determine obscenity, established by the U.S. Supreme Court in *Roth* v. *United States:* "whether to the average person, applying contemporary community standards, the dominant theme of the material taken as a whole appeals to prurient interest."

search engine the tool used to locate information in an online computer database.

selective perception the concept that different people perceive different messages differently.

sender (or source) the agency that puts a message on a channel (for example, a local cable company).

server a computerized storage system used to send programs and data to consumers, using cable, phone lines or other networks.

set-top box the device that sits on top of a TV set and links viewers to cable systems (and, in the future, to the new communications network).

share an abbreviation for *share-of-audience,* which compares the audience for one show with the audience for another. *Share* means the percentage of the audience with TV sets on that is watching each program.

situation comedy a television program that establishes a fixed set of characters in either a home or work situation.

small presses book publishers with fewer than 10 employees.

spiral of silence a phenomenon in which people are unlikely to voice disagreement with the prevailing climate of opinion embraced by the media.

studio system the movie industry system of hiring stars and production people under exclusive contracts.

subsidiary rights the rights to market a book for other uses—to make a movie, for example, or to print a character from the book on T-shirts.

sweeps the months when TV ratings services gather their most important ratings—February, May and November. (See *rating.*)

syndicates agencies and news organizations that sell articles for publication to appear in many different outlets simultaneously.

syndicators services that sell programming to broadcast stations and cable.

tabloid a small-format newspaper that features large photographs and illustrations along with sensational stories.

tabloid journalism (or jazz journalism) a newspaper format style that combines large pictures and headlines to emphasize sex and violence.

telco an abbreviation for *telephone company.*

telco-cable cross-ownership used to describe a telephone company that owns a cable company or a cable company that owns a telephone company.

30-year rule a theory about how long people take to completely adopt a new technology, developed by futurist Paul Saffo.

time-shifting recording a television program using a DVR or VCR, so that someone can watch it later.

two-step flow the transmittal of information and ideas from mass media to opinion leaders and then to their friends and acquaintances.

universal service the concept that everyone in the United States should have access to affordable telecommunications services.

V-chip a microchip device that allows parents to program TV sets to eliminate objectionable programs.

vertical integration the process by which one company controls several related aspects of the media business simultaneously.

yellow journalism highly emotional, often exaggerated or inaccurate reporting that emphasizes crime, sex and violence.

Media Research Directory

This directory is designed to familiarize you with some of the publications that will help you find background and current information about the media. Also included is a list of associations that can provide information about specific media businesses.

The study of media covers many areas of scholarship besides journalism and mass communication. Historians, psychologists, economists, political scientists, and sociologists, for example, often contribute ideas to media studies. This directory therefore includes a variety of information sources from academic and industry publications as well as from popular periodicals.

MEDIA SOURCES YOU SHOULD KNOW

The Wall Street Journal is the best daily source of information about the business of the media. Although you won't find articles specifically about the media every day, you will find regular reports on earnings, acquisitions, and leaders in the media industries. *The Wall Street Journal Index* will help you find the articles you need.

The *Los Angeles Times* daily section "Calendar" follows the media business very closely, especially television and movies, because the majority of these companies are based in Los Angeles. The *Los Angeles Times Index* lists stories in the *Times.*

The New York Times and the *Washington Post* also carry media information and both are indexed.

Advertising Age publishes special issues throughout the year focusing on newspapers, magazines, and broadcasting.

Columbia Journalism Review and *American Journalism Review* regularly critique developments in the print and broadcast industries. *Columbia Journalism Review* is published by New York's Columbia University Graduate School of Journalism. The University of Maryland College of Journalism publishes *American Journalism Review.*

Communication Abstracts, Communication Research, Journal of Communication and *Journalism Quarterly* offer scholarly articles and article summaries about media issues. Journals that cover specific media topics include *Journalism History, Journal of Advertising Research, Newspaper Research Journal,* and *Public Relations Review.*

U.S. Industrial Outlook, published each year by the U.S. Department of Commerce, projects the expected annual earnings of American businesses, including the mass media industries.

Advertising Age publishes regular estimates of actual advertising receipts as each year progresses. McCann-Erickson in New York publishes annual projections of advertising revenue in a publication called *Insider's Report.* Included are ongoing tables on total advertising revenue for each year as well as a breakdown of national and local advertising.

The Veronis, Suhler & Associates Communications Industry Forecast, published annually in July, follows all the media industries. The *Forecast* offers historical media tables, tracking past performance, as well as projections for future media industry growth.

Since 1973, Paine Webber in New York has sponsored an Annual Conference on the Outlook for the Media. Conference speakers include experts on newspapers, broadcasting, cable, advertising, and magazine and book publishing, as well as media investment specialists. The results are published in an annual report, *Outlook for the Media,* issued each June.

Broadcasting & Cable Yearbook is an annual compilation of material about the broadcast industry. Also listed are syndicators, brokers, advertising agencies and associations.

Editor & Publisher Yearbook, published annually, lists all U.S., and many foreign, newspapers. The yearbook also publishes newspaper statistics—the number of daily and weekly newspapers published in the U.S., for example.

The Encyclopedia of American Journalism by Donald Paneth (New York: Facts on File, 1983) is a very useful alphabetical guide to events and people in the history of journalism.

Ulrich's International Periodicals Directory lists magazines alphabetically and by subject.

Standard Directory of Advertisers lists advertisers by the types of products they sell—all of the advertisers that handle automobile manufacturers, for example. *Standard Directory of Advertising Agencies* shows advertising agencies alphabetically, along with the accounts they manage.

WORKING THE WEB

Thousands of Web sites on the Internet offer useful material. What follows is an alphabetical list of the specific sites listed at the end of each chapter. If you can't reach the Web site at the address listed, search using the site's name, listed in **bold type.** Also, if you can't find a Web site as listed, try changing the search engine you are using. Common search engines are AltaVista, Yahoo! and Lycos.

To find a group of Web sites on a specific media topic, check Working the Web at the end of each chapter.

Media Web Sites

Advertising Age
www.adage.com
Advertising Council
www.adcouncil.org
All Media Email Director (e-mail addresses for key editors, columnists, correspondents and executives in magazines, newspapers, radio, TV and news syndicates across the United States and Canada)
www.owt.com/dircon
Amazon.com Online Booksellers
www.amazon.com

American Advertising Federation
www.aaf.org
American Association of University Presses
aaup.pupress.princeton.edu:70
American Society of Journalists and Authors
www.asja.org/cwpage.htm
American Society of Newspaper Editors Minority Employment Report
www.asne.org/kiosk/diversity/97minsrv.htm
An Appraisal of Technologies of Political Control
jya.com/atpc.htm

Associates Press Wire
www.latimes.com/HOME/NEWS/AUTOAP/ICBT
OPAP.html

Association for Asian Studies
www.easc.indiana.edu/~aas

Barnes & Noble
www.barnesandnoble.com

BBC News
news.bbc.co.uk/default/htm

Bookfinder
www.bookfinder.com

Borders Books and Records
www.borders.com

**Canadian Broadcasting Corporation (CBC)
Newsworld**
www.newsworld.cbc.ca

**Canadian Broadcasting Corporation (CBC)
Radio (audio and text)**
www.radio.cbc.ca/radio/programs/news/head-
line-news

Communications Topics Website
www.syr.edu/~bcfought

Computer Assisted Reporting
home.att.net/~bdedman/index.html

CD Now (CD Sales)
www.cdnow.txt

**CNN Audioselect (audio tracks of all CNN
channels)**
www.cnn.com/audioselect/

Communications Decency Act
www.findlaw.com/casecode/supreme.html

Copyright on the Net
www.benedict.com/home/htm

**Copyright Principles Proposed by the National
Humanities Alliance**
www.ninch.cni.org/ISSUES/COPYRIGHT/PRIN-
CIPLES/NHA_Compact.html

Corporate Watch
www.corpwatch.org

Cross Media Ownership Rules Campaign
www.alliance.aust.com/CMOC

David Letterman
www.cbs.com/lateshow

Denver Post
www.denverpost.com

Digital Entertainment Network
www.den.net

Dilbert (Scott Adams' comic)
www.unitedmedia.com/comics/dilbert

**Directory of Public Relations Agencies and
Resources on the Web**
www.webcom.com/impulse/prlist.html

Diversity in Electronic Media
www.mediaaccess.org/program/diversity/
index.html

Drudge Report
www.drudgereport.com

Editing for Magazines
www.well.com/user/mmcadams/copy.editing.html

Editor & Publisher Interactive
www.mediainfo.com/ephome/news/newshtm/st
op/st120597/htm

Electronic Frontier Foundation
www.eff.org

Electronic Rights Defense Committee
www.erights.qc.ca

The Electronic Telegraph
www.telegraph.co.uk

Entertaindom (Time Warner)
www.entertaindom.com

Entertainment Weekly Online Magazine
cgi.pathfinder.com/ew

ESPN Sportzone
www.sportzone.com

ESPN Sportszone Fantasy Baseball
www.zebrasports.com/baseball/default.htm

The Exile (from Moscow)
www.exile.ru/index/htm

Fair—Fairness and Accuracy in Reporting
www.fair.org

Fair Use on the Net
www.fairuse.stanford.edu

Federal Trade Commission
www.ftc.gov

Freedom Forum
www.freedomforum.org

Grateful Dead Concerts Online
www.deadradio.com

Hispanic Magazine Online
www.hisp.com

Hotline (politics)
www.cloakroom.com

Industry Standard
www.thestandard.com

Inside Radio
www.insideradio.com

Internet Movie Database
www.us.imdb.org/Movies/credits.html

Investigative Journalism on the Internet
www.vir.com/~sher/julian.htm

Jerusalem Post
www.jpost.co.il

Journal of Electronic Publishing
www.press.umich.edu/jep

Los Angeles Times
www.latimes.com

Links to American Publishers
www.lights.com/publisher

Market Guide to the Motion Picture Industry
www.marketguide.com/MGI/INDUSTRY/
movies.htm

Media History Project on the Web
www.mediahistory.com

Mediapolis
mediapolis.es

Miami Herald
www.miamiherald.com

MIT Media Lab Project
casr.www.media.mit.edu/groups/casr/papert.html

Motion Picture Industry Book
www.studentcenter.com/where/ndustry/IN7822
.htm

Motion Picture Industry: Behind the Scenes
library.advanced.org/10015

MP3
www.mp3.com

National Public Radio
www.realaudio.com/contentp/nrp.html

The New Media Monitor
www.gpnet.it/dallomo/

Newspaper Association of America
www.naa.org/

**Newslink to Most Major Newspapers,
Magazines and Broadcasts**
www.newslink.org

New York Times
www.nytimes.com

Old Radio
www.oldradio.com

Online Public Relations
www.connectingonline.com/anchors/online_pu
blic_relations.html

Public Broadcasting Service (PBS)
www/pbs.org/Welcome.html

People Magazine Online
www.people.com

Political Junkie
www.politicaljunkie.com

Public Journalism Bibliography
poynter.org/research/biblio/bib_pj.htm

Public Relations Society of America
www.prsa.org

The Radio Archive
www.edu/radio-archive-homepage.html

Radio History
home.luna.nl/~arjan-muil/radio/history.html

Radio-Television News Directors Ethics Codes
www.missouri.edu/~jourvs

Real Networks (audio on the Internet)
www.real.com

Recording Industry Association of America
www.riaa.com

Reporters Committee for Freedom of the Press
www.rcpf.org/rcfp

Salon Magazine
www.salon.com

The San Francisco Chronicle
www.sfgate.com

San Jose Mercury News
mercurycenter.com

Seattle Post-Intelligencer
www.seattlep-i.com

Slate Magazine
www.slate.com

**Small Business Resources Index for Public
Relations Resources**
www.inc.com/idx_t_cc.html

Smoking Gun
www.smokinggun.com

**Society for the History of Authorship,
Reading and Publishing**
www.indiana.edu/~sharp

Sony
www.sony.com

**Surfing the Aether: Radio and Broadcasting
Technology History**
www.northernnet.com/bchris/home.html

The Tonight Show
www.nbctonightshow.com

USA Today
www.usatoday.com

U.S. Government Documents Online
www.access.gpo.gov/su_docs

**Vernon Stone's University of Missouri
Broadcasting Employment Website**
web.missouri.edu/~jourvs/indix/html

Virtual recordings
www.virtualrecordings.com

Wall Street Journal Interactive Edition
www.wsj.com

The Washington Post
www.washingtonpost.com

Women in Film
www.cinema.ucla.edu/women

World Net Daily
www.WorldNetDaily.com

UNCOVERING MEDIA HISTORY

The Journalist's Bookshelf by Roland E. Wolseley and Isabel Wolseley (Indianapolis: R. J. Berg, 1986) is a comprehensive listing of resources about American print journalism.

The classic history of American magazines is Frank Luther Mott's *History of American Magazines* (New York: D. Appleton, 1930).

An overview of radio and television history is provided by Christopher H. Sterling and John M. Kittross in *Stay Tuned: A Concise History of American Broadcasting,* 2nd ed. (Belmont, Calif.: Wadsworth, 1990). The classic television history is Eric Barnouw's *Tube of Plenty* (New York: Oxford University Press, 1975).

A History of Films by John L. Fell (New York: Holt, Rinehart & Winston, 1979) and *Movie-Made America* by Robert Sklar (New York: Random House, 1975) provide a good introduction to the history of movies.

Sterling and Kittross's *Stay Tuned* (listed earlier) provides some information about the recording industry. *This Business of Music* by Sidney Shemel and M. William Krasilovsky (New York: Billboard Publications, 1985) explains the way the recording industry works.

John P. Dessauer's *Book Publishing: What It Is, What It Does* (New York: R. R. Bowker, 1974) succinctly explains the book publishing business. A historical perspective and overview is available in *Books: The Culture & Commerce of Publishing* by Lewis A. Coser et al. (New York: Basic Books, 1982).

Three histories of American advertising are *The Making of Modern Advertising* by Daniel Pope (New York: Basic Books, 1983), *The Mirror Makers: A History of Twentieth Century American Advertising* by Stephen Fox (New York: Morrow, 1984), and *Advertising the American Dream* by Roland Marchand (Berkeley: University of California Press, 1985).

In 1923, Edward L. Bernays wrote the first book specifically about public relations, *The Engineering of Consent* (Norman: University of Oklahoma Press, reprinted in 1955). For an understanding of today's public relations business, you can read *This Is PR: The Realities of Public Relations* by Doug Newsom, Alan Scott, and Judy VanSlyke Turk (Belmont, Calif.: Wadsworth, 1993).

The most comprehensive academic journals specifically devoted to media history are *American Journalism,* published by the American Journalism Historians Association, and *Journalism History,* published by the History Division of the Association for Education in Journalism and Mass Communication.

For information about historical events and people in the media who often are omitted from other histories, you can refer to *Up from the Footnote: A History of Women Journalists* by Marion Marzolf (New York: Hastings House, 1977), *Great Women of the Press* by Madelon Golden Schilpp and Sharon M. Murphy (Carbondale: Southern Illinois University Press, 1983), *Minorities and Media: Diversity and the End of Mass Communication* by Clint C. Wilson and Felix Gutiérrez (Newbury Park, Calif.: Sage, 1985), *Gender, Race and Class in Media* by Gail Dines and Jean M. Humez (Newbury Park, Calif.: Sage, 1994), and *Facing Difference: Race, Gender and Mass Media* by Shirley Biagi and Marilyn Kern-Foxworth (Newbury Park, Calif.: Pine Forge Press, 1997).

FINDING THE BEST INDEX

Another good place to begin specific mass media research is with an index. Indexes provide quick, comprehensive access to listings of articles about the mass media industries. Pick a subject heading about your topic (if you need help defining the heading to use, see the subject heading list beginning on page 402). Then check the most likely index from the following print index list that catalogs information about your topic. You may have to check two or more indexes to locate all of the citations you need.

Print Indexes

Access: The Supplementary Index to Periodicals
Arts and Humanities Citation Index
Business Index
Business Periodicals Index
Communication Abstracts
Film Literature Index
Graphic Arts Literature Abstracts
Humanities Index
Index to Legal Periodicals
Journalism Monographs
Library Literature
Popular Periodicals Index
Readers' Guide
Trade and Industry Index
Ulrich's Periodicals Index

MAGAZINES FOR MEDIA RESEARCH

Many magazines publish information about the mass media industries and support industries. The following is an alphabetical listing of the major magazines in each subject area. If a periodical is indexed, the name of the index appears in parentheses.

Advertising

Advertising Age (Business Periodicals Index)
Adweek/Adweek: National Marketing Edition (Business Periodicals Index)
Journal of Advertising (Business Periodicals Index)
Journal of Advertising Research (Business Periodicals Index)

Broadcasting

Broadcasting & Cable (Business Periodicals Index)
Cablevision (Ulrich's Periodicals Index)
Electronic Media (Ulrich's Periodicals Index)
Emmy, published by the Academy of Television Arts and Sciences (Access: The Supplementary Index to Periodicals)
Federal Communications Law Journal (Index to Legal Periodicals)

Journal of Broadcasting and Electronic Media, published by Broadcast Education Association (Communication Abstracts)

RTNDA Communicator, published by the Radio-Television News Directors Association

Television Digest

TV Guide (Access: The Supplementary Index to Periodicals)

Video Week (Ulrich's Periodicals Index)

Magazine and Book Publishing

AB Bookman's Weekly, collector books (Library Literature)

Bookwoman, published by the Women's National Book Association

COSMEP Newsletter, published by the Committee of Small Magazine Editors and Publishers

Folio, the magazine for magazine management (Trade and Industry Index)

Publishers Weekly, the journal of the book industry (Business Periodicals Index)

Movies

American Film (Arts and Humanities Citation Index)

Film Comment, published by the Film Society of Lincoln Center (Arts and Humanities Citation Index)

Hollywood Reporter

Variety (Business Index)

Video Review, covers video for home viewing

Newspapers

Editor & Publisher: The Fourth Estate (Business Periodicals Index)

Journalism Monographs, published by the Association for Education in Journalism and Mass Communication (Communication Abstracts)

Newspaper Financial Executive Journal, published by International Newspaper Financial Executives (Encyclopedia of Business Information Sources)

Newspaper Research Journal, published by the Association for Education in Journalism and Mass Communication (Communication Abstracts)

Presstime, published by the Newspaper Association of America (Graphic Arts Literature Abstracts)

Quill, published by the Society of Professional Journalists (Humanities Index)

Public Relations

Public Relations Journal (Business Periodicals Index)

Public Relations Quarterly (Business Periodicals Index)

Public Relations Review (Communication Abstracts)

Recordings

Billboard (Business Periodicals Index)

Cash Box (Encyclopedia of Business Information Sources)

Down Beat (Readers' Guide)

Music Index, a separate index that covers articles on the music industry

Music Review (Ulrich's Periodicals Index)

Rolling Stone (Popular Periodicals Index)

Digital Media and the Web
The Industry Standard (Business Periodicals Index)
Wired (Business Periodicals index)

Global Media
Advertising
Affiliated Advertising Agencies International, Colorado (Ulrich's Periodicals Index)

International Journal of Advertising, England (Ulrich's Periodicals Index)

Broadcasting
Broadcast Weekly, London (Broadcasting & Cable Yearbook)
Cable and Satellite Europe, London (Broadcasting & Cable Yearbook)
Eastern European & Soviet Telecon Report, Washington, D.C. (Broadcasting & Cable Yearbook)

Movies
Young Cinema and Theatre/Jeune Cinéma et Théâtre, cultural magazine of the International Union of Students, Czech Republic

Newspapers
International Media Guide, Newspapers Worldwide, Connecticut

Periodicals
InterMedia, London (Broadcasting & Cable Yearbook)

Public Relations
Public Relations Review, England (Ulrich's Periodicals Index)

Recordings
Musical America International Directory of the Performing Arts, ABC Leisure Magazines, Inc., New York

Other
World Press Review
Media International, England (Ulrich's Periodicals Index)
OPMA Overseas Media Guide (Overseas Press and Media Association), England (Ulrich's Periodicals Index)

Media-Related Topics
Censorship News, published by the National Coalition Against Censorship
Communication Research (Communication Abstracts)
Communications and the Law (Index to Legal Periodicals)
Entertainment Law Reporter, covers motion pictures, radio, TV, and music (Index to Legal Periodicals)
News Media and the Law, published by Reporters Committee for Freedom of the Press (Index to Legal Periodicals)
Nieman Reports, published by the Nieman Foundation for Journalism at Harvard

FINDING SUBJECT HEADINGS
FOR MASS MEDIA INFORMATION

Because mass media information is often scattered throughout different
types of references in the library, what follows is an alphabetical list of subject headings as they appear in the Library of Congress Subject

A—B

Academy Awards (motion pictures)
Advertising, Magazine
Advertising, Newspaper
Advertising, Political
Advertising agencies
Advertising and public relations (often public
    relations is not listed separately)
Audio-equipment industry
Audio-visual equipment
Audio-visual materials
Authors
Blacks—Communication
Blacks in literature
Blacks in motion pictures
Blacks in television broadcasting
Blacks in the press
Book editors
Book industries and trade
Broadcast advertising
Broadcast journalism
Broadcasters

C—E

Cable television (see also individual companies,
    such as Home Box Office)
Cable television advertising
Children—Books and Reading
Children in advertising
Children in literature
Children's literature
Communication
Compact disc industry
Compact disc players
Compact discs
Editing
Editors
Ethics

F—L

Fiction
Films
Foreign correspondents
Foreign news

Government advertising
Government and the press
Journalism
Journalistic ethics
Journalists (see also individual names, such as
    Peter Jennings)
Law
Libel and slander
Literary agents
Literary ethics
Literature

M—O

Magazines
Marketing
Mass media
Minorities
Motion picture industry (see also individual com-
    panies, such as Sony Pictures Entertainment)
Motion pictures
Music
News
News agencies
News photographers
News radio stations
News recordings
Newspapers (see also individual companies, such
    as Knight-Ridder Newspapers, Inc.)
Nielsen family
Nonfiction novel
Novelists

P—R

Periodicals
Phonograph
Photography
Photography, Advertising
Photography—Films
Press
Press and journalism in literature
Press and politics
Press law
Press releases
Printing industry
Public relations

Publishers and Publishing (see also individual
companies, such as HarperCollins)
Radio advertising
Radio broadcasting
Radio journalism
Radio programs
Radio stations
Reporters and reporting

S—T

Sound
Sports journalism
Television
Television advertising
Television and reading
Television broadcasting
Television journalists
Television programs
Television sound

Television stations
Television writers
Terrorism and mass media
Terrorism in television
Terrorism in the press

U—Z

Underground literature
Underground press
United States, Journalists
Video recordings
Video tape recorders and recording
Women and journalism
Women—Communication
Women and literature
Women authors
Women broadcasters
Women in advertising
Women in mass media

FINDING MEDIA ORGANIZATIONS

These organizations compile statistics and useful information about specific
industries for their members and for the public. (To find out an association's
current address and telephone number, check the *Encyclopedia of Associations,*
available in printed form and as an online database.) The public information
office or the office of research usually handles these requests.

A—B

American Advertising Federation
American Association of Advertising Agencies
American Black Bookwriters Association
American Booksellers Association
American Library Association
American Society of Newspaper Editors
Asian American Journalists Association
Associated Press Managing Editors
Association of American Publishers
Association for Education in Journalism and
Mass Communication
Association of Independent Television Stations, Inc.
Association of National Advertisers
Audit Bureau of Circulations
Black American Cinema Society
Black Women in Publishing
Broadcast Education Association

C—O

Cabletelevision Advertising Bureau
Hispanic Journalists Association
International Association of Business
Communicators

Investigative Reporters and Editors
Magazine Publishers of America
Motion Picture Association of America
National Association of Black Journalists
National Association of Broadcasters (each state
also has its own state association)
National Association of Hispanic Journalists
National Black Public Relations Society
National Cable Television Association
Native American Journalists Association
Newspaper Association of America (each state
also has its own state association)

P—Z

Public Relations Society of America
Radio Advertising Bureau
Radio-Television News Directors Association
Recording Industry Association of America
Task Force on Minorities in the Newspaper
Business
Television Bureau of Advertising
Women in Communications
Women in Film
World Institute of Black Communications/CEBA
Awards

Notes

Chapter 1: You in the New Information Age

1. George Gilder, "Life After Television, Updated," *Forbes,* Feb. 28, 1994, Dow//Quest ID#0000385340ZF.
2. Ibid.
3. Melvin L. DeFleur and Everette E. Dennis, *Understanding Mass Communication,* 2nd ed. (Boston: Houghton Mifflin, 1986), p. 5. This is an abbreviated and modified version of DeFleur and Dennis' definition.
4. Ibid.
5. Thomas R. King, "News Corp.'s Twentieth Century Fox Forms Unit to Make 'Mainstream' Films," *The Wall Street Journal,* Aug. 23, 1994, p. B-5.
6. Ibid.
7. Knight-Ridder Newspapers, "Launching the Info Revolution," *The Sacramento Bee,* Jan. 12, 1994, p. G-1.
8. Bart Ziegler, "Building the Highway: New Obstacles, New Solutions," *The Wall Street Journal,* May 18, 1994, p. B-1.
9. Ibid.
10. Philip Elmer DeWitt, "Electronic Superhighway," *Time,* April 12, 1993, p. 53.
11. Ziegler.
12. Ibid.
13. "It's the End of the World As We Know It...And I Feel Fine," *The Economist* 330 no. 7850 (Feb. 12, 1994):17.
14. *The Veronis, Suhler & Associates Communications Industry Forecast* 1999–2003; Arbitron, *Radio Today,* 1997; Nielsen Media Research, as reported in *Computerworld,* August 31, 1998.
15. This is a projected estimate based on *The Veronis, Suhler & Associates Communications Industry Forecast* 1999–2003.
16. *The Wall Street Journal,* March 30, 1992, p. B1.
17. Anthony Smith, *Goodbye Gutenberg* (New York: Oxford University Press, 1980), p. 6.
18. Plato, *Collected Works* (Princeton, N.J.: Phaedrus, 1961), pp. 520–21.
19. Smith, p. 5.
20. Ibid., p. 8.

Chapter 2: Newspapers

1. Richard Saul Wurman, *Information Anxiety* (New York: Doubleday, 1989), p. 33.
2. Livingston Rutherford, *John Peter Zenger* (Gloucester, Mass.: Peter Smith, 1963 [reprint of the first edition]), pp. 121–23.
3. Marion Marzolf, *Up from the Footnote* (New York: Hastings House, 1977), p. 2.
4. Ibid., pp. 1–11.
5. Edwin Emery and Michael Emery, *The Press and America,* 6th ed. (Englewood Cliffs, N.J.: Prentice-Hall, 1988), p. 36.
6. Lauren Kessler, *The Dissident Press* (Beverly Hills: Sage, 1984), p. 21.
7. Madelon Golden Schilpp and Sharon M. Murphy, *Great Women of the Press* (Carbondale: Southern Illinois University Press, 1983), p. 125.
8. Ida B. Wells, *The Crusade for Justice: The Autobiography of Ida B. Wells,* ed. Alfreda M. Duster (Chicago: University of Chicago Press, 1970), p. 42.
9. Emery and Emery, p. 137.
10. W. A. Swanberg, *Citizen Hearst* (New York: Bantam Books, 1971), p. 68.
11. Emery and Emery, p. 241.
12. Emery and Emery, p. 35.
13. James N. Dertouzos and Timothy H. Quinn, "Bargaining Responses to the Technology Revolution: The Case of the Newspaper Industry," *Labor Management Cooperation Brief,* U.S. Department of Labor, September 1985, p. 7.
14. Anthony Smith, *Goodbye Gutenberg* (New York: Oxford University Press, 1980), p. 52.
15. Patrick M. Reilly, "Newspapers Are Paging Young Readers," *The Wall Street Journal,* May 6, 1991, p. B-1.
16. Karen Jurgenson, "Diversity: A Report from the Battlefield," *Newspaper Research Journal* 14, no. 2 (Spring 1993):92.
17. Reilly.

Chapter 3: Magazines

1. Shirley Biagi, *NewsTalk I* (Belmont, Calif.: Wadsworth, 1987), p. 110.
2. Madelon Golden Schilpp and Sharon M. Murphy, *Great Women of the Press* (Carbondale: Southern Illinois University Press, 1983), p. 44.
3. Donald Paneth, *Encyclopedia of American Journalism* (New York: Facts on File, 1983), p. 208.
4. Ida Tarbell, *All in the Day's Work* (New York: MacMillan, 1939), pp. 235–39.
5. W. A. Swanberg, *Luce and His Empire* (New York: Scribner's, 1972), p. 57.
6. Deidre Carmody, "A Guide to New Magazines Shows Widespread Vitality," *The New York Times,* Feb. 25, 1991, p. C-1.

7. Ibid.

8. *The Magazine Hand Book 1992–1993*, Magazine Publishers of America, p. 39.

9. James B. Kobak, "1984: A Billion-Dollar Year for Acquisitions," *Folio* 14, no. 4 (April 1985):82–95.

10. Karlene Lukovitz, "The Next 10 Years: 24 Predictions for the Future," *Folio* 11, no. 9 (September 1982):103.

Chapter 4: Books

1. E. B. White, *Letters of E. B. White*, ed. Dorothy Lobrano Guth (New York: Harper & Row, 1976), p. 571.

2. U.S. Department of Commerce: *The Veronis, Suhler & Associates Communications Industry Forecast 1997–2001.*

3. Lewis A Coser, Charles Kadushin, and Walter W. Powell, *Books: The Culture & Commerce of Publishing* (New York: Basic Books, 1982), p. 7.

4. Ibid.

5. James D. Hart, *The Popular Book* (Berkeley: University of California Press, 1950), p. 9.

6. Ibid., p. 57.

7. Ibid., p. 138.

8. Ibid., p. 151.

9. Ibid., p. 185.

10. John P. Dessauer, *Book Publishing: What It Is, What It Does* (New York: R. R. Bowker, 1974), pp. 3–4.

11. Hart, p. 274.

12. Kenneth C. Davis, *Two-Bit Culture: The Paperbacking of America* (Boston: Houghton Mifflin, 1984), p. xii.

13. Ibid., p. 316.

14. Dessauer, p. 8.

15. Ibid.

16. U.S. Department of Commerce, pp. 27–29.

17. Ibid., p. 14.

18. Ibid., p. 43.

19. Laura Landro, "Publishers' Thirst for Blockbusters Sparks Big Advances and Big Risks," *The Wall Street Journal*, Feb. 3, 1986, p. 21.

20. Alex S. Jones, "For Waldenbooks, Reading Is More than a Pastime," *The New York Times*, reprinted in *The Sacramento Bee*, April 30, 1984, p. C-3.

21. U.S. Department of Commerce, pp. 27–29.

22. Coser, Kadushin, and Powell, p. 35.

Chapter 5: Radio

1. A. M. Sperber, *Murrow: His Life and Times* (New York: Freundlich, 1986), p. 168.

2. *Radio Marketing Guide and Fact Book for Advertisers 1997*, Radio Advertising Bureau, *Media Guide 1997*, Radio Advertising Bureau.

3. Irving Settel, *A Pictorial History of Radio* (New York: Citadel Press, 1960), p. 17.

4. Erik Barnouw, *Tube of Plenty* (New York: Oxford University Press, 1978), p. 9.

5. Ibid., p. 11.

6. Ibid., p. 13.

7. Ibid., p. 15.

8. Settel, p. 32.

9. Ibid., p. 39.

10. John R. Bittner, *Broadcast Law and Regulation* (Englewood Cliffs, N.J.: Prentice-Hall, 1982), p. 57.

11. Settel, p. 52.

12. Barnouw, p. 145.

13. Ibid.

14. Peter Fornatale and Joshua E. Mills, *Radio in the Television Age* (New York: Overlook Press, 1980), p. 20.

15. David R. MacFarland, *The Development of the Top 40 Radio Format* (New York: Arno Press, 1979), p. 46.

16. Ibid., p. 44.

17. Ibid., p. 53.

18. *The Veronis, Suhler & Associates Communications Industry Forecast*, June 1992, p. 86.

19. Fornatale and Mills, p. 64.

20. Eric Zorn, "Radio Lives!" reprinted from *Esquire* in *Readings in Mass Communication*, 6th ed., eds. Michael Emery and Ted Curtis Smythe (Dubuque, Iowa: Wm. C. Brown, 1986), pp. 340–41.

21. Ibid., p. 339.

Chapter 6: Recordings

1. R. Serge Denisoff, *Solid Gold* (New Brunswick, N.J.: Transaction Books, 1975), p. 1.

2. Robert Metz, *CBS: Reflections in a Bloodshot Eye* (Chicago: Playboy Press, 1975), pp. 147–48.

3. Ibid., p. 153.

4. James D. Harless, *Mass Communication: An Introductory Survey* (Dubuque, Iowa: Wm. C. Brown, 1985), p. 201.

5. David Pauly, "A Compact Sonic Boom," *Newsweek*, Dec. 6, 1985, p. 47; *U.S. Industrial Outlook 1991*, pp. 32–33.

6. *Billboard Magazine* 52, no. 104 (Dec. 26, 1992):14, 99.

7. Jeffrey Zaslow, "New Rock Economics Make It Harder to Sing Your Way to Wealth," *The Wall Street Journal*, May 21, 1985, p. 1.

8. Ibid.

9. Stephen Dreider Yoder, "Digital Tape Is Inevitable; So Why the Delay?" *The Wall Street Journal*, Aug. 12, 1986, p. 29.

10. *Revving Fast Forward*. Recording Industry Association, 1995, p. 34.

11. Louis P. Sheinfeld, "Ratings: The Big Chill," *Film Comment* 22, no. 3 (May–June 1986):10.

12. Robert Epstein, "Now It's the Recording Industry's Turn to Face the Music," *Los Angeles Times*, Nov. 22, 1990, p. F-1.

13. Jeffrey A. Trachtenberg, "Music Industry Fears Bandits on the Information Highway," *The Wall Street Journal*, August 2, 1994, p. B-21.

14 Chris Nelson, "David Bowie to Sell Hours...Online," Sonicnet.com, Aug. 31, 1999.

15 Michael Marriott, "New Ways to Play MP3 Music, Without Plugs or Speakers," *The New York Times*, Aug. 19, 1999, D11.

16. James R. Smart, *A Wonderful Invention: A Brief History of the Phonograph from Tinfoil to the LP* (Washington: Library of Congress, 1977), p. 6.

17. Metz, p. 146.

Chapter 7: Television

1. Jeff Greenfield, *Television: The First Fifty Years* (New York: Abrams, 1977), p. 11.

2. Ibid., pp. 52–53.

3. Erik Barnouw, *Tube of Plenty* (New York: Oxford University Press, 1975), p. 17.

4. Les Brown, *Television: The Business Behind the Box* (New York: Harcourt Brace Jovanovich, 1971), p. 43.

5. Ibid.

6. Shirley Biagi, *NewsTalk II* (Belmont, Calif.: Wadsworth, 1987), p. 140.

7. Ibid.

8. Newton Minow, *Equal Time: The Private Broadcaster and the Public Interest* (New York: Atheneum, 1964), p. 51.

9. Ibid., p. 317.

10. Ibid., p. 336.

11. Ibid., p. 339.

12. Greenfield, p. 234.

13. Christopher H. Sterling and John M. Kittross, *Stay Tuned: A Concise History of American Broadcasting,* 2nd ed. (Belmont, Calif.: Wadsworth, 1990), p. 414.

14 Kathy Chen and Martin Peers, "FCC Relaxes Its Rules on TV Station Ownership," *The Wall Street Journal,* Aug. 6, 1999, A-3.

15. "Year in Review: Sports," *Electronic Media* 10, no. 2 (Jan. 7, 1991):54.

16. John Lippman, "Southwestern Looks to Enter Cable Race," *Los Angeles Times,* Nov. 5, 1993, p. D-1.

17. Julie Amparano Lopez and Mary Lu Carnevale, "Fiber Optics Promises a Revolution of Sorts, If the Sharks Don't Bite," *The Wall Street Journal,* July 10, 1990, p. A-1.

18. Ibid.

Chapter 8: Movies

1. Jason E. Squire, ed., *The Movie Business Book* (New York: Simon & Schuster, 1983), p. 3.

2. Ibid., p. 2.

3. Robert Sklar, *Movie-Made America* (New York: Random House, 1975), p. 9.

4. Tino Balio, *The American Film Industry* (Madison: University of Wisconsin Press, 1976), p. 27.

5. Sklar, p. 16.

6. Ibid., p. 36.

7. Ibid., p. 40.

8. Balio, p. 75.

9. Jack C. Ellis, *A History of American Film,* 2nd ed. (Englewood Cliffs, N.J.: Prentice-Hall, 1985), p. 43.

10. Balio, p. 112.

11. *Moving Picture World,* Feb. 1, 1919, p. 619.

12. Motion Picture Association of America, *Motion Picture Production Code,* 1954, p. 2.

13. Ibid., pp. 2–5.

14. Balio, p. 209.

15. Ibid., p. 213.

16. Dalton Trumbo, *Additional Dialogue: Letters of Dalton Trumbo: 1942–1962* (New York: M. Evans, 1970), p. 301.

17. Balio, p. 372.

18. Ibid., p. 315.

19. Sklar, p. 389.

20. *The Veronis, Suhler & Associates Communication Industry Forecast,* June 1991, p. 108.

21. Squire, p. 345.

22. John Lippmann, "Movie Ticket Revenue Rose 8% in '99, While Number of Admissions Grew 4%," *The Wall Street Journal,* Jan. 7, 2000, B-2.

23. Michael Cieply and Peter W. Barnes, "Movie and TV Mergers Point to Concentration of Power to Entertain," *The Wall Street Journal,* Aug. 21, 1986, p. 1.

24. Squire, p. 155.

25. Ibid., p. 150.

26. Squire, p. 298.

27. Thomas R. King, "Theater Chain Has Plans to Jolt Movie Viewers," *The Wall Street Journal,* Aug. 18, 1994, p. B-1.

28. "The World Is Hollywood's Oyster," *Business Week* 3195 (Jan. 14, 1991):97.

Chapter 9: Digital Media and the Web

1. David Shaw, "Newspapers Take Different Paths to On-line Publishing," *Los Angeles Times,* June 17, 1997, A–1.

2. Roger Fidler, *Mediamorphosis* (Thousand Oaks, Calif.: Pine Forge Press, 1997), pp. 100–101.

3. Ibid., 103.

4. *The Veronis, Suhler & Associates Communications Industry Forecast, 1997–2001,* 371.

5. Fidler, 209.

6. "The Book of the Future," *Frames* (January 1996: 51), 1.

7. Mick LaSalle, "Get a Really Good Picture—for Only $250,000," *San Francisco Chronicle,* Jan. 13, 1998, E1.

8. Fidler, 180, 233.

9. Ibid., 22–23.

10. Ibid.

11. Ibid., 26.

12. Veronis, Suhler, 372.

13. Ibid., 373.

14. Ibid.

15. "Paul Saffo and the 30-year Rule," *Design World,* 24 (1992): 18.

16. Veronis, Suhler, 372.

17. Robert Wright, "The Man Who Invented the Web," *Time,* May 19, 1997, p. 68.

18. Craig McKie, personal interview with the author, January 12, 1998.

19. David Shaw, "Internet Gold Rush Hasn't Panned Out Yet for Most," *Los Angeles Times,* June 19, 1997, A–1.

20. Ibid.

21. Ibid.

22. Julia Angwin, "Now You Got to Pay to Play Online," *San Francisco Chronicle,* June 20, 1997, B–1.

23. Shaw, "Internet Gold Rush."

24. Ibid.

25. Ibid.

26. Ibid.

Chapter 10: Advertising

1. Daniel J. Boorstin, "The Rhetoric of Democracy," in *American Mass Media: Industries and Issues,* 3rd ed., eds. Robert Atwan, Barry Orton, and William Vesterman (New York: Random House, 1986), p. 37.

2. Ibid.

3. Robert Atwan, "Newspapers and the Foundations of Modern Advertising," in *The Commercial Connection,* ed. John W. Wright (New York: Doubleday, 1979), p. 16.

4. Edgar R. Jones, *Those Were the Good Old Days* (New York: Simon & Schuster, 1979), p. 35.

5. Ibid., p. 44.

6. Atwan.

7. Stephen Fox, *The Mirror Makers: A History of American Advertising and Its Creators* (New York: Morrow, 1984), p. 15.

8. Ibid., p. 32.
9. Ibid., p. 155.
10. Ibid., p. 210.
11. Ibid., p. 212.
12. Ibid.
13. Boorstin.
14. Ibid.
15. Ibid.
16. Ibid.
17. Jib Fowles, "Advertising's Fifteen Basic Appeals," in *American Mass Media: Industries and Issues,* p. 43.
18. Ibid., pp. 46–52.
19. Michael Schudson, *Advertising: The Uneasy Persuasion* (New York: Basic Books, 1984), p. 13.
20. Louis C. Kaufman, *Essentials of Advertising,* 2nd ed. (New York: Harcourt Brace Jovanovich, 1987), p. 510.
21. Schudson, p. 13.
22. Jonathan Price, "Now a Few Words About Commercials . . . " in *American Mass Media: Industries and Issues,* p. 63.
23. Radio Advertising Bureau, *Radio Facts for Advertisers 1989–1990* (New York: Radio Advertising Bureau), p. 28.
24. Sally Goll Beatty, "Seagram Flouts Ban on TV Ads Pitching Liquor," *The Wall Street Journal,* June 11, 1996, p. B-1.
25. Kaufman, p. 514.

Chapter 11: Public Relations

1. Fraser P. Seitel, *The Practice of Public Relations,* 2nd ed. (Columbus, Ohio: Charles E. Merrill, 1984), p. 40.
2. Theodore Lustig, "Great Caesar's Ghost," *Public Relations Journal,* March 1986, pp. 17–19.
3. Doug Newsom and Alan Scott, *This Is PR: The Realities of Public Relations,* 3rd ed. (Belmont, Calif.: Wadsworth, 1986), p. 40.
4. Scott M. Cutlip, Allen H. Center, and Glen M. Broom, *Effective Public Relations,* 6th ed. (Englewood Cliffs, N.J.: Prentice-Hall, 1985), p. 36.
5. Quoted in Sherman Morse, "An Awakening on Wall Street," *American Magazine* 62 (September 1906):460.
6. Cutlip, Center, and Broom, p. 39.
7. Edward L. Bernays, *The Engineering of Consent* (Norman: University of Oklahoma Press, 1955), pp. 3–4.
8. Craig Randall, "The Father of Public Relations: Edward Bernays, 93, Is Still Saucy," *United* 30, no. 11 (November 1985):50.
9. Newsom and Scott, p. 47.
10. Doris E. Fleischman, "Public Relations—A New Field for Women," *Independent Woman,* February 1931, p. 58, as quoted in Susan Henry, "In Her Own Name?: Public Relations Pioneer Doris Fleischman Bernays," a paper presented to the Committee on the Status of Women Research Session, Association for Education in Journalism and Mass Communication, Portland, Oregon, July 1988.
11. Doug Newsom and Alan Scott in *This Is PR* are especially diligent about chronicling women's contributions to public relations. This specific information appears on p. 49.
12. "Interview: Henry Rogers," *PSA* 21, no. 10 (October 1986):70.

13. Newsom and Scott, p. 50.
14. *Occupations of Federal White and Blue Collar Workers,* U.S. Office of Personnel Management, 1989.
15. James K. Gentry, "The Best and Worst Corporate PR," *Washington Journalism Review* 8, no. 7 (July 1986):38–40.
16. Joanne Lipman, "As Network TV Fades, Many Advertisers Try Age-Old Promotions," *The Wall Street Journal,* Aug. 26, 1986, p. 1.
17. Lawrence G. Foster, "The Role of Public Relations in the Tylenol Crisis," *Public Relations Journal,* March 1983, p. 13.
18. Jeff Blyskal and Marie Blyskal, "Making the Best of Bad News," *Washington Journalism Review* 7, no. 12 (December 1985):52.
19. Mark Glover, "Juice Maker in PR Mode: Odwalla's Ads Explain Status," *The Sacramento Bee,* Dow/Quest SBEE9632600056.
20. The U.S. Department of Labor, Bureau of Labor Statistics unpublished statistics from the current population survey: 1992 annual averages.
21. *County Business Patterns 1989,* U.S. Bureau of the Census, December 1991.
22. *Public Relations Journal* 49, no. 3, March 1993; Newsom and Scott, p. 69.
23. "Japanese Said Lagging in PR," *Los Angeles Times,* reprinted in *The Sacramento Bee,* Dec. 8, 1986, p. C-3.
24. Summarized from a list of work assignments listed in Cutlip, Center, and Broom, p. 64.
25. Jeff Blyskal and Marie Blyskal, *PR: How the Public Relations Industry Writes the News* (New York: Morrow, 1985), p. 46.
26. Craig Bromberg, "Goliath Pitch Behind Times' 'David Story,'" *Manhattan, inc.* 4, no. 4 (April 1987):18.
27. Joanne Angela Ambrosio, "It's in the Journal, But This Is Reporting?" *Columbia Journalism Review* 18, no. 6 (March/April 1980):35.
28. Bromberg.
29. Blyskal and Blyskal, *PR,* p. 82.

Chapter 12: Mass Media and Social Issues

1. Lynn Smith, "Calls to L.A. Domestic Abuse Lines Jump 80%," *Los Angeles Times,* June 24, 1994, Dow/Quest.
2. Deb Kollars, "Callers Flood AIDS Hotlines; Johnson Cheered on 'Arsenio,'" *The Sacramento Bee,* Nov. 9, 1991, p. A–22.
3. William L. Rivers and Wilbur Schramm, "The Impact of Mass Communications," in *American Mass Media: Industries and Issues,* 3rd ed., eds. Robert Atwan, Barry Orton and William Vesterman (New York: Random House, 1986), pp. 11–12.
4. David M. Potter, *People of Plenty* (Chicago: University of Chicago Press, 1954), p. 167.
5. Robert M. Liebert and Joyce Sprafkin, *The Early Window,* 3rd ed. (New York: Pergamon Press, 1988), p. 161.
6. "Synopsis of FTC Staff Report on Television Advertising to Children," in *The Commercial Connection,* ed. John W. Wright (New York: Dell, 1979), pp. 340–42.
7. Scott Ward, cited in George Comstock et al., *Television and Human Behavior* (New York: Columbia University Press, 1978), p. 199.

8. James David Barber, *The Pulse of Politics: Electing Presidents in the Media Age* (New York: Norton, 1986), p. 150.
9. Ibid., p. 246.
10. Thomas E. Patterson and Robert D. McClure, *The Unseeing Eye: The Myth of Television Power in National Elections* (New York: Putnam, 1976), p. 113.
11. Joseph C. Spear, *Presidents and the Press* (Cambridge, Mass.: M.I.T. Press, 1984), p. 52.
12. Personal telephone conversation with Herbert Alexander, April 8, 1987.
13. Herbert E. Alexander, *Financing the 1980 Election* (Lexington, Mass.: D.C. Heath, 1983); Herbert E. Alexander and Brian A. Haggerty, *Financing the 1984 Election* (Lexington, Mass.: D.C. Heath, 1987). Herbert E. Alexander, Citizens' Research Foundation, University of Southern California.
14. Dow Jones News Service, "Feinstein Victory Over Huffington Official," Dec. 15, 1994.
15. Barber, p. 6.
16. Joshua Meyrowitz, *No Sense of Place* (New York: Oxford University Press, 1985), p. 92.
17. Ibid., p. 242.
18. Mark Fetler, "Television Viewing and School Achievement," *Mass Communication Review Yearbook*, vol. 5 (Beverly Hills: Sage, 1985), pp. 447–61.
19. Walter Lippmann, *Public Opinion* (New York: Free Press, 1965), p. 61.
20. Tania Modleski, *Loving with a Vengeance: Mass-Produced Fantasies for Women* (New York: Methuen, 1982), p. 113.
21. Carolyn Martindale, "Only in Glimpses: Portrayal of America's Largest Minority Groups by *The New York Times* 1934–1994," a paper presented at the Association for Education in Journalism and Mass Communication Annual Convention, Washington, D.C., August 1995.
22. "Don't Blink: Hispanics in Television Entertainment, 1994–1995," Center for Media and Public Affairs for the National Council of La Raza.
23. M. L. Stein, "Racial Stereotyping and the Media," *Editor & Publisher*, Aug. 6, 1994.
24. Art Nauman, "Comics Page Gets Serious," *The Sacramento Bee*, April 11, 1993.
25. Ibid.
26. Neil Postman, *Amusing Ourselves to Death* (New York: Viking Penguin, 1985), pp. 160–61.
27. Ibid.

Chapter 13: Media Ownership and Press Performance

1. James Madison, letter to W. T. Barry, Aug. 4, 1822, in *Letters and Other Writings of James Madison, Fourth President of the United States, Vol. 3, 1816–1818* (Philadelphia: J. B. Lippincott, 1854), p. 276.
2. Walter Lippmann, *Public Opinion* (New York: Free Press, 1965), p. 229.
3. Additional information that has not appeared in preceding chapters is from Ben H. Bagdikian, *The Media Monopoly* (Boston: Beacon Press, 1983); Newspaper Association of America; *Broadcasting & Cable Yearbook 1993* (New Providence, N.J.: Reed Reference Publishing Co., 1993); *U.S. Industrial Outlook 1993*, sec-

tion 24, p. 11; *Advertising Age*, April 15, 1996, p. 520. Steven Levy, "A Blow to the Empire," *Newsweek*, Dec. 29, 1997/Jan. 5, 1998, 58–60.
4. A. J. Liebling, *The Press* (New York: Ballantine, 1961), pp. 4–5.
5. Michael J. Robinson and Ray Olszewski, "Books in the Marketplace of Ideas," *Journal of Communication* 30, no. 2 (Spring 1980):82.
6. Joanne Lipman, "Ad Agencies Feverishly Ride a Merger Wave," *The Wall Street Journal*, March 9, 1986, p. 6.
7. Mark Landler, "Westinghouse to Acquire 98 Radio Stations," *The New York Times*, Sept. 20, 1997, Y–23.
8. Benjamin M. Compaine, *Who Owns the Media?* (White Plains, N.Y.: Knowledge Industry Publications, 1979), p. 26.
9. William A. Henry III, "Learning to Love the Chains," *Washington Journalism Review* 8, no. 9 (September 1986):16.
10. Compaine, p. 26.
11. Philip Weiss, "Invasion of the Gannettoids," *The New Republic*, Feb. 2, 1987, p. 18.
12. Ben H. Bagdikian, "Conglomeration, Concentration, and the Media," *Journal of Communication* 30, no. 2 (Spring 1980):60.
13. David H. Weaver and G. Cleveland Wilhoit, *The American Journalist in the 1990s, Preliminary Report* (New York: The Freedom Forum, 1992), pp. 1, 2, 7.
14. Ibid.
15. Herbert J. Gans, "Are U.S. Journalists Dangerously Liberal?" *Columbia Journalism Review* 24, no. 4 (November/December 1985):32–33.
16. See William A. Dorman, "Peripheral Vision: U.S. Journalism and the Third World," *World Policy Journal*, Summer 1986, pp. 419–46.
17. Herbert J. Gans, "The Messages Behind the News," in *Readings in Mass Communication*, 6th ed., eds. Michael Emery and Ted Curtis Smythe (Dubuque, Iowa: Wm. C. Brown, 1986), pp. 161–69.
18. James Reston, *The Artillery of the Press* (New York: Harper & Row, 1966), p. 49.
19. Norman Corwin, *Trivializing America: The Triumph of Mediocrity* (Secaucus, N.J.: Lyle Stuart, 1986), p. 33.
20. Times Mirror, *The People & the Press* (Los Angeles: Times Mirror, 1986), p. 30; Times Mirror, *The People & the Press* (Los Angeles: Times Mirror, 1989), pp. 25–26.
21. Times Mirror, *We're Interested in What You Think* (Los Angeles: Times Mirror, 1987), p. 8.

Chapter 14: Law and Regulation

1. Tom Wicker, *On Press* (New York: Viking, 1978), p. 260.
2. Leonard W. Levy, *Emergence of a Free Press* (New York: Oxford University Press, 1985), pp. 272–73.
3. Ralph L. Holsinger, *Media Law* (New York: Random House, 1987), p. 14.
4. Ibid., p. 61.
5. Rodney A. Smolla, *Suing the Press* (New York: Oxford University Press, 1986), p. 46.
6. Peter Braestrup, *Battle Lines: Report of the Twentieth Century Fund Task Force on the Military and the Media* (New York: Priority Press, 1985), p. 29.

7. Holsinger, p. 35.

8. Sanford J. Ungar, *The Papers & The Papers: An Account of the Legal and Political Battle over the Pentagon Papers* (New York: Dutton, 1975), pp. 306–307.

9. Holsinger, pp. 48–49.

10. Jeff Blyskal and Marie Blyskal, *PR: How the Public Relations Industry Writes the News* (New York: Morrow, 1985), p. 15.

11. "Notes and Comment," *The New Yorker* 66, no. 51 (Feb. 4, 1991):21.

12. Thomas B. Rosenstiel, "The Media Take a Pounding," *Los Angeles Times,* Feb. 20, 1991, p. A1.

13. Carl Bode, *Mencken* (Carbondale: Southern Illinois University Press, 1969), pp. 272–76.

14. Holsinger, pp. 332–33.

15. Ibid., pp. 340–41.

16. National Coalition Against Censorship, *Books on Trial: A Survey of Recent Cases* (New York: National Coalition Against Censorship, 1985), pp. 6–20.

17. Madalynne Reuter and Marianne Yen, "Censorship Rose 35 Percent over Previous Year, Study Finds," *Publishers Weekly,* Oct. 24, 1986, p. 13.

18. Smolla, p. 18.

19. Ibid., pp. 29–30.

20. Ibid., p. 50.

21. Holsinger, p. 161.

22. Peter McGrath and Nancy Stadtman, "What the Jury—and *Time* Magazine—Said," *Newsweek,* Feb. 4, 1985, p. 58.

23. Bee News Services, "$25 Million Judgment in 'Jenny Jones' Case," *The Sacramento Bee,* May 8, 1999, A–1.

24. "Media and Libel: Rising Losses," *Folio* 17, no. 7 (July 1988):89.

25. Ibid., p. 34.

26. Kyle Pope, "ABC Network Loses Libel Suit Over '20/20,'" *The Wall Street Journal,* December 19, 1996, p. B-1.

27. "Media and Libel: Rising Losses," *Folio,* p. 92.

28. Smolla, p. 257.

29. Holsinger, pp. 191–92.

30. Ibid., p. 192.

31. G. Christian Hill, "It's War! The Battle for the Telecommunications Dollar Is Turning into a Free-for-All," *The Wall Street Journal,* Sept. 16, 1996, p. R-1.

32. Ibid.

33. Ibid., p. 2.

34. Ibid.

35. Benton Foundation, *The Telecommunications Act of 1996 and the Changing Communications Landscape* (Washington, D.C.: Benton Foundation, 1996), p. 2.

36. Ibid.

37. Catherine Arnst, "Telecom's New Age: The Coming Telescramble," *Business Week,* April 8, 1996 (America Online).

38. Mike Mills, "Burning the Midnight Oil on New Phone Rules," *Washington Post,* July 10, 1996 (Dow Jones News Retrieval).

39. Bloomberg Business News, "Playboy Wins a Hold on 'Scrambling' Rule; Victory in Court Likely, Judge Says," *Chicago Tribune,* March 9, 1996 (Dow Jones News Retrieval).

40. Benton Foundation, pp. 7–8.

41. Peter H. Lewis, "Judges Turn Back Law Intended to Regulate Internet Decency," *The New York Times,* June 13, 1996 (America Online).

42. Christopher Stern, "The V-chip First Amendment Infringement vs. Empowerment Tool," *Broadcasting & Cable,* Feb. 12, 1996 (Dow Jones News Retrieval).

43. Sylvia Rubin, "New TV Ratings Unveiled—To Renewed Criticism," *San Francisco Chronicle,* Dec. 20, 1996, p. A-1.

44. Ralph L. Holsinger, *Media Law,* 2nd ed. (New York: McGraw-Hill, 1991), p. 502.

45. Fraser P. Seitel, *The Practice of Public Relations,* 2nd ed. (Columbus, Ohio: Charles E. Merrill, 1984), p. 428.

46. Holsinger, p. 416.

Chapter 15: Ethics

1. Anthony Brandt, "Truth and Consequences," *Esquire* 102, no. 4 (October 1984):27.

2. John Hulteng, *The Messenger's Motives: Ethical Problems of the News Media* (Englewood Cliffs, N.J.: Prentice-Hall, 1985), p. 221.

3. Tom Goldstein, *The News at Any Cost* (New York: Simon & Schuster, 1985), p. 217.

4. Ibid., p. 218.

5. "ABC: Walters Wrong to Be Iran Messenger," *The Sacramento Bee,* March 17, 1987, p. 1.

6. Ibid.

7. "Federal Judge Finds Winans, Two Others Guilty," *The Wall Street Journal,* June 25, 1985, p. 2.

8. M. L. Stein, "Survey on Freebies," *Editor & Publisher,* May 31, 1986, p. 11.

9. Alan Prendergast, "Mickey Mouse Journalism," *Washington Journalism Review* 9, no. 1 (January/February 1987):32.

10. Richard Harwood, "What Is This Thing Called 'News'?" *Washington Post,* March 12, 1994, Dow//Quest ID#0000096451WP.

11. Richard M. Levine, "Murder, They Write," *The New York Times Magazine,* Nov. 16, 1986, p. 132.

12. Jonathan Alter with Peter McKillop, "AIDS and the Right to Know," *Newsweek,* Aug. 18, 1986, p. 46.

13. Dale Van Atta, "Faint Light, Dark Print," *Harper's* 273, no. 1,638 (November 1986):57.

14. Ibid.

15. Elizabeth Jensen, "NBC-Sponsored Inquiry Calls GM Crash on News Program a Lapse in Judgment," *The Wall Street Journal,* March 23, 1993, p. B10.

16. Kevin Helliker, "CNN Got Its Story About Poisoned Eagles, But Rancher Cries Foul," *The Wall Street Journal,* Nov. 25, 1997, p. A–1.

17. Ibid.

18. Clifford G. Christians, Kim B. Rotzoll, and Mark Fackler, *Media Ethics,* 2nd ed. (New York: Longman, 1987), pp. 9–17.

19. Andy Rooney, "The Journalist's Code of Ethics," in *Pieces of My Mind* (New York: Atheneum, 1984), pp. 59–60.

20. Society of Professional Journalists Code of Ethics, Sept. 1996

21. Radio-Television News Directors Association, Code of Broadcast News Ethics, January 1988.

22. Public Relations Society of America, Code of Professional Standards for the Practice of Public Relations, rev. 1983, p. 1.

23. Mike Wallace, "The Press Needs a National Monitor," *The Wall Street Journal*, Dec. 18, 1996, Dow/Quest J9635300131.

24. Ibid., pp. 215–16.

25. John Hulteng, "Get It While It's Hot," *feed/back* 12, nos. 1 and 2 (Fall 1985/Winter 1986):16.

Chapter 16: A Global Media Marketplace

1. "Nigeria Cracks Down on Media," *San Francisco Chronicle*, July 24, 1993, p. A-18; Michael Williams, "'Gaman' Adds Spice to Japanese Life and to Its TV Fare," *The Wall Street Journal*, March 5, 1993, p. A-1; Mark Fineman, "Iraqis Plugging In to Youth TV," *Los Angeles Times*, Aug. 3, 1993, p. H-2; Kevin Helliker, "Drop That Remote! In Britain, Watching TV Can Be a Crime," *The Wall Street Journal*, Sept. 27, 1993, p. A-1.

2. Fred S. Siebert, Theodore Peterson, and Wilbur Schramm, *Four Theories of the Press* (Urbana: University of Illinois Press, 1963), p. 135.

3. Lowndes F. Stephens, "The World's Media Systems: An Overview," *Global Journalism: Survey of International Communication*, 2nd ed. (New York: Longman, 1991), p. 62.

4. Ibid., p. 68.

5. Manny Paraschos, "Europe," *Global Journalism: Survey of International Communication*, 2nd ed. (New York: Longman, 1991), pp. 93–128.

6. Ibid., p. 96.

7. Philip Revzin and Mark M. Nelson, "European TV Industry Goes Hollywood," *The Wall Street Journal*, Oct. 3, 1989, p. A-18.

8. Tyler Marshall, "East Germans Dazzled by Western Press," *Los Angeles Times*, July 31, 1990, H–8.

9. Blaine Harden, "'Maniacs' on TV Wake Up Poland," *Washington Post*, March 11, 1990, p. A-20.

10. Associated Press, "Media Chiefs Fired; Allegedly Backed Coup," *The Sacramento Bee*, Aug. 27, 1991, p. A-11.

11. Everette E. Dennis and Jon Vanden Heuvel, *Emerging Voices: East European Media in Transition* (New York: Gannett Center for Media Studies, October 1990), p. 2.

12. Mort Rosenblum, "TV Takes the Center Stage in Romanian Revolution," *The Sacramento Bee*, Dec. 17, 1989, p. A-11.

13. Paraschos, p. 124.

14. The Associated Press, "Ads for Comrades: Soviets Run U.S. Commercials," *The Sacramento Bee*, May 18, 1988, p. E-1; Mark J. Porubcansky, "Soviet Paper Finally Prints Capitalist Ads," *The Sacramento Bee*, Jan. 4, 1989, p. C-4; *Baltimore Sun*, "Censorship Outlawed in U.S.S.R.," *The Sacramento Bee*, June 13, 1990, p. A-8.

15. Laurie Hays and Andrea Rutherford, "Gorbachev Bids to Crack Down on Soviet Press," *The Wall Street Journal*, Jan. 17, 1991, p. A-8.

16. Dennis and Vanden Heuvel.

17. Christine Ogan, "Middle East and North Africa," *Global Journalism: Survey of International Communication*, 2nd ed. (New York: Longman, 1991), p. 130.

18. Ibid., p. 135.

19. Ibid.

20. Charles P. Wallace, "Radio: Town Crier of the Arab World," *Los Angeles Times*, Jan. 7, 1988, p. 1.

21. Ogan, pp. 139–40.

22. L. John Martin, "Africa," *Global Journalism: Survey of International Communication*, 2nd ed. (New York: Longman, 1991), p. 161.

23. Ibid.

24. Ibid.

25. Ibid., p. 190.

26. Sydney W. Head, *World Broadcasting Systems* (Belmont, Calif.: Wadsworth, 1985), p. 89.

27. Ibid., p. 90.

28. S. Karene Witcher, "Fairfax Group to Be Placed in Receivership," *The Wall Street Journal*, Dec. 11, 1990, p. A-4.

29. Anne Cooper Chen and Anju Grover Chaudhary, "Asia and the Pacific," *Global Journalism: Survey of International Communication*, 2nd ed. (New York: Longman, 1991), p. 214.

30. Ibid., p. 240.

31. "Publish and Be Ideologically Damned," *The Economist*, October 26, 1996, p. 41.

32. Michael B. Salwen, Bruce Garrison, and Robert T. Buckman, "Latin America and the Caribbean," *Global Journalism: Survey of International Communication*, 2nd ed. (New York: Longman, 1991), pp. 274–85.

33. Ibid.

34. Head, p. 27.

35. Salwen, Garrison and Buckman, p. 305.

36. Ibid., p. 302.

37. Robert G. Picard, "Global Communications Controversies," *Global Journalism: Survey of International Communication*, 2nd ed. (New York: Longman, 1991), p. 74.

38. Head, p. 381.

39. Elizabeth Jensen, "ABC and BBC to Pool Their Radio-TV News Coverage," *The Wall Street Journal*, March 26, 1993, p. B-1.

40. "Murdoch to Expand Television in India," *Dow Jones International News*, Feb. 15, 1994, Dow//Quest.

41. Andrew Pollack, "Japan's Master Maverick of the Internet," *The New York Times*, Nov. 21, 1993, section 3, p. 3.

42. Ray Josephs and Juanita Josephs, "Public Relations the U.K. Way," *Public Relations Journal*, April 1, 1994, Dow//Quest ID#0000403889ZF.

43. John Lippman, "Tuning In the Global Village," *Los Angeles Times*, Oct. 20, 1992, p. H-2.

44. Ibid.

45. "Wired Planet," *The Economist* 330, no. 7850 (Feb. 12, 1994):12.

46. "China Refuses to Switch Off," *The Economist* 332, no. 7870 (July 2, 1994):35.

47. Lippman, p. H-1.

48. "Wired Planet," *The Economist*, p. 18.

Index